D0872223

Feminist Perspectives
in Therapy

WILEY SERIES IN
PSYCHOTHERAPY AND COUNSELLING

Series Editors

Franz Epting
Dept of Psychology
University of Florida

Bonnie Strickland
Dept of Psychology
University of Massachusetts

John Allen
Dept of Community Studies
Brighton Polytechnic

Feminist Perspectives in Therapy

An Empowerment Model for Women

JUDITH WORELL and PAM REMER
University of Kentucky, USA

JOHN WILEY & SONS
Chichester · New York · Brisbane · Toronto · Singapore

Other Wiley Editorial Offices

John Wiley & Sons, Inc., 605 Third Avenue,
New York, NY 10158–0012, USA

Jacaranda Wiley Ltd, G.P.O. Box 859, Brisbane,
Queensland 4001, Australia

John Wiley & Sons (Canada) Ltd, 22 Worcester Road,
Rexdale, Ontario M9W 1L1, Canada

John Wiley & Sons (SEA) Pte Ltd, 37 Jalan Pemimpin #05–04,
Block B, Union Industrial Building, Singapore 2057

Library of Congress Cataloging-in-Publication Data

Worell, Judith, *1928–*
    Feminist perspectives in therapy : an empowerment model for women
/ Judith Worell and Pam Remer.
        p. cm.—(Wiley series in psychotherapy and counselling)
    Includes bibliographical references and index.
    ISBN 0-471-91860 1 (ppc)
    1. Feminist therapy. I. Remer, Pam. II. Title III. Series.
RC489.F45W69 1992
616.89'14—dc20   91–30785
                                                       CIP

British Library Cataloguing in Publication Data

A catalogue record for this book is
available from the British Library.

ISBN 0-471-91860-1 (ppc)

Typeset in 10/12 pt Times by Cambridge Composing (UK) Ltd
Printed and bound in Great Britain by Biddles Ltd, Guildford and King's Lynn

To our four feminist daughters,
Amy, Beth, Randa, and Wendy

Contents

Part 2: Lifespan Issues in Counseling Women

Part 3: Becoming a Feminist Therapist

Contents   xi

Series Preface

The Wiley Series in Psychotherapy and Counselling is designed to fulfil many different needs in advancing science and practice in the helping professions. One of the areas of most concern in this field has been making clear the specific concerns of women in this enterprise. There have been great strides made along these lines with special sections being formed in professional organizations focused on women, new books and journals appearing at a steady pace, and degree programs in Women's Studies being established at major universities. Even with this progress much remains to be accomplished as illustrated by recent findings that women have not been included in research populations dealing with basic health conditions and diseases, (e.g. research projects dealing with heart disease). This book by Worell and Remer on *Feminist Perspectives in Therapy* will help to ensure that women's concerns and issues will not be passed over in the development of the scientific study of therapy and counseling.

While there have been other books focusing on therapy with women, none of these come close to covering the range of topics of the current volume nor cover them in such detail. As noted by one of the reviewers of this book, 'this book is literally filled with factual information which is both accurate and current'. In the three main sections of the book, the authors cover the foundations of a feminist perspective, basic lifespan issues in women's lives, and the essential procedures needed for becoming a feminist therapist.

While the authors have adopted an explicit feminist perspective, they have been very inclusive in their use of therapeutic techniques which cover the gambit from cognitive–behavioral to humanistic approaches. The authors have also put forth great effort in order to engage the reader in the material through the use of thought-provoking self-assessment questionnaires and procedures at the beginnings of the chapters. They have made a point of illustrating the application of this material in client dialogue and in specific case examples of concepts presented. Because of the way this book has been written, it can be used in many different ways. The authors were wise to include in their introductory remarks their recommendations on how to use this book. In addition to the professional worker using the book for instruction and training, the book can be easily used in the college classroom and can be understood by any person who is interested in becoming more knowledgeable about the feminist approach to therapy. The authors have found a way to keep the richness of the professional presentation of the topic and at the same time make it accessible to people who do not have a specific professional background.

It is with a great deal of enthusiasm that this volume is welcomed to the series. It will be no surprise if this book sets a new standard of excellence in this field.

FRANZ EPTING
Series Editor

Preface

The field of counseling and psychotherapy with women is relatively new. The first book on counseling women was published in the 1970s. On a parallel track, the development of a feminist approach to counseling and psychotherapy is also relatively recent. Several new journals have appeared that address the psychology of sex roles and women, as well as therapeutic issues in treating women clients. Thus, the research is expanding, new applications of feminist principles are beginning to appear in the literature, and more theorists are paying attention both to the goals and the process of feminist therapy with women. As new applications and insights develop, there is a need to organize current views, to integrate them within contemporary theoretical positions, and to suggest applications of these insights to practical case materials.

There are a number of core issues related to the mental health of women that suggest the need for a specialty in counseling and therapy with women. Among these issues are (a) the special problems that women bring into the therapeutic setting; (b) sex-role socialization in the development of women; (c) the inadequacies of contemporary theory, research, and practice in addressing the lives of women; and (d) the development of alternative approaches to conceptualization and intervention with women. The application of feminist principles to counseling and psychotherapy with women requires additional integration of theory with practice. Finally, important topics such as diagnosis and assessment, ethical practices in counseling with women, research applications, and the training of counselors and psychotherapists require consideration.

This book addresses core issues in counseling women within the context of two major theoretical positions and a sample of client concerns. The book will be useful both to beginning graduate students who desire an introduction to counseling women, as well as to more advanced and professional clinicians. Advanced professionals may want to discover and integrate these emerging approaches into their therapeutic repertoire, or may selectively adapt text materials for workshops and continuing education training. Each chapter contains a self-assessment pretest on knowledge or attitudes, an introductory overview, a chapter summary, and self-awareness activities. The self-assessment and self-awareness exercises are excellent learning strategies for students, and contribute to the usefulness of this book as a classroom or continuing education text. The underlying theme of the text emphasizes that effective counseling with women clients requires an awareness of personal stereotypes about this client population, an understanding of self in relation to women, and a sensitivity to the special psychological and social environments within which women's development takes place.

The authors are both feminist clinicians with wide experience in the teaching, research, and practice of counseling and psychotherapy with women clients. As educators, we have an understanding of the principles of effective instruction, and we include components in the text that contribute to the learning process. As clinicians, we have both been active in the establishment and administration of a community mental health clinic. In this capacity, we infused our ideas about feminist principles into the values and operation of the agency. Many of the ideas in this book have grown out of our experiences with putting feminist ideas into action.

Coming from clearly different theoretical viewpoints, and employing a contrasting range of therapeutic goals and strategies, we each contribute to this project in unique ways. Through exposition in theory and case materials, we demonstrate how therapists with differing views can apply the principles of feminist counseling with women, and can integrate these principles into their practice. Thus, the approach may be useful for individuals who prefer differing theoretical positions and who may differentially emphasize experiential, affective, cognitive, or behavioral strategies in their practice. In view of the fact that over two-thirds of all clients in non-residential settings are women, it is incumbent upon the therapist in training to become knowledgeable and competent in the important issues surrounding the well-being of women.

We acknowledge a limitation in our expertise. As white middle-class women, we draw upon our own experiences with clients and with our personal lives. Where possible, we have attempted to include data on minority groups and applications to women from other cultures and nationalities, but we necessarily view them through our own lens. The reader who wishes to apply the principles in this book to groups other than those we cover may wish to supplement the suggested references with further reading. We also recognize a limitation in the range of topics discussed in this book. We mention briefly many issues for women that require a much lengthier volume: body image, eating disorders, multiple concerns with health, sexuality, growing older and aging, distressed relationships, multicultural issues, and so on. We hope that the selected sample of women's concerns will provide a model for feminist practice and research with other issues as they arise in your professional experiences.

We believe it is important to communicate to the reader about the way in which the book was written. As committed feminists, we dedicated ourselves to a collaborative and cooperative project. We view collaboration as a process in which each contributor has an equal part, but in which each may contribute in differing ways. For us, the collaborative venture involved an interrelated set of processes that included trust, protection, egalitarianism, respect, flexibility, self-disclosure, and affirmation.

In trusting ourselves and one another, we felt free to take risks with ideas and suggestions without fear of ridicule or criticism. In respecting each other's identity, we each valued and validated the other's theoretical and epistemological views. Neither of us attempted to mold the other to her own image. In maintaining an egalitarian working relationship, we each reserved the right to contribute our own knowledge, skills, and expertise to the format and content, and to contribute more substantially to those chapters in which we felt most competent. In doing so, we each maintained respect for the other's expertise and the legitimacy of her views, even when disagreements occurred, as indeed they did. In negotiating conflict, we each valued the other's perspective as real and legitimate, and we tried to apply our counseling skills to the process of active listening and offering constructive feedback. Throughout the process of writing this book, we attempted to maintain flexibility and openness to looking at each issue from alternative perspectives.

In applying feminist principles to the lives of other women, we tried as well to apply them to ourselves. In this context, we valued personal self-disclosure, and shared the events in our lives that helped to frame current perspectives. We discovered that we are both survivors; between our two lives we have experienced incest, rape, wife abuse, sexual harassment, career and employment discrimination, dual-career marriages, motherhood, divorce, single parenting, and the professional superwoman syndrome. We have coped with "Woman's Body" through menstruation, pregnancy, child-birth, hysterectomy, menopause, growing older, and an endless obsession with staying thin. For us, then, the personal became political as we considered the external forces that shaped our lives and the personal triumphs that enabled us to emerge with strength and self-affirmation.

We have come to realize that all women are survivors, having faced and met special challenges as a result of our being women in a society that devalues women. We celebrate our success in meeting stress and challenge with creative solutions. In writing this book about "Woman as Problem", we shift the focus to "Woman as Survivor". In doing so, we acknowledge our own strengths as we affirm one another. And we celebrate and appreciate the many wonderful and courageous women whose lives have contributed to the collective tapestry of this book.

Acknowledgements

First and foremost, we want to extend a very special appreciation to Rory Remer and Bud Smith for their continuing support and encouragement.

We also want to recognize the many people who were important to us in the process of completing this task: friends, students, mentors, clients, family, reviewers, and the many women whose lives construct the fabric of this book. Naming some of these people probably leaves out some others—in particular the following played important roles:

Diane Banic
Adena Bargad
Franz Epting
Bonny Gardner
Amy Hack
Rachel Hare-Mustin
Toni Gayle Holland
Carl Hollander
Diana Villaseñor Hollander
Janet Hyde

Shirley Lange
Jeanne Marecek
Joellen Popma
Carolyn Gatliff Provence
Damon Robinson
Mary T. Terlau
Rhoda Unger
Carrie Wilkinson
Alice Zollicoffer

Prologue

We are born into, grow up, and grow old in a society that teaches us that the democratic phrase 'all men are created equal' does not include women. (Benokraitis & Feagin, 1986.)

This is a book about women, but it is also a book about yourself. In reading this book and its perspectives on the lives of women, you may arrive at a place that is different from where you started. You may revise your views and thinking about some theories, clinical interpretations, and information about women's experiences in contemporary society. In your journey through the book, you may begin to revise some of your attitudes toward women's roles and your ideas about the value of feminism in professional practice. We hope you begin to view the world through a different lens.

The self-assessment "Self and World Views" below will be a useful way for you to evaluate some of the ways in which your ideas and attitudes change. Before you start to read the book, take a few minutes to complete the inventory and to score yourself on the four factors on the profile. At the end of the book, we ask you to complete the inventory once more, thereby evaluating the extent of change, if any, on each of the four factors. We hope this exercise will lead to some insights for you. The best way for you to determine its utility is to commit yourself to a pre-post assessment. Your scores should be your own personal property, but sharing the outcomes with a partner or friend may be an enlightening experience. Please try it.

Self-assessment: Self and World Views

Below you will find a series of statements. Some of these statements represent ideas about how the world works. Other statements are about how people might describe themselves. Read each statement carefully and decide to what degree it currently describes you or your ideas about the world. Then select *one* of the five answers that best describes your present agreement or disagreement with the statement.

For example, if you *strongly agree* with the statement, "I like to return to the same vacation spot year after year," you would rate the statement with the number *5* in the space provided as shown below. Remember to read each statement carefully and decide to what degree you think it describes your views at the present time.

1	2	3	4	5
Strongly disagree	Disagree	Neither agree nor disagree	Agree	Strongly agree

_____ (1) I don't think there is any need for an Equal Rights Amendment; women are doing well.

_____ (2) I used to think that there isn't a lot of sex discrimination, but now I know how much there really is.

_____ (3) I just feel like I need to be around people who share my feminist point of view right now.

_____ (4) I want to work to improve women's status.

_____ (5) I think that most women will feel most fulfilled by being a wife and a mother.

_____ (6) It only recently occurred to me that I think it's unfair that men have the privileges they have in this society simply because they are men.

_____ (7) Being a part of a feminist community is important to me.

_____ (8) On some level, my motivation for almost every activity I engage in is my desire for an egalitarian world.

_____ (9) I've never really worried or thought about what it means to be a woman in this society.

_____ (10) When you think about most of the problems in the world—the threat of nuclear war, pollution, discrimination—it seems to me that most of them are caused by men.

_____ (11) My social life is mainly with women these days, but there are a few men whose friendship I enjoy.

_____ (12) I have a lifelong commitment to working for social, economic, and political equality for women.

_____ (13) If I were a woman married to a man and my husband was offered a job in another state, it would be my obligation to move in support of his career.

_____ (14) It makes me really upset to think about how women have been treated so unfairly in this society for so long.

1	2	3	4	5
Strongly disagree	Disagree	Neither agree nor disagree	Agree	Strongly agree

_____ (15) I share most of my social time with a few close friends who share my feminist values.

_____ (16) It is very satisfying to me to be able to use my talents and skills in my work in the women's movement.

_____ (17) I do not want women to have equal status with men.

_____ (18) Recently, I read something or had an experience that sparked a greater understanding of sexism.

_____ (19) Especially now, I feel that the women around me give me strength.

_____ (20) I care very deeply about men and women having equal opportunities in all respects.

_____ (21) I think that men and women had it better in the 1950s when married women were housewives and their husbands supported them.

_____ (22) When I see the way most men treat women, it makes me angry.

_____ (23) If I were to paint a picture or write a poem, it would probably be about women or women's issues.

_____ (24) I feel that I am a very powerful and effective spokesperson.

_____ (25) I don't see much point in questioning the general expectation that men should be masculine and women should be feminine.

_____ (26) I am angry that I've let men take advantage of women.

_____ (27) Particularly now, I feel most comfortable with others who share my feminist point of view.

_____ (28) I am very committed to a cause that I believe contributes to a more fair and just world for all people.

_____ (29) I am not sure what is meant by the phrase "women are oppressed under patriarchy."

_____ (30) I am willing to make certain sacrifices to effect change in this society in order to create a non-sexist, peaceful place where all people have equal opportunities.

_____ (31) Generally, I think that men are more interesting than women.

_____ (32) I think that rape is sometimes the woman's fault.

Scoring

The scale that you have just completed is a revised version of the Feminist Identity Scale (FIDS) discussed in Chapter 13. It is important to note that both women and men can use this scale for self-assessment. To score your responses, please follow the format below. For each factor, add the numbers you assigned to each item in the scale to form a sum total. Then, divide by the number of items in the factor: insert this score in the grid provided below, under the column for Pre-test.

Factor   I: Items 1, 5, 9, 13, 17, 21, 25, 29, 31, 32.   Total/10
Factor II: Items 2, 6, 10, 14, 18, 22, 26.   Total/7
Factor III: Items 3, 7, 11, 15, 19, 23, 27.   Total/7
Factor IV: Items 4, 8, 12, 16, 20, 24, 28, 30.   Total/8

		Score	
Factor		**Pre-test**	**Post-test**
I:	Acceptance	☐	☐
II:	Revelation	☐	☐
III:	Embeddedness	☐	☐
IV:	Commitment	☐	☐

At the completion of the book, we ask you to take the scale once more. After scoring your responses again, insert the factor scores in the column under Post-test. Assess any change and discuss with a friend or colleague. What have you discovered? See p. 327 for a display of scores.

Foundations of Feminist Therapy

The groundwork for becoming a feminist therapist extends far beyond a discussion of theory and technique. Working with women who seek help requires that you are aware of and understand the full context of their experiences and development across the lifespan. Part 1 provides the foundation for feminist therapy by offering a perspective and context within which to view women's life experiences. The three introductory chapters set the stage for a consideration of women's lives in contemporary context. First, we provide a rationale for viewing the field of counseling and therapy with women as a separate discipline. Within this framework, we explore concepts related to sex, gender, and feminism, and we outline an empowerment model of feminist counseling and therapy. Next, we review the changing roles for women and men in contemporary Western societies, and relate these changes to the issues that women bring to counseling. We then consider the psychological world of the developing girl, and review research on gendered socialization practices which support divergences between the developmental experiences of girls and boys.

The remaining three chapters of Part 1 expand the discussion of feminist therapy and explore its application to diagnosis, assessment, and theory transformation. First, we compare several models of feminist therapy with more traditional approaches to psychological intervention, and we expand the empowerment model with specific feminist counseling goals. We then assist you in integrating your current theorizing about how to do counseling and therapy within a feminist format. Finally, we present a critique of traditional assessment and diagnosis and offer alternative strategies that are more compatible with a feminist perspective.

You will note that each chapter begins with a self-assessment, and ends with one or more experiential exercises and further readings The self-assessments are designed to encourage you to be reflective about your attitudes, values, and beliefs about women and men. Many of the self-assessments involve stereotypes that are commonly held by members of Western cultures. Although you may like to believe that you are unbiased, we challenge you to complete these self-assessments conscientiously, and to consider how your current attitudes may reflect stereotyped thinking. An interesting assignment might be to retake each self-assessment after you have read the chapter, and to compare your two sets of responses. The exercises, on the other hand, bring you into more personal contact with the material covered in the chapter by asking you to apply some of the concepts to your own experiences. The exercises may be completed alone, but you will find it more enjoyable and enlightening to share your responses with a colleague or friend. At the end of the book, your final assignment is to retake the "Self and World Views" scale, and to consider how your progress through this book has altered your overall views and attitudes about women and men, and about yourself.

CHAPTER 1

Gender and Sex-role Issues in Counseling

Self-assessment: Beliefs About Women*

For each of the statements listed below, write a number on the line to the right of the statement that describes your response to this statement. Your responses can range from strongly disagree (1) to strongly agree (5). Use the scale below to determine how to score your response.

Disagree		**Neutral**	**Agree**	
Strongly	Somewhat		Somewhat	Strongly
1	2	3	4	5

Women are less decisive than men.   _____

Women are less dominating than men.   _____

Women are more passive than men.   _____

Women have more emotional insight than men.   _____

Women are more interpersonal than men.   _____

Women are less career interested than men.   _____

Women are more vulnerable than men.   _____

Women are less intelligent than men.   _____

Women are less decisive than men.   _____

Women are less sexual than men.   _____

Women are more appearance-conscious than men.   _____

---

* From Belk & Snell, 1986, with permission of Sage Publishing Co.

Women are sexual teases.   _____

Women are more moral than men.   _____

Women act sillier than men do.   _____

Menstruation debilitates women.   _____

Scoring

Now, review your responses. If you marked any of these statements with other than 3 (neutral), you tend to stereotype women in some ways. After you read Chapter 1, it may be helpful for you to discuss your responses with a colleague or friend.

Overview

New approaches to women's mental health have emerged in the wake of the revitalized women's movement. Since 1970, two decades of progress have achieved public recognition of the separate forces that impact on women in Western societies. National and world-wide organizations were born to address the inequalities in the treatment of women's physical and psychological problems and to lobby for change. New scholarship and research on the psychology of women introduced the "second sex" into the medical and psychological literature and brought the lifespan issues of women into sharper focus. The social construction of gender relocates women's problems from individual and internal to societal and external. The feminist construction of gender redefines the nature of women's and men's relationships in terms of the expression and maintenance of power. Emergent client populations were "discovered" where problems were never thought to exist. The challenges of these new client populations stimulated the development of theories, research, and procedures to address their concerns. The combined efforts of women's groups in both the lay and professional communities have resulted in a new agenda for women's mental health. The base of this agenda is rooted in the history and expression of feminism, which nurtures and promotes the goal of equality between women and men everywhere.

This chapter presents an overview of these historic trends and provides an introduction to the remainder of the book. After reading Chapter 1, you will be able to:

(1) Discuss the rationale for a specialty in counseling women.
(2) Differentiate the concepts of gender, sex, and sex role.

(3) List the advantages and drawbacks of both alpha and beta bias in considering gender.
(4) Present at least three differing views of feminism.
(5) Apply these views of feminism to the principles of feminist counseling.

Rationale for a Specialty in Counseling Women

This is a book about women in contemporary context. As a result of the Women's Movement of the late 1960s and beyond, a revolution has occurred in the conceptualization of women's and men's roles in Western society. As emergent ideologies challenged traditional views, the field of psychology began to expand in new directions. The result of this expansion has been a wealth of new knowledge about women and men, revised theories to explain and account for psychological development, and a demand for new applications to prevent and remediate human problems. Within the past 20 years, a new discipline of the Psychology of Women has been established, providing the foundation for an applied science dedicated to Counseling Women.

In the field of mental health, the consideration of sex and gender in the prevalence, etiology, diagnosis, and treatment of a range of human problems has long been neglected. Recent surveys of both clinical and community samples reveal that a high proportion of individuals with signs of depression, anxiety, panic, anorexia, simple phobia, and agoraphobia are women (Eichler & Perron, 1987). In the United States, overall health and community mental health utilization rates are higher for women than for men. Women are prescribed a disproportionate share of psychoactive drugs, many of which have deleterious or unknown side-effects (McBride, 1987). Dissatisfaction with existing theories, knowledge base, and treatment approaches motivated a call for change.

Dissatisfaction with Traditional Treatment

What was the impetus for seeking alternative approaches to women's well-being? The catalyst for change came from many directions, as researchers and clinicians voiced their concerns. Expression of these concerns covered a broad range of issues that addressed both the deficits in our psychological knowledge about women and the problems that existed with current intervention models and practices in the mental health field. A sample of the sources of this concern are listed below.

(1) Dissatisfaction with traditional theories of female and male development and behavior that depicted male-typed traits as the norm and

females as deficient by comparison (Broverman et al., 1970; Doherty, 1976; Gilbert, 1980).

(2)   Frustration with the continuing omission of women from the knowledge base of psychology (Grady, 1981; McHugh, Koeske, & Frieze, 1986).

(3)   Challenging sex-role stereotypes that define "femininity" for women and "masculinity" for men as the most desirable and psychologically healthy adjustments (Bem, 1974; Broverman et al., 1970; Constantinople, 1973.)

(4)   Recognition that many of the reported psychological sex differences in behavior, personality, and psychopathology reflect inequalities in social status and interpersonal power between women and men (Henley, 1977; Unger, 1979).

(5)   Uncovering evidence of sex bias and sex-role stereotyping in counseling and psychotherapy (American Psychological Association, 1975; Hare-Mustin, 1978; Schlossberg & Pietrofesa, 1978; Sherman, 1980).

(6)   Consideration of sex stereotyping and sex bias in the diagnosis of psychopathology (Franks, 1986; Kaplan, 1983; Rothblum & Franks, 1983).

(7)   Determination that women's "intrapsychic" problems frequently originate from sources external to themselves (Brown & Harris, 1978; Miles, 1988, Rawlings & Carter, 1977).

(8)   Concern about the disregard by many mental health professionals for the validity of women's self-reported experiences (Hare-Mustin, 1983; Holroyd, 1976).

(9)   Challenging the practice of attributing blame and responsibility to women for their experiences of sexual and physical violence (Resick, 1983; Walker, 1978).

(10) Rejection of "mother-blaming" in family functioning that pathologizes women's interdependence and involvement and removes responsibility from men for their abuses of power (Bograd, 1986; Caplan & McCorquodale, 1985).

(11) Concern for the increasing medicalization of women's psychological problems, including issues of diagnosis and prescriptive drugs (McBride, 1987; Worell, 1986).

(12) Unwillingness to tolerate the continuing neglect of women's mental health concerns (Brodsky & Hare-Mustin, 1980; Sobel & Russo, 1981).

Catalysts for Change

In response to these concerns, new approaches to intervention with women were envisioned. The emergence of a specialty area in counseling and psychotherapy with women was predicated on four factors that supported its development (Worell, 1980):

(1) The Psychology of Women became a reality, a substantial body of theory and knowledge about the biological, cultural, and psychological characteristics of women.
(2) New client populations emerged "whose non-traditional counseling needs and goals support the development of alternative intervention strategies" (Worell, 1980, p. 477).
(3) New mental health agendas for research on women were initiated and supported by the broad professional community.
(4) Alternative counseling models were developed that addressed the unique characteristics and goals of underserved populations.

In the wake of these developments, training programs in the specialty of counseling and psychotherapy with women have been initiated and implemented. We will discuss each of these factors further in terms of their contributions to the specialty of counseling and psychotherapy with women.

Throughout this book, you will note that we tend to use the terms "counseling" and "psychotherapy" interchangeably. Although these two terms converge in their meanings, in some respects they differ. Counseling has been applied historically to interventions that assist clients in understanding and resolving ongoing problems in living. As such, counseling tends to focus on positive health and well-being. Psychotherapy, in contrast, has been applied traditionally to medical or illness models that locate problems within persons and aim to remediate pathology in patients. Although we adhere to a counseling model, we recognize that feminist intervention may cover a wide range of theoretical positions. The legacy of feminist applications to women's mental health issues is based on early advocacy of "feminist therapy." We will therefore use these terms interchangeably, with the recognition that readers may interpret and apply them in individual ways.

The Psychology of Women and Gender

The first requirement for the development of a new discipline and specialty area is the accumulation of a body of knowledge that serves as a database for theory, research, and applications to practice. Four major outcomes of innovative research on women and gender included: (1) new information about women and their lives in contemporary society; (b) revised views of gender, sex, sex roles, and gender-related behavior; (c) the rise of feminist theory, which serves as a guide to further research and practice; and (d) the applications of these innovations to professional practice.

New Information about Women

Sex-related comparisons

In exhaustive searches of the literature published between 1967 and 1982, Mary Roth Walsh (1985) found over 13 000 citations related to the psychology of women; Kay Deaux (1985) reported 18 000 citations that covered sex differences and sex roles. In the early publications, attention centered on sex comparisons, or how girls and women compared with boys and men on a range of characteristics. These characteristics included, among others, intellectual abilities, achievement variables, career development, interpersonal relationships, aggression, dominance, and prosocial behavior.

Comprehensive reviews of this research by Eleanor Maccoby and Carol Jacklin (1974), and later meta-analyses reported by Janet Hyde and Marcia Linn (1986), concluded that only a few sex differences were reliably established. On the basis of analyses over a wide range of studies, researchers concluded that sex differences have been over-emphasized, and account for no more than 1–5% of the variance in female and male responses (Deaux, 1984; Hyde & Linn, 1986). Thus, on any characteristic, the differences within groups of women and men exceed the discrepancies between them.

Situational contexts

Later research broadened the areas of interest and focused on situational, personality, and contextual correlates of sex-related behaviors on a variety of tasks. These studies looked at such areas as expectancies and attributions for success and failure; interpersonal interactions and group processes; leadership and power tactics; masculinity, feminity, and androgyny; and sex-related attitudes and stereotypes. In these areas, the sex differences obtained were found to vary with the nature of the task, the sex of the experimenter or target persons, and the sex-related attitudes and stereotypes of the individuals involved. Sex was seldom the sole determinant of behavior. Nevertheless, the study of how women and men do or do not differ remains salient in literature on the psychology of women. We discuss this issue below in the context of gender.

Women's lives

More recently, research on women has looked at the meaningful contexts of their lives. This research brought us new information about women in relation to the roles they occupy (e.g. daughter, wife, mother, worker), the discriminatory practices that restrict their opportunities (e.g. in education, employment, politics, and public life), the victimization and violence they experience (e.g. incest, rape, sexual harassment, physical battering), the diverse groups with which they identify (e.g. women of color and differing subcultures, lesbians, older women, disabled), and their psychological processes (e.g. well-being, self-esteem, stress, anger, depression, anxiety). As women's experiences are explored in the context of their real lives, innovative research strategies and approaches have been developed to answer the complex questions that were not previously considered or examined.

Considering Gender, Sex, and Sex Roles

Although the call for change rallied around the issues that faced contemporary women, it soon became clear that women's concerns could be reinterpreted in the broader context of gender. That is, researchers in the field hypothesized that behaviors and attitudes previously believed to be determined by sex (female or male) were societally and situationally created rather than intrinsic to the individual. Some research provided evidence that women's and men's behaviors could be understood in the context of the status inequalities between the two sexes (Eagly, 1987; Henley, 1977). Thus, many of the obtained sex-related behaviors could be interpreted as evidence of unequal power relations between women and men (Crawford & Marecek, 1989; Sherif, 1982). These insights with respect to gender lead us to redefine our constructs and to revise our research strategies.

Gender

Gender is the one of the most salient categories by which people judge and evaluate others (Deaux, 1984). We define *gender* as culturally-determined cognitions, attitudes, and belief systems about females and males. Gender is a concept that varies across cultures, that changes through historical time, and that differs in terms of who makes the observations and judgments.

According to many scholars, the language that we use to describe our experience of the world and that of others profoundly influences our cognitions (Gergen, 1985). From this point of view, we construct a reality about gender that represents a shared social agreement about what is "really" there. The *social construction of gender* defines our knowledge, attitudes, and beliefs about women and men. We take the position here that the characteristics we attribute to gender are not "true" attributes of females and males, but are socially constructed categories that function to maintain female–male dichotomies and male-dominated power structures (Hare-Mustin & Marecek, 1988; Unger, 1983, 1989).

The social construction of gender creates in each of us a self-image of who we are as females and males and how we should behave. From this perspective, the cognition that "I am a woman" functions to activate my entire experience of femaleness in society, and serves as a general schema that shapes my current and future activities (Frieze et al. 1989). Gender also structures the expectations and behaviors of those with whom we interact, resulting in self-fulfilling prophecies that shape our behavior to meet the expectations of important others (Towsen, Zanna, & McDonald, 1989). In Chapters 2 and 3 we review research that demonstrates how the social construction of gender influences socialization practices with girls and boys, and traditional views of the separate roles of women and men.

For many professionals in the field, gender becomes the major issue in working with women.

> The social construction of gender plays a major role in the definition and diagnosis of illness, timing and expression of symptoms, treatment strategies, and theoretical explanations. Thus, mental illness is as much a social as a personal event (Cheryl Brown Travis, 1988, p. 2).

Throughout this book we caution you to be aware of your gender stereotypes and to sensitize yourself to the ways in which your gender conceptions may influence the therapeutic process. We shall have more to say about gender issues in later chapters.

The meaning of gender differences

It is important to consider two major approaches to gender-related characteristics, those that exaggerate the differences between females and males and those that ignore them. Rachel Hare-Mustin and Jeanne Marecek (1988) refer to these two stances as alpha bias and beta bias. They maintain that bias toward either approach to gender is problematic for women.

Alpha bias assumes an "essentialist" position, that there are real and enduring differences between the orientations, abilities, and values of women and men. This position tends to dichotomize women and men, to support different roles based on their natural dispositions, and to encourage separatism. Examples of alpha bias that heighten the valuing of women include beliefs about women's special "ways of knowing" (Belenky et al, 1986), and views of woman as intrinsically relational, caring, and connected (Chodorow, 1978; Gilligan, 1982).

Examples of alpha bias that are used to devalue women are found in the fields of sociobiology and endocrinology. Here, obtained gender differences are attributed to genetic determinism (Kendrick & Trost, 1989; Wilson, 1975) or to the presumed effects of androgens on brain functioning. In the former case, men's "promiscuity" and social dominance are regarded as natural and rooted in genetic survival of the fittest. In the latter case, sex differences in performance, such as in spatial relations, are attributed to the selective effects of male androgens on the right cerebral hemisphere (brain lateralization). In both examples, gendered patterns of behavior are assumed to result from endogenous or biological variables that reflect "true" sex differences. Based on her examination of extensive data, Ruth Bleier, a biologist, concludes that there is no firm evidence for a biological basis of behavioral differences between females and males (Bleier, 1984, 1988).

Alpha bias becomes useful, however, in asking new questions about women's experience and in looking at the particular circumstances of their lives apart from those of men. We see in Chapter 13 that a feminist approach to research suggests that specific questions about the lives of women may be generated as a result of their unique psychological environments.

Beta bias ignores or minimizes differences between women and men. Traditional psychological research has erred in the direction of beta bias by (a) ignoring questions related to the lives of women, and (b) assuming that findings based on male samples could be generalized to explain women's experience and behavior. Minimizing sex differences frequently leads to disadvantaging women, such as assuming that they have equal access to resources and equal opportunities in relationships, employment, and leadership positions. Ignoring questions about women's lives has created a void in the psychological literature about one-half of the human population. Hare-Mustin and Marecek (1988) caution the helping professional in particular that either alpha or beta bias in the context of the counseling setting can be disadvantageous to the client.

Sex

In contrast to the cultural determinants of gender, we refer to *sex* as a descriptive, biologically-based variable that is used to distinguish females from males. In the research literature, sex has been used in two contexts: as a subject variable, and as a stimulus variable (Unger, 1979). As a subject variable, sex is used to define two categories of people, female and male. Aside from certain physical and reproductive capabilities, few if any characteristics can be explained by sex alone. In contrast, sex as a stimulus variable serves to structure and define what is observed by others, so that comparisons between females and males become reflections in the eye of the observer. We refer to many of these observations as *sex stereotypes*, or generalizations about a person's behavior on the basis of membership in a particular observable group (female or male).

At this point, you may wish to review the responses you made to the self-assessment exercise at the start of this chapter. Do any of your ratings reflect stereotypes about women?

Because sex-related attributions and expectations are so heavily dominated by gender conceptions, we may never be able to extricate the "true" effects of sex from those of gender; that is, the direct influence of gender begins at birth, thus confounding the two variables. In Chapter 3, we discuss the influence of gender expectations on the development of girls and boys. Until gender no longer serves to frame social conceptions of female and male behavior, we believe that sex should remain as a purely descriptive, rather than an explanatory, concept.

Sex roles

The concept of *sex role*[1] refers to patterns of culturally approved behaviors that are regarded as more desirable for either females or males. The social construction of gender in any culture will function to determine broad expectations for female and male sex roles. Thus, gender conceptions define what we believe is appropriate behavior in various situations for ourselves as well as for other women or men.

Sex roles in any society are influenced by a large number of variables, and will vary within different subcultures and across historical time. We conceptualize the individual's sex-role functioning as multidetermined: by societal forces, by life development events, and by the person's own psychological processes. These variables are displayed in Figure 1.1. Consistent with our discussion of gender, we assume that being female or male influences the expression and experience of each variable in the model.

It can be seen from this model that a change in a person's sex-role conceptions and behavior (the gendered self) can be influenced by any of the variables in the display. For many psychologists, one goal of psychological development is to eliminate the gendered self, so that sex roles become obsolete and non-functional. With a transcendence beyond sex roles, both women and men would perceive themselves and others as humans with equal options for alternative behaviors (Bem, 1987; Lott, 1985a; Worell, 1981).

In Chapters 2 and 3 we discuss traditional and emerging nontraditional sex roles. In Chapter 4, we review psychological theories that envision a gender-free individual. One of the aims of a feminist approach to counseling is to assist individuals in freeing themselves from the constrictions of rigid sex-role prescriptions. The goal of a gender-free self for women, however, is far from realized in a societal structure in which gender determines so many of their life-course events. In Figure 1.1, however, we place feminism at the base of the social forces, to suggest that the goals of the feminist agenda fit the ideals of a gender-free society.

Feminist Psychology

Research and scholarship in the psychology of women is not necessarily feminist. There is a great deal of overlap, of course, and the major scholarly

---

[1]Although gender role is frequently used to describe socially constructed expectations for females and males, we use the term sex role with the same understanding.

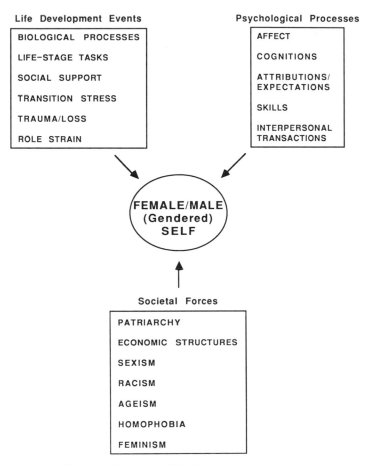

Figure 1.1. A model of sex-role functioning

journal in psychology, *The Psychology of Women Quarterly*, is feminist in its goals, procedures, and content (Worell, 1990, in press). In this section, we define feminism and provide examples of feminist orientations to personal and social issues, and applications to clinical practice. Feminist research is covered in Chapter 13. Feminist assessment, counseling, and psychotherapy are explored in greater detail in Chapters 4, 5, and 6.

Defining feminism

Feminism is defined in *Webster's New World Dictionary* (1978) as (a) "The principle that women should have political, economic, and social rights equal to those of men", and (b) "the movement to win such rights for women"

(p. 514). With this seemingly benign definition, we wonder why we frequently meet with a negative reaction when one of us says "I am a feminist". If you are not a feminist within this definition, do you then believe that women should not have rights equal to those of men?

In reality, the range of belief systems attached to the term "feminist" is broad. In Table 1.1 we provide a sample of some alternative attitudes toward feminism on the part of women (Worell, 1984). These attitudes may differ according to the dominant political position of the woman[2] as well as the topic or area that her attitude targets. We display only four possible targets here: attitudes toward men, other women, work, and the Equal Rights Amendment. Many other targets can be influenced by attitudes toward feminism.

At the extreme left of Table 1.1, for example, we see the woman who opposes the feminist position and who accepts women's submissive status with respect to men. Some of the clients we discuss in later chapters fit this model. Some of these women do have paid employment outside the home, but maintain an oppositional view toward having equal power with men. Thus, these schemata are only suggestive of typical positions toward feminism, and may not fit any one individual accurately in all areas. Which position do you fit? Do you match with all four target areas for this position? Perhaps this table will assist you to perceive that the label of *feminist* is attached to many possible meanings and can be associated with a range of different attitudes and behaviors.

Defining feminist psychology

The applications of the diverse views of feminism have resulted in conflicting definitions in the professional field. Since we take a constructionist view of gender, we shall also do so for feminism: that is, by agreement, we select certain characteristics of the feminist agenda that we believe are most reflective of the values and beliefs to which we subscribe. We are indebted to Barbara Wallston (1986), however, for her cogent articulation of a similar set of feminist values. At the base of these views is the conviction that women's problems cannot be solved in isolation from the gender politics of the larger social structure.

For our purposes, feminist psychology embraces five major tenets:

(1)   We recognize that the politics of gender are of central concern and are reflected in women's lower social status and women's oppression in most societies.

---

[2]There are many ways to categorize the diversity of feminist political positions. Our labels do not coincide exactly with some frequently used categories of feminist beliefs (e.g. liberal, radical, socialist), and should not be confused with them.

Table 1.1. *Will the Real "Feminist" Please Stand Up! Women's Attitudes Toward Feminism—what kinds of experiences would fixate a person at one level or facilitate movement to another? (From Worell, 1984, with permission.)*

Sample target areas	Oppositional *Submissive*	Traditional *Accommodating*	Exploitive *Manipulative*	Contemporary *Egalitarian*	Activist *Confronting*	Radical *Avoidant/hostile*
Men	Men should have financial and political power. Takes subservient role; dependent. Men determine the rules. Role is to please men.	Accepts role of traditional wife/ mother, daughter. Accepts status quo in male–female relations.	Uses men to get what she wants. Tries to please spouse, boss and co-workers (male). Accepts male power structure and uses for own purposes.	Wants egalitarian role at home, work, play. Wants men to be androgynous, participants, partners.	Wants egalitarianism. Male power is the issue. Males will take power and dominate unless women assert themselves. Supports male liberation.	Rejects male companionship and male organization. These are the dominant groups and cannot be dealt with.
Career	Full-time homemaker. Antagonistic to "working mothers". May do volunteer work or help spouse.	Career/job secondary to home/family. Financial reasons for work—not career development. Spouse career takes precedence. Accepts homemaker role; volunteer.	Sees own career as important— work ethic—I made it on my own with hard work and persistence.	Accepts interrupted career but wants full-time; upwardly mobile, wants equal pay and opportunity for self.	Career development critical to women's economic independence— money is power, women need equal access to power/money.	Women must take care of women completely, at home, work, production of goods and services.

(Continued overleaf)

Table 1.1. (continued)

	Oppositional	Traditional	Exploitive	Contemporary	Activist	Radical
Sample target areas	Submissive	Accommodating	Manipulative	Egalitarian	Confronting	Avoidant/hostile
ERA	Opposed, believes it will take away her right to be protected and cared for.	Antagonistic or neutral—doesn't see need for it, believes women have equal opportunity and status.	Supports—will guarantee equal pay and working conditions. May deny that she has ever experienced sex discrimination.	Supports—recognizes inequalities between sexes and wants equality across the board.	Promotes actively—sees male power structure as root of women's lower status—women must change the system.	May actively support or else withdraw from contact with other women's groups. Separatist.
Women	Feels alliance to friends who also stay at home. Antagonistic to competent women in responsible positions.	Feels alliance to peers, wives of spouse's colleagues.	Keeps women powerless. Competitive—I'm better than they, made it without them.	Accepts as colleagues, likes women, cooperates in joint ventures.	Sisterhood and woman power is the only way to achieve equality—nurture each other. May serve as mentor to other women.	May reject heterosexual women because they collude in their own domination.

(2) We seek equal status and empowerment in society not only for women, but for all oppressed minority groups.
(3) We value and seek knowledge about women's experience.
(4) We acknowledge that values enter into all human enterprises and that neither science nor practice can be value-free.
(5) We are committed to action for social and political change.

You may be able to detect the outlines of the *Webster's Dictionary* definition of feminism here, but we advance further. The feminist agenda looks at the uses of power and how status hierarchies deprive women of their freedom and equality. We include other oppressed groups, because the politics of racism, ageism, homophobia, and poverty also deprive individuals of their human dignity and liberties. In valuing women's experiences, we legitimize the study of women as a scientific enterprise, and we encourage innovative methods of research to explore these experiences. We reject the notion of a totally "objective" science or practice related to behavior, and call upon researchers and practitioners to acknowledge their values and biases.

Finally, we believe that few individual women can achieve equity alone, and that the commitment to feminism requires both individual and collective action for social and political changes. Therefore, our feminist counseling approach seeks a dual outcome: assisting the woman toward empowerment in her own life, and seeking change in the social power structure that forms the basis of many of her problems.

Implications for Training and Practice

The advances of the new Psychology of Women in terms of theory and knowledge provide exciting implications for training programs in counseling and psychotherapy. In Chapter 13, we offer a model of training that incorporates this knowledge and uses it in the service of educating and sensitizing prospective practitioners. As a student, we want you to be aware of the gender stereotypes you may hold, your attitudes toward non-traditional or gender-free roles for women and men, and your understanding of the politics of gender. In particular, you will want to understand the social impact of violating traditional sex roles and the price that women (and men) pay for doing so.

An effective program for training counselors for women incorporates a research component that avoids gender bias in method and content and that explores the lives of women. The program also includes a feminist analysis of client issues and careful supervision to provide constructive feedback to the therapist. We believe that without such awareness, you are likely to impose your stereotypes on your clients. In doing so, you may unwittingly support them in "adjusting" to the status quo and in remaining in subordinate life positions. As you read this book, please complete all the self-assessment and awareness activities. These activities are designed to assist you in evaluating, and changing if necessary, your social constructions of sex and gender. The goal of these activities is to promote the effective and ethical treatment of women.

Emergent Client Populations

The second requirement for a new discipline in counseling women is a client population whose needs and goals are not being met by traditional practices and procedures. How does the population of women clients differ from those of the past? What are their special needs that require advanced knowledge, skills, and specialized training?

Changing Times

Family role shifts

First, the dramatic changes in the formation and maintenance of family roles in the past 20 years has lead to a shift in women's life-styles, in the situations that they face, and the problems with which they cope. In particular, women are remaining single more frequently and for longer periods of time, finding partners or marrying later, having fewer children, entering the paid labor force at an unprecedented rate, developing new career paths, separating and divorcing more often, coping with single parenting, re-entering higher education at later ages, experiencing interrupted careers, and recoupling or remarriage. They are growing older and living longer, and may find themselves "sandwiched" between growing children and elderly parents, or living alone. New definitions of "family" have encouraged marginalized groups such as lesbian and bisexual women to confront their relationship needs more openly. Each of these life events may present situational coping problems and issues for which women seek help.

The increase of women in the paid labor force confronts them with a host of new issues: managing multiple roles, negotiating dual-career and egalitarian relationships, coping with role conflict and role strain, non-traditional career development and change, employment discrimination, professional isolation, sexual harassment, management training, assertiveness concerns, workforce re-entry, and retirement.

The prevalence of singleness and high divorce rates opens up issues of finding new relationships, establishing sexual satisfaction, developing social support networks, divorce counseling, child custody decisions, managing step-children and reconstituted familes, and coping with financial stress and loneliness. Chapters 7 and 10 consider clients for whom family and work-related conflicts motivate them to seek counseling.

Women and violence

Second, the exposure of violence and sexual assault to public scrutiny in the past 15 years has had two positive effects on client populations. First, women are seeking assistance following violent experiences such as rape or wife abuse. Second, women who have been sexually abused through incest or assault as children are coming to terms with their early victimization. The establishment of crisis centers for sexual assault and wife battering has encouraged many women to seek assistance who formerly would have suffered in silence. The "normalization" of this violence may appear frightening when we look at the prevalence rates, but the public attention to violence has had the salutary effect of encouraging women to say "No more secrets." Chapters 8 and 9 deal with clients who were physically and sexually abused.

Women and body

Third, certain syndromes have increased in reported frequency as society places continuing demands on women to conform to sex-role standards, and as women are becoming concerned with the care and maintenance of their bodies. Here, we find a rising prevalence of women concerned with body image and weight control, as evidenced by eating disturbances such as anorexia, bulimia, and obesity. Women also seek psychological help in dealing with medical and physical concerns: AIDS, mastectomy, menstruation-related distress, reproductive issues including pregnancy, unplanned pregnancy and infertility, and problems concerning the abuse of addictive substances such as alcohol and prescription drugs.

Women in high risk groups

Finally, we are increasingly aware of high risk group membership for women. Women in high risk groups are those for whom their issues as women in society are compounded with exclusion and discrimination as a result of experiences of racism, ageism, homophobia, and poverty (see Figure 1.1). Women from high risk groups have been reluctant to seek help from the mental health community, partly because they anticipate and frequently experience a re-enactment of societal discrimination in psychotherapy. As new approaches such as cross-cultural counseling are initiated, more of these women are encouraged to seek help in dealing with their multiple issues. We discuss two of these high-risk groups in Chapter 11: lesbian women, and women of color.

Implications for Research and Practice

The emergence of multiple and complex lifespan issues for women in contemporary Western societies provides a sufficient rationale for the development of new approaches for addressing these issues. The implications of this emergent client population for both research and practice are evident.

First, there is a pressing need for increased research to broaden the knowledge base about women's mental health concerns. The issues that face contemporary women have only begun to attract the attention of the scholarly community. More information is required before we can gain a firm understanding of the factors that contribute to women's stress and distress as well as to their strengths and resilience. This knowledge should be extended to all groups of women:

> As women's lives become the focus of investigation, researchers have explored questions about women of color, women in poverty, and women with non-traditional affectional preferences. Ignored and neglected populations are targeted for greater understanding into the themes of their lives and the meanings that are transmitted to them as a function of their minority status. As each new generation of researchers explores issues of personal relevance and value, they will uncover new truths about women and men that may change the "facts" that underlie our current understandings. (Worell, 1989, p. 216.)

In the section below, we discuss the Women's Mental Health Agenda (Eichler & Perron, 1987) developed under the auspices of the National Institute of Mental Health, which outlines some priorities for research and development with particular attention to underserved populations.

Second, it is evident to many of us in the professional arena that traditional approaches to prevention and intervention for women are inadequate. Traditional models of treatment that label the woman as disordered and that locate the problem within her biology, personality, or deficient skills, are insufficient to address the multiple forces that impact on her well-being. We take the position here that "fixing" the woman to return to her former status and adjustment is unsatisfactory and unacceptable. The psychiatric concept of "remission" as a definition of a positive outcome for psychotherapy exemplifies this traditional approach. Models of counseling and psychotherapy that aim to reduce stress and remove "pathology" are frequently inappropriate for women and have targeted only one side of women's lives. Innovative approaches and strategies are clearly required. Chapters 4, 5, and 6 present a framework for reconstructing an alternative view of the counseling process for women.

Research Agendas for Women's Mental Health

The third requirement for a specialty in counseling and psychotherapy with women is a firm foundation of research related to their mental health concerns. At the present time, this research base is deficient and in need of concerted support and expansion. On the basis of a series of conferences, the National Institute of Mental Health (NIMH) (Eichler & Perron, 1987) developed an Agenda for Research in Women's Mental Health.

The National Institute of Mental Health Agenda

From the diverse possibilities for research activities, a panel of experts recommended five areas for further study and funding. These included:

(1) Diagnosis and treatment of mental disorders in women.
(2) Mental health issues for older women.
(3) Stressors affecting the mental health of women: multiple roles.
(4) Causes and mental health effects of violence against women.
(5) Stressors affecting the mental health of women: poverty.

We offer these research priorities as examples of the public realization that women's mental health issues have been ignored and that the time is ripe for action on many fronts.

New Models and Emergent Procedures

The final step in developing a specialty in counseling and psychotherapy with women commits us to introduce innovative models and procedures. Dissatisfactions with and perceived limitations of traditional therapies paved the way for three major changes in the treatment of women.

First, the development of feminist approaches to intervention with women signalled a dramatic break from previous therapies in many aspects of values and procedures. Second, specialized interventions for underserved or inappropriately served client groups have been formulated that target the unique issues and concerns of these groups. Third, ethical principles in counseling women have been developed by feminist groups that outline and detail appropriate ethical issues in treatment procedures for women.

Feminist Counseling and Psychotherapy

The development of feminist principles and procedures in counseling stretches from the early beginnings of consciousness-raising groups (Brodsky,

1973; Kravetz, 1980) to the establishment in 1982 of the Feminist Therapy Institute for advanced psychotherapists (Rosewater & Walker, 1985). Between these two developments, many talented practitioners and scholars, too numerous to cite here, have contributed creatively to the growing literature in this field. We credit our thinking to the accumulated writings, dialogue, and practical experiences of a host of our colleagues.

Feminist principles

There are several approaches to feminist therapy that differ on specific beliefs and procedures, but they contain many elements in common (Marecek & Hare-Mustin, 1987). Among these common elements are:

(1) A consciousness-raising approach: clients are helped to differentiate between the politics of the sexist societal structure that influence their lives and those problems over which they have realistic control. Consequently, intrapsychic causation for problems in living is supplanted by exploration of sex-role messages and societal expectations.
(2) An egalitarian relationship between client and therapist: the client is encouraged to set personal goals and to trust her own experience and judgement. Power differentials between client and therapist are minimized.
(3) A woman-valuing and self-validating process: women are encouraged to identify their strengths, to value and nurture themselves, and to bond with other women. Language forms that devalue women are reframed from weakness to strengths (e.g. terms such as "enmeshed and fused" may be reframed as "caring, concerned, and nurturing").

An Empowerment Model

In this book, we present an empowerment model of counseling that incorporates and expands on the three principles expressed above. Empowerment is conceptualized in two ways. First, the individual is empowered in dealing with her life situations through achieving flexibility in problem-solution, and developing a full range of interpersonal and life skills. She learns to identify and cherish her personal strengths and assets as well as to recognize her responsibility for change. Second, empowerment encourages women to identify and challenge the external conditions of their lives that devalue and subordinate them as women or as members of minority groups, and that deny them equality of opportunity and access to valued resources. Feminist approaches to empowerment thus incorporate both internal and external contributions to personal distress and well-being, and assist the woman to discriminate between them. This discrimination functions to free her from feelings of being "crazy" and out of control, and replaces her sense of powerlessness with strength and pride in her ability to cope. Chapter 4 describes the empowerment model within the context of three Principles of Feminist Therapy and provides a set of therapeutic goals that match each principle.

Feminist strategies

The tenets of feminist counseling cut across diverse theories and specific techniques. Feminist therapists endorse a range of theoretical views and employ many different kinds of strategies and specific interventions. The two authors of the present volume are personally committed to two different, but not incompatible, theoretical views: cognitive–behavioral, and psychodrama. Each of us has adapted our basic theoretical orientation and techniques to render it compatible with Feminist Therapy principles and procedures. In Chapter 5, we provide a method for transforming a theory of counseling so that it is compatible with feminist views. Some theories may be more conducive to this transformation process than others, depending upon the extent to which they endorse sex-biased concepts or procedures.

Across various theories, however, some techniques are used commonly by most feminist therapists. Examples of strategies that are common to feminist approaches include sex-role analysis, power analysis, and demystifying methods. In *sex-role analysis*, clients are helped to identify how societal structures and expectations related to traditional gender arrangements have influenced their lives. *Power analysis* explores the power differential between women and men (and/or between oppressed and dominant groups) in Western societies and assists clients in understanding both the destructive and effective uses of power. In *demystification*, clients are provided with information that teaches them about the process of change and provides them with the tools for evaluating and monitoring their own progress. While demystification is not unique to feminist approaches, it is used strategically as a means of reducing the power differential between client and therapist and thus empowering the client. Each of these strategies, as well as many others typically used in feminist therapy, is described more fully in Chapter 4.

Specialized Interventions

In addition to the introduction of feminist approaches to counseling, specialized interventions have been created that address the needs of particular population groups. One issue of *The Counseling Psychologist* (1979, **8** (1)) contains no less than 17 sets of procedures for differing groups of women clients. For each group, differing sets of knowledge, attitudes, and skills are proposed for ethical and competent intervention with that particular group.

In other contexts, recent advances in specialized counseling procedures include career development, rape crisis, counseling survivors of incest and sexual abuse, counseling bulimic and anorexic clients, lesbians, agoraphobics, survivors of wife-battering, minority women from many subcultures, older women, re-entry women, and many more. For each of these special groups, particular sets of knowledge, attitudes, and skills may be required. In Chapter 11, we present a model for feminist cross-cultural counseling and some special groups with whom the model might be applied.

Ethical Principles

Finally, a third area in which new approaches to women have been advanced is in the development of ethical principles specifically designed for intervention with women. Following a major survey in which sex-biased practices of psychotherapists were uncovered (American Psychological Association, 1975), several groups within the American Psychological Association formulated ethical principles in practice with women. These principles are further described and explained in Chapter 12. The principles are not required for licensing in any states but Kentucky and Rhode Island (according to our knowledge). Efforts are currently being directed toward integrating these principles into standard ethics procedures.

One indicator of the legitimacy of a discipline or field is the presence of an ethical code. We believe that the adoption of ethical procedures should become routine for all the helping professions, working not only with women but with all minority or oppressed groups.

Directions for Change

Feminist views of intervention with women incorporate a mandate for public action and social change. It is insufficient to "fix" the woman for functioning in a dysfunctional society. Our model of intervention includes an outreach component that includes action on three levels: community involvement, consumer enlightenment, and social policy.

At the community level, we involve ourselves with agencies and local groups that are working on behalf of women's issues. The consumer enlightenment level encourages us to disseminate information about women to relevant groups, so that this information can be integrated toward modifying prevailing attitudes, beliefs, and practices. Relevant groups might include law enforcement, parents, teachers, schools, and the public media.

Action on social policy goes further to influence legislation, funding, and public policies that will eliminate gender-based stereotypes, prevailing power differentials, and support of discriminatory practices. As professional practice, consumer enlightenment, and social policy work together to effect social change, we will see new visions of what we are and what we can become.

Summary

In this chapter, we have presented the outlines for developing and implementing a specialty in Counseling Women. The requirements for this specialty include a field of knowledge about the psychology of women, a population of clients whose needs are not being met by current approaches, a research agenda that provides a blueprint for future research needs, and a therapeutic counseling approach that is tailored to the population of clients being served. The outlines for this specialty require new training programs to implement the guidelines for change, and an outreach plan that effects changes in policies across educational, government, and political structures.

Activities

A
As a woman—look back at your life as a woman. Consider the challenges you faced, and assess your strengths as you met and survived these challenges. Appreciate and take pride in your strengths. Share your thoughts with a partner or friend.

B
As a man—think about the important women in your life. Select one or several and consider the challenges they faced as women. Assess their strengths as they met these challenges. Appreciate and take pride in their strengths. Share your ideas with a partner or friend.

Further Readings

Deaux, K. (1984). From individual differences to social categories: Analysis of a decade's research on gender. *American Psychologist*, **39**, 105–116.
Gilbert, L. A. (1980). Feminist Therapy. In A. M. Brodsky & R. Hare-Mustin (Eds.), *Women and Psychotherapy*, (pp. 245–266). New York: Guilford.
Worell, J. (1989). Images of women in psychology. In M. Paludi & G. A. Steuernagel (Eds.), *Foundations for a Feminist Restructuring of the Academic Disciplines*, (pp. 185–224). New York: Harrington Park.

CHAPTER 2

Changing Roles for Women

Self-assessment: Women and Men in Society*

The Social Order Scale

Respond to each statement by circling the number on the right that best describes your position.

		Agreement			Disagreement		
		Strong	Moderate	Mild	Mild	Moderate	Strong
(1)	At the present time, both women and men have equal opportunities in education and employment.	1	2	3	4	5	6
(2)	Women have more to gain than to lose by asking for complete equality.	1	2	3	4	5	6
(3)	Housekeeping and raising children cannot keep most women satisfied as a full-time job.	1	2	3	4	5	6
(4)	Most women have only themselves to blame for not doing better in life.	1	2	3	4	5	6

* From Worell & Worell, 1977, with permission.

	Agreement			Disagreement		
	Strong	Moderate	Mild	Mild	Moderate	Strong
(5) Women are usually less reliable on the job than men because they tend to be absent more often and to quit more often.	1	2	3	4	5	6
(6) The special courtesies extended to women have frequently kept women feeling helpless and in their place.	1	2	3	4	5	6
(7) Children of employed mothers are often less well adjusted than children of unemployed mothers.	1	2	3	4	5	6

Questions 8–14: what is your opinion of the following?

	Agreement			Disagreement		
(8) The US constitutional Equal Rights Amendment for women.	1	2	3	4	5	6
(9) Educational counseling and training to help women select careers appropriate for their sex.	1	2	3	4	5	6
(10) If both parents are employed, child-rearing responsibilities assumed mainly by mothers.	1	2	3	4	5	6
(11) If both parents are employed, housekeeping shared equally by each.	1	2	3	4	5	6
(12) Publicly supported day-care facilities for children of employed parents.	1	2	3	4	5	6

		Agreement			Disagreement		
		Strong	Moderate	Mild	Mild	Moderate	Strong
(13)	Preferential consideration to men in hiring, salary and/or promotion, since most men are the family breadwinners.	1	2	3	4	5	6
(14)	The Women's Liberation Movement.	1	2	3	4	5	6

Your responses to the Social Order Scale reflect your general attitudes toward new social roles for women and men. Your scores reflect the degree to which you believe in traditional or non-traditional roles in the areas assessed by these 14 questions.

Scoring

Add your scores in the following manner:

(1)	Total questions 1, 4, 5, 7, 9, 10, 13	21 or less	= traditional
		21–35	= emergent
		35–42	= contemporary
(2)	Total questions 2, 3, 6, 8, 11, 12	28 or higher	= traditional
		14–28	= emergent
		6–14	= contemporary

Overview

The focus of this chapter is on the impact of changing social and personal roles on the issues that women bring to the counseling setting. Changes brought about in the latter half of the twentieth century—movement of women into the workforce, altered expectations for marital and motherhood status, and revised conceptions of appropriate sex-role behaviors—leave both women and men with changing norms for personal well-being and life adjustment. These changes also lead to new sources of personal and culturally-based stress. It is important for helping professionals to consider the sociocultural sources of women's mental health issues if they are to be of optimal assistance in facilitating productive change. After completing Chapter 2, the reader will be able to:

(1) Compare traditional wife and motherhood roles with new options for women in terms of expectations and outcomes for personal well-being and sources of stress.
(2) Describe the major groups of single women, and summarize important issues that therapists may want to consider in working with these women.
(3) List and explain the benefits and costs of paid employment outside the home for women, including outcomes in both family and work-related settings.
(4) Contrast traditional and emergent views of appropriate sex-role behaviors and evaluate their implications for women's personal well-being.
(5) Discuss the concept of androgyny in terms of its advantages and limitations as a model of mental health.

Evolving Social Roles

During the second half of the twentieth century, dramatic changes have occurred in the home and work-life of women in industrialized Western societies. Four major changes are notable:
(1) Delay in the age of marriage and child-bearing.
(2) A reduction in the size of families.
(3) A move from primarily family and child-care orientation of women to increased participation in the paid workforce.
(4) An increase in the incidence of single status and single-parenting.

These events have important implications for women's roles as wife, mother, and worker, and for women's development as individual human beings.

Women as Wives

Traditional wives

In traditional marriages, women have been expected to assume the role of wife as a major goal in their lives. Social expectations, as well as legal requirements, encouraged the woman to change her name, give up her interests and friends in favor of those of her husband, move to her husband's residence and relocate with his employment changes, and to depend upon him for economic security, social status, and personal identity. The loss of personal identity through marriage has been reflected in the traditional reference to a married woman as "Mrs" followed by her husband's name, whereby both her first and last names disappear and become merged with his. Thus, Mary Jones becomes Mrs John Smith, and in effect becomes an extension of his identity. In traditional marriages, women are younger, smaller, and less educated than their husbands, further encouraging the woman to depend upon her husband for protection and support.

In most parts of the Western world, legal aspects of the marital contract provided the woman with limited rights to jointly-owned property, family finances, and freedom from marital rape and physical abuse. According to social convention, her major occupational role is that of housewife, a position which is accompanied by low social status, little recognition, and no direct pay. Her major rewards come through keeping a clean home, raising accomplished children, and being a "good wife." She is able to gain social recognition and status mainly through her husband's occupation and achievements (Sales, 1978; Unger, 1979; Worell & Garret-Fulks, 1983).

Although their work within the home holds no exchange value as a marketable commodity, women contribute to their husbands' careers and achievements by freeing them from home and child-care responsibilities. Wives have typically served as housekeeper, cook, child-care worker, nurse, social secretary, transportation agent, and general keeper of the peace. Husbands have expected that in return for their part in providing economic support, their wives would provide for them a haven of rest and tranquility.

Variations in aspects of the traditional wife role may be found according to both ethnic group and socioeconomic status. Black women, for example, have typically worked outside the home, and therefore have been less dependent upon husbands for economic support and social status. Prevailing social mores and marital laws, however, have generally supported a system in which a woman's social and legal positions were subordinate to those of her husband.

Changing views of marriage

The women's movement challenged the ideal of a husband-dominated marital arrangement, and spurred on both legal and social modifications in marital roles. In the United States, as well as in other Western countries, many of the laws that denied financial, property, and personal rights to married women have been removed, and women have been changing their expectations for the marital relationship. As women delay marriage in favor of increased educational and career development, their expectations for the marital relationship also change. Adding the roles of paid worker and educated person to the marital contract decreases women's traditional economic dependency and encourages them to regard the relationship in a more egalitarian manner.

As women's goals for marriage become more egalitarian, the role expectations for "wife" have been modified. Increased education and career plans encourage the wife to consider her own needs, plans, and goals, as well as those of her family. She increases her expectations for equal sharing of household tasks, child-care, and decision-making. She may also expand her conceptualization of the ideal marital relationship, becoming more concerned with achieving a sharing and communal partnership (Lange & Worell, 1990; Worell, 1988). She may begin to view the marriage as one in which companionship, communication, friendship, and intimacy are important parts of the contract. These expanded expectations may put added burdens on some relationships that were launched with more traditional conceptions of wife as helpmate and homemaker by one or both partners.

As women increasingly seek equality in their intimate relationships, men have experienced pressure to make some adjustments in their concepts of marriage. Most research finds that men remain more traditional than women in their ideals of marital relationships. Men, more than women, prefer that their spouse remain at home and not be employed full-time, and few men want an employed wife where there are preschool children in the home (Herzog, Bachman, & Johnson, 1983; Komarovsky, 1976; Yorburg & Arafat, 1975). Women who intend to pursue full-time careers following marriage are still viewed as the least desirable mates by college men (Hollender & Shafer, 1981).

Contemporary marriage

The majority of contemporary marriages in the United States are dual-earner relationships, however, in which women are working both for economic support and personal satisfaction. New approaches to role-sharing in marriage require that both partners remain flexible and open to alternatives. The fact that women in dual-earner marriages continue to assume the major share of household and childcare duties, as we shall see, results in potential role-strain and is a source of continuing dissatisfaction for many women. Studies on marital satisfaction reveal that where a discrepancy exists between the spouses, it is usually the wife who expresses a discontent (Locksley, 1980; Ryne, 1981; Steil & Turetsky, 1987). Although modern marriages assume both traditional and non-traditional forms, many couples are struggling to resolve the balance of role-sharing and division of tasks in their relationships. In the most traditional marriages, in which the wife chooses the role of full-time homemaker, satisfaction may be generally high for both spouses, although somewhat more for the husband. Wives who either stay home because their husbands expect them to do so, or work outside the home by necessity rather than choice, experience more distress and depression than wives in traditional or egalitarian marriages (Krause, 1983).

In favor of the more egalitarian marriage, there is evidence that husbands and wives who are both employed by choice and who share household duties may experience the greatest mutual psychological benefits of marriage and the least degree of personal stress (Gray-Little & Burks, 1983; Ross, Mirowsky, & Huber, 1983; Steil & Turetsky, 1987).

Single Women

Although the role of wife is normative in the stream of women's development, an increasing proportion of women over the age of 18 live alone. Either by choice or by circumstance, singleness is becoming a stable lifestyle for many women. Who are the single women and how do they fare in society as non-wives? Single women can be divided into three major groups: those who have delayed or rejected marriage, those who are divorced or separated, and those who are widowed. Although many of these women will eventually marry or remarry, the single style of life is becoming an acceptable and desirable life choice for some women. A fourth group, composed of lesbian women, may be either single and unattached or may be living in a committed same-sex partner relationship. Although some lesbian women do marry, as a group they are more likely to retain single status.

Delaying or rejecting marriage

Women who are single by choice tend to be well-educated, professional, and invested in their careers. Studies on single career women provide us with evidence that in general they have high self-esteem and are satisfied with their lives. They believe that they live rich and interesting lives, and they highly value their independence (Gigy, 1980; Lowestein et al., 1981). Cultural stereotypes portray the single woman as a "spinster" or "old maid" who is single not by choice but because she was not "chosen." Social attitudes are changing, however; three-quarters of the respondents in a recent national survey believed that being single was as acceptable as being married. In contrast, a similar survey 20 years previously found that three-quarters of the respondents believed that singleness reflected both maladjustment and questionable morality (Institute for Social Research, 1976). Probably, satisfaction with single status increases as the woman has a successful career, substantial income, a network of friends, and good health. For many single women, however, few or none of these conditions may be met.

Some single women reject traditional heterosexual marriage in favor of attachments to other women. These women may live alone or with another woman, but are usually legally single, since marriage between same-sex partners is proscribed in every culture. Research on the life-styles of lesbian women suggests that lesbian and heterosexual women are similar on a variety of mental health criteria (Sophie, 1982). In their close relationships, however, lesbian women tend to value autonomy, role flexibility, and egalitarianism (Caldwell & Peplau, 1984). The unique issues for lesbian women center on their minority and devalued status in Western cultures and the societal stigma with which they all live.

Terminating marriage

The next group of single women are divorced or separated. In the United States, about 40% of all marriages terminate in divorce, so that the population of single women in this category remains relatively high. Because divorce is a traumatic and emotionally disturbing process, even when desired by the individual, women in the process or aftermath of divorce comprise a steady clientele for the counseling professional. The first 2 years following divorce tend to find the woman beset by economic stress, depression, loneliness, and second thoughts about her marriage (Bloom, Asher, & White, 1978; Hetherington, Cox, & Cox, 1982). If there are young children, she is doubly strapped by overload and financial insufficiency. If she is over 55, she may be faced with new demands for independence and employment that strain her present skills and capabilities. Although the social status of the divorced woman is stigmatized less today than 20 years ago, it still remains an unstable societal position accompanied by negative public attitudes (Worell & Garret-Fulks, 1983).

Widowed and older women

The population of older women is the fastest growing group in the United States. Of these women, over two-thirds are widowed, living alone, and at high risk for poverty, loneliness, poor health, and depression. The older widow is less likely than her male counterpart to remarry and to have an adequate retirement income, and is more likely to live in substandard housing. These conditions are even more visible for minority women, those who are Black, Hispanic, or otherwise non-Caucasian (Eichler & Perron, 1987; McBride, 1987). Although they may require our services even more than do other groups, older women are the least likely to come to the attention of mental health professionals (McBride, 1990). A recent survey of services offered by psychologists revealed that only 2.7% of services were provided to older people (VandenBos, Stapp, & Kilburg, 1981).

Lesbian women

Finally, the population of lesbian women, previously invisible in a heterosexual society, has begun to emerge as a group voicing legitimate interests and special needs. As more lesbian women choose to live openly in society with respect to their life-style, their personal issues have come to the attention of the mental health community, and the professional literature has expanded accordingly (see, for example, Martin & Lyon, 1984; Moses & Hawkins, 1982). As a group, lesbian women face massive societal and interpersonal homophobia (fear and denigration of homoerotic life-styles), stigmatization and oppression as a minority group, and conflicts about how to deal with the issues that arise in the context of their personal orientation. Counseling lesbian women has become a subspecialty for some professionals, reflecting the complexities of living a homoerotic life-style in a heterosexist culture. Chapter 11 will consider in more detail some of the issues that lesbian women may bring to psychotherapy.

Single women—summary

For all groups of single women, their anticipated and culturally sanctioned role as someone's wife has been replaced by reconstructed roles that require new skills and a fresh view of alternative life-styles. The costs and benefits of the single life-style are important to consider, and for many women the balance clearly favors singlehood. For some women, affectional and sexual attachments to other women are paramount in their lives. A lesbian style of life involves benefits and costs in addition to those of other non-married women.

Women as Mothers

Traditional mothers

In almost all societies, women are given primary responsibility for childcare. Women's reproductive capabilities and ability to nurse the infant, of course, made them the more likely candidates for the mothering job. Until recently, women had little control over their reproductive functioning, and were likely to spend a substantial portion of their lives pregnant, nursing, or caring for minor children.

In the role of "primary parent," mothers have been held accountable for the progress as well as the problems of their offspring. Mothers have been typically idealized as the all-loving, caring, accepting, sacrificing, and ever-present parent, and have been expected to place the needs of their children above those of their own. Mothers who worked outside the home were held responsible for obtaining appropriate childcare and were expected to leave work when the child was ill. But mothers who placed their children in daycare have also been seen as putting their children at great psychological risk (Hare-Mustin, Bennett, & Broderick, 1983). Although recent studies have demonstrated amply that appropriate daycare may be just as advantageous to children's development as full-time care with a primary parent (Etaugh, 1980), both the lay public and the professional community continue to place responsibility on the woman when problems arise.

In a recent survey of major clinical journals, covering 125 professional articles published over a span of 12 years, two researchers found that mothers were "blamed" for 72 kinds of psychopathology in their children. In comparison to mothers or both parents, fathers were least likely to be seen as responsible for the personality and behavior problems of their children (Caplan & Hall-McCorquodale, 1985). Mothers have been blamed for spending too little time (neglect) or too much time (overprotection) with their children, for providing insufficient love (maternal deprivation) or excessive love (maternal smothering), for disciplining too much (the demanding mother) or for providing too little control (the indulgent mother). The "Jewish mother" is famous for instilling inescapable guilt in her children.

The traditional role of mother, then, left the woman with a tenuous and risky path to achieving recognition and personal fulfillment, since she was expected to attain these goals through her children. Studies of marital happiness indicate that satisfaction is highest either before the birth of children, or following their departure in late adolescence (White, Booth, & Edwards, 1986). Consistent evidence suggests that the constant care of young children, in particular, has negative effects on women's psychological well-being and is associated with both depression and physiological symptoms (Hetherington, Cox, & Cox, 1982; Kessler & McRae, 1981). Full-time housewives whose children are all in school are beset by low self-esteem and high psychological symptomology (Hoffman & Nye, 1974). Although the rewards of motherhood may be high, the costs are also considerable.

New options for motherhood

The introduction of widely available birth control methods and increased options for elective termination of pregnancy have contributed to the contemporary phenomenon of delay in marriage and childbearing, reduction in number of children in families, and a rise in voluntary childlessness (Cook, West, & Hammer, 1982; Faux, 1984; Hoffman, 1977; Yogev & Vierra, 1983). As a result of increased life periods during which women are freed from childcare responsibilities, personal choice has been expanded and more options for lifespan personal development are available to women.

Changing expectations about wife/mother roles are revealed in studies with both high-school seniors anticipating their future lives, and with older adult women at varying stages in their life development. Recent studies with large samples of high-school seniors found that students believe parenting should be shared by mothers and fathers, and that fathers should not be relieved of childcare involvement. In the areas of household tasks, there is some discrepancy in the expectations of women and men for egalitarian role assumption; fewer males than females rate equal sharing of household tasks as desirable or at least acceptable (Herzog & Bachman, 1982; Herzog, Bachman, & Johnston, 1983; Tittle, 1981).

In a lifespan study comparing younger women (age 18–34) with middle-age (35–54) and older (over 60) women, the younger women rated five traditional women's tasks as less important to their lives than did the older samples. These tasks included selecting a mate, learning to live with a marriage partner, starting a family, rearing children, and managing a home. The three groups of women were drawn from a wide range of economic circumstances and represented a variety of ethnic respondents (26% were Black). It is notable, however, that on a rating scale from least to most important in their lives, even the younger group of women rated all five tasks at the upper end of their value scales (Meriam & Hyer, 1984). These data support the proposition that as today's younger women face expanded options for life planning, traditional tasks of childrearing and home management assume reduced salience in their lives.

Despite these changes in family expectations and the timing and structure of parenthood, women who become mothers are still assuming the major responsibilities for the daily care of the children and for the multiple tasks involved in running a household (Gilbert, 1985; Kellerman & Katz, 1978). Traditionally female tasks, such as everyday family cooking, cleaning up after meals, cleaning the house, doing the laundry, purchasing food, caring for preschool children and for children after school hours and when they are ill, are still assumed primarily by wives, regardless of whether or not they are employed outside the home (Nyquist et al., 1985). Even in households in which both parents are employed full-time, only 30% of the fathers in a recent study participated meaningfully in both household and childcare tasks (Gilbert, 1985). Figure 2.1 displays relative participation in childcare and household tasks by wives and husbands.

These data from many sources suggest that although attitudes about women's roles have become less traditional with regard to mothering and household responsibilities, in practice women remain the primary parents and the major keepers of the home. The influence of this division of labor on the process and outcomes of children's socialization and on women's experiences of stress and "role strain" are considerable. The expectation that a woman will be the primary parent also influences child-custody decisions following divorce and the status and well-being of women who become single parents.

Single mothers

In the United States, 20% of all families with minor children are mother-headed, and the number of one-parent families is increasing at 10 times the

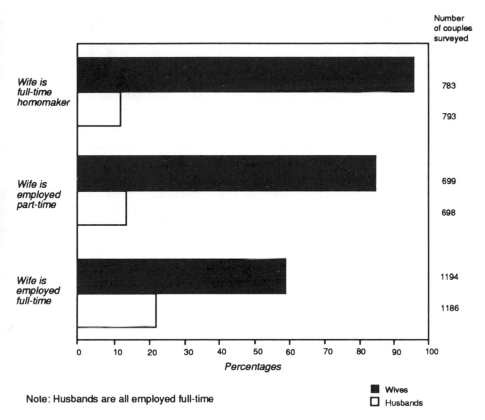

Figure 2.1. Who does the housework? Percentage of husbands and wives who do over 10 hours weekly. Adapted from Blumstein and Schwartz (1983)

rate of two-parent families (United States Bureau of the Census, 1980). Between 30% and 40% of all American children will live in a single-parent home during their formative years, 98% of which are mother-headed (Glick, 1979). Among Black families, the rate of single parenting is double that of White families (Emery, Hetherington, & DiLalla, 1985). Considering the high incidence of single-parent homes, it appears that these family arrangements are indeed normative in contemporary society.

Single-parent mother-headed homes consist of three types: divorced or separated mothers, never-married mothers, and lesbian mothers (who may be from either of the two groups). All single mothers experience similar stresses and problems in daily living, but each type of single parent experiences additional sources of culturally-induced stress. For all single mothers, three types of stress predominate: economic insufficiency, role strain, and social isolation (Worell, 1988; Worell & Garret-Fulks, 1983).

At the economic level, grim statistics remind us that the income of one-parent families in the United States is only one-third that of two-parent families, and almost half of all families below the poverty level are headed by a woman (Weitzman, 1985). Role overload is a common stressor in the lives of single mothers. They are juggling the responsibilities of dual parenting, as well as all the requirements of the traditional wife, mother, and worker roles. Finally, social isolation is more common for single than for married mothers, and is characterized by fewer sources of emotional and family support and less frequent contact with anyone other than co-workers and children (Barnett & Baruch, 1987; Keith & Schafer, 1982; Leslie & Grady, 1985, Weinraub & Wolf, 1983). In comparison to single fathers, moreover, single mothers experience less appreciation from their children and less positive feedback about their parenting role (Ambert, 1982). As a mediator of perceived stress, social support affects both the appraisal of life events and the coping skills that are mobilized for problem-solution (Brownell & Schumaker, 1984).

Single mothers, facing multiple stressors, are at high risk for incidence of depression, low self-esteem, and feelings of personal incompetency and helplessness (Kazak & Linney, 1983; Keith & Schafer, 1982). Never-married and lesbian mothers experience the additional stressors of negative community evaluations, and legal risks in losing their children in adoption or custody battles (Lenwin, 1981). The consequent over-utilization of mental health facilities by single mothers may further stigmatize them as inadequate parents (Guttentag, Salsin, & Belle, 1980).

Elective non-mothers

Although over 90% of American women do become mothers, the attractions of childlessness are motivating some contemporary women to take another look at motherhood. Consonant with advances in the control of reproduction and revised attitudes toward motherhood, increasing numbers of women are electing to remain childless. In tandem with opportunities for control of fertility, expanded educational and career orientations may induce some women to select a childless life-style. Among professional women, in particular, the rate of childlessness exceeds that of the general population, and younger married women are choosing to have fewer children than did their foremothers (Yogev & Vierra, 1983).

Women's motives for voluntary childlessness range across commitment to work, desires for personal freedom and growth, and interest in maintaining a companionate marriage (Bram, 1984). Attitudes toward "Woman as Mother" remain strong in the general population, however, and childless families frequently find that family and friends demand explanations about why they chose not to have children. Studies with college students find that attitudes toward voluntarily childless women are substantially negative, viewing them as selfish, immature, and unloving (Peterson, 1983; Ross & Kagan, 1983). These negative attitudes do not match the findings on personal and marital satisfaction of childless couples, however, which suggest that they are generally well-adjusted and happy individuals (Houseknecht, 1979). Further, in an intensive set of interviews with a large sample of 719 older women (age 60–75), both childless women and those who had children reported satisfaction with their own life-style, and perceived more rewards to their own life-style choice and more costs of the opposite choice (Houser, Berkman, & Beckman, 1984).

Women as Workers

As we have seen, most women no longer believe that being a wife and mother are the only important goals in life. Although over 90% of high-school and college women plan to marry and have children, they also intend to combine a job or career with their family lives (Herzog, Bachman, & Johnson, 1983; Meriam & Hyer, 1984).

Paid employment

Women are entering the paid labor force at an unprecedented rate. The traditional family of an employed father and full-time mother of two or more children is now becoming atypical rather than the norm. In the United States, only 7% of families conform to this pattern (United States Department of Labor, 1985). The majority of women of working age in Western industrialized nations are working outside the home, from over 60% in the United States to about 75% in Sweden (Lott, 1987). Of these women, over half are married with preschool children. How does the world of work affect the changing roles of women?

We are using the concept of work here to denote paid employment, usually outside the home. Although women who take sole responsibility for home and children, or who volunteer for community projects, are certainly working in terms of time, effort, and expertise, their work differs in several ways from paid employment in the external labor force. Full-time homemakers receive no direct wages, they are seldom rewarded with recognition for their efforts and skills, and they have difficulty in restricting their hours of working to a predictable 8-hour schedule. They also have no opportunity for advancement or for bettering their position or remuneration.

Women generally seek paid employment for the same reasons that men do (Voydanoff, 1980). Paid employment outside the home provides multiple sources for stimulation and self-esteem: interesting personal contacts, exciting or stimulating work tasks, opportunities to be relieved temporarily of constant childcare, achieving recognition and self-fulfillment, freedom to develop and expand personal skills and creativity, and opportunities to earn money (Beckman, 1978). Of course, not all paid employment provides these benefits, and women who work in low-paid service and industrial settings may continue to work at tedious or unchallenging jobs primarily out of economic necessity. Almost half of all employed women in the United States are single, and many families require two paychecks to maintain a minimally comfortable standard of living (US Department of Labor, 1985).

In contrast to the majority of men, however, women face many obstacles to satisfaction and achievement in the workplace. Among these obstacles are lower wage-scales, job segregation into low status positions (secretary, sales clerk), fewer employment benefits, less opportunity for advancement and fewer opportunities to use experience and education, higher layoff and job-loss rates, sexual harassment, and devaluation of personal motivation and competence. In addition, working women, more than men, face the ever-present tasks of home and childcare, and suffer from work overload and role-strain.

As a result of societal sexism and discrimination, all working women must cope daily with many of these obstacles to job satisfaction. We shall see that, as a function of their socialization experiences, women tend to take the blame for their job-related stress, and attribute to their own ineptitude the problems that are clearly more a function of external discrimination and sexism. The issues surrounding personal, as compared to external, barriers to achievement in the workplace are prime targets for counseling with employed women. Chapter 10 discusses issues in career counseling.

Women in male-dominant professions

As women increase their opportunities and aspirations for career development and personal accomplishment, they are moving into professions previously occupied mainly by men. In addition to the issues discussed above for women in the workplace, the position of women in work-settings traditionally reserved for men place them at greater risk for social isolation, sexual harassment, and pressure to perform as token woman. Jeanne Lemkau (1986) aptly points out that these women are both highly visible and are treated in stereotypic ways by the men with whom they work. In their professions, they are expected to be assertive, competent, and to show leadership and autonomy, all of which may violate their own and their male co-workers' expectations for women's typical behavior. Lemkau suggests that the combination of women's double bind regarding their required and socialized sex-role behaviors, their attributional styles of self-blame for work-related difficulties, and their occupational isolation and lack of support, all contribute to high risk for developing symptoms of depression.

Because these tend to be independent and ambitious women prior to entering a male-dominated profession, they may show additional symptoms of the superwife/supermom syndrome, believing that they must do everything well. Due to their socialization as women in society, they experience guilt for being the "working mother" of their children. As autonomous women, they may deny their need for support, thus cutting themselves off from the willingness to ask for help when they can't "do it all." As a result, these women may experience not only stress and depression, but overwhelming loneliness. Lemkau (1986) offers counseling interventions that target the focal issues of these non-traditional working women. We shall discuss these interventions in Chapter 10.

Changing Roles for Women—Summary

In summarizing the changing roles for women as wives, mothers, and workers, it is important to separate our personal ideals and preferences from the realities of women's lives. As women face new choices, the decision-making tasks become more difficult. Both counselors and clients need to adjust their conceptions and solutions to the actualities of today's families and the new expectations that confront both women and men. As these role expectations change, moreover, we experience revised conceptions of how women and men ought to behave as females and males. The changing conceptions of appropriate sex-role behavior in contemporary society is certainly one of the more important advances in the lives of contemporary women. At this point in your reading, you may want to review your responses to the self-assessment at the beginning of the chapter. Would you classify your views of women's social roles as traditional, neutral, or emergent? Let us examine the traditional and changing expectations for gender-related behavior called sex roles.

Emergent Sex Roles

We saw in the preceding section that the impact of gender on lifespan experiences is profound. The status of being a woman or man in all societies has provided a framework around which role prescriptions and life opportunities have been organized. These role prescriptions are accompanied by stereotyped expectations about appropriate behaviors to be displayed by women and men in a variety of situations, expectations that are moderately consistent across cultures and historical times.

We have previously defined psychological sex roles as clusters of expectations for behaviors and activities that are considered to be desirable for either females or males in any society (Bem, 1974; Kelly & Worell, 1977; Worell,

1978, 1981, 1982, 1988, 1989b). These expectations are stereotypes in that they reflect simplified generalizations about females and males that are intended to apply to all individuals within each of the two groups. Some of these sex-role stereotypes may be true for some individuals (e.g. men are stronger than women), but they are seldom useful when understanding a particular person.

Traditional Sex Roles

Psychological theorists have attempted to understand the process by which women and men develop sets of personal behaviors that fit many of the cultural stereotypes. This process has been referred to as "sex typing," or the means by which females and males develop "feminine" and "masculine" behaviors, attitudes, preferences, and life goals (Huston, 1983). Feminine orientations are those believed to be proper and healthy for women, and masculine behaviors are thought to be more appropriate and healthy for men. As individuals develop, they learn what these expectations are for their gender group, and they tend to adapt themselves accordingly.

Sex typing has been shown to include a wide range of human behaviors, including personality traits, attitudes about how women and men should behave, choice of clothing, language, non-verbal mannerisms, occupational and career decisions, and leisure activities. Traditional sex typing of personality traits encourages women to be kind, nurturing, submissive, expressive of feelings, and dependent upon others; and men to be assertive, achieving, dominant, autonomous, less inclined to display feelings, and self-determined. Indeed, in studies on college populations, the majority of women and men have described themselves in terms similar to these sex-typed conceptions (Rosenkrantz et al., 1968). More recent research on personality stereotyping finds little change over time. On 53 of 54 traits comparing the "typical" woman or man, respondents decribed the typical woman in terms of an "expressive" cluster of traits as more emotional, home-oriented, considerate, understanding, excitable, and devoted to others. The "competency" characteristics of self-confidence, independence, and decisiveness were attributed more frequently to men (Ruble, 1983). Although people are less likely to stereotype themselves than others, cultural sex-role stereotyping has clearly not disappeared.

The implications of these sex-role stereotypes for women's development and well-being in society are considerable. Sex-role conceptions affect the way we think about and evaluate ourselves, the way that others regard us and deal with us, and the opportunities that society affords the individual for personal growth and development. In particular, traditional sex-role stereotypes about desirable behaviors and personality traits have serious implications for women's personal well-being.

Challenges to Traditional Sex-role Behavior

The challenge to traditional ideas about appropriate sex-role behaviors for women and men emerged as a companion to changes in women's social roles. As women and men move toward more equality in their work and family activities, sharp distinctions between their effective skills begin to lose whatever function they may previously have had. Concepts of healthy adjustment have become less attached to gender-based criteria and are more attuned to the situations in which people actually function. Mounting evidence that traditional forms of sex-role behavior might be damaging to personal well-being and effective social functioning have resulted in efforts to develop alternative models of healthy and optimal human behavior. Two streams of research were particularly impactful in turning attention toward new models of well-being: first, that of Broverman and her associates (1970), who examined attitudes of mental health professionals toward the "healthy" man or woman; and second, the work of Sandra Bem (1974) in developing and testing a new measure of sex-role functioning that assesses "masculine" and "feminine" traits independently of their gender base.

Mental health stereotypes

In a landmark study exploring the attitudes of mental health professionals toward women, Broverman et al. (1970) reported that the healthy woman was rated differently than the healthy man on a set of sex-typed trait descriptors. The healthy man was rated similarly to the healthy adult as relatively independent, decisive, and assertive, but the healthy woman was seen as more emotional, submissive, and dependent than the healthy man. These trait descriptions of the well-adjusted woman by mental health professionals served to highlight the prevailing conception that good adjustment was characterized by conformity to sex-role stereotypes. Broverman et al. interpreted these findings as a demonstration of a double standard of mental health, whereby the healthy woman was evaluated in more negative terms by the mental health community. A recent replication of this study with college students revealed that contemporary men still judge women and men differently on standards of mental health. Women respondents, on the other hand, judged both women and men in similar terms (Brooks-Gunn & Fisch, 1980).

The damaging aspects of a double standard for evaluating appropriate healthy behavior are twofold. First, it provides a source of negative evaluation, both external and personal, for women who conform to sex-role standards by relegating them to an inferior status and labeling them as less well-adjusted. Second, it puts the non-conforming woman at risk for censure if she violates the standard, thereby placing her in an impossible bind with

Table 2.1. *Items on the Bem Sex-role Inventory that were Judged to be More Desirable for the Typical American Man (Masculine) or for the Typical American Woman (Feminine). (Adapted from Bem, 1981.)*

More desirable for men	More desirable for women
Defends own beliefs	Affectionate
Independent	Sympathetic
Assertive	Sensitive to needs of others
Strong personality	Understanding
Forceful	Compassionate
Has leadership abilities	Eager to soothe hurt feelings
Willing to take risks	Warm
Dominant	Tender
Willing to take stand	Loves children
Aggressive	Gentle

no acceptable alternatives. Studies on sex-role stereotyping have found that both women and men who violate sex-role standards tend to be judged more negatively than those who conform (Coie, Pennington, & Buckley, 1974; Zeldow, 1976).

Measuring androgyny

A second line of important research on sex roles challenged the traditional conception of masculinity and femininity as bipolar end-points of a single measurement continuum (Constantinople, 1973). The standard approach to sex-role functioning was to designate an individual as either more or less masculine, so that as masculinity decreased, femininity increased. Thus, an individual could not be characterized by both sets of traits. New methods of measuring sex-typed personality traits were developed, bringing with them a radically different conception of healthy sex-role functioning.

Sandra Bem (1974) proposed that the "feminine" and "masculine" components of personality are complementary rather than competing dimensions. Accordingly, she developed a scale (the Bem Sex-role Inventory or BSRI) that assessed these two dimensions separately, allowing the individual to obtain an independent score on each set of traits. Table 2.1 displays the items on the short form of the BSRI (Bem, 1981). Bem further proposed a new model of healthy functioning, suggesting that individuals with both sets of sex-typed personality traits should benefit by being more flexible and adaptive across a variety of social settings (Bem, 1974, 1975). Bem's formulation of equality in the display of sex-typed personality traits was labeled *psychological androgyny*.

Subsequent research with similar sex-role trait scales suggested that androgyny may be conceptualized as a high degree of both "masculine" and "feminine" characteristics, and that these may be better seen as "instrumental" and "expressive" clusters of traits or self-presentation styles (Spence, Helmreich, & Stapp, 1975). According to the androgyny formulation, the sex-typed person is one who displays a majority of characteristics that are gender-congruent. Thus, the "feminine" woman would endorse more of the expressive traits than the masculine or instrumental traits. In contrast, androgynous persons should see themselves as having both sets of traits available to them, depending upon the demands of the situation.

The androgyny model of psychological functioning captured the imagination of the research community, and stimulated a wide variety of studies designed to assess its utility. How does the androgyny model of healthy functioning compare with competing models, and what are its implications for the psychological well-being of women?

Androgyny and Psychological Well-being

For feminist therapists, a central issue in androgyny research concerns the status of androgyny as a model of mental health. Do androgynous individuals demonstrate higher personal effectiveness, better psychological functioning, and greater life satisfaction than sex-typed persons? Is the androgynous person at lesser risk than the sex-typed one for serious psychological disorders? Should the changing roles for women and men include dramatic revisions in the way in which we view our own sex-role functioning, in the manner in which we socialize our children, and in the behaviors that we support and encourage in our clients?

The answers to these questions are confounded by the complex nature of sex-role behavior, and by the wide range of strategies through which researchers have attempted to evaluate the androgyny concept. In particular, researchers have looked at personality traits, situational behaviors, self-esteem and life satisfaction, rates of psychological disturbance, and interpersonal interactions. It would be difficult and unrealistic to presume that simple measures of expressive and instrumental personality traits (such as those displayed in Table 2.1) can predict individual adjustment and well-being across all life situations. First, it has been shown that sex-role assessment across traits, activities, and beliefs are generally uncorrelated (Orlofsky & O'Heron, 1987; Spence & Helmreich, 1980). Second, it has become clear that sex-typed personality traits do not remain constant over time, and are reciprocally affected by the situation in which the individual operates as well as by the life-stage and current life-role requirements (Nash & Feldman, 1981; Spence & Sawin, 1985; Worell, 1981). Thus, a comparison across competing models becomes a tenuous task. Finally, the concept of androgyny has received serious challenges from the academic community (Lott, 1985a).

Evaluating Androgyny

The interpersonal domain

In her early work, Sandra Bem explored the hypothesis that individuals who scored androgynous on the BSRI were more likely to fit her "flexibility/ adaptive" model across a range of situations than were persons who saw themselves in traditional sex-typed terms. In comparison to sex-typed males, she found that androgynous males exhibited higher levels of nurturant and playful behavior (Bem, 1975; Bem, Martyna, & Watson, 1976), and androgynous women and men were more responsive in an empathic interpersonal situation (Bem, Martyna, & Watson, 1976). Androgynous persons were also less uncomfortable than sex-typed individuals when asked to engage in cross-sex activities regarded as more appropriate for the other sex—men asked to iron or women to hammer a nail, for example (Bem & Lenney, 1976).

In tempering the generalizability of these findings, other researchers have pointed out that (a) women and men did not always behave similarly within sex-typed categories, and (b) Bem used different people across situations, thus not entirely validating the idea that the same person in the androgyny model would be equally effective in any situation. Nevertheless, Bem's research was important in demonstrating the possibility that traditional sex-typed behavior was not necessarily the better model of effective functioning.

Subsequent research on interpersonal skills, however, tends to support the utility of self-reported androgyny in relation to effective social behavior (Ickes & Barnes, 1978; Kelly, O'Brien, & Hosford, 1981), and willingness to provide nurturant and emotional support (Worell, Romano, & Newsome, 1984). In adolescence, androgynous girls are rated higher on social acceptance and good peer relationships than are sex-typed girls, a finding that certainly runs counter to traditional expectations (Massad, 1981; Wells, 1980). In interpersonal situations, it appears that the social skills involved in initiating a relationship and maintaining effective communication may well be reflected in both the instrumental and expressive traits or self-presentations represented by the androgyny typology. Studies such as these have important implications for the personality of the counselor as well, suggesting that an androgynous self-concept may be an effective stance in some counseling situations (Petry & Thomas, 1986).

The well-being domain

Aside from interpersonal skills, research to evaluate the androgyny model has examined two broad groups of behaviors: those that suggest effective psychological functioning, such as measures of self-esteem, life satisfaction, and effective coping skills; and those that signal dysfunction, such as signs of anxiety and depression, social isolation, substance abuse, and over-utilization of mental health facilities. The results are mixed. When the instrumental and expressive characteristics are examined separately, it appears that the two sets of traits contribute independently, each providing a positive set of outcomes. Little evidence exists that the combined interaction or blending of these traits of self-concepts is more advantageous than either set of scores alone (Cook, 1987).

Across many studies, moreover, the instrumental or "masculinity" model seems to hold an advantage over androgyny (Whitely, 1983), whereby individuals who score high on assertive and dominant traits reflect equal or higher levels of self-esteem, general adjustment and freedom from depression and anxiety (Basoff & Glass, 1982; Cook, 1987; Orlofsky & O'Heron, 1987; Whitely, 1983). The "masculinity" model was empirically derived from outcomes on a wide range of sex-role research, suggesting that the instrumental traits of autonomy and assertiveness will lead to more effective functioning because they are more highly valued in society and lead to higher rewards for the individual who uses them (Kelly & Worell, 1977).

For women in particular, the evidence suggests that the traditional convergence model of psychological development is the least advantageous. That is, women who are relatively unskilled or unassertive in situations requiring independence, competence, and mastery are likely to experience some problems in coping with both internal and external sources of stress. The woman with a sex-typed self-concept in today's society is more likely to suffer from low self-esteem, higher levels of anxiety and depression, lower peer acceptance, and social withdrawal (Burchardt & Serbin, 1982; Feather, 1985; Whitely, 1984). We are particularly concerned about the higher incidence of symptoms of depression in women with traditional orientations. That is, an interpersonal style that is characterized by compliance, passivity, low assertiveness, and prioritizing the needs of others ahead of her own, places the woman at high risk for the development of negative personal outcomes. For both adolescent and adult women, the contributions of the instrumental components of personal functioning suggest that these traits or self-perceived attributes are important for psychological well-being across varying life stages.

Beyond Androgyny

Despite the mounting evidence that restricted personality traits or sex-typed self-concepts in both personal and social realms may not be the most advantageous to women, the androgyny model has experienced some criticism. In designating "masculine" and "feminine" expectations for behavior, it may be that we are perpetuating a gender-based view of human functioning. In response, several researchers and theorists have called for a moratorium on descriptions of behavior based on gender.

Gender-free theory

Sandra Bem proposes a gender-free approach, in which the most advantageous position is to respond to situations without attention or concern for their gender implications. People with gender-free schemata, she contends, tend to perceive others in terms of their human characteristics, independently of their gender-stereotyped behavior (Bem, 1983). She calls for a gender-free society in which both children and adults will be free to express their personalities in ways that are not restricted to being a girl or boy, woman or man.

Transcendence theory

A second view of progress beyond androgyny calls for sex-role transcendence (Rebecca, Heffner, & Olenshanksy, 1976). In the transcendent model, the individual progresses through three stages, from the undifferentiated responding to gender of the preschool child, to sex-typed dichotomies corresponding to female and male stereotypes, and finally to a stage in which individuals respond in unique ways that are independent of gender. The transcendent model assumes that children learn sex-role stereotypes as a normal aspect of cognitive development, in attempting to develop categories to organize the environment.

   Although gender-free and transcendent theories of sex-role responding appear to arrive at similar conclusions, their assumptions about development and child-rearing appear to differ dramatically. That is, gender-free approaches propose that children should be socialized to reject gender stereotypes and to develop behavior patterns that are independent of being a girl or boy. Since stereotyping of gender-related images and activities characterizes most cultures, parents who endorse a gender-free society need to challenge these stereotypes with their children and to encourage children to do the same (e.g. girls can be doctors and daddies are not always the boss). In contrast, a view that believes that gender-stereotyping is "normal" at certain ages would allow instances of children's stereotyped thinking to persist, thus encouraging the development of sex-typed behaviors and sexist orientations to oneself and others.

Toward empowerment

In contrast to either sex-typing, androgyny, gender-free or transcendence models of psychological well-being, we have proposed an alternative model of personal *empowerment*. Chapter 1 presented the outlines of this empowerment model and we shall be returning to it throughout the book. An empowerment model incorporates both a personal and a social component, dealing not only with intrapsychic functions but considering as well the person within the context of the larger social environment and its institutions. The empowerment model assumes that individuals cannot be fully in a state of well-being if they must function in environments that are patriarchal and sexist. The personal factor provides for flexibility and competence in all areas of personal functioning (not just sex-typed traits). The environmental factor envisions a society that is free of stereotypes and barriers based on gender, race, age, sexual orientation, disability, and other status characteristics that limit individual freedom and opportunity for life satisfaction and well-being.

In comparing the empowerment model to androgyny, two differences are apparent. First, the concept of androgyny is restricted to a limited set of sex-typed personality traits, and thus fails to encompass a full range of potentially healthy and adaptive behaviors. Second, the androgyny model places the source of women's adjustment within themselves, thereby denying the important contributions of external opportunities, supports, and barriers to the well-being of the person. In contrast, an empowerment model encompasses both the individual as she functions in her life space, as well as the characteristics of her present and past environments that impact her. To the extent that these environments continue to confront her with discriminatory messages and practices, her mental health and well-being will be at risk. We will address these issues further in Chapters 3, 4, and 6.

Comparing competing models

Since there is very little research specifically addressing the models that go beyond androgyny, how can we evaluate them? Clearly, one solution is to increase our research efforts to explore the psychological benefits or costs to individuals who are relatively androgynous, gender-free, transcendent, or empowered in their thinking and behavior. Certainly, we hold a gender-free society as our ideal community, in which all individuals grow and develop in a culture that is devoid of stereotypes, barriers, and social/economic arrangements that restrict the well-being of women (Lott, 1985a). From a practical position, however, we maintain that society, as currently organized, has far to travel before it reaches the stage of transcendence or gender neutrality. As people function in an environment that continually reminds them of who they are and what is expected of them as women or men, it seems important to develop strategies to confront and counteract the debilitating effects of sex-role stereotyping and rigid social roles.

Although androgyny in personal functioning and self-presentation may not be our final resting place, we believe that the theory has contributed an important perspective, drawing our attention to the ways in which women and men have restricted their interpersonal behavior and conceptualizations.

To the extent that we can attend to these considerations in the counseling situation, we may be able to raise the level of awareness of clients toward understanding and dealing not only with the role-constricted behaviors that may impede and limit their personal well-being and social functioning, but to the societal conditions that support these behaviors.

Implications for Counseling

Changes in the social and interpersonal roles of contemporary women and men have contributed in dramatic ways to the process and outcomes of counseling and psychotherapy. At least three important issues have been brought to bear on the therapeutic experience:

(1) How we look at personal well-being and conceptions of psychological disorder.
(2) How we evaluate and intervene in the sources of stress in women's lives.
(3) Our conceptions of realistic opportunities and goals for personal growth and change.

Psychological Well-being and Disorder

As individuals reorient their life styles and behavior, patterns of adjustment that formerly appeared "normal" or "deviant" now take on a new set of perspectives. The average family no longer exists, and expected roles within families are continually undergoing revision. Employed mothers, single career women, and "househusbands" may become as normal tomorrow as the traditional nuclear family of yesteryear. Mental health professionals are also revising their understandings of what contributes to effective functioning for women, and are supporting women as they consider new options that extend beyond traditional social roles.

As our understanding of positive well-being changes, conceptions of deviance and disorder become modified as well. Diagnostic approaches to women's symptomology have increasingly questioned the traditional categories that determine decisions about psychopathology (Franks, 1986; Kaplan, 1983; Rosewater, 1985a). The over-representation of women in such disorders as depression, anorexia nervosa (refusal to eat), and agoraphobia (fear of leaving the house), to name only a few, suggests that many normally socialized behaviors in women overlap with diagnoses of psychopathology (Landrine, 1989). Researchers and clinicians are considering how oversocialization into society-sanctioned role behaviors may function to determine our conceptions of normality and deviance. From the perspective of the clinician, it will be important to understand the social bases of these sex-typed clusters of behaviors, and to interpret to clients how their conformity to sex-role expectations has been damaging to their well-being. Feminist approaches to assessment, counseling, and psychotherapy are considered in Chapters 4, 5, and 6.

Sources of Stress

A second set of issues relating to innovations in social and sex-role functioning suggests new ways of looking at the sources of stress in women's lives. We can define stress as the sum of cognitive, affective, and physiological reactions to situations in which individuals perceive that environmental demands exceed their coping abilities (Lazarus & Folkman, 1984). Traditional assumptions about the protective function of the home for women and the stresses of the workplace for men have been challenged by new findings that point to the increased risks for illness and depression in mothers with preschool children, and the rise in psychological well-being for women who add employed worker to their wife and mother roles (Barnett & Baruch, 1986). At the same time, these new roles for women engender health risks that may be important issues for counseling: role overload and role strain, conflicts and guilt about "abandoning" one's children to the care of others, harassment and segregation in the workplace, and economic fallout resulting from divorce, discrimination, and ageing.

Recent research points out that none of these situations in itself engenders stress reactions. Rather, it may be the quality of other life situations, the amount of social support from significant others, and the amount of perceived control over alternative options that contribute to the experience of high or low stress (Barnett & Baruch, 1987). In particular, multiple roles have been considered in the light of two competing hypotheses. First, the *scarcity hypothesis* proposes that each role we assume requires energy, and that each additional role compounds the behavioral requirements, resulting in role strain and overload. The alternative hypothesis, called the *expansion hypothesis*, states that new roles that add reward, prestige, and recognition may improve well-being and reduce stress (Barnett & Baruch, 1987). In considering the degree and sources of stress in clients' lives, it is important to consider both hypotheses as contributing to the issues that women bring to therapy. Both hypotheses have received research support, and both may be operating in particular situations. For example, we have seen that satisfaction in the employed worker role for women is highly dependent upon the amount of support she receives in home and child-care tasks, as well as in the quality of her situation and opportunities for advancement in the workplace.

In addition to our understandings of new dimensions in social roles, we are beginning to apply concepts introduced by androgyny and other personality researchers to the counseling encounter. In particular, the view of women as appropriately passive, dependent, and compliant has been replaced by alternative approaches that link these attributes to feelings of helplessness and lack of personal control over life events. As a result, therapists working with women have attended more carefully to the encouragement of coping skills that mediate women's perceptions of inescapable life events and that provide clients with positive options for dealing with situational stress. We will discuss these coping skills in later chapters.

Opportunities for Change

A final issue raised by changes in social and personal roles deals with the conceptual distinction between what women need to change in themselves in order to increase their well-being, and what needs to change in the social and economic arena. No longer can mental health professionals hope to solve women's personal issues by helping their clients to gain insight into their personal conflicts and to change specific behaviors. Women can be fruitfully encouraged to relate their personal concerns to the structure of the society that produces internal and external barriers to women's (and men's) optimal development. Women can be educated to the ways in which the destructive and limiting messages of their gender-based heritage have led them into the dilemmas they now face. Women can be helped to lead more productive and self-enhancing lives by exploring for themselves the full meaning of the emerging social and personal roles for both women and men.

Summary

Chapter 2 discussed the evolving roles of women in relation to singlehood, coupling and marriage, parenthood, and paid employment outside the home. Traditional approaches to women's social roles were contrasted with changing attitudes and options. In particular, we noted an increase in singlehood, in expectations for equity within marital relationships, in the choice to remain childfree, and in the amount and type of participation in the paid workforce. Variations in these options for ethnic minority women were noted. Each of these emergent role changes is accompanied by advantages and hazards for women that may be appropriate topics for counseling interventions. Recent attention to the advantages and drawbacks of an androgyny model of mental health were reviewed. Recommendations for interventions emphasized that changes in sociocultural structures and practices must occur if women's mental health needs are to be addressed.

Activity (Adapted from Rekers, 1985)

Draw a family tree representating at least three generations of your family. Gather information about your mother and about as many female family members as you can for the following areas: occupations, childbearing pattern (mother's age at births, number and spacing of children, miscarriages), partner patterns (marriage, divorce, remarriage, death of partner, singlehood, same-sex partner, age at marriage or partnering, divorce or death of partner), nature and quality of female–male relationships in each family grouping (power differential, dysfunctional patterns), nature and quality of female–female relationships in each family grouping, significant characteristics of each female family member, female members who were outcasts/black sheep in the family. What traumas were experienced and how did the women cope with them? This information can be collected by reflecting back on family stories you have heard, looking at family photo albums and interviewing other family members.

The major goal of the exercise is for you to get an intergenerational picture of what it means to be female and the nature of female–male relationships in your family. Listen for sex-role messages that have been passed on verbally or modeled from one generation to the next. Look for the commonalities and differences in the lives of females in your family's history. What positional status or power do women have in your family? What are their strengths? What have been the barriers to their full development as people? How are you currently living in accordance with or in reaction to the gender legacies of your family?

Further Readings

To expand and extend your understanding and knowledge of social and personal roles, you may want to read the following resources:

Cook, E. P. (1985). *Psychological Androgyny*. New York: Pergamon Press.
Lott, B. (1987). *Women's Lives: Themes and Variations in Gender Learning*. Monterey, CA: Brooks/Cole.
Worell, J. (1981). Lifespan sex roles: Development, continuity, and change. In R. M. Lerner & N. A. Busch-Rossnagel (Eds.), *Individuals as Producers of their Development*. New York: Academic Press.
Worrell, J. (1989). Sex roles in transition. In J. Worell & F. Danner (Eds.) *The Adolescent as Decision-maker: Applications for Development and Education*. New York: Academic Press.

CHAPTER 3

Socialization for Womanhood:
A Sex-role Analysis

Self-assessment: Rules for Women and Men*

Each of the statements below represents a rule or message about how to behave appropriately as a woman or man in Western society. For each of the statements, decide whether it applies mostly to women, mostly to men, or applies about equally to both women and men. Check your answers in one of the three columns to the right for each rule.

Rule	Women	Men	Both
Be sensitive to others	⎯⎯	⎯⎯	⎯⎯
Be understanding and accommodating	⎯⎯	⎯⎯	⎯⎯
Be strong physically	⎯⎯	⎯⎯	⎯⎯
Be in control	⎯⎯	⎯⎯	⎯⎯
Don't argue or fight	⎯⎯	⎯⎯	⎯⎯
Don't be the boss	⎯⎯	⎯⎯	⎯⎯
Be financially successful	⎯⎯	⎯⎯	⎯⎯
Support the family	⎯⎯	⎯⎯	⎯⎯
Get married and have children	⎯⎯	⎯⎯	⎯⎯
Take primary responsibility for home and childcare	⎯⎯	⎯⎯	⎯⎯
Do well in sports	⎯⎯	⎯⎯	⎯⎯

* Adapted from Blankenship, 1984.

Rule	Women	Men	Both
Your career comes first	——	——	——
Don't make more money than your spouse does	——	——	——
Don't be smarter than the other sex	——	——	——
Make decisions for the family	——	——	——
Don't show your emotions	——	——	——
Be attractive and well groomed	——	——	——
Put the family's needs before your own	——	——	——
Be the dominant one in the relationship	——	——	——
Be smarter than the other sex	——	——	——

Scoring

Now add up your scores for each of the three columns. Half of these statements were judged to be messages given to girls as they grow up and half were judged to be messages given to boys. Now, do you want to go back and reconsider any of your responses?

Overview

We know that females and males grow up in environments that are psychologically different in important ways. Even as new social roles and revised expectations for social behavior emerge, the culture continues to transmit traditional messages that encourage the integration of women into institutionalized social structures. We consider sex-role socialization in terms of rule-governed learning about how to be an appropriate female or male within society. All levels of the sociocultural environment have been found to exert significant pressures on developing individuals to conform to prevailing expectations for sex-typed behavior. These influences on sex-role socialization include the family, the educational system, the media, public, political, and religious institutions, and the workplace.

Socialization influences on individual development will be viewed here from four major perspectives: the family, the media, the educational system, and the workplace. Implications of these socialization agents for personal and interpersonal functioning are considered. Finally, we examine these processes for their contributions to the problems and issues that women bring to counseling.

After reading Chapter 3, readers should be able to:

(1) Explain socialization as a rule-governed process.
(2) Describe the dimensions of family socialization that differentiate the experiences of girls and boys.
(3) List the contributions of the media, schools, and the workplace to the barriers that face today's women.
(4) Summarize the relationship between traditional sex-role messages and the following issues of concern to women: depression, body image, dependency, sexual and physical abuse, and career and achievement conflicts.

Learning the Rules

We view the process of sex-role socialization as a life-long journey. Although earlier theories of sex typing assumed that gender identity and preferences were developed by middle childhood, recent formulations support the lifespan approach (Katz, 1979; Worell, 1981). That is, we can consider sex-role orientation as a composite of attitudes, beliefs, interests, skills, and activities that becomes integrated with gender in ways that are qualitatively and quantitatively different across major life periods. Early learning can predispose individuals to accept and enact traditional sex-typed behaviors and attitudes. Later experiences, however, may dramatically alter our perceptions and values. New demands on our time and skills may precipitate a reorganization of values and priorities. Exposure to new settings and opportunities can expand our behavioral range, and encourage us toward greater openness and flexibility in gender-related activities. Thus, we assume that sex-role learning is an organic process and not a completed product at any particular life period.

Rule-governed Learning

Nevertheless, most of us develop and mature in families that transmit many traditional messages about "appropriate" behavior for girls and women. We are also surrounded by a culture that is predominantly patriarchal in its structures and institutions (Benokraitis & Feagin, 1986). In this chapter, we view the process of sex-role socialization as rule-governed learning, whereby the differential treatment and responses to females and males are abstracted by each individual into generalized rules for living (Constantinople, 1979; Pleck, 1985). These gender-related rules are applied to self and others in two general forms: (1) gender stereotypes that serve as personal guidelines or ideals for behavior in many situations (e.g. rules for being the good girl, good woman, or good mother), and (2) self-imposed expectations and standards that function as personal mandates (I can, I should, I must), or restrictions (I can't, I'd better not, I won't). Thus, each individual learns many of the prevailing gender stereotypes that characterize our cultural heritage. She also incorporates specific learning as a function of her own experiences within her family, school, and community.

The consistency of children's knowledge about gender rules is well established by middle childhood (Huston, 1983; Worell, 1982). Elementary schoolchildren typically can verbalize what behaviors are expected of girls and boys, and their adult occupational choices are impressively sex-typed. Children know the rules for "appropriate" language (girls don't swear), for social behavior (girls don't hit), for body behaviour (keep your legs crossed when you sit), for life-career aspirations (grow up to be a teacher, nurse, secretary, or wife/mother), for achievement outcomes (girls don't boast about their success), for family relationships (father is the boss), and for adult household roles (mothers should clean, cook, and take care of the children). In your self-assessment at the start of this chapter, did your ratings for women's and men's roles differ?

Gender-related Belief Systems

As adults, we continue to incorporate many of these rules into our personal guidelines for living. As a result, we tend to feel virtuous and appropriately female when we conform to personal gender beliefs, and we may feel uncomfortable, threatened, or "unfeminine" when we violate them. As an example of this gender-learning process, the self-assessment for Chapter 3 includes a sample of rules for women and men reported in a study by Mary Blankenship (1984). In this study, considerable consistency was found in the perceptions of gender-related rules for social behavior for women in four age groups, from Junior High through late adulthood. When individual rules were collapsed into broad categories, four major mandates prevailed. Women believed that as adult females, they were expected to (a) be attractive and well groomed at all times; (b) be acquiescent to men in both home and work-related settings; (c) display passive, compliant, and "happy" behavior in social situations; and (d) take major responsibility for the household and childcare. Across major age groups, these women expected to obtain social approval for gender-role compliance, and social sanctions or disapproval for violating these rules.

Another way to approach gender-based social rules is to consider prevailing stereotypes about women and men in contemporary society, and to view them as organizing rules for those who endorse them. As an example,

Richard Ashmore and Fran Del Boca (1984) developed an attitude survey containing 400 gender-related items. Responses to these items were factored into a taxonomy with four major variables: (a) beliefs about personal attributes (women tend to be gullible; women are helpful); (b) attitudes toward women and men in relationships (it bothers me to see a man being told what to do by a woman; it's a woman's own fault if a man forces sex on her); (c) attitudes toward family and work roles (in marriage, the man should take the lead in decision-making; many jobs should be closed to women because of physical requirements); and (d) attitudes about gender in society (women need to work together to achieve political and social rights; abortion should be available to all women).

With the exception of the last category on general social policies, these two taxonomies are very similar. Both taxonomies embrace societal perceptions of women that are consistent, pervasive, and widely held. When individuals endorse such stereotypes, they tend to convert them into mandates or rules for personal behavior (Huston, 1983).

Rules as Communication

One of our goals in counseling women is to help clients become aware of the unwritten rules or messages they use to guide their lives. Although we use the language of communication in referring to "messages", it is likely that most of these rules are not within active awareness for most women. Gender-related messages may need to become explicit if clients are to assume meaningful control over their daily lives. The technique of *sex-role analysis* encourages women to examine the gender rules that guide their thoughts, feelings, and behavior. In the process of gaining sex-role awareness, women can explore how the rules were learned, can consider how well these rules function for them now, and can make decisions about which of their gender-driven messages they would like to revise.

In our work with women, we have encountered a range of self-reported gender messages that emerge from the process of sex-role analysis. Table 3.1 displays some typical messages that women recall as they become aware of their own socialization experiences. The messages are organized here according to the first three stereotype categories in the taxonomy formulated by Ashmore and Del Boca (1984). Viewing this set of messages may be useful to clients in their efforts to recall, formulate, or recognize the gender rules that characterize their childhood, adolescence, or present situation.

In Table 3.1, notice that each message contains an implicit set of corollary behaviors which may impose a rigid framework of rules that many women still follow. For example, the rule that home and children come before job or career is embedded in a network of daily and intermittent tasks. These tasks are usually controlled by rules about who in the family plans meals,

Table 3.1. *Typical Sex-role Messages for Women*

Personal attributes

Do Be a lady: wear feminine clothes, speak softly, keep your knees together, smile, be agreeable, be happy and congenial.

Don't Swear, hit, be aggressive physically or verbally, interrupt others, get angry, do male activities, be athletic or muscular.

Relationships with men

Do Be daddy's little girl, compliant, pleasing, listen, be flirtatious and coy, dress to please, seek approval, take second place, ask permission, have a man in your life, take care of the relationship, initiate and carry on conversation.

Don't Compete with him, act more intelligent, challenge his authority, beat him in a game, initiate a date, take the lead in sex, earn more money than he does.

Family and work

Do Take responsibility for home, meals, children, put home and children before self and career, prioritize spouse career ahead of own, recognize father as most important family member.

Don't Be the boss, allow work to interfere with family plans or meals, neglect your children, let the house get dirty.

---

shops for food, plans and manages social contacts, picks up a sick child from school, calls and arranges childcare, mends a torn shirt, does the laundry, shops with children for clothes, arranges (or does) the house-cleaning chores, visits the school on PTA night and consults with teachers, bakes cookies for the homeroom party, plans and officiates at the children's birthday parties (or weddings), etc. These are only a sample of the tasks involved in home and child management. The fact that women who are wives or mothers do the majority of these tasks (see Chapter 2) is clearly related to the traditional socialization of women for the wife/mother role.

Although women in dual-career families are attempting to equalize the home/child responsibilites, their gender-socialized messages, as well as those of their partners, frequently interfere with their egalitarian intentions. When home and childcare tasks are left undone, women, more than men, are likely to feel uncomfortable and guilty. The process of sex-role analysis may be useful and therapeutic to a woman struggling with the self- and externally-imposed demands of home care and childcare. In the process of sex-role analysis, she may be helped to understand why she feels she must assume the major portion of these tasks in addition to her employment outside the home, and how she can plan to disengage her self-messages from those imposed by others. In the application of sex-role analysis to women's socialization messages, it is helpful to understand the social processes through which gender-related rules have been adopted by each of us. We can then interpret these processes to clients and assist them in meaningful plans for change.

The Role of Social Institutions

Social institutions teach gender rules according to essentially similar principles. Because gender stereotypes are common throughout most cultures, individuals learn these rules as a natural part of their environments. In addition to explicit gender teachings, the total effect of institutional gender rules provides a "hidden curriculum" (Worell & Stilwell, 1981), in which the messages are frequently implicit rather than explicit. The subtle and pervasive existence of both explicit and implicit gender messages at all levels of the external culture informs women about who they are, what they may become, and how they should view themselves.

An important agenda of the women's movement has been to articulate and make public the sexist and discriminatory practices that exist at all levels of the social community. As a result, revised social practices as well as numerous legal remedies have moderated the extreme effects of societal sexism. Nevertheless, recent studies on the influences of families, the public media, schools, and working environments attest to the persistence of gender-stereotyped messages in both the private and public domains.

Socialization in Families

Families form the earliest classroom in which gender stereotypes and rules are learned. We speak of families in the broadest sense, including the two-parent, the one-parent, and the siblings who may live with the family or become frequent visitors. Although most parents deny that they treat their girls and boys differently, observational studies in homes, schools, and clinical settings support the contributions of parents to the gender-defined training of their children.

Teaching The Rules

The degree to which parents actively participate in gender-typing varies by individual family, as well as by sex of the parent, socioeconomic class, racial or ethnic group, and the parents' own sex-role beliefs. One of the most salient variables here is the sex of the parent, with fathers more than mothers being relatively traditional in expectations for their daughters and sons. The more traditional orientations of fathers appear in both direct behavior toward their children, and in their role behaviors within the home (Block, 1979; Barry, 1980; Fagot, 1978; Langlois & Downs, 1980).

Personal sex-role beliefs can also mediate one's parenting behaviors. Parents who are flexible and less traditional in their sex-role beliefs have been found to stereotype less in their parenting behaviors and to produce more sex-role-flexible children (Brooks-Gunn, 1986; Jackson, Ialongo, & Stollak, 1986; Kelly & Worell, 1976; Spence & Helmreich, 1978). Some limited research on Black families suggest that Black mothers may be less sex-typed in their expectations and behaviors toward their daughters (Gump, 1980; Lynn, 1979; Malson, 1983). Black women, as we have seen in Chapter 2, are themselves less willing than most White women to conform to traditional societal sex-typing, and tend to have more egalitarian family relationships. Black fathers, on the other hand, were found in one study to sex-type both their daughters and sons more than a comparison sample of White fathers (Price-Bonham & Skeen, 1982).

In the following section, we explore some general findings on parental socialization practices suggested by current research, and we consider the differential messages that girls and boys receive in the family setting. In individual or group work with women, however, it will be important for each client to explore her personal gender training as she experienced it, and as it impacted on her behavior and on the messages she continues to give herself.

How Families Teach

Families socialize for gender-related behavior in four major ways:

(1) By modeling patterns of behavior that are observed by children and that provide expectations about future behavior.
(2) By providing direct contingencies for gender-related behavior through attention and reinforcement for approved actions and ignoring or punishment for those behaviors they wish to discourage.
(3) By instructing and teaching gender-related content and skill development.
(4) By providing differential environmental structure and opportunities for exploration and new learning.

We consider each of these family socialization functions below.

Modeling

First, families are *models* themselves of traditional or flexible behavior. The activities and roles that parents perform within the household provide patterns for current behavior and expectations about future goals and relationships. Mothers who work outside the home, for example, are more likely to have daughters who assume responsibility for themselves, work during adolescence, work outside the home when they become mothers themselves, and have higher levels of career aspirations and success than daughters of home-bound women (Hoffman, 1979). It is likely that in these homes, fathers are also playing a less traditional role, providing daughters with a more cooperative and flexible model of family relationships.

Parents also model patterns of interpersonal relationships. Children can observe and learn about how people in families express love, detachment, control, and dominance. Most families present patterns of father dominance, control over important decisions, and access to favored resources. Some families provide patterns of paternal violence, wife battering and rape, child incest and abuse, and desertion. Children in these families are learning about the place of girls and women in relationships and about how women (their mothers and themselves) cope with unavoidable violence and abuse. Both boys and girls in violent and abusive families develop dysfunctional beliefs and behaviors related to interpersonal affection and control. These children may carry over such patterns into their future relationships. Persistence of issues related to family violence and abuse will be detailed further in Chapter 9.

Contingency training

Second, families provide *direct contingencies* for gender-related behaviors. For example, parents tend to give preschool children more positive attention when they are engaged with sex-typed toys and play, and they tend to reprimand cross-sex play (Langlois & Downs, 1980). Fathers engaged in a learning task with their preschool children were more likely to steer their boys back to task completion and their girls toward interpersonal socializing and play (Block, Block, & Harrington, 1975). These differential parent patterns may not be verbalized by the child, but they carry clear messages about what activities the parents believe are desirable and appropriate.

Reinforcement of passive and compliant behavior may be highlighted for girls who experience paternal or sibling incest. In these families, the girl is given attention and praise for "colluding" with the sexual perpetrator, "cooperating" with the abuse and for "keeping the secret" from others. Experiences in which compliant behavior to male sexual abuse is repeatedly reinforced in childhood may predispose the girl to further compliance with later abuse. This is part of the process of "revictimization," which we discuss in Chapters 8 and 9.

Direct instruction

Third, parents actively *instruct and teach* their children with gender-related messages and skill development that prepare them for distinctive future roles. Girls are more often instructed in domestic skills, for example, while boys are taught to throw balls. Boys, on the other hand, are taught not to cry, while girls are encouraged to be less active and to "behave like a lady." In an observational study with preschool children, Fagot (1978) found that parents encouraged girls to play with dolls rather than with blocks or manipulative toys, and criticized girls for running, jumping, and climbing. These parents were also more likely to respond to girls' requests for help, while expecting boys to solve their own problems. These findings suggest that, in some families, the groundwork for encouraging passivity, helplessness, and dependency in girls may start at an early age.

Opportunity

Finally, parents provide a great deal of *structure and opportunity* to establish gender-related skills and expectation for future roles. Especially salient here are the distinctive clothes and toys that parents provide, the freedom they allow both within and away from the home, and the expectations they communicate about future educational and occupational commitment. Girls' clothes are less conducive than are boys' clothes for active play. Girls' toys encourage quiet play in proximity to parents, and are frequently imitative and uncreative (tea sets, make-up kits, housekeeping toys). Parents also encourage girls to remain closer to home than boys, and are more concerned with their supervision and monitoring (Block, 1983; Huston, 1988).

Several studies have found that parents hold differing expectations for their adolescent boys and girls. Boys, more than girls, are expected to enroll in advanced math courses (Parsons, Adler, & Kaczala, 1983) and to attend college or graduate school (Rosen & Aneshensel, 1978). When asked about goals for their children, parents in a large national sample were likely to name occupational success, work, intelligence, advanced education, and ambition in relation to boys. For daughters, parents were more likely to emphasize being kind, unselfish, loving, attractive, having a good marriage and being a good parent (Hoffman, 1977). It is not difficult to conclude that many parents construct different psychological environments for their girls and boys that may convey important and distinctive messages about present abilities and future opportunities.

Teaching New Rules

With a change in personal and cultural attitudes toward traditional sex roles, many families are attempting to break new ground. In all four areas outlined above, many families have attempted to provide egalitarian role models, to monitor carefully their sex-differentiated practices, to teach their girls and boys about equal opportunity, and to increase the non-sexist environment of their children. While doubtless these efforts have had some success (Katz & Boswell 1986), parents also find that the patterns for gender-distinct expectancies are rampant in the culture, as mediated by television, magazines and books, and the realities of social institutions (Weinraub & Brown, 1983). Even the most "liberated" parent may feel frustrated by the transmission of societal messages that conflict with values and ideals practiced at home. Both authors have been told at some time by their young daughters that they could not possibly be "doctors" because doctors are men!

Cognitive Outcomes

Jeanne Block (1983) proposed that parental practices establish "meta-messages" that communicate important developmental information about the self in relation to the environment. As parents interact with children in a multitude of ways, they are telling girls and boys about their self-worth, their personal goals, and their world views. These meta-messages help to channel children into directions for development that are functionally different for girls and boys.

Meta-messages

Block (1983) described three identifiable meta-messages communicated to children during early socialization that have implications for later cognitive functioning: (a) the responsiveness of the environment to one's actions; (b) the opportunities that are available for engaging in novel and exploratory behavior, and (c) the skills that one develops with respect to problem-solution. On the basis of an extensive review of research, Block suggested that, in contrast to boys, girls tend to develop the following orientations: low self-efficacy or belief in one's ability to master important tasks; less curiosity and independent exploration of the environment; and low risk-taking behavior in the face of requirements for problem-solution. These aspects of cognitive orientation, according to Block, leave the girl child with impaired strategies and skills for independent action in the face of conflict, and inadequate skills for mastery and overcoming obstacles.

Aletha Huston (1988) proposed that the close supervision of girls and their continual proximity to adults, especially the mother, leads girls to become compliant, attentive to the wants of others, obedient, quiet, and unassertive. Close bonding with adult socialization agents, however, also fosters "communal behaviors promoting group cohesion and caring about others" (p. 16). Huston emphasizes that the high degree of structure that characterizes the socialization of girls leads to increased internalization of social norms and a mechanism for transmission of cultural values and norms. The close contact with adult agents, moreover, results in women's capacity for maintaining close emotional ties with others.

In a similar approach, Lois Hoffman (1977) reviewed relevant research on parental socialization practices, concluding that documented differences in socialization have important implications for female development. She suggested that parental messages about one's abilities may induce girls to "feel more vulnerable, less confident in their independent abilities to cope and explore, short-changed with respect to certain kinds of cognitive learning experiences, and less pressured to achieve in competitive and occupational spheres" (p. 651). Hoffman also suggested that what girls do learn is their importance in the expressive–relational process, and the expectations for them to be the child-bearer and nurturer. Hoffman concluded, however, that as sex roles become less traditional, these socialization differences may decrease, especially in relation to the trend toward women's employment outside the home.

Finally, the emphasis in families on affectional behavior expressed by girls and independent mastery behavior by boys may communicate to girls that relationships are both their major source of self-definition and their primary responsibility (Cancian, 1987; Miller, 1976). In future encounters, women are likely to believe that they must be attached to a man if they are to find meaning in their lives. Further, that if a relationship fails, it is their "job" to mend it and their fault when one partner exits. As a result of these meta-messages, a common issue presented by women in psychotherapy centers on intimate relationships, as women struggle with "finding them, understanding them, untangling them, changing them, repairing them or escaping them" (Worell, 1988). The focus on women as care-taker of the relationship further reduces a woman's power and control over important resources in her life, and renders her dependent on the intimate partner to fulfill her self-image.

Implications for Counseling

The concept of meta-messages may be useful for clients who experience a sense of helplessness, despair, and self-defeat when facing a seemingly insurmountable problem. A relevant example here is Clara, who is further described in Chapter 9. Clara was living with a physically abusive spouse who also had an alcohol problem. Clara "knew" that she should not tolerate the abuse, yet she appeared unable to draw upon her resources to resolve the situation. She believed that she was nothing without her partner and that she could not possibly live without him. We see clients who remain in an aversive and dangerous relationship, who present themselves as "helpless" to change the relationship yet "unable" to leave it. We shall consider the concept of meta-messages further in Chapter 9 when we examine the situation facing the abused woman.

The family is only one of the cultural agents that constructs a framework of sex-role messages for women's development. We now consider some of the other social institutions that form a background for family transmission of gender information. In particular, the general media, schools, and work environments all contribute their share of gender stereotypes, sexist belief systems, and discriminatory practices.

Media Messages

We consider the public media from three sources: language, television, and videotapes. We recognize also that other media sources may influence our gender messages, including music, art, dance, books, magazines, and newspapers. Assume, if you can, that these media sources probably add to (or perhaps multiply) the effects of the major sources of public media gender learning.

Language

By the time they enter school, most children have a rich vocabulary of spoken language and a much larger repertoire of comprehension. Gender rules embedded in written and spoken language inform children (and adults) about the place and value of women. Susan Basow (1986) asserts that "language plays a major role in defining and maintaining male power over women" (p. 129). She suggests that this outcome is accomplished through three major formats: ignoring, labeling, and deprecating.

Ignoring

Women are ignored most blatantly in the public media through the widespread use of the generic masculine. That is, masculine pronouns and wordforms are used to denote all persons, both male and female. Examples of male-linked wordforms include "manpower," "mankind," "salesman," as well as many words associated with achievement: "mastery," "fellowship," and "bachelor's degree," to name only a few. The generic "he" appears frequently in the public media to refer to all persons, regardless of sex; it has been estimated that the average individual will encounter the generic "he" over 10 million times in a lifespan (MacKay, 1980). The generic masculine eliminates women from the public domain, rendering them invisible. It has also been demonstrated to influence the evaluations and perceptions of both children and adults. When individuals of both sexes are presented with a sentence such as "All men are created equal," both their verbal and visual images are primarily those of a man (Wilson & Ng, 1988).

Judy Cornelia Pearson (1985) reviewed the literature on the effects of both generic masculine and male-linked wordforms. She concluded that these language forms bias perception by focusing on males, influencing responses to "wanted" advertisements for employment, and directing the assignment of important jobs (e.g. Chairman) to men. Current usage of generic masculine language has decreased, notably in textbooks and in public television news reporting. The American Psychological Association adopted non-sexist language guidelines for all its publications in 1981 (American Psychological Association, 1983). The recent efforts at resurrecting the invisible woman in the public domain by means of non-sexist language remains to be extended throughout the media as well as in our personal communication in daily life.

Labeling and deprecating

Two other sources of gender-based social messages include labeling and deprecation. Labels for women are frequently differentiated in such a way that the woman is thrown into a subordinate role. Examples here include the "man and wife" wedding ceremony, and "Mrs John Smith" following marriage. The traditional order of gender referencing also implies male primacy. Notice in most books and public documents that boys and girls, men and women, are described in that order. Which of the two sexes is presumed to be more important? We hope you have recognized by now that in this book, we have tried to reverse the custom by referencing women before men. Deprecation of women occurs when language referring to them is derogatory ("bitch"), belittling ("girls"), or depersonalizing ("chick"). Many researchers have demonstrated that deprecating words are applied more frequently to women than to men (Holland & Davidson, 1984; Pearson, 1985).

Television and Video

We see two issues of concern regarding portrayals of women and men in the televised/video media. First, the portrayal of women in unfavorably stereotyped roles and behaviors encourages viewers of all ages to accept these images of women. Second, the depiction of violence against women, and especially violent sex, increases the probability that male viewers will entertain violent thoughts about women and will increase their acceptance of prevalent rape myths (Briere & Malamuth, 1983; Malamuth, 1981). (Chapter 8 discusses rape myths in detail.)

Television

The average child watches between 4 and 5 hours of TV every day and views about 20 000 commercials each year. All aspects of televised programming present stereotypes that are disadvantageous to women: children's programming, prime time, daytime soaps, and especially the commercials. Overall, women appear less frequently than men and are almost invisible in some popular children's shows. More than men, women tend to be portrayed as home-oriented or employed in traditional jobs (teacher, nurse). Women in all these contexts tend to show manipulative, deferent, submissive, incompetent, or helpless behavior, and to be concerned with their appearance and that of their floors, laundry, and furniture. Portrayal of women on afternoon "soaps" shows women who are frequently divorced, raped, abandoned, misunderstood, or otherwise in some kind of personal difficulties (Pearson, 1985).

Children and adults are receiving some clear messages from commercial television: that men are more important, more competent, and they make the major decisions. Television serves as a constant reminder of traditional societal stereotypes of women and men. Further, the more that people watch TV, and the stronger their initial stereotypes, the more entrenched they become in traditional views of women and men (McGhee & Freuh, 1980; Morgan, 1982). Although some effort has been made to include women as competent role models (*Cagney and Lacey*, for example), the proportion of competent to incompetent women remains unfavorable for purposes of effective modeling outcomes.

Videos

Videotapes that are commercially available for rental or purchase in thousands of retail outlets are a major source of portrayals of both sexual and non-sexual violence against women (Cowan et al., 1988). Gloria Cowan and her associates (1988) surveyed a sample of widely available X-rated videos in California, reporting that physical violence against women appeared in 73% of the films. Further, 82% of the films portrayed exploitation of women, and 51% of the films showed a man raping a woman.

In a detailed review of the effects of violence in the media, Daniel Linz and his associates (Linz et al., 1986) concluded that (a) depictions of violence against women influence the viewer's attitudes toward violence and aggression, and (b) the pairing of sex and aggression may encourage the association of violence with sexual arousal for men and lowers the threshold for subsequent aggressive acts. Repeated exposure to violent sexual acts towards women reduces male empathy for the victim and increases his belief that she enjoys being violated. Furthermore, exposing men to violent pornography results in subsequent aggressive responses to a female confederate.

In view of the increased availability of sexually explicit and sexually violent videos, it seems clear that adults as well as children are being socialized in gender-specific ways. Our concern here is with the lessons that are being learned and the messages that are transmitted about the permissibility of sexual and non-sexual violence toward women. The willingness of video producers to modify their products is tied to the capital return on their investment; as long as sexually violent videos are consumed, their messages will persist.

The Educational System

Children spend about one-third of their waking lives in school. Although children arrive at school with well-established gender stereotypes, all aspects of the school setting have been shown to contain gender messages. These gender messages are transmitted through personnel and administrative arrangements, textbooks, curriculum, teacher and counselor behavior, and through differential allocation of resources, such as in athletics.

What Children Learn

Children are learning about who has the power. The large majority of elementary and high school teachers are women and most principals and school superintendents are men. Children are also learning to consolidate their previous stereotypes about how to be a girl or boy, and what they may expect to become as they mature into women and men.

Textbooks

In their assigned school readings, children are learning about who the culture believes to be important and worthy of admiration and respect. Textbooks tend to be heavily gender-stereotyped, with higher frequencies of men and boys in both text and pictures, and role-restricted portrayals of girls and women.

Girls have been more frequently depicted in school texts as passive, fearful, unwilling to take risks, and asking for help when in trouble. Girls have been less frequently shown in heroic, brave, adventurous, and achieving roles (Stockard et al., 1980). In a comprehensive review of illustrations in elementary textbooks, Weitzman and Rizzo (1974) found that White men were shown in 150 different occupations, while women were shown in only four occupations. These same authors also found that by the sixth grade, there were four pictures of males in school texts for every one of females. The messages are clear. Biased presentations of females and males in school texts has been a major source of sex-role instruction.

Curriculum

Curriculum arrangements have encouraged girls to enter language and home economics courses and boys to focus on advanced math and technical training. Counselors have frequently not been helpful in encouraging the educational aspirations of girls toward economic self-sufficiency and non-traditional career choices. Athletic programs have been heavily weighted in favor of boys' participation and competition and programs for girls and women are still insufficiently financed and supported.

Teachers

Finally, children are learning some subtle messages from their teachers. Studies on direct interactions with teachers at all levels suggest that, unknowingly, many teachers are encouraging and supporting the maintenance of traditional gender roles for both girls and boys. Although schools may not be the primary vehicle for gender-related learning, research supports the view that schools are doing little to counteract or modify traditional sex-role stereotypes and beliefs (Eccles & Hoffman, 1984; Huston, 1983; Stockard et al., 1980; Worell, 1982, 1989a).

What Teachers Teach

Most teachers are unwilling to declare that they view girls and boys differently, or that they interact with girls in any way other than they deal with boys. Some research supports these egalitarian views. However, many studies suggest otherwise.

Stereotypes

First, it is important to note that many teachers subscribe to the same stereotypes as the general population, that is, tending to see girls as emotional, neat, quiet, concerned about appearance, easily hurt, and harboring a dislike for math and science (Wise, 1978). It seems unlikely that teachers who believe in stereotyped sex differences can avoid transmitting those attitudes to their students in various ways.

Differential expectations

Second, teachers tend to respond to boys with both more praise and attention for good academic achievement, and more disapproval for off-task behavior (Brophy & Good, 1974; Dweck et al., 1978; Good, Sikes, &

Brophy, 1973; Sadker & Sadker, 1985; Serbin et al., 1973). In the study by Thomas Good and his associates (1973), boys with high expected achievement levels received the majority of positive teacher feedback, teacher-initiated attention, and positive affect. Of particular significance for later occupational attainment is the finding in a more recent study that boys with high math achievement were praised more often and received more teacher interaction than girls with similar math abilities (Parsons, Kaczala, & Meece, 1982).

Carol Dweck and her associates (1978) further found that boys received more teacher praise for intellectual competence, while girls were praised more than boys for being neat. Teachers criticized girls for intellectual inadequacy almost twice as frequently as for boys, attributing girls' failures to their lack of competence and boys' failures to their lack of effort. These documented differences in teacher behavior toward the achievement efforts of girls and boys led Dweck and her associates to hypothesize that girls will be more likely to attribute their failures to lack of ability, leading to less persistence following a difficult task. These authors suggested that the pattern of criticism experienced by girls in school may result in an orientation toward "learned helplessness," whereby positive coping and achievement behaviors are not mobilized in the face of a challenging problem.

Further, we may propose that the contrast in total attention to boys in classrooms may well teach girls that they are less important than boys and that their achievement efforts are less worthy of praise. Although girls receive grades in school that are at least as good as those received by boys, girls' interest and engagement with math and science begins to dwindle at about the seventh grade. Lack of interest in math by adolescent girls has been associated with its identification as a field "for boys," as well as with active teacher discouragement of mathematically talented girls (Fox, Brody, & Tobin, 1980).

Finally, as more women enter advanced educational institutions, both overt and covert discriminatory practices follow them through the halls of ivy. In the Project on the Status and Education of Women, Bernice Sandler (1982) identified over 35 kinds of situations that functioned to create "a chilly climate in the classroom" for women students in institutions of advanced education. This large-scale study concluded that both female and male faculty undermine women's self-confidence and career aspirations. Examples of these discriminatory situations included: (a) overt discrimination (disparaging comments in class, questioning women's career commitment, sexual harassment); (b) subtle discrimination (being more attentive to men students); and (c) rendering women invisible (interrupting them more, ignoring women who volunteer, calling on women less frequently). Thus, at all levels of education, women can expect to find a differential atmosphere of academic encouragement and equity.

Cognitive Outcomes

We see at least three outcomes of the schools' traditional support of stereotyped gender-related behaviors: career choice, problem-solving capabilities, and cognitive mediators of success and failure. First, the continuation of traditional socialization practices by schools and teachers discourages girls from exploring productively the range of options in the world of work. We shall have more to say about this issue in Chapter 10. Second, we have seen that girls who are encouraged to remain close to adults, who are dependent on adult approval, and who fail to persist in the face of difficulty or failure, are at risk of developing inadequate problem-solving skills.

Finally, the patterns of reinforcement and criticism observed in some classrooms may reinforce the tendency of many girls to attribute their successes to luck and their failures to a lack of ability. These attributional patterns tend to lead toward lowered pride in one's work following success or a competent performance, and less persistence following failure (Bar-Tal & Frieze, 1978).

Viewing the Future

The patterns of educational bias outlined above have been under siege in the United States since Congress passed Title IX of the educational amendments to the 1964 Civil Rights Act. Once the regulations were written in 1976 this legislation provided the basis for massive changes in how the schools treated girls and women. Title IX forbids discrimination in school admissions, entrance to curriculum, segregation of schools by sex, athletic programs, services and materials provided by counselors, and employment of educational personnel (Stockard et al., 1980).

Title IX legislation says nothing, however, about curriculum materials, teacher behavior, or specific advice provided by counselors. Thus, while this legislation provides the mechanism for reducing discrimination against girls and women, it does not guarantee a change in attitudes or behavior of those who guide the educational system. Figure 3.1 displays the relationship between legislation and its effects on subsequent behavior, attitudes, and societal norms. It can be seen that legislation will affect directly some personal and institutional behavior in the direction of compliance to new laws. Revised attitudes and social norms about women's capabilities and opportunities follow gradually, as legal structures become translated into stabilized practices that encourage gender-free education.

As a result of the indirect influences of legislation on teacher and administrative attitudes, gender-free education is not yet a reality. Parents who are concerned about messages transmitted by the hidden curriculum of sex bias and discrimination still need to remain vigilant and actively involved

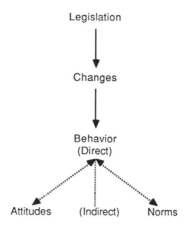

Figure 3.1. Direct and indirect effects of legislative change

in the experiences of their children at school. Some research with non-sexist materials supports the belief that children's and teachers' stereotyped attitudes can be changed following exposure to non-traditional texts and experiential training (Flerx, Fidler, & Rogers, 1976; Guttentag & Bray, 1976; Remer & Ross, 1982).

Implications for Counseling

These current and past experiences with school-based sexism can provide rich materials for exploration with women who have career or achievement conflicts. In considering some of the messages they may have learned at school, these women can begin to reconsider the sources of their work-related distress. When women experience institutional sex-based discrimination, they tend to attribute their difficulties to their personal characteristics or lack of competency. In Chapters 7 and 10 we discuss how to help clients untangle their sex-role messages from academic contexts and the realities of their work situations, thereby releasing them from the torments of self-deprecation and depression.

The Workplace

Women are socialized to the expectations of the workplace long before they seek employment outside the home. From early childhood through adolescence, we have seen that young girls maintain traditional stereotypes about what jobs are "appropriate" for women. Accordingly, their aspirations have been restricted by the cultural stereotypes that surround them at home, in school, and in the media. Women have expected to work at a restricted range of jobs, to earn less than their male counterparts in the same or similar jobs, and to accept discriminatory limits placed on their promotion and advancement. For women who continue to follow traditional lines of employment, the messages they may carry with them convey low status, a lack of control over their workplace conditions, and little hope for a better tomorrow.

Recent changes in attitudes toward women's work and career aspirations have motivated many women to challenge the boundaries of sexism and to seek education and job placement in fields that have been traditionally reserved for men. As women begin to infiltrate the male world of work, new demands and sources of stress enter their lives. Women in non-traditional jobs face many of the barriers and stresses of women in all employment settings (discrimination in the form of lower wages than men, sex stereotypes, sexual harassment, and restricted opportunity for advancement). They are meeting new obstacles as well, through biased expectations of competent women, isolation as token female, denial of access to higher level positions, and a lack of powerful role models (Kanter, 1977; Lott, 1985b). It is important for women to understand that barriers to equality in the paid labor market may provide continuing sources of stress and negative messages that contribute to the development of destructive symptomology: anxiety, self-deprecation, exhaustion, and depression.

We have selected three workplace variables for discussion that are common denominators of women's employment-related socialization: gender and racial segregation; biased employment practices; and sexual harassment. These variables are by no means inclusive of all sources of labor-force discrimination toward women, but they represent important facets of workplace socialization that confront most employed women.

Gender Segregation

Women are segregated in the labor market by whole industries, by specific occupations, and by segmentation within internal markets. Table 3.2 displays the earnings of women workers in the United States in selected occupational categories. Women are concentrated in the lowest-paid occupations, and are over-represented in the service areas such as retail sales clerks, maids, clerical workers, and teachers (except college) (Fox, 1987; LaCroix & Haynes, 1987; United States Department of Labor, 1985). Highly unionized and well-paying jobs such as transportation, construction, and mining are still held primarily by men. And despite the purported gains by women in recent years, high status jobs, such as those in law, medicine, engineering, architecture, University teaching, and politics, are still filled mainly by White men. In 1988, for example, the Congressional Senate of the United States was represented by 99 men and one woman.

Table 3.2. *Median Weekly Earnings of Full-time Workers.* (*From United States Department of Labor, Bureau of Labor Statistics, 1985, with permission.*)

Occupation	Women ($)	Men ($)	Earnings ratio women:men
Total	259	400	64.8
Professional	394	534	73.8
Executive/managerial	358	568	63.0
Sales	212	403	52.6
Household service	130	208	62.5
Clerical/secretarial	257	380	67.6
Precision production	254	401	63.3

Within organizations, women are assigned to lower rank positions and are seldom represented in top management levels. Women hold fewer than 1% of top management positions, 2% of the directorships of corporations, and 7% of the middle-level executive positions (Benokraitis & Feagin, 1986). In educational systems, less than 3% of school superintendents in the United States are women. In the university in which the two authors teach, women represent 10% of the Full Professors, 5% of the Department Heads, and 2% of the Deans and major administrators (American Association of University Professors, 1990).

Minority women, especially Black and Hispanic, occupy "the bottom rungs of the occupational ladder" (McNett, Taylor, & Scott, 1975). Minority women experience the double risk of gender and ethnicity, and frequently have difficulty in separating sexism from racism as sources of discrimination (Reid, 1988; Terrelonge, 1984). Although some writers believe that racism is the major deterrent to equitable employment for minority women, gender remains the best overall predictor of low employment status and income for women of color (Terrelonge, 1984).

The messages women receive from the structure of contemporary employment segregation are these: (a) women are less important than men; (b) women are worth less than men; (c) women are less competent than men; (d) women will have a tough time gaining entry to high status, well-paying positions; and therefore (e) women should be satisfied with low-level, low-paying jobs.

Many women are ignoring these messages, however, and are attempting to enter the labor market in areas previously reserved for men in both professional and blue-collar occupations. Women who select non-traditional job or career paths encounter a variety of biased employment practices that may threaten their job security, advancement, and personal well-being.

Biased Employment Practices

In addition to occupational segregation, women experience employment discrimination in many forms. Examples of employment bias include: (a) hiring and promotion practices that focus on women's marital or motherhood status, appearance or age; (b) lower salaries than men for the same or similar jobs; (c) differential criteria for advancement and pay raise; (d) isolation of the token woman in all-male units; (e) hiring practices such as part-time work that deny women access to unemployment and pension benefits; (f) assignment to lower-level tasks with less latitude and control even within the same occupational category; and finally (g) sexual harassment that is frequently ignored or allowed to persist (Benokraitis & Feagin, 1986; Fox, 1987; LaCroix & Haynes, 1987, Matlin, 1987).

Explanations for the existence of employment bias and discrimination range from concepts about economic or capitalistic power policies to gender stereotypes and myths about working women. Regardless of the economic base of gender and racial bias, stereotypes that operate at the local employment level have been demonstrated to affect practices in selection, retention, and promotion of women.

Thomas Ruble and his associates (1984) reviewed the research on occupational stereotyping, concluding that "sex stereotypes . . . operate in various ways to limit equal employment opportunities for women." These authors point out that women's performance tends to be evaluated differentially, such that high levels of performance may be attributed to transitory causes (luck, effort, easy job) rather than to stable causes (ability and skill). Further, reward allocations may be mediated by performance attributions, so that attributing performance to high ability results in increased likelihood of a raise or promotion. Conversely, women's failures tend to be explained as lack of ability, leading to lower probabilities of retention and promotion. Bernice Lott's (1985b) review of women's performance evaluations concluded that in most areas of high achievement, women's competence tends to be devalued in comparison to men with identical credentials.

A model for explaining the process of performance evaluation was proposed by Diane and Thomas Ruble (1982). The diagram in Figure 3.2 includes four major factors that "may result in negative biases concerning women's potential . . . the evaluator's prior set of beliefs, the observed performance, the evaluator's causal explanations for the observed performance, and the consequences of the process" (p. 211). At all levels of the model, gender stereotypes will influence the performance evaluation process.

The outcomes of performance discrimination mirror those of gender segregation. But because the contributions of subtle bias and gender stereotypes are complex and interact in unknown ways with actual job performance, women in non-traditional occupations are at particular risk for attributing

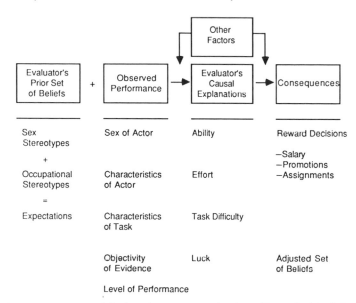

Figure 3.2. A process model of performance evaluation. (From Ruble & Ruble, 1982. Reprinted with permission of Greenwood Publishing Group, Inc. All rights reserved.)

their employment stress to their personal inadequacies. Jeanne Parr Lemkau (1986) contends that women's "self-attributions of blame block awareness of sexism" (p. 36), rendering these women more vulnerable to guilt and depression. She suggests that educating women about institutionalized sexism in the workplace, combined with connections to a supportive female network, will reconnect these women with their sense of personal power and control.

Sexual Harassment

A third barrier to women's occupational progress is the persistence of sexual harassment in the workplace. Sexual harassment is defined by interpersonal behaviors of a sexual nature that are one-sided, unsolicited, unwanted, unwelcome, repeated, and not under the control of the victim (Thomas & Wiener, 1987).

In the most comprehensive study to date, a nationwide survey of 23 000 federal workers revealed that 42% of the women reported some level of sexual harassment on the job (United States Merit Systems Protection Board, 1981). Harassing situations included actual or attempted rape, sexual advances and personal phone calls, touching, fondling, coercing the victim against walls or in her office, pressure for dates, and tasteless remarks. Frequently, harassing behaviors were accompanied by threats of retribution, denial of promotion, and loss of employment. Women in non-traditional job placements, and those in settings with a greater proportion of men, were more likely to be subjected to sexual harassment. These data have been replicated with essentially the same results in a number of other studies (Coles, 1986). A more recent survey of women in engineering, science, and management found that 75% of these women in non-traditional occupations experienced some form of sexual harassment (Lafontaine & Tredeau, 1986). Single and divorced women were over twice as likely to be sexually pressured as were married women.

The deleterious effects of sexual harassment have been documented in many studies. As with victims of rape, sexually harassed women experience anger, depression, humiliation, shame, fear, helplessness, guilt, and aliena-tion. Victims may also experience somatic symptoms, sleeplessness, loss of appetite, headaches, and fear of returning to work. Victims frequently blame themselves, preferring not to report the experience to anyone, and then take responsibility for the harassment. Some women eventually quit their jobs rather than be confronted with continuing "manhandling" and sexual coer-cion (Coles, 1986). In Chapter 7 we discover that sexual harassment at work was a significant contributor to Andrea's depression.

Fortunately, there are federal, state, and local regulations currently in place that forbid sexual harassment in most employment settings. Victims who do report harassing behavior to their employers are in a favorable position to receive retribution and relief. At the present time in the United States, women in small business operations are the most vulnerable to continued harassment, since federal legislation does not extend to them.

Clients who disclose a sexual harassment situation to the therapist should be advised of their legal rights and offered support and assistance in keeping records, informing supervisors, and filing formal complaints of sexual harass-ment. The management of a sexual harassment case is a sensitive one that will challenge the skills of even the most experienced therapist. This is also an area in which few therapists have had experience, so that informing oneself on legal and procedural issues is essential for providing optimal service to the victimized client.

Personal Outcomes

Interpreting Stress

The effects of traditional sex-role socialization and discriminatory sexist practices at all levels of the social community are complex and multideter-mined. House (1974) presented a model for understanding the impact of occupational stress that seems applicable to all the sources of socialization discussed above. Figure 3.3 displays the House model, which begins at box 1

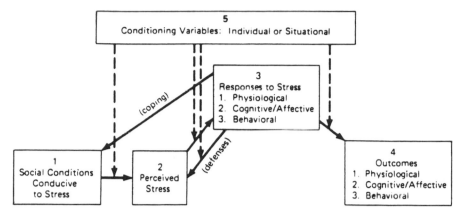

Figure 3.3. A model of occupational stress. Solid arrows between boxes indicate presumed causal relationships among variables. Dotted arrows from the box labeled 'conditioning variables' intersect solid arrows, indicating an interaction between the conditioning variables and the variables in the box at the beginning of the solid arrow in predicting variables in the box at the head of the solid arrow. (Reprinted from House, 1974, with permission of the author and the American Sociological Association.)

with social conditions conducive to stress and ends at box 4 with physiological, cognitive/affective, and behavioral outcomes. Mediating or "conditioning" variables (box 5) help determine the degree to which an individual will be influenced by cultural or situational stressors, and include such factors as gender, age, race, education, and quality of social support.

Applications to Clients

We like to use this model to propose that the cultural messages provided to women, as well as the barriers they meet along the path of self-development, will impact women differentially. When we see women in clinical consultation who present syndromes of adjustment to their life situations that appear dysfunctional for them, we look first to the societal influences on these presenting issues. We then explore how the client has interpreted and internalized the messages she receives from her social environment, and we consider how these messages have contributed to the distress and pain in her current life.

Consider a sample of the clients who arrive at our office with syndromes that appear to be intimately connected with widespread cultural messages. Sylvia was distraught over her latest romantic break-up, and showed signs of depression (sleeplessness, loss of appetite, self-deprecation) and anxiety (gastric upset, fear of being alone). She was certain that life would never be better for her and that she could never find another man to love her.

Irene confessed that she had been taking diet pills for years and feared that she was addicted to them. Nevertheless, she was proud of her slim figure and terrified to relinquish the assurance offered by the medication that she would remain attractive to others. Despite a medical assessment that she was well within her weight range for her age and height, she insisted she was "too fat" and wanted referral to a diet center.

Joyce was brought to the office by her husband because she refused to drive alone. She seldom left her house, was convinced she would have a panic attack and become "stranded" if she were to leave home alone. She remained essentially home-bound except when her husband accompanied her.

Clara, described earlier, had withstood an abusive marriage for 12 years with marginal progress toward leaving her husband. She had convinced herself (with the help of her spouse and family) that she could never "make it on her own" and that her only hope for a better life was to try to please her husband more and to avoid getting him angry.

Marge was struggling with the management of a household, four school-age children, and an assembly-line job at a local manufacturing plant. She presented symptoms of exhaustion, guilt about leaving her children in daycare after school, and concern that her eldest boy was becoming a delinquent. She was caught between wanting to leave her job, pressure for economic survival, and, as it turned out, fear of her manager who was demanding sex after hours.

We could enumerate many more concerns that women bring to counseling that have interconnections to the cultural messages that women receive and take in. It becomes important for these clients to understand that they are similar to many other women in their stressful situations, and that the troubles facing them may have important antecedents in their cultural conditioning. This is not to avoid the contributions of each woman's ongoing behavior to the outcomes of her personal life. Through a sex-role analysis, however, she is helped to distinguish between the messages she receives from others and those she continues to provide for herself.

Summary

This chapter has reviewed the contributions of the family, the public media, the educational system, and the workplace, to the socialization experiences of women and men. We have viewed sex-role socialization as a rule-governed process through which the differential treatment of women and men is abstracted by each individual into gender-specific rules for living. These rules are then translated into stereotypes about others as well as into internalized standards for personal behavior. We explored how major social institutions provide a variety of gender messages that limit and restrict opportunities for women and that erect barriers to women's full development and well-being. We considered the implications of women's socialized sex-role messages for the problems that women present in psychotherapy in the areas of depression, body image, excessive dependency, marital abuse, home–career conflicts, and sexual harassment.

Activities

Select one of the cases discussed in the final section of this chapter (pp. 79–80) and complete the following:

A
(1) List the possible socialization factors that might have contributed to the presenting problem.
(2) Generate at least two messages that the client may have internalized (i.e. accepted as her own) that may be serving to maintain her present dysfunctional patterns.
(3) For each self-generated message you listed in (2) above, restate the message in terms that might enable the client to view the issue differently and more productively for herself.

B
For the same client you considered above, list the concrete ways in which her environment can be changed in relation to her personal goals for change.

Further Readings

Benokraitis, N. V., & Feagin, J. R. (1986). *Modern Sexism: Blatant, Subtle, and Covert Discrimination.* Englewood Cliffs, NJ: Prentice-Hall.

Block, J. H. (1983). Differential premises arising from differential socialization of the sexes: Some conjectures. *Child Development*, **54**, 1335–1354.

Figueira-McDonough, J., & Sarri, R. (Eds.) (1987). *The Trapped Women: Catch 22 in Deviance and Control.* Newbury Park: Sage.

Pearson, J. C. (1985). *Gender and Communication.* Dubuque, IA: Wm C. Brown.

Stockard, J., Schmuck, P. A., Kempner, K., Williams, P., Edson, S. K., & Smith, M. A. (1980). *Sex Equity in Education.* New York: Academic Press.

CHAPTER 4

A Feminist View of Counseling and Therapy

Self-assessment: Counseling Values

Indicate to the left whether you agree (3); are undecided or neutral (2); or disagree (1) with each statement below.

_____ (1) Selecting the goals of counseling is primarily the therapist's responsibility.

_____ (2) Therapy should focus primarily on changing the client's behavior, thoughts, values and/or feelings.

_____ (3) Therapy should focus primarily on changing oppressive/detrimental environmental conditions.

_____ (4) The power of a therapist should be minimized.

_____ (5) Therapists should keep their values out of the counseling process.

_____ (6) Counselors should remain anonymous; should not self-disclose very much.

_____ (7) A major goal of therapy is to help clients adjust successfully to their social environments.

_____ (8) Clients and therapists should be equal partners in the therapeutic process.

_____ (9) Therapists should be neutral observers of human behavior.

_____ (10) Clients should be fully informed about the process of therapy.

_____ (11) Therapists' values should be clearly stated to clients.

_____ (12) Clients' problems can be understood apart from the specific society in which they live.

_____ (13) Due to their extensive training, therapists know clients better than clients know themselves.

_____ (14) Problematic behaviors by individuals most often represent adaptive responses to a "sexist" society.

_____ (15) Therapists having emotional distance from clients is preferable to therapists having emotional connection to clients.

Scoring

In order to get an interpretable summary, items 1, 2, 5, 6, 7, 9, 12, 13 and 15 must be "reverse scored," meaning that a "1" needs to be converted to a "3", a "3" needs to be converted to a "1" and a "2" stays the same. Items 3, 4, 8, 10, 11, and 14 are to be scored as you originally marked them. Once you have converted, find your total score by adding up your points for each item.

The range of scores is from 15 to 45. Scores near the 15 end of the continuum indicate that your values about therapy more closely resemble sexist approaches. Scores near the 45 end of the range indicate that your values more closely match feminist therapy values. Scores in the mid-range indicate a mixture of values.

Overview

The purposes of this chapter are to define traditional, non-stereotyped and feminist approaches to counseling, to explicate in depth the assumptions, principles, goals, and strategies of feminist therapy, and then to demonstrate the contrasting perspectives of non-stereotyped, traditional, and feminist therapies on a specific client case. More specifically, readers will:

(1) Be able to discuss the major differences between traditional and non-stereotyped and feminist therapies.
(2) Know the assumptions and values that form the foundation of feminist counseling.
(3) Know the three basic Principles of Feminist Therapy.
(4) Become familiar with the goals and strategies of feminist therapy.
(5) Be able to compare their own belief and value systems with those of feminist therapy.
(6) Become familiar with the techniques of sex-role and power analyses.

Traditional, Non-stereotyped, and Feminist Therapies

Traditional, non-stereotyped and feminist approaches to counseling differ primarily in the value systems that underlie them. This value and belief "foundation" in turn influences the goals and techniques used in counseling. We believe that it is not possible to have a value-free approach to therapy. Since the values of both the therapist and of the therapist's theoretical orientation have such a strong influence on the process and content of therapy, the values and beliefs of traditional, non-stereotyped and feminist approaches to therapy will be the focus of comparison.

Traditional Therapies

In this book, traditional models of therapy are defined as those therapies that put an emphasis on therapist objectivity, analytical thinking, therapist expertness and control of procedures, emotional distance from clients, and intrapsychic dynamics. Traditional therapies can be sexist in a variety of ways, involving gender-biased stereotyping and diagnostic labeling, andro-centric interpretations, and intrapsychic assumptions.

Gender-biased stereotypes

Traditional therapies often embrace the belief that women and men should behave in traditionally sex-role stereotyped "appropriate" ways. Thus, therapists using these approaches may believe that for women to be mentally healthy, they should be emotionally expressive, submissive, and nurturant, and achieve fulfillment through their roles as wives and mothers. They may assume that for a man to be mentally healthy, he must be aggressive, independent, unemotional, competitive, and economically successful. Heavy emphasis is often placed on assumed biological differences between women and men in determining what is appropriate for females and males. Traditional therapy may promote traditional sex roles and advocates that clients conform to these traditional sex-role ideals (Sturdivant, 1980).

As an example of traditional stereotyping, a therapist might encourage a female client who has interests and abilities related to the medical field to choose nursing as a career, while encouraging a male client with the same interests and abilities to be a physician. Believing (in accordance with traditional sex-role norms) that women should be the primary caretakers of children and of marriage relationships, a sexist therapist might encourage a female client who is being abused by her husband to stay in the marriage and learn to be more understanding of her husband's stress. Success of therapy might be evaluated on a female client's improving her physical appearance. Treatment goals for female and male clients may differ, based solely on the client's gender. For example, a male's progress in therapy might be measured by how assertive and independent he becomes, while a woman's progress might be measured by an increase in the quality of her care-taking abilities.

Biased labeling

Traditional therapists also may apply diagnostic categories and labels differentially to females and males. For example, they might diagnose a female client "hysteric," while labeling a male client with the same characteristics as "anti-social" (Ford & Widiger, 1989). They may label a woman who has had several sex-partners "promiscuous" while labeling a similarly behaving man a "Don Juan." In Chapter 6, we review ways in which assessment and diagnosis may be sexist.

Androcentric interpretations

Many sexist therapeutic approaches are "androcentric," i.e. based on male norms. The male perspective and male stereotyped traits are more highly valued than the female way of doing things. For example, it is androcentric to value being logical and analytic more highly than being intuitive and emotionally expressive. Androcentric theories also use the male experience as the norm and compare females to that male standard. Deviations by females from this male standard are then evaluated as being "less than." For example, the Freudian concept of women having "penis envy" is rooted in the androcentric perspective that having a penis is better than having a vagina and uterus.

Intrapsychic assumptions

Sexist traditional therapy ignores the role that clients' social, political, economic, and cultural environment plays in the problems that clients are experiencing (Greenspan, 1983; Sturdivant, 1980). Rather, these therapies tend to focus solely on the client's intraphsychic make-up, locating the problem in how the client is feeling, thinking and/or behaving. Total attention to the client's internal conflicts without considering the role that the client's external environment contributes to the client's issues leads therapists to blame clients for aspects of their problems that are societally induced (Greenspan, 1983). Feminist therapists call this phenomenon "blaming the victim" because the individual is blamed/held responsible for displaying behavior, thoughts, and feelings that are developed to cope with a restricting and oppressive environment. For example, a sexist traditional therapist might label a woman "masochistic" because she stays in an unhappy marriage. She stays in the marriage because, according to the sex-role beliefs she has internalized from her environment, she will be a "failure" if the relationship fails. Also she cannot financially support her children and herself (she originally made a choice to be a sex-role appropriate female and stay home to raise the children). The therapist ignores the impact of these sex-role stereotyped messages and locates the problem solely in the individual woman. Most of our counseling theoretical orientations are based on an intrapsychic model. If a theory or therapist focuses solely on factors internal to the client, then that approach or practitioner is sexist along this dimension.

Traditional therapies—summary

In summary, there are several ways in which traditional therapies tend to be sexist. The sexist aspects of these therapies may be blatant or subtle. First, the use of gender-biased stereotypes prescribes different behaviors and personality characteristics as appropriate for females and males. Second, sexist therapists use labels and diagnostic categories differentially for females and males. Third, traditional therapies are often androcentric in their perspective. Finally, traditional therapies focus solely or primarily on intrapsychic causes of clients' problems and ignore the social conditions that often give rise to these problems. These approaches are built on an "adjustment to the environment" model of mental health, in that a good therapy outcome is for clients to accommodate successfully to their environment, whether that environment is positive, neutral, or negative. Further, traditional sex-role stereotypes and institutionalized sexism are viewed as positive societal forces.

Non-stereotyped Therapies

Non-stereotyped therapies are more difficult to define. Some authors describe them as gender-neutral (Sturdivant, 1980), while others describe them as feminist therapy without the political components (Foxley, 1979; Rawlings & Carter, 1977). Non-stereotyped approaches occupy a middle position on the continuum between sexist traditional and feminist therapies and represent a complex range of therapeutic approaches. In order to reconcile the differences in definitions of non-stereotyped therapy in the existing literature, we will discuss the continuum of that range from gender-neutral to androgynist.

Gender-neutral approaches

The first category of non-stereotyped therapeutic approaches is closer to the traditional end of the continuum. Approaches fitting the gender-neutral end of the continuum do not adhere to traditional sex-role stereotypes as appropriate norms for females and males. They believe that individual needs and talents should be the guides for individual choices. Thus, females and males can be anything they want to be and should not be restricted by sex-role norms. However, there is a tendency for these therapists to overvalue male traits and to encourage women to be more like men, e.g. to be more assertive, dominant, analytic (Brickman, 1984). Differential labels and diagnoses for females and males are not used.

Gender-neutral therapists do not acknowledge the destructive impact of growing up and living in a patriarchal society. Thus, gender-neutral approaches tend to focus intrapsychically, ignoring sex-role socialization and institutionalized sexism. They view the world as benign or neutral with regard to gender. Individuals are encouraged to develop their full potential, thus emphasizing the client's individual power. The environment is not viewed as imposing major blocks to that development. To the extent that these approaches do not acknowledge the environmental sources of clients' issues, they can end up "blaming the victim" and thus still contain a major source of sexism. Therapists in this category would be supportive of a woman who wanted to be a physician or of a man who wanted to be a nurse. However, they might not encourage consideration of those choices if the client does not initiate exploration of those choices first. Further, they would not initiate an exploration of societal roadblocks to and strategies for overcoming societal barriers to these clients' non-traditional choices. They would not initiate an exploration of a client's sex-role socialization history.

Androgynist approaches

Androgynist therapy is closer to the feminist therapy end of the continuum. Therapists in this androgynist category espouse values and beliefs very similar or identical to feminist views. Thus, the androgynist therapist values an androgynous model of mental health in which women and men are encouraged to develop all aspects of themselves. Clients are encouraged to develop a large repertoire of behaviors and characteristics and to balance traditional female and male traits. Sex-role reversals are not labeled pathological (Rawlings & Carter, 1977). Differential diagnoses and desired treatment outcomes are not based on gender.

Sex-role socialization is viewed as a major source of the client's problems. Androgynist therapists educate clients about the effects of sex-role socialization and encourage clients to explore the external as well as the internal sources of their problems. Androgynist therapists may or may not acknowledge the existence of sexism in our educational, political, religious, legal, and economic institutions. Therapists in this category do not advocate political action by themselves or by their clients (Gilbert, 1980) and they avoid the use of the label "feminist therapist," even though their belief systems match closely.

Non-sterotyped therapies—summary

In summary, non-sterotyped approaches to therapy encompass a wide range of beliefs and can be divided into at least two categories. The gender-neutral category, which is closer to the traditional end of the continuum, does not prescribe adherence to traditional sex roles, but still uses a basically intra-psychic model of therapy that ignores the effects of a sexist environment on individuals. The androgynist category is closer to the feminist therapist end of the continuum. Both internal (intrapsychic) and external (especially sex-role socialization) sources of clients problems are explored and an androgyn-ous model of mental health is embraced. Androgynist therapists may or may not consider themselves feminists and prefer the label "non-sexist therapist" to "feminist therapist".

Feminist Therapies

In Chapter 1, you may recall that we defined feminism in several different ways. We pointed out that feminists of all persuasions endorse gender equity, but on specific topics they embrace a wider range of beliefs. Similarly, feminist therapy is also not a single, unified approach. Marececk and Hare-Mustin (1987) identify three different types of feminist therapies: radical, gender-role, and woman-centered. The first, *radical feminism*, attributes the differences between females and males primarily to the unequal distribution of power in societal conditions that exist for women and men. The major goal of radical feminist therapists is to equalize women's and men's power in all of society's institutions. The second group of feminist therapies, *gender-role*, attributes personality differences between females and males to differ-ential sex-role socialization. Their focus is on individual development rather than social change. The major goals of this gender-role group are to resocialize clients to become more androgynous and to facilitate clients' personal growth. The third group, *woman-centered*, composed of both cultural feminists and psychodynamic therapists, believes that there are fundamental differences in the psychological make-up of women and men; differences that are not due solely to sex-role socialization. Therapists in this group highlight female-stereotyped characteristics such as cooperation, empathy, and altruism, resulting in a positive re-evaluation of female traits traditionally perceived as deficits. Feminine qualities are viewed as a desir-able source of possible societal transformation. Counseling goals for this woman-centered approach are to facilitate clients' positive valuing of their femaleness and trusting of their perspective of their experiences, i.e. devel-oping a woman-focused consciousness.

An empowerment model

Thus, even within feminist therapy there is much diversity. In this book we are presenting an approach to feminist therapy that represents our integration of this diversity. The Empowerment Model of Feminist Therapy introduced in Chapter 1 incorporates many of the ideas from all three types of feminist therapy. However, our Empowerment Feminist Therapy Model most closely resembles the one labeled "radical feminist therapy" by Marecek and Hare-Mustin (1987), since we focus on women's low social power as the basis of their problems and we believe that both social and individual changes are needed.

In the remainder of this chapter, the assumptions, principles, goals, and techniques of our Empowerment Model of Feminist Therapy will be explored in detail. Because feminists' assumptions about the world form the foundation of feminist therapy, and because these beliefs influence the choice of therapeutic goals and techniques, the world-view assumptions of Empowerment Feminist Therapy will be presented first.

Empowerment Feminist Therapy: World View Assumptions

Feminist therapy approaches were created as a result of the feminist movement of the 1960s. As we discussed in Chapter 1, leaders of the feminist movement criticized traditional therapists for being agents of society, for encouraging women to adapt to traditional sex roles, while also labeling women "sick" when their adaptation was too complete, e.g. labeled "masochistic" for being submissive to their abusive husbands (Caplan, 1985). Consciousness-raising and self-help groups were developed as an alternative to traditional therapy. Some of the people who participated in those consciousness-raising groups were traditionally-trained mental health professionals, who took the newly-acquired awareness about themselves as women and men and about institutionalized sexism and created a new therapeutic approach to working with female and male clients. This new approach, called "feminist therapy," was based on feminist beliefs. Feminist therapists embrace a wide range of counseling theoretical orientations, e.g. psychoanalytic, cognitive behavioral, family systems, gestalt, etc. Some feminist therapists consider their theoretical orientation to be that of "feminist therapist." While their therapeutic goals and techniques may vary in accordance with their various theoretical orientations, the goals, techniques, and concepts which emerge from their theoretical orientations are evaluated against the feminist belief system that feminist therapists embrace. Concepts and techniques in each therapist's repertoire that violate that feminist belief system must be modified or replaced. Thus, this core set of beliefs forms the foundation upon which our Empowerment Feminist Therapy is built and can be stated as a set of basic assumptions. The assumptions presented below are a synthesis of the existing literature (Gilbert, 1980; Greenspan, 1983; Rawlings & Carter, 1977; Russell, 1977; Sturdivant, 1980).

(1) Women have individual problems because of living in a society that devalues them, limits their access to resources and discriminates against them economically, legally, and socially. Thus, sexism is institutionalized in all areas of our society—families, religion, education, recreation, the work place, and laws. "The inferior status of women is due to their having less political and economic power than men" (Rawlings & Carter, 1977, p. 54). Institutionalized sexism is a major source of problems for people.

(2) Contrary to theories of biological determinism, feminist therapists believe that women may differ from men primarily because of the differences in how women and men are socialized. This sex-role-stereotyped socialization process limits the potential of all human beings. All people have the capacity for all characteristics and behaviors. Both sexes are victims of sex-role socialization. Sex-role socialization is a major source of individual pathology for both women and men.

(3) Women and men do not have equal status and power. Women are oppressed and in a subordinate power position.

(4) Psychopathology is primarily environmentally induced. This concept is called "cultural determinism."

(5) Females and males "should have equal opportunities for gaining personal, political, institutional, and economic power" (Rawlings & Carter, 1977, p. 50).

(6) All societal opportunities should be open to both women and men regardless of race, ethnicity, age, affectional preference, handicaps, or economic circumstances. Gender or identified groupings should not determine individual behavior or restrict opportunities for personal competence and flexibility in all areas of living.

(7) Racial, economic, handicapped, heterosexist, and ageist oppression are also important sources of societal pathology. Social change needs to encompass all oppression.

(8) Relationships between people should be egalitarian. Marriage should be a partnership between equals. Traditional, hierarchical power differentials between women and men are detrimental to women.

(9) Women and men tend to be socialized toward different value systems. For example, more men than women value analytical thinking, independence, competition, and assertiveness. More women than men value nurturance, cooperation, intuition, empathy, and relationship

interdependence. Women are taught one value system (female-stereo-typed) while living largely in an environment based on male-stereo-typed values. This duality may result in a values conflict for women.

(10) Traditional therapeutic approaches have developed primarily from the male perspective and are based on a male-stereotyped value system. For example, women's economic dependence on men has been over-emphasized as a deficit, while men's independence has been overval-ued. Men's relationship dependence on women has been ignored.

(11) The female perspective, the female value system, and female experi-ence should be given equal weight and focus to the male perspective.

(12) An end to sexism in society requires both a change in how females and males are socialized and structural changes in society's major insti-tutions. Political, institutional change is necessary to eradicate sexism and oppression of minority groups.

(13) Therapy is a value-laden process. All therapists have values that they communicate in the therapy session with or without their awareness. Therapists who are aware of their own values and explicitly state their relevant values to clients minimize the imposition of their values on the client.

Principles of Empowerment Feminist Therapy

Three basic principles of feminist therapy—the Personal Is Political, Egali-tarian Relationships, and Valuing the Female Perspective—emerge from the feminist belief system and guide the work of feminist therapists. These principles represent how feminist beliefs and assumptions are applied to the content and process of therapy. These principles form the core beliefs about the nature and conduct of counseling. The goals of feminist therapy encom-pass a wide range of possibilities which reflect both the therapist's theoretical orientation and the specific issues of individual clients. However, certain goals are generally shared by most feminist therapists and are related to each of the principles of feminist therapy. In this section, the three Principles of Empowerment Feminist Therapy and related counseling goals are presented.

I. *The Personal Is Political*

Principle

The Personal Is Political principle encompasses feminist beliefs about sex-role stereotyping, institutionalized sexism, and oppression. Since traditional sex-role socialization and the institutionalized separation and discrimination of people based on gender are judged to oppress and limit the potential of all individuals, the external environment is considered the main source of clients' problems. Thus, the primary source of a client's pathology is *not intrapsychic or personal*, but rather *is social and political* (Gilbert, 1980). The acknowledgment of the societal sources of women's individual issues is the core of feminist therapy (Sturdivant, 1980).

Separating the external from the internal. Feminist therapy focuses on helping clients identify the influence of social rules, sex-role socialization, institutionalized sexism and other kinds of oppression on personal experience, so that they can separate the external and internal sources of their problems. This process involves several steps. First, individuals must recognize the existence of, and the negative influence on their lives, of patriarchal societal practices. Second, they must begin to see a relationship between these external experiences and the issues they have brought to counseling. Third, they must decide whether they want to change themselves (their internalized sex-role messages) and their environment (social change). Finally, they implement the desired changes. The priority in Empowerment Feminist Therapy is given to identifying dysfunctional environmental factors rather than concentrating on intrapsychic factors. Further, the focus is on changing the unhealthy external situation and on changing the internalized effects of that external situation, rather than on helping the client adapt to a dysfunctional environment.

Reframing pathology. Individuals are not blamed or pathologized for thinking, feeling, and behaving in ways that are congruent with living in an oppressive society. Their "symptoms" are seen as strategies for coping with an unhealthy environment (Greenspan, 1983; Sturdivant, 1980). For example, women's depression may be seen as a natural, logical response to being oppressed and discriminated against (Greenspan, 1983). The recognition that there is not something inherently wrong with them ("I'm not crazy"), that their reactions are "normal" given the patriarchal society in which they live, empowers clients to make changes in themselves and in their environments. A natural outcome of consciousness-raising about the external sources of women's issues is for women to become angry at their oppression. Feminist therapists believe that it is not only important for women to learn to express their anger (contradicting traditional sex-typed messages not to be angry), but that it is also crucial for women to use their anger as a source of energy for changing their environments and themselves. Individuals are not to blame for how they are, but are responsible for working toward change.

One focus of this change is on helping clients modify their internalized beliefs about what is appropriate behavior for females and males. Feminist therapists encourage clients to develop all aspects of themselves, aspects considered to be traditionally appropriate for only males or for only females. Individuals are encouraged to develop a full repertoire of behaviors.

Initiating social change.   Changing of clients' sex-role stereotypes and sex-role-stereotyped self-talk is not sufficient (Greenspan, 1983). Even children who are raised in gender-free families still have to live in a world of discrimination and oppression. The ultimate goal of feminist therapy is to create a society in which sexism and oppression of minority groups does not exist. Thus, change of our institutions (the family, schools, religion, the workplace, economics, laws, political structure, etc.) is crucial, since these are the means by which society perpetuates sexism and oppression. Mental health cannot be achieved solely by women acquiring healthier behaviors. Society must be changed and women from all groups must have increased social power as well as increased personal power (Marecek & Hare-Mustin, 1987).

These social change goals of feminist therapy are difficult to integrate into the individual focus of counseling. One way to accomplish this integration is to view social change as having a continuum of levels—from large, macro-levels to smaller, micro-levels. For example, a macro-level social change would be a change in policies by a political party, e.g. including more female and minority convention delegates. Another macro-level change example is the change in rape laws that has occurred in the last decade. An example of change at a micro-level is a woman confronting her boss about discriminatory or sexist practices in the workplace and the resulting changes in office procedures and/or her boss's attitude. Clients' working for environmental changes, especially at the micro level, is often a spontaneous outcome of identifying the external sources of one's problems, of not blaming the victim. Social change that is facilitated by feminist therapy is more likely to occur at the micro level. However, micro-level changes made by individuals often result in macro-level societal changes, e.g. the changing roles of women that were discussed in Chapter 2. Macro-level changes are also accomplished by a group of individuals working for social and political change. Feminist therapists encourage clients to join groups where they can work with others for these changes. This group alliance increases the individual's social power.

Feminist therapists also involve themselves in their communities in working for social change. They model skills directed at institutional change. This institutional change involvement is also important as a preventive strategy—changing the environmental conditions so that they will not continue to cause problems for women, i.e. to make environments healthier.

Counseling goals

The following statements are possible feminist therapy goals which are related to the Personal Is Political principle. Counselors help clients to:

(1) Become aware of their own sex-role socialization process.
(2) Identify their internalized sex-role messages/beliefs.
(3) Replace sex-role stereotyped beliefs with more self-enhancing self-talk.
(4) Develop a full range of behaviors that are freely chosen, not dictated by sex-role sterotypes, i.e. to become more flexible and competent and less sex-typed.
(5) Evaluate the influence of social factors on personal experiences.
(6) Understand how society oppresses women.
(7) Understand that individual women's experiences are common to all women.
(8) Identify sexist and oppressive societal practices that negatively affect them.
(9) Acquire skills for enacting environmental change.
(10) Restructure institutions to rid them of discriminatory practices.
(11) Develop a sense of personal and social power.

II. *Egalitarian Relationships*

Principle

Feminist therapists believe that interpersonal relationships should be as egalitarian as possible. This principle is related to the feminist beliefs that women in our society do not have equal status and power with men, and that minority groups are subordinate in status to majority groups.

One of the major complaints by the women's movement of traditional therapy was that therapists used their power to encourage and/or coerce women to adapt to an unhealthy environment, and thus were agents of patriarchal social control. The sex-role-stereotyped values of the therapist negatively influenced the client (Rawlings & Carter, 1977). Feminist therapists believe that it is crucial to build an egalitarian relationship between the client and counselor for two reasons. First, egalitarian client–counselor relationships minimize the "social control" aspects of therapy (Sturdivant, 1980). In an egalitarian therapeutic model, counselors have less of a power base from which to impose their values on clients. Second, the client–counselor relationship should not reproduce the power imbalances women experience in society. The therapeutic relationship should be a model for egalitarian relationships in general.

Empowering the client.   In Empowerment Feminist Therapy, clients and counselors are considered to be of equal worth. One is not the "expert" and the other "sick". Therapy is to be a collaborative process in which the client is considered to be an expert on herself. There are no outside experts on the woman's experience (Brickman, 1984). The counselor's expertise is based on her specialized training (knowledge of human behavior, of therapy, and of institutionalized sexism) and on her own life experiences as a woman. Feminist therapists use several strategies to minimize the power differential between them and their clients. First, because therapy is a value-laden process, feminist therapists make their relevant values known to their clients in the beginning of counseling. This declaration of values by the counselor minimizes the counselor's imposition of her values on the client, i.e. the client is free to accept or reject the counselor's values if they are made explicit. Feminist therapists share their beliefs about society and educate their clients about the theory and process of feminist therapy. This allows clients to make an informed choice, to be an educated consumer about therapy (Gilbert, 1980; Greenspan, 1983; Sturdivant, 1980). Clients are encouraged to shop around for a therapist. Feminist therapists teach their clients relevant therapeutic skills. Counseling goals are collaboratively determined by the client and counselor and written contracts are often used to spell out the conditions of therapy.

Balancing power. Contrary to many traditional approaches to therapy, feminist therapists self-disclose (share information about their current and past life experiences) and self-involve (share their here-and-now reactions) with clients. A female counselor's self-disclosure to a femal client facilitates identifying the common social conditions that they share as women. This is an important way to move from an intrapsychic focus to a social, external focus (Greenspan, 1986). Self-disclosure also reduces the role distance and power differential between client and therapist. Self-involving responses conveying how the therapist is emotionally reacting to the client, or to what the client is saying, are important for several reasons. First, the client gets feedback about how she is impacting another person. Second, the therapist allows her own vulnerability to be present by sharing her feelings. Third, the therapist models effective communication skills, including modeling direct expression of anger—an emotion that is discouraged for women by traditional sex-role socialization. (Greenspan, 1986). Self-disclosure and self-involvement must be used with care. They are used when they are relevant to the client's issues, when they can be appropriately handled by the client and when their use will be in service of the client's psychological growth.

In advocating egalitarian client–counselor relationships and counselor self-disclosure, Empowerment Feminist Therapy embraces a female perspective on the therapeutic process that conflicts with many beliefs of traditional therapies which are based on stereotyped male values. The objective, emotionally-distant, expert-therapist model of many traditional therapies is replaced by a model that emphasizes empathy, sharing of common experiences, nurturance, and mutual respect (Greenspan, 1983). Client "transference" issues are also treated differently. Client reactions to the therapist are not treated solely or primarily as transference of previous relationships to the therapeutic relationship. Rather, much consideration is given to the reality of the client–counselor relationship—that the client is having legitimate here-and-now reactions to the real attributes and behaviors of the therapist. Thus, in feminist therapy these client reactions are not usually interpreted as transference, but are accepted as valid (Greenspan, 1983). The counselor–client relationship is explored and counselors are open to the client's feedback. This feedback is especially important when clients express anger at the therapist. Since females are systematically taught not to express their anger, a major goal of feminist therapy is to facilitate clients' expression of anger. For therapists to interpret clients' anger towards them as really being transferred anger invalidates clients' angry feelings, punishes their initial attempts at expressing their anger, and violates the feminist concept of clients being experts on themselves.

Affirming the woman. In further promotion of egalitarian therapeutic relationships, feminist therapists emphasize identification of client strengths in addition to exploration of problems. Often identification of these strengths involves reframing of previously negatively valued traits, ones that are negatively valued using an androcentric perspective, but are reappreciated from a gynocentric perspective. This revaluing of self is a part of the third Principle of Feminist Therapy which will be discussed later in this chapter.

Egalitarian therapeutic relationships are difficult to achieve. The establishment of an egalitarian relationship with clients is more of an ideal that is continually strived for, rather than an accomplished reality for all or even most therapeutic relationships.

Counseling goals

The following statements are possible feminist therapy goals which are related to the Egalitarian Relationship principle. Counselors help clients to:

(1) Develop egalitarian relationships—both in therapeutic relationships and in the client's life generally.
(2) Be economically autonomous. Most feminist therapists believe that women must be financially independent in order to not be in a "one-down," subordinate position (Greenspan, 1983, Sturdivant, 1980).
(3) Develop a balance of independence and dependence (interdependence) in relationships.
(4) Develop a full range of interpersonal and life skills.

(5) Be appropriately assertive.
(6) Develop skills for dealing with the interpersonal conflict that comes from living in a sexist environment.
(7) Express and use anger in service of implementing constructive change.
(8) Identify personal strengths and assets.

III *Valuing the Female Perspective*

Principle

A common misconception about feminist therapy is that its goal is to make women more like men. On the contrary, a major premise of Empowerment Feminist Therapy is that women and men need to be able to increase their appreciation of the female perspective of life and of female value systems.

In Chapter 1, we pointed out that socially constructed conceptions of gender have segregated and devalued many sets of behaviors that are traditionally socialized in women. Reconstruction of our gender conceptions requires that we re-evaluate the female-stereotyped traits and affirm them as important and valuable human characteristics for both women and men. Feminist therapy assists women in identifying the devalued aspects of their socialized selves and in reconceptualizing weakness into strength and negative deficit into positive advantage.

The devaluation of female-related characteristics results in a kind of double bind for women. They are reinforced for being "appropriately" female and at the same time are devalued for being that way. For example, women are taught to be nurturing of their families, to put their family members' needs before their own and to devote their life energies to "making the home." Yet women are criticized for being "enmeshed" with their families and for being "dependent" on a man economically. The concept of "codependency," typically applied to women, is a prime example of how women are pathologized for providing the nurturance and attachment behaviors they were taught to give to men (van Wormer, 1990). Women are expected to nurture others. Yet nurturance is devalued in society at large, as is evidenced by the low pay associated with "nurturant" professions like nursing and teaching, and by the low status that nurturing by the therapist has in most traditional therapy approaches. Women usually internalize this androcentric double bind by following the sex-role norm, while devaluing themselves and their femaleness (Greenspan, 1983). Societal, male-stereotyped norms invalidate the female's experience.

Revaluing the woman. Thus, feminist therapists believe that women need to reject androcentric definitions of womanhood, to learn to value their female characteristics, and to validate their own, woman-centered views of the world. Women are encouraged to self-define themselves, based on trusting their own experiences. Sturdivant (1980) calls this phenomenon the "woman-defined-woman" (p. 92). Feminine characteristics that have been defined as deficits when compared to male characteristics are "revalued" as strengths in feminist therapy. Thus, empathy, nurturance, cooperation, intuition, interdependence, and relationship focus are valued and given priority. Needs for nurturance and interdependency are viewed as legitimate and not as pathological. Peaceful negotiation is valued against competitive and aggressive solutions to conflict. Heterosexuality is not seen as healthier than homosexuality.

Outcomes of revaluing women.   This revaluing and redefining process has many implications for both women and the feminist therapy process. First, learning to value previously devalued characteristics facilitates women's use of a large role repertoire, i.e. they not only acquire desirable additional traits they have been taught to suppress (becoming more androgynous), but also prize and use desirable traditional female-typed traits. They also learn to value other women and their relationships with other women. Increased bonding with other women is seen as an important way for women to understand the common social conditions that underlie the life problems that they have. Thus, consciousness-raising groups and all-female therapy groups are viewed as very desirable alternatives to replace or augment individual therapy. These groups are ways for women to heal women, and for women to see that their individual power is bound to the power of women as a group. Women can not be "empowered" solely through intrapsychic change. Real empowerment of women can only be realized through social change (Greenspan, 1983). A second implication of the revaluing process is that women learn to nurture themselves (Gilbert, 1980).

Third, feminist therapy encorporates this female-based value system. Clients are treated as experts on themselves. Meeting client needs (rather than frustrating them), nurturing clients, being empathic, and establishing collaborative, egalitarian relationships are important aspects of feminist therapy (for a more detailed account of how androcentric values influence traditional therapeutic approaches, see Greenspan, 1983). Feminist therapists believe that when clients experience therapists' empathic understanding and support, they are more likely to love and nurture themselves (Greenspan, 1983).

Counseling goals

The following statements are possible feminist therapy goals related to the Valuing the Female Perspective principle. Therapists help clients to:

(1)   Trust their own experiences as women.
(2)   Redefine womanhood from a female perspective.
(3)   Appreciate female-related values.
(4)   Trust their intuition as a legitimate source of knowledge.
(5)   Identify personal strengths.
(6)   Identify and take care of their own needs and nurture themselves.
(7)   Value themselves as women.
(8)   Value other women and their relationships with women.
(9)   De-emphasize androcentrically defined physical attractiveness.
(10) Accept and like their own bodies.
(11) Define and act in accordance with their own sexual needs rather than someone else's sexual needs.

Techniques of Feminist Therapy

Feminist therapists use a wide variety of techniques to accomplish the goals of feminist therapy. Some techniques, such as sex-role analysis and power analysis, are unique to feminist therapy, while others are drawn from other theoretical orientations. All techniques that feminist therapists use must first be evaluated for their compatability with feminist therapy principles. Those techniques that violate these principles must either be modified or discarded. For example, most feminist therapists do not use paradoxical interventions, such as prescribing the symptom (Levant, 1984), if the therapist uses the technique without the client being aware of its purpose. This "manipulation" of the client violates the egalitarian relationship principle. In the next section, we will define and discuss several techniques that are used by most feminist therapists. These techniques of feminist therapy are displayed in Table 4.1.

Sex-role Analysis

Sex-role analysis is designed to increase clients' awareness of how societal sex-role-related expectations adversely affect them and of how women and men are differentially socialized (Sturdivant, 1980). The first step of sex-role analysis is for clients to identify the direct and indirect sex-role messages (verbal, non-verbal, modeled) they have experienced across their lifespan (see the exercises in Chapters 2 and 3 for examples). Second, they identify both the positive and negative consequences to them of those sex-role messages. Third, they identify how they have internalized these external messages in the form of conscious and unconscious self-talk. Fourth, they decide which of these internalized messages they want to change. Fifth, they develop a plan for implementing the change (e.g. cognitive restructuring). Sixth, they implement the change. They also learn skills for counteracting

Table 4.1.   *Techniques of Feminist Therapy*

Principle	Techniques
I: The Personal Is Political	Sex-role analysis Power analysis Bibliotherapy Reframing Assertiveness training Consciousness-raising
II: Egalitarian Relationships	Demystifying strategies Bibliotherapy Assertiveness training C-R Groups
III: Valuing the Female Perspective	Relabeling Bibliotherapy C-R groups

negative environmental reactions to their implemented changes. Sex-role analysis can be used in many variatons (one structured exercise on sex-role analysis is presented in the Activities section at the end of this chapter). Many feminist therapists believe that sex-role and power analyses are more effectively done in groups of women (Kravetz, 1980).

Power Analysis

Power analysis is designed for two purposes: (a) to increase clients' awareness of the power differential existing between women and men in Western societies (Sturdivant, 1980); and (b) to empower clients to have influence on the interpersonal and institutional externals affecting their lives. We define power as the ability to access personal and environmental resources in order to effect personal and/or external change. One's actual use of power depends on access to and/or possession of different kinds of power, one's decision to use that access, and the ways in which the power is exerted.

Power analysis can involve several steps. First, both the therapist and client can review the variety of existing definitions of power and then choose the one that best fits for them. Second, clients are taught about the different kinds of power (e.g. role, resource, legal, institutional, normative, reward, physical, referent, etc.). Third, information can be given about the differential access women and men generally have to these kinds of power (Lips, 1981; Johnson, 1976). Clients are encouraged to identify which kinds of power they possess or to which they generally have access.

Fourth, clients can be introduced to Johnson's (1976) structure for understanding the various ways power can be exerted, e.g. direct vs. indirect, personal resources vs. concrete resources, and competence vs. helplessness. Since Johnson concludes that women generally exert power through indirect, personal resources, and helplessness means, women clients especially need to identify the modes they typically use in exerting power and to learn about alternative strategies. Fifth, clients are asked to explore how sex-role messages (internalized sex-role stereotyping) and environmental barriers (institutionalized sexism) are affecting their use of power. Challenging and changing their internalized messages is an important prerequisite to clients' using a wider range of kinds of power and of power strategies. The final step in power analysis encourages clients to try out additional or alternative kinds of power and power strategies, thereby increasing their power role repertoire.

Both female and male clients can benefit from analyzing the destructive and effective uses of power. Both sides of the power structure are analyzed, especially the "effects of too little power and authority on women and the effect of too much power and authority on men" (Brickman, 1984, p. 61).

Assertiveness Training

Traditional sex-role socialization of women prohibits women from acting assertively and directly (Jakubowski, 1977). Thus, training to be assertive, to stand up for one's own rights while not trampling the rights of others, is crucial for women if they are not to be powerless victims. Assertive skills are important for women to possess in order to impact the environment effectively and to bring about social change. Since assertiveness skills are so important to both effecting institutional change and to having egalitarian relationships, feminist therapists must possess assertion-training skills (Gilbert, 1980). Jakubowski (1977) has developed a four-component assertiveness training program for women, which includes teaching clients to differentiate between assertive, passive, and aggressive behaviors, to develop a belief system that supports their rights to assert their needs and have them met, to reduce psychological blocks (e.g. traditional sex-role messages) to their being assertive, and to develop assertiveness skills through behavioral rehearsal.

Consciousness-raising Groups

Consciousness-raising (C-R) groups, a creation of the Women's Movement, are groups of women meeting regularly to discuss their lives as women. As the women in a C-R group share information about their individual lives, they begin to identify the commonalities in their experiences and then to see the social/external roots of those experiences that are related to living in a sexist environment. The women explore their sex-role socialization process and its negative and positive effects on their lives (sex-role analysis) and they examine the one-down power position of women in society (power analysis). Generally, C-R groups are leaderless and egalitarian, are growth-oriented, and focus on working toward social change. The content may range from cognitively-oriented discussions to more personal, emotional sharing. They share similarities with self-help groups (Kravetz, 1980). The C-R group goals and format are often adapted by feminist therapists to counseling women in an all women's group with the therapist as leader. These all-women therapy groups follow the Feminist Therapy Principles and are seen as having several advantages over individual counseling. First, the interpersonal sharing is spread over many individuals, rather than just the client and counselor, thus providing a wider base for identifying the commonalities in the female experience. Second, the women are sources of healing for each other, often taking turns in being the healed and the healer—a process which helps turn "victims" into "survivors" (Figley, 1985) and empowers the individual woman. Third, the women can work toward social change more effectively together than alone.

Bibliotherapy

Feminist therapists often encourage clients to read books and articles relevant to their therapeutic issues. The client's learning about herself and her environment through reading is called bibliotherapy. Resocialization (away from traditional sex-role stereotypes) and education of clients about sexism is facilitated by clients' reading (Sanders & Steward, 1977). Bibliotherapy is also a good way for clients to learn life-coping skills. Bibliotherapy can also increase the expertise of the client vis-à-vis the therapist, thereby reducing the power differential between them.

Reframing and Relabeling

In the family therapy literature, "reframing" is a technique in which the counselor changes the frame of reference for looking at an individual's behavior. It usually refers to a shift from an intrapersonal to an interpersonal definition of the client's problem (Grunebaum & Chasin, 1978). In feminist therapy, the reframing shift is usually from intrapersonal/individual to societal/political, and is accomplished by identifying the contribution of the external invironment to the individual's problem. Thus, reframing is a very useful technique for the Personal Is Political principle of feminist therapy. "Relabeling" usually refers to counseling interventions that change the label or evaluation applied to the client's behavior or characteristics, usually shifting the focus from a negative to a positive evaluation. Related to the Valuing the Female Perspective principle of feminist therapy, clients learn to relabel previously evaluated weaknesses (based on androcentric norms) as strengths (based on gynocentric norms).

Therapy-demystifying Strategies

Feminist therapists use a variety of techniques to demystify the therapy process for clients. The more clients know about therapy in general and specifically about therapy with this particular therapist, and share in decisions related to their therapy, the greater is the chance for developing an egalitarian relationship between the therapist and client.

Having access to information is one way to increase women's personal power. Feminist therapists teach clients about therapy so that they can be informed consumers. In initial sessions with clients (some feminist therapists provide this session free of charge), feminist therapists describe their theoretical orientation and therapeutic strategies, their relevant personal and professional values, their general expectations for both themselves as therapists and for clients, and the client's rights as a consumer of therapy. Fees for therapy are also negotiated. They often encourage clients to "shop around" for a therapist by interviewing other therapists and finding the best match for them. For example, the New York Chapter of the National Organization for Women (1978) has published a booklet entitled *A Consumer's Guide to Non-sexist Therapy* to educate potential clients about their rights and to help them in their search for a therapist.

Once the client has decided on a therapist, the client and feminist therapist develop a therapeutic contract (either verbal or written) that articulates the conditions of therapy (fee, session time, length of therapy, etc.) and the therapeutic goals towards which they will work. The goal setting is done collaboratively, with input from both the client and counselor and with the client having the final say.

Feminist therapists also teach relevant counseling skills to clients. For example, many counseling skills are basically good interpersonal communication skills that can be important for clients to add to their behavioral repertoire. Self-awareness and self-monitoring skills give clients control over their behaviors, and thus increase their choices. Feminist therapists also teach and encourage clients to evaluate the counseling relationship and to evaluate progress toward therapeutic outcomes. Identifying and expressing needs and wants is an important change for many women due to the female-stereotyped sex-role rule that dictates that women should subordinate their needs to the needs of others. By giving feedback to the therapist about how the therapist is impacting the client, and by evaluating whether their needs are being met in therapy, clients learn how to assert themselves.

Demystifying strategies are not the exclusive domain of feminist therapists. Indeed, they are strategies for applying ethical practices in counseling sessions for all kinds of therapies (Hare-Mustin et al., 1979). However, in feminist therapy they serve the additional purpose of reducing the power differential between client and therapist, thus increasing the possibility of an egalitarian therapeutic relationship.

Characteristics of Feminist Therapists

First and foremost, feminist therapists must have a commitment to the beliefs of feminism and a set of values that are consistent with the Principles of Feminist Therapy (Rawlings & Carter, 1977). Sturdivant (1980) believes that feminist therapists must have applied feminist principles to their own lives and should continue to model the incorporation of these principles. Thus, feminist therapists should have been through their own consciousness-raising process. They should also be involved in their communities in bringing about social change. They need to be knowledgeable about the psychology of women and about women's issues, especially about the external sources of women's concerns. They use this professional and personal awareness in the counseling process to listen to what clients say and to conceptualize and reframe client experiences from a feminist perspective. They are active in the therapeutic process. They initiate explorations of how sex-role socialization and environmental sexism impact client issues. They challenge clients to consider a full range of choices. For example, if a female client expressed interest in nursing and medical technology, the feminist therapist would encourage her to add physician to her list of career alternatives. Feminist therapists are often advocates on behalf of clients (Rawlings & Carter, 1977; Sturdivant, 1980).

Sturdivant (1980) suggests that feminist therapists also need to be warm, empathic and spontaneous—to be capable of expressing their feelings and of being willing to self-disclose and self-involve. Feminist therapy de-emphasizes therapist "objectivity," since the need to be objective distances both the client and counselor from their own feelings. Feminist therapists value emotional involvement with clients as well as having cognitive understanding. Since expression of anger is important for women, counselors must be comfortable with their own expression of anger and with clients' expressions of anger in sessions.

Comparative Case Analysis

In this section, traditional, feminist, and non-stereotyped approaches to therapy will be compared by applying them to a client case. Our intention is to show you contrasting, possible strategies that each of these orientations might use to treat this case, rather than to give you a complete, comprehensive case analysis of how each would do therapy with the client, an incest survivor.

"Nina" is a 31-year-old female who comes to therapy because of periodic bouts of "unexplained" depression, a low level of sexual desire, and low self-esteem. She is the only female stockbroker in a medium-sized company. She and her husband have two children and have recently been in marriage counseling for their sexual difficulties (unmatched levels of sexual desire). She entered individual therapy because she felt that the sexual difficulties were "her fault." She was repeatedly sexually abused by her older brother from the time she was 5 years old until she was 11 years old. She repressed these memories. She never told anyone about the abuse. As she begins therapy she does not remember that she was sexually abused. After 3 months of therapy, Nina reports terrifying, frightening nightmares in which she sees her brother in her bedroom and she awakens feeling frightened.

Sexist Traditional Strategies

There are many ways in which counselors can be sexist in their work with Nina: accepting incest myths, minimizing the trauma, blaming the victim or her mother, engaging in sexual misconduct, and setting inappropriate counseling goals. The first way is for the therapist to believe in societal myths about incest (O'Hare & Taylor, 1983). For example, the sexist therapist may treat Nina's nightmares as fantasies or wish-fulfillment. This interpretation can be based on society's beliefs that incest is a rare occurrence and is often "made up" by the victim. Therapy based on this assumption would focus on identifying and resolving other factors contributing to Nina's presenting problems, e.g. her "inability" to accept her traditional wife and mother role, her self-blame, her need to control everything and everyone around her, and/or her need to prioritize and organize her multiple roles more efficiently. Her presenting symptoms would be viewed as pathological and she likely would be given a diagnosis that labeled *her* rather than her trauma. Nina might finish therapy without recognizing that she was an incest survivor.

Even if the nightmares are explored and the incest is acknowledged as having happened, there are other ways for the therapist to be sexist. The therapist might minimize the seriousness of Nina's trauma since she experienced only "brother–sister sex play" (O'Hare & Taylor, 1983). The therapist might interpret the brother's behavior as "affectionate" and thus not harmful. The sexist therapist might blame Nina for the abuse, i.e. ask her to assume responsibility for her part in the abuse by pointing out that she didn't tell anyone, that she was orgasmic, that she led her brother on, that her brother did not use physical force, and/or by accusing her of seducing her brother. The therapist could also blame Nina's mother for allowing the abuse to occur or for causing Nina's brother's acting out by her inadequate mothering. No mention will be made about her father's role since family relationship dynamics are not traditionally men's responsibilities. Thus, the incest would be seen as being caused by women (Brickman, 1984). The most harmful sexist practice would be for Nina's therapist to take advantage of her vulnerability by approaching her sexually. Therapists' sexual relationships with clients, while always unethical, deliver a double blow to Nina because by sexually abusing Nina, the therapist would recreate the original trauma and revictimize Nina. (Sexual misconduct by therapists will be discussed in Chapter 12.)

Counseling goals would also be vulnerable to sexism. The therapist might impose his/her own goals or Nina's husband's goals on Nina. For example, if the therapist primarily values women's biological roles, priority would be given to working on Nina's sexual problem so that she could again be a "functioning" wife. Little emphasis would be given to Nina's pain, but rather to how her trauma affects her husband's comfort (Brickman, 1984). Her depression might be interpreted as resulting from her trying to do too much. She might be encouraged to reduce her work commitments so that she could be a better wife and mother.

Empowerment Feminist Strategies

Feminist therapists would approach Nina's issues quite differently. They would reject incest myths, assess for sexual trauma, educate about incest and sexual violence, reinterpret family power dynamics, remove blame from the victim, and empower the client to become a survivor.

Assessing for sexual trauma

Because feminist therapists are well educated about the reality of women's lives, e.g. high occurrence rate of rape, sexual abuse, spouse abuse, they routinely assess for these experiences in all their clients. For example, at the beginning of therapy, the therapist would ask Nina if she had had "any uncomfortable, unwanted, or unpleasant sexual experiences". Also, because of their knowledge about specific women's issues, feminist therapists would know about the range of symptoms often found in incest survivors and would recognize that Nina's three presenting issues (depression, sexual difficulties, and low self-esteem) are symptomatic of sexual abuse trauma (Finklehor, 1986). Nina's nightmares would be seen as possible confirmation of these symptoms. Because the client is seen as an expert on herself, and because the therapist acknowledges the high incidence of childhood sexual abuse, Nina's nightmares would be viewed as possible flashbacks or resurfacing of traumatic memories, rather than as fantasies. (It is beyond the scope of this discussion to show how a therapist would facilitate Nina's exploration of her nightmares so that the real basis of them could be uncovered.)

Removing victim blame

As the memories of the incest surface, the therapist would share her knowledge about incest with Nina, helping her to connect her present behavior and feelings to her trauma. This reduces Nina's feelings that she is going crazy. Brother–sister incest would not be viewed as less traumatic than parent–child incest. Nina's brother would be held responsible for his abusive behavior and his behavior would be defined as rape, an act of sexual violence. Feminist therapists believe that the victim is never to blame. Intrusive, abusive offenders use their power to achieve self-gratification in a way that traumatizes a resistant but powerless victim (Brickman, 1984). Nina would learn that orgasm can be a purely physiological response to genital touch and that her orgasmic response to her brother did not signify that she wanted to be abused, nor that she really wanted to have sex with her brother.

Re-interpreting family power dynamics

In Empowerment Feminist Therapy, power and authority are seen as important underlying issues. The power that Nina's brother had because he was older and male would be explored, as would Nina's and her mother's possible lack of power as females in the family. Nina's mother would not be held solely responsible for not protecting Nina. Nina's father's role (as an equally responsible co-parent) in not having protected Nina would be explored. Since the dynamics of an individual family are strongly influenced by the societal norms of male dominance, it is important for the power differential between males and females in Nina's family and in society in general to be addressed (Herman, 1981).

Challenging of incest myths

Society's view of incest, as depicted in incest myths and the media, would also be discussed. More than likely Nina's experience of the sexual abuse would be different from society's depiction of incest. By helping Nina challenge the myths she has learned, the therapist facilitates Nina's beginning to trust her own feelings and perspective. The role of sexual violence in helping to keep women subjugated through fear would be addressed. Incest is directly connected to men having sexual power over women (Brickman, 1984).

Equalizing power

The feminist goal of building egalitarian therapeutic relationships would be especially important with Nina so as not to recreate, in the therapy relationship, the controlling victimizer–helpless victim dynamics of her abuse. The feminist therapist would appropriately self-disclose. If the therapist is herself a rape or incest survivor, she would share some of her own experiences as a victimized female and as a survivor. Goals would be collaboratively decided upon and might include claiming her sexuality for her own pleasure (rather than restoring her sexual functioning for her husband), learning to like and nurture her own body, trusting her own perspective and experience of her trauma, valuing her femaleness, nurturing herself, identifying her strengths as a survivor, increasing her assertion skills, learning not to blame herself, expressing all of her feelings related to the incest, especially anger, and learning to channel her anger for effecting external change.

Re-interpreting "symptoms"

Nina's "symptoms" would be viewed as normal reactions to traumatic experience, not as indicators of pathology. The counselor and Nina would explore how her symptoms are connected to her specific trauma and how they helped her to cope with the trauma. Nina would probably be encouraged to join a therapy group for incest survivors. Through group sharing, Nina would learn to feel less different and isolated. She would also have the opportunity to help other victims to heal, an experience which Figley (1985) says is important in becoming a "survivor." Finally, the feminist therapist and/or Nina might work at changing society, especially its contribution to the existence of incest and society's myths about incest. Social change is seen as crucial.

However, Nina's incest trauma is only one source of her "symptoms." Nina's depression and low self-esteem also would be partially viewed as normal reactions to Nina's being a woman in a patriarchal society, i.e. they are a reflection of her societal subordination as a woman. The feminist counselor would inquire about Nina's experiences as the only professional woman in her office and of her experiences pursuing a non-traditional career. In what ways is she being discriminated against in the workplace? Nina's possible role strain and role overload would also be discussed. Strategies for changing her environment and others' expectations of her (rather than giving up her work) would be explored.

Nonstereotyped Strategies

The non-stereotyped therapist's approach to Nina is more difficult to predict. The non-stereotyped therapist would probably not blame Nina for her victimization. On the contrary, some gender-neutral family therapists would label Nina's family as dysfunctional and would use an orientation in which no one individual was to blame. Everyone involved might be viewed as a victim (Brickman, 1984). Or a family systems approach (gender-neutral) might look at what each family member contributed to the problem and thus, hold everyone partly responsible for the incest, including Nina. (Most feminist therapists judge this joint assessment of responsibility as sexist.) Most non-stereotyped, humanistic therapists emphasize personal, individual power, while ignoring real differences in the role, resource, and physical powers that exist between women and men. Thus, in a non-stereotyped approach, external, institutionalized barriers (social realities) are minimized and Nina's personal psychological power to create her own life would be emphasized. Especially in the gender-neutral end of the continuum, therapists may end up subtly blaming Nina for not exercising her personal power to disclose about or end the abuse.

Androgynist therapists would employ similar strategies to feminist therapists. These strategies might be establishing an egalitarian relationship, not blaming Nina for the sexual abuse, looking at the role that sex-role socialization played in the sexual abuse (i.e. men socialized to be abusers, women socialized to be subordinate), establishing collaborative counseling goals, using a stress model for understanding normal reactions to trauma (Figley, 1985) and de-emphasizing diagnosis of Nina's pathology. However, androgynist therapists would not include a power analysis, or acknowledge the relationship of institutionalized sexism (e.g. society's norm of male dominance) and the existence of incest. Likewise, they probably would not be involved in changing societal attitudes or practices regarding incest and rape, or in encouraging Nina to channel her newly discovered power and anger to bring about societal change.

Other similarities and differences between non-stereotyped therapists and feminist and traditional therapists would depend upon non-stereotyped therapists' accurate knowledge about incest, their theoretical orientation, their ability to handle a client's deep emotional pain, and their own myths and biases about rape and sexual abuse.

Summary

The three principles of feminist therapy—I. The Personal Is Political; II. Egalitarian Relationships; and III. Valuing the Female Perspective—constitute a therapeutic approach very different from most traditional therapies. The Empowerment Feminist Therapy approach requires that all of one's gendered perspectives and assumptions about both the world and therapy be considered anew. Becoming a feminist therapist means putting one's androcentrically-defined view of the world, and one's androcentrically-based professional training, in a basket, mixing up the contents and then putting them into a feminist-designed sieve that requires major reconstruction and/ or disposal of existing gender-related concepts. Correspondingly, clients of feminist therapists acquire a whole new way of looking at and responding to their world. For both the counselor and the client, this shared journey of empowerment can be frightening, angering, and exhilarating.

Activities

A
After reading this chapter, you can retake the *Counseling Values Self-assessment* to see if you have changed any of your values.

B
Sex Role Analysis Exercise. This is an exercise designed to help you identify the advantages and disadvantages to you of sex-role messages you learned while growing up, and by which you may still continue to be influenced. Complete the following steps:

(1) *Sex-role message identification*. Beginning with your early childhood experiences and continuing developmentally up to the present day, write down all the messages you received about how you should and should not behave because you were female or male. Make two lists: one of "Shoulds" and one of "Shouldn'ts." These lists represent the composite of the sex-role rules that you have learned.

   Remember that these messages may have been verbal or non-verbal, may have been reflected in ways you were rewarded, punished, and ignored, and may have been modeled by others. These messages may have come from a variety of sources: significant others, acquaintances, the media, printed materials, and from institutional structures and policies. In recalling these messages, it is useful to work with developmental periods of your life, e.g. junior high, and to focus on those factors and people who were influential in your life during that period.

(2) *Sex-role restructuring*
   (a) *Look over the lists you have just made*. Put a check mark by each message that still influences your present behavior. Select one of these check-marked messages to explore further here.
   (b) *Identification of original sources of messages*. Think about how and where you originally learned this message, e.g. in your family, in school, in church, from peers, on TV, etc. Write down all the sources from which you learned this sex-role rule.

(c) *Current reinforcers and punishments.* In what ways and by whom are you currently reinforced for behaving in accordance with, or punished for not behaving in accordance with, your sex-role rule?

(d) *Cost–benefit analysis.* What benefits do you gain by following your sex-role rule? What does this sex-role rule cost you: how does it limit you? What benefits do you see that society gains by women (or men) living in accordance with your sex-role rule? What are the costs to society of this sex-role rule?

(e) *Decision to change.* Based on your personal and societal cost–benefit analysis, you now need to decide if you want to change this internalized sex-role message. If you decide not to change it, stop here. If you decide to change it, proceed to the next step.

(f) *Reconstructed message.* Re-write your sex-role rule into a self-message that is more self-enhancing and less restricting. What behaviors do you need to change to live in accordance with your newly constructed message?

(g) *Implementation of new message.* Brainstorm strategies that will help you implement your new message and its corresponding behavior changes. Make a commitment to yourself about which of these strategies you will use.

Further Readings

To expand your understanding of feminist therapy, you may want to read the following resources:

Gilbert, L. A. (1980). Feminist therapy. In A. M. Brodsky, & R. T. Hare-Mustin (Eds.) *Women and Psychotherapy* (pp. 245–265). New York: The Guilford Press.

Greenspan, M. (1983). *A New Approach to Women and Therapy.* New York: McGraw-Hill.

Marecek, J., & Hare-Mustin, R. T. (1987). Feminism and therapy: Can this relationship be saved? (Unpublished manuscript.)

Rawlings, E. I., & Carter, D. K. (1977). *Psychotherapy for Women.* Springfield, Il: Charles C. Thomas.

Sturdivant, S. (1980). *Therapy with Women: A Feminist Philosophy of Treatment.* New York: Springer.

Feminist Transformation of Counseling Theories

Self-assessment: Clarifying Your Theoretical Position

Before you begin to use feminist theory in your practice with clients, you will want to develop a clear conception of your theoretical position in psychotherapy and counseling. That is, how do you currently use theoretical conceptions in your approach to human functioning and behavior change? Before reading Chapter 5, complete the following format for clarifying your theoretical approach to therapy. At the end of this chapter, we will ask you to apply your understandings of Feminist Therapy Principles to revising and adapting the theory of your choice to a feminist format.

(1) History: briefly trace the historical basis of the theory. Who were the theoretical grandparents, and how did they gather data to develop and support their theorizing?

(2) List the key constructs or concepts of the theory.

(3) How does the theory explain personality development and change?

(4) How does the theory explain psychopathology, mental illness, maladjustment, or problems in living that bring clients into contact with the helping professional?

(5) What is the role of assessment and diagnosis?

(6) What is the role of the therapist and of the client?

(7) List the major therapeutic techniques or strategies.

(8) Develop a brief statement about how this theoretical approach fits your personal views of human functioning and behavior change.

Overview

The purpose of this chapter is to develop an understanding of how to integrate traditional theoretical views with feminist principles of psycho- therapy and counseling. We start with a comparison of traditional and feminist models to theory-building and we provide a format for assessing the compatibility of any theory with Feminist Therapy Principles. Two theoretical approaches to psychotherapy and counseling are offered as examples of the adaptation process: cognitive–behavioral theory and psychodrama. Readers are challenged to perform a similar transformation exercise on a theory of their choice. After reading Chapter 5, the reader will be able to:

(1) Outline eight steps in the conception of a chosen theory of psycho- therapy or counseling.
(2) Compare traditional with feminist-compatible models of theory construction.
(3) Determine the compatibility of the theory with feminist therapy principles.
(4) Revise the chosen theory to fit compatibly with feminist therapy principles.

SECTION ONE:
A GUIDE TO THEORY TRANSFORMATION

Searching for a Theory

Feminist therapists embrace a wide range of theoretical orientations. We believe that therapeutic change is most effectively accomplished when therapists are well grounded in a cohesive theory that enables them to conceptualize the client's issues and to anticipate the effects of specific interventions. In contrast to theory-based interventions, the eclectic approach takes a pragmatic stance, using whatever techniques or strategies appear to be useful in each situation. Surveys of practicing clinicians suggest that pro- fessional helpers are about evenly split between adhering to an established theoretical approach or relying on eclectic pragmatism (Garfield & Kurtz, 1974). Regardless of personal choice, it will be most useful for you to identify a favored theory or theories in order to apply the feminist transformation process to a personally-endorsed set of constructs and interventions.

Advantages and Drawbacks in Counseling Theory

The adoption of a theory-based approach to counseling and psychotherapy has both advantages and drawbacks.

Theory vs. eclecticism

On the positive side, a theory provides a consistent resource for conceptualizing functional and dysfunctional behavior patterns and for selecting interventions that are tailored to the needs of the client. Thus, theory-based interventions are more likely to follow a rational process of hypothesis-testing and revision of strategy than a trial-and-error approach that attempts "whatever will work." Theory-based interventions are also more likely than randomly-chosen techniques to be subjected to systematic research evaluation. A research base can provide valuable information to the clinician about how the intervention functions with differing types of problems and with various client populations.

Many practitioners find that a single theory becomes too restrictive and confining, however, and prevents the therapist from using techniques that might be useful but are extra-theoretical (Jacobson, 1987; Levine & Sandeen, 1985). Successful eclectics report that they do develop personal theories that increase their range of intervention options without inviting therapeutic chaos (Garfield & Kurtz, 1977). Other therapists have attempted to integrate the concepts and strategies from several theories to provide increased flexibility and richness of conceptualization (Goldfried, 1982; Wachtel, 1977). Finally, some therapists may adopt a major theoretical orientation, yet borrow judiciously from other theories when particular situations and/or strategies appear to enrich the treatment plan (Jacobson, 1987; Lazarus, 1981). In these instances, therapists can usually articulate how they use extra-theoretical strategies to supplement the central model from which they operate.

The delicate negotiation between theoretical purity and strategic flexibility is ultimately a personal decision. It seems probable that the eclectic practitioner does base hypotheses and strategies on some aspects of favored theories at differing times and with selected clients. We believe that for the purposes of working effectively with women clients, one's theoretical assumptions and working hypotheses should be explicit, rather than implicit, in the awareness and functioning of the clinician. As we shall point out later in this chapter, the feminist therapist may want to adopt a central theoretical approach while borrowing relevant strategies from other theories that facilitate the stated goals of counseling.

Traditional vs. feminist theory

A second drawback to many theories of counseling and psychotherapy is the incompatibility of concepts and interventions drawn from the theory with the Principles of Feminist Therapy. In our view, most contemporary theories of psychotherapy and counseling contain elements that render their application undesirable for use with women clients. Some theories of behavior development and change are more conducive to integration with feminist views than others. Please review your responses to the self-assessment exercise and try to identify elements and concepts from your chosen theory that appear incompatible with the Principles of Feminist Therapy. Then continue to read the chapter for how to analyze a theory to accommodate to a feminist format. The following sections offer a format for how to analyze a current theory of behavior change for its compatibility with feminist principles. First, we summarize the characteristics of theories that are inconsistent with effective treatment strategies for women. Then, we suggest four criteria for developing a feminist format for theories of counseling and psychotherapy. We complete the analysis with a set of guidelines for transforming a given theory into a format that meets the criteria for feminist counseling.

Characteristics of Traditional Theories

The purpose of a psychological theory is not to mirror nature but to present an image of nature that appears useful for understanding individuals (Levy, 1970). Similarly to the concept of gender, a theory is a construction of reality, and reflects the understandings that exist at the time of social history in which the theory is developed (Gergen, 1985; Morowski, 1987). Many psychological theories were born during a period in history in which gender was viewed as a dichotomous property of the state of being female or male. Observed social arrangements were assumed to be rooted in the nature of gender, so that women and men were assumed to possess different characteristics and to follow divergent life pathways. Consequently, some theories currently in use bear the reflections of our historical heritage regarding the "true" nature of women and men.

The following analysis presents six characteristics of traditional theories that reflect biased or outdated assumptions about the place of gender in human functioning. These characteristics are displayed in the left-hand column of Table 5.1. A theory can be gender-biased if its content and constructs can be characterized in any of the following ways: (a) androcentric, (b) gendercentric, (c) ethnocentric, (d) heterosexist, (e) intrapsychic, or (f) deterministic. Each of these concepts is described and examples are provided below.

Androcentric

An androcentric theory constructs the lives of persons according to an understanding of the lives of men (Doherty, 1978; Katz, 1979, Rosser, 1990; Worell, 1981, 1989b). The theory may use male-oriented constructs such as

Table 5.1. *Characteristics of Theories*

Traditional	Feminist
Androcentric ——————┐	
Gendercentric ———————┘ ——————→ Gender-free	
Ethnocentric ——————┐	
Heterosexist ————————┘ ——————→ Flexible	
Intrapsychic ——————————————→ Interactionist	
Deterministic ————————————→ Lifespan	

"penis-envy," or may draw assumptions about "normal" human development from an observation of men's developmental sequences of behavior. Examples of androcentrism are found in Freud's (1948; 1965) description of male identity development, in which the boy's defensive identification with a father figure leads to the formation of a healthy superego and internalization of high moral standards. Since girls do not progress through the same Oedipal sequence as boys, their superego development is never quite as consolidated, resulting in a lower level of moral development in women. Women, in Freud's view, are by nature passive, emotional, masochistic, narcissistic, and have a lesser sense of justice.

Other examples of androcentric theories are found in Erikson's (1963, 1968) description of identity development in women and men. For the adolescent male, a sense of secure identity comes from adopting a philosophy of life and choice of a career. For women, however, identity is normally deferred until "they know whom they will marry and for whom they will make a home" (1968, p. 123). A woman's identity is therefore not defined by ideology or career commitment, but by her fusion with the roles of wife and mother.

Some theories contain a male-defined conception of the healthy personality. Family systems theories, for example, emphasize hierarchy, differentiation, and interpersonal boundaries (Bograd, 1986). In Murray Bowen's theory, the differentiated self (ideal adjustment) is characterized by a rational and objective stance, and the capacity to free the self from relationship contexts (Hare-Mustin, 1978). Michele Bograd (1988) points out that by these male-defined standards, women are viewed as "enmeshed, undifferentiated, or over-involved, where the prototypically male pole is valued and the prototypically female pole is defined as unhealthy" (p. 97).

Clinicians who base their understandings of women and men on either of these theories may arrive at conclusions about women clients that are male-biased and inaccurate for any particular woman. Although thoughtful therapists might argue that these parts of Freud's, Erikson's, or Bowen's theories do not play a role in their current therapy, it seems possible that unverbalized influences may exist.

Gendercentric

Gendercentric theories propose two separate paths of development for women and men. The theories of Freud and Erikson discussed above are both gendercentric as well as androcentric. Other theories that posit separate paths of development, however, do not necessarily devalue women but view them as separate and different from men in their personality structure, needs, or values. An example here is object relations theory (Chodorow, 1978; Miller, 1976). Recent formulations of psychoanalytic approaches to personality structure and development propose that women and men differ fundamentally in their needs for attachment and separation, and in their valuing of intimacy and connection in relationships. The differences in personality structure are assumed to evolve from early experiences with the mother, who functions as a prime force in determining the female and male orientation to self and others.

Therapists who adopt a gendercentric theory reveal alpha bias (see Chapter 1). They tend to view women and men as dichotomous in their relationship needs and skills, emphasizing how women and men differ rather than how they intersect (Worell, 1988). Although there are some demonstratable differences between women and men in relationship styles, these differences are small, overlapping, and frequently a function of self-presentation strategies rather than personality structure (Deaux, 1984). We believe that it is counterproductive to attribute patterns of behavior to sex or gender, rather than to sets of attitudes and beliefs that are modifiable. Although we may focus on socially-based gender messages that women and men internalize as they mature, these messages are viewed as changeable, rather than deeply rooted in personality structure or biological sex.

Ethnocentric

Ethnocentrism is built into the structure of many theories that base their observations on Anglo-European populations. Ethnocentric theories assume that the "facts" of development and human interaction are similar across races, cultures, and nations. Examples of ethnocentrism in theorizing are seen in assumptions about "normal" family functioning, including the hierarchy of the two-parent family, the relative power position of women and men in families, and the place of children within the family structure. Assumptions about "working mothers," day-care, extended family arrangements, and who should have jurisdiction over children in contested custody suits, can all be influenced by the clinician's theoretical view of appropriate family functioning.

Some family therapy approaches that use a systems theory model may impose a traditional role structure on women within the family setting (Bograd, 1986; Hare-Mustin, 1978, 1980; Margolin, 1982). Therapists who adhere to traditional systems theory may also impose their values on Black, Hispanic, Asian, or other ethnic group families, whose concepts and values about appropriate family functioning may vary considerably from White, middle-class American culture. Conceptions about appropriate amounts of "enmeshment" and "individuation" (or attachment and separation) for example, may vary across ethnic groups, allowing the potential for misuse of these constructs with families that adhere to culturally different life-styles. Clinicians from diverse theoretical persuasions may need to examine their assumptions and their beliefs about healthy family functioning in order to avoid an ethnocentric position with clients. We examine strategies for working with minority and cross-cultural clients in Chapter 11.

Heterosexist

Psychology has been generally heterosexist in its theory and research. Most traditional theories of psychological development and therapeutic change view heterosexual orientation as normative and desirable, and they devalue life-styles that are oriented toward same-sex partners. In classical psychoanalytic theory, for example, a homosexual orientation was viewed as a failure to achieve normal gender identity, and therefore the preference for same-sex partners was treated as a personality disorder. Heterosexism was built into earlier diagnostic systems, and only in 1973 did the American Psychiatric Association remove homosexuality as a category of mental illness from the Diagnostic and Statistical Manual (DSM-II).

New avenues of research suggest the need for at least two revisions of classical heterosexist theory: (a) preference for same-sex partner (gay or lesbian) or for partners of either sex (bisexual) is a stable historical fact and is evidenced in well over 10% of the population (Weinstein & Rosen, 1988); (b) personality functioning in gay men and lesbian women differs mainly from heterosexual samples in that these individuals tend to be more androgynous and less sex-typed in their interpersonal behavior (Blumstein & Schwartz, 1983; Kurdek & Schmitt, 1986). Clinicians who remain loyal to unsupported theories about homosexual development and behavior may reveal homophobic and biased attitudes in their counseling interviews. We discuss counseling strategies with lesbian clients in Chapter 11.

Intrapsychic

Theories that attribute all behavior to intrapsychic causes may fall into the position of "blaming the victim." When theories of development and therapeutic change minimize the influence of the external environmental on past and current behavior patterns, the woman will bear total responsibility for her actions and for the situations in which she finds herself. Examples here include both object relations theory and some theories of cognitive change. In object relations theory (Chodorow, 1978; Marcus, 1987), women's failure to differentiate and separate from the mother figure may be seen as a factor in their unwillingness to leave an abusive marital relationship. In some rational cognitive–behavioral theories (Ellis, 1962), the client may be held responsible for her current situation because of her "irrational and faulty" thinking.

Although we do not propose that clients be exempted from their individual contributions to the problems they encounter in life, or from their responsibility for change, an intrapsychic causation model suggests that changes should occur only with the client and not with her environment. Clinicians who adopt an intrapsychic model will tend to emphasize how the client's personality, thoughts, or behaviors have contributed to her predicament, and will tend to ignore or minimize situational constraints and environmental stressors. Clients may be assured that they can "fix" themselves within a maladaptive situation by adjusting their behavior and thinking patterns.

Deterministic

Deterministic theories of development and behavior assume that current patterns of behavior were developed and fixed at an early stage in life. Concepts of causality tend to be linear, with past events predicting current behavior. As a result, sex-role conceptions and orientations become an inflexible part of one's personality and are relatively intractable at later stages. Clinicians who adhere to a deterministic view will tend to expect an orderly sequence of change with clients, and may assume that behavior is less affected by current situations than by past history and/or stable personality traits. A deterministic view of personality development may encourage clinicians to apply diagnostic labels that describe a stable property of the person (dependent personality, for example) rather than to describe situational behavior patterns (e.g. allows husband to make decisions for her).

In summarizing the characteristics of many traditional psychological theories, we find that they may contain attributes of androcentrism, gendercentrism, ethnocentrism, heterosexism, as well as intrapsychic and deterministic assumptions that are detrimental to effective counseling with women. In the following section, we offer an alternative format within which any theory can be evaluated for compatibility with a feminist view.

A Format for Feminist Theory

Whether you decide to adhere strictly to one theoretical approach, or you wish to develop a combination of theoretical strategies, you can examine your assumptions, concepts, and techniques for their compatibility with a feminist model. In contrast to the characteristics of traditional theories described above, the feminist format provides four criteria for evaluating a theory: (a) gender-free, (b) flexible, (c) interactionist, and (d) lifespan (see Table 5.1).

Gender-free

Gender-free theories view women and men as similar in psychological make-up. These theories avoid stereotypes, or language that labels one sex as more socially desirable, mature, or valued than the other. Gender-free theories explain differences between women and men in terms of socialization processes, self-presentation strategies, and developmental aspects of cognitive and affective processing. That is, the theory avoids incorporating into its structure and concepts the sexist or stereotyped concepts of the broader culture. Gender-free theories promote change toward reduced sex-role stereotyping in social roles and interpersonal behavior.

Flexible

A flexible theory uses concepts and strategies that apply equally to individuals or groups of any age, culture, race, gender, or sexual/affectional preference. A flexibility model can account for within- as well as between-sex differences in behavior, and allows for a range of healthy and satisfying sex roles and life-styles for both women and men. A flexibility model suggests the possibility of multiple interpersonal arrangements and options for change, rather than prescribing the desirability of one outcome over the other. A flexible theory should enable the therapist to remain vigilant to the special needs of each client group without devaluing the chosen life-style of the client.

Interactionist

A theory that hypothesizes a reciprocal interaction between the individual and a range of internal and external variables is essential to a feminist model.

Interactionist theories contain concepts that are specific to the individual (affective, behavioral, and cognitive) as well as those that can encompass the situation or the broader environment (institutions, power, barriers). Interactionist theories consider multiple causes and influences on behavior, such that the individual cannot be understood outside the context of all relevant variables. Interactionist theories invite the possibility of change in both individuals and situations.

Lifespan

A lifespan view assumes that development is a life-long process, in which behavior changes can occur at any time. Therefore, "maturity" is not an end-state, neither can an ideal state be determined. Lifespan theories describe behavior according to multiple determinants that may induce continual change rather than emphasizing traits or orderly sequences of behavior (Baltes, Reese, & Lipsett, 1980). As applied to gender-related behavior, a lifespan theory suggests that these behaviors are not fixed in people, time, or situations, but are potentially in flux. From a lifespan perspective, individuals are embedded in their social–historical environment, but remain capable of choice and self-determined change (Worell, 1981). Lifespan theories invite an open approach to behavioral change that encourages alternative options at all ages and stages.

In summarizing the requirements of a feminist-compatible theory, we see that they encompass four characteristics: gender-free, flexible, interactionist, and lifespan. In the next section, we offer a procedure to use in examining your preferred theory. With this procedure, you will look at a selected theory for evidences of traditional concepts that are detrimental to counseling women, and will be able to transform the theory to a format that is more compatible with Feminist Therapy Principles.

Transforming a Theory to a Feminist Format

For a theory to become compatible with a feminist therapy approach, the theory should be thoroughly analyzed and compared to at least seven criteria. First, the theory should meet the four requirements (gender-free, flexible, interactionist, lifespan) described in the previous section. Second, the theory should not violate the three Principles of Feminist Therapy. In this section we present guidelines for adapting one's theoretical orientation to a feminist therapy approach. Table 5.2 depicts five steps involved in transforming a theory to a feminist format.

Table 5.2.   *Theory Transformation Steps*

Steps	Comparison criteria

I Identify sources of bias in the theory (compare each area below to the criteria in the list to the right)
    (A) Historical development of theory
    (B) Key theoretical concepts
    (C) Theory of personality development
    (D) Sources of client's problems
    (E) Language and label usage
    (F) Role of diagnosis and assessment
    (G) Role of therapist and client
    (H) Therapeutic techniques
	Feminist Theory Format
	Gender-free: women and men similar in make-up; differences due to socialization
	Flexible: a wide range of healthy lifestyles is acceptable. Theory applies to diverse client groups
	Interactionist: individual functioning is the result of interactions between individual and environmental variables

II Restructure or eliminate sexist components	*Lifespan*: development is a lifelong process
III Determine whether theory is still viable	**Feminist Therapy Principles**
IV Identify ways in which theory is compatible with feminist criteria	I The personal Is Political II Egalitarian Relationships
V Highlight components from chosen theory and add components from other theories that facilitate accomplishment of counseling goals related to Principles I, II, III.	III Valuing the Female Perspective

Step 1: Identify Sources of Bias

The first step in the transformation process is to analyze all major aspects of a particular theoretical orientation in order to identify the sources of sex bias in the theory. Different aspects of the theory are delineated and compared against the seven criteria listed in Table 5.2. There are eight substeps to this analysis.

Historical development of theory

Since many sources of theoretical bias are covert or subtle, it is important to know how the theory was developed and how the social–cultural era in which the theoretician lived influenced the development of the theory. More specifically, what were the cultural beliefs about appropriate roles for women and men during the time the theory was conceived? How are these beliefs reflected, ignored or rejected in the theory? Whom did the theoretician observe or study in deriving the theory's constructs? If the criterion sample is restricted to one sex, social class, race, age, etc., then application to other samples is likely to have androcentric, ethnocentric, and/or gendercentric biases. For example, Super's (1957) theory of career development was based on studying the career development of middle-class, White males (androcentric, ethnocentric). His theory has been applied to the career development of people in general.

Key theoretical concepts

What are the key constructs in a particular theory? How are the concepts applied to women and men? That is, are different constructs used for females and males (gendercentric)? Are the constructs applied similarly or differentially to females and males? What value judgments about femaleness and maleness are conveyed by the constructs? Do the constructs reflect a male perspective or male-valued traits, e.g. independence, differentiation, hierarchical power (androcentric)?

Theory of personality development

Gender bias in a theory is often most clearly evident in how personality development is explained by the theoretician. How are any differences between females and males explained? Does female or male development serve as the norm against which the other sex is evaluated? How are mental illness and mental health defined? Are they defined differently for females and males? Are different roles prescribed for females and males (gendercentric)? What is the relative emphasis on a client's deficits vs. strengths? What is the role of the environment in personality development (intrapsychic)? Is behavior seen as the result of single or multiple determinants? Are one's personality traits fixed at an early stage of life, and thus seen as difficult or impossible to change (deterministic)?

Sources of clients' problems

Most current psychotherapies focus primarily on the source of problems as located in the client (intrapsychic) or at least as being within the client's control. Even the theories that do acknowledge the impact of environmental events and environmental context on individual behavior often frame the goals of counseling to focus solely on intrapsychic change. In accordance with the "Personal Is Political" principle, a feminist approach needs to incorporate environmental change goals. What are the internal and/or external sources of problems and pathologies in personality development? What are the roles of environment and culture on individual behavior? Is the theory primarily intrapsychic or interactionist? What are the goals of counseling? Does the theory "blame the victim" (and/or the victim's mother)?

Language and label usage

Traditionally, theories have been written using the "generic he" to refer to all persons. Only recently have writers and publishers suggested or required substituting plural nouns and pronouns for the "generic he". Most theoretical orientations are written with the "generic he" because they were developed before these publishing changes occurred. The problem is that research has consistently shown that when individuals read "he" references, they are more likely to perceive that the subject matter applies to males than to females. Thus, most of our older theories have to be read compensating for the use of the "generic he." (See Chapter 3 for further discussion of the generic masculine.)

The labels applied to the theory's constructs are also crucial. What labels are used for the constructs? Are the same behaviors in females and males labeled differently? What value judgments are conveyed by the labels used (gendercentric)? Do the constructs reflect bias about age, race, sexual preference, handicaps (ethnocentric, heterosexist)?

Even if the constructs and labels of a theory are neutral (e.g. family systems theory), the writings that explain the theory can apply it in a sexist manner. Thus, analyzing case examples given in the writings about the theory is important. Do the case examples of functional behavior reflect the client's traditional sex-role stereotypes? Do the case examples of dysfunctional behavior reflect departure from traditional sex-typed behavior?

Role of diagnosis and assessment

As we will elaborate in Chapter 6, diagnosis and assessment can be sexist in many ways. One's theoretical orientation usually specifies roles for the use of assessment strategies and diagnostic labels. Theories which use sexist diagnostic labels or diagnostic systems closely connected to Freudian theory are the least compatible with a feminist therapy approach. Diagnostic categories and labels which closely parallel traditional sex-role stereotypes usually pathologize/blame individuals for their own socialization (accuse them of masochism, for example). Theories which advocate a client–therapist collaborative approach to assessment and diagnosis are more compatible with feminist therapy. A feminist theory also needs constructs and techniques for measuring external/environmental variables.

Role of therapist and client

According to Principle II, egalitarian relationships between client and therapist are valued because they do not recreate the power imbalances that women experience in society. Thus, theoretical orientations that advocate a distant, expert role for the therapist vis-à-vis the client are incompatible with a feminist therapy approach. How are the desired roles of client and therapist described by the theory? How are counseling goals decided? How much validity is given to the client's perspective? How is client transference viewed? Is therapist self-disclosure permitted by the theory?

Counseling techniques

Techniques which emphasize a large power differential between the therapist and client are incongruent with feminist therapy. Are the therapeutic techniques manipulative or hidden, as in paradoxical directives? How are the techniques and client-counselor therapeutic interactions related to collobor-ative or non-collaborative setting of counseling goals? How are empathy, self-disclosure and other relationship-building techniques integrated into the theory?

Step 2: Restructure Theory's Sexist Components

In Step 1, the sexist components of the theory were identified. In Step 2, these identified components must be modified so that they are non-sexist. If modification is not possible, those aspects of the theory must be eliminated.

Step 3: Determine Viability of Theory

Once sexist components have been restructured or eliminated, the theory is re-evaluated for its continued viability. If too many components have been eliminated or modified, the theory may have lost its basic structure and/or congruence. If the theory is judged to be no longer viable, then another theory which is more compatible with the principles of feminist therapy must be sought. If the theory is judged to be viable, then one moves to Step 4.

Step 4. Identify Compatibility with Feminist Criteria

The theoretical and applied aspects that have survived Steps 1, 2, 3 and 4 are appreciated for their compatibility with a feminist therapy approach. They are also recognized for their potential contribution back to the practice of feminist therapy, i.e. aspects of this theoretical orientation which can be borrowed by feminist therapists using differing primary theories. These contributions to other feminist orientations are the focus of Step 5.

Step 5: Highlight Feminist Components

Many theories have unique contributions to make to feminist therapy. Many constructs and techniques from diverse theories facilitate the accomplishments of Principles I, II, and III goals. At this step, these contributions from other theories are evaluated for possible inclusion into one's own theory.

SECTION TWO: APPLICATIONS OF THEORY TRANSFORMATION

In the following two sub-sections, we demonstrate the process of theory transformation with two selected theories: cognitive–behavioral, and psychodrama. Each of the two authors of the present volume employs a preferred theory in conjunction with a Feminist Therapy approach, and discusses her view of how the theory can be integrated with feminist principles. You should observe that the steps in theory transformation may vary according to both the theory and the individual who applies it. Thus, each application of theory transformation may be unique, despite some basic similarities. Here, we demonstrate a process of theory application and revision. As a prospective or practicing clinician, you will want to select and apply the theory of your choice in a similar manner.

Cognitive–behavioral Interventions

Cognitive–behavioral (CB) theory and strategies embrace a liberal range of learning-based approaches. The scientific and philosophical foundations of learning theory are reflected in the efforts of CB therapists to establish research-based support for their interventions. The emphasis on empirical validation of CB interventions encourages the use of theoretical constructs that can be clearly defined and measured, and the development of therapeutic procedures that can be replicated across clinical settings. Recent extensions of CB to interventions with women emphasize multiple assessment strategies that are relevant to the individual lives of women (MacDonald, 1984).

In this section, we examine CB theory using an abbreviated version of the format for transforming a theory (Table 5.2). In the following, we: (a) briefly overview the historical background and common components of CB interventions; (b) provide a rationale for CB theory in terms of its compatibility with feminist therapy; and (c) suggest revisions in CB concepts and procedures that increase its compatibility with feminist principles.

Historical Background

CB theory has a complex history, and integrates concepts and strategies from at least five differing sources. Table 5.3 displays five of the most significant models, along with representative treatment goals and techniques, that reflect

Table 5.3. *Historical Roots of Cognitive–behavioral Theory*

Model	Treatment goals	Representative strategies
Respondent/classical	Reduce conditioned emotional reactions; decrease avoidant behavior	Stimulus control Relaxation techniques Desensitization In vivo practice
Operant	Rearrange external contingencies, facilitate a reinforcing environment	Contingency management Differential reinforcement Contracting
Social learning	Facilitate self-regulation of thoughts and behavior: client as change agent	Modeling, role play Skill training Self-management Information-giving Bibliotherapy
Cognitive	Modify dysfunctional beliefs, attributions, standards, expectancies	Cognitive restructuring Relabeling Reattribution training Problem-solving
Cognitive–behavioral	Assist client to learn new cognitive, emotional, interpersonal and behavioral skills	All the above plus: Coping skills Self-instruction Stress inoculation

the historical roots of CB approaches: respondent conditioning, operant conditioning, social learning, cognitive, and CB theories. Additionally, several other theories are drawn into the formulations, most notably information-processing, and attribution theory. For purposes of simplicity, we have chosen to omit these here. However, in your further readings, you may encounter concepts that relate to either of these two theories; for example, attribution theory is closely related to the concept of *learned helplessness*, which is used by some cognitive therapists to understand abusive relationships (Abramson, Seligman, & Teasdale, 1978; Douglas & Strom, 1988).

It can be seen from Table 5.3 that clinicians who self-describe as cognitive-behavioral in their orientation tend to employ a variety of inter-related techniques and procedures. Some recent therapists have also proposed integrative approaches that expand the boundaries of a strict learning or cognitive point of view (see Epstein, Schlesinger, & Dryden, 1988; Jacobson, 1987; Kanfer & Goldstein, 1986; Kanfer & Schefft, 1988; Kendall & Hollon, 1979; Levine & Sandeen, 1985). A comprehensive survey of the range of concepts and techniques used by cognitive and behavioral therapists can be found in The Dictionary of Behavior Therapy Techniques (Bellak & Herson, 1985).

Common Features of Cognitive–behavioral Interventions

Donald Meichenbaum (1986) has identified some of the commonalities among the diverse range of CB interventions. He points out that CB interventions tend to be relatively short, moderately structured, and encourage an active role by both counselor and client. CB therapists typically engage the client in a collaborative alliance, whereby the two parties embark on a "shared adventure" to understand and reconceptualize the client's problems. Although therapists frequently take the role of a teacher, they do not presume to be the expert. Rather, they engage clients in an "egalitarian relationship" in which they serve "as a consultant who is prepared to provide special skills, rather than as authority who can provide certain answers" (Piasecki & Hollon, 1987, p. 143).

Across CB approaches, Meichenbaum (1986) suggests that the therapist works with clients to:

(1) Help them better understand the nature of their presenting problems.
(2) View their cognitions ("automatic" thoughts, images) and accompanying feelings as hypotheses worthy of testing rather than as facts or truths.
(3) Encourage them to perform "personal experiments" and review the consequences of their actions as "anomalous data" or "evidence" that is contrary to their prior expectations and beliefs.
(4) Learn new behavioral, interpersonal, cognitive, and emotional regulation skills (p. 347).

The right-hand column of Table 5.3 displays a sample of the wide range of interventions that may be applied.

Rationale for Cognitive–behavioral Theory

We believe that CB theory is a comfortable choice for feminist therapists because so many of its tenets are compatible with our view of effective treatment for women. CB constructs and interventions meet the criteria for a feminist format discussed earlier, in that they are gender-free, flexible, interactionist, and lifespan.

Feminist format

Traditional learning and cognitive theories use language and concepts that are gender-free, and can be flexibly applied to any group of individuals. Concepts such as *reinforcement, generalization, expectancy*, and *self-efficacy* are not embedded in a developmental structure that defines females and

Table 5.4. *Cognitive–behavioral Strategies: Congruence with Feminist Therapy Principles*

Strategy	Principle	Application to feminist therapy
Modeling	I, II, III	Allows therapist to demonstrate competent behavior, wide role repertoire, flexibility
Contracting	I, II	Provides equal participation in goal-setting and choice of strategy, encourages client to initiate change in self and situation
Functional analysis	I, II	Enables therapist and client to collaborate in determining situational and personal antecedents and consequences of problems
Self-monitoring	I, II, III	Assists client in identifying her thoughts and feelings in relation to situational events
Self-reinforcement	II, III	Enables client to nurture and empower self
Stress inoculation	I, II, III	Strengthens client coping skills, enables her to identify and appreciate her strengths
Assertiveness training	I, II, III	Assists client in meeting her needs, raising self-esteem, achieving personal goals. Leads to empowerment and personal pride
Cognitive restructuring	I, II, III	Provides for sex-role analysis, power analysis, reframe deficits as strengths

males in differing terms. Social Learning theory in general has emphasized that a reinforcing environment encourages flexibility of behavioral repertoires, and has discouraged the use of negative procedures because they inhibit prosocial behavior. The concepts of cognitive and behavioral theories are free of age-related restrictions, and can be applied to thoughts, feelings, and behaviors at any age or stage of life. CB interventions may thus be tailored for use with individuals from differing age or gender groups, and from diverse ethnic and subcultural populations.

Feminist Therapy Principles

How can we match the broad range of CB interventions and concepts with the Principles of Feminist Therapy? A sample of this matching procedure is presented in Table 5.4. The articulation of CB and feminist therapy is further elaborated below for Principles I and II.

I:The Personal Is Political.   First, the early learning theory concepts of *respondent* and *operant conditioning* emphasize that all behavior is embedded in context and can be changed only in relation to the social and cultural situations in which it occurs (Hayes, 1987). Standard learning theory concepts can be used to encompass the external variables that influence women's well-being. These external factors include sources of stress in women's lives (*punishment* or *reinforcement deficit*) as well as sources of satisfaction (*reinforcing events*). For example, in behavioral marital therapy (Jacobson & Margolin, 1979), attention is given to the frequency and ratio of critical and positive spouse comments (punishment and reinforcement), and to pleasing activities that the couple shares (reinforcing events). These variables, among others, are targeted for intervention, with the general goal of increasing pleasurable activities and positive partner comments and decreasing negative communications.

Second, the social learning theory concepts of *observational learning* and *modeling* (Bandura, 1977b) are useful in sex-role analysis for conceptualizing social and historical influences on women's stereotyped images and messages. Bandura's (1978) concept of *reciprocal determinism* suggests that psychological functioning is a continuous reciprocal interaction between cognition, affect, behavior, and environmental consequences. Bandura points out that in this process, "the environment is influenceable, as is the behavior it regulates" (1978, p. 195). The idea of an "influenceable environment" clearly sets the stage for implementation of social change, and coincides with our emphasis on assisting clients to effect change, whether small or substantial, in their life space.

Finally, the cognitive and CB components (Bandura, 1977a, 1977b, 1986; Beck, 1976; Ellis, 1962; Kanfer & Schefft, 1988; Meichenbaum, 1977; Rotter, 1954; Thoreson & Mahoney, 1974) are useful in a variety of procedures that integrate ongoing thought processes with procedures for overt behavioral change. These procedures may include cognitive restructuring (reframing, relabeling), reattribution (revising the causality of events), anxiety management, problem-solving, stress inoculation, and self-management. These strategies provide the client with self-managing coping skills that assist her efforts to effect change in both self and situation.

II: Relationships Are Egalitarian.   In the three procedures of *functional analysis* (assessment), *goal-setting*, and *contracting*, the client's role in CB therapy is one of negotiated partnership. Therapist and client together attempt to discover what is the problem, and to negotiate a contracted set of goals and possible alternatives. Meichenbaum's (1986) description of the process of CB therapy presented above clearly highlights the collaborative nature of CB interventions. Instructions, suggestions, and "homework" activities are carefully explained and are consensual rather than prescribed. Failure to complete the self-managed activities between therapy sessions is seen as a problem to be explored and resolved, rather than to be interpreted as client "resistance."

Two additional characteristics of CB interventions contribute to client empowerment. First, attention to *skills training* in domains that have been underdeveloped has been useful in such areas as career skills and situational assertiveness. Second, wherever possible, *self-management* procedures (*self-monitoring, self-instruction, self-evaluation*) are initiated and encouraged, to fully empower the client as an active agent in her own therapy and behavior change.

Revising Cognitive–behavioral Theory to a Feminist Format

The forgoing discussion suggests that many aspects of CB theory are well suited to feminist therapy. This section will review three modifications of CB theory that we believe increase its compatibility with Feminist Therapy Principles: (a) relabeling of pathologizing concepts; (b) focus on feelings; and (c) integration of social role theory.

Relabeling pathologizing concepts

Although most concepts in CB theory and its historical relatives are generally bias-free with respect to gender, we encounter some examples of CB concepts that may be detrimental to women. In particular, certain cognitive concepts implicate individual pathology as the "cause" of individual problems, while placing minimal emphasis on the context in which the behavior occurs. Three such examples are *distortion, irrationality,* and *faulty thinking*. Some cognitive therapists in particular tend to use cognitively-pathologizing concepts that locate the problem solely within the client's "illness," in effect blaming the client for her symptoms.

Since the feminist therapist accepts the client's experience as "real," terms that label her thinking as "irrational" or "faulty" deny the client's perceptions and drive her further from trust in herself. Alternative ways to conceptualize client behavior when it does not appear to match "reality" should be considered.

First, it may be that the client's perceptions do match the realities of her life situation. Extensive research on the accuracy of perception in depressed persons, for example, indicates that depressed persons probably see reality *more* accurately than those who optimistically believe that the environment is beneficial and that they can control their outcomes (Hammen, 1988). Lynn Rehm (1988) further amplifies the depressed process, noting that "perception of the objective world is not distorted in depression. Depressed individuals accurately report specific events in their lives . . . (but) . . . depressed persons are more negative about themselves" (p. 167). Indeed, it appears that non-depressed persons show the most cognitive distortion; they tend to be higher in "illusions of personal control," show inflated (unrealistic) expectations of future success on experimental tasks, maintain a "self-serving bias" in attributions for positive outcomes, and they over-estimate the amount of positive feedback they receive (Alloy & Abramson, 1988). Now, who are the real "distorters of reality"?

In contrast to the expansive cognitive bias of non-depressed individuals, the negative self- and world-views of many depressed clients lead us to explore the realities of their lives as well as the "distortions" in their thinking processes. The pessimistic attributions and expectations should cue the therapist to obtain a fuller understanding of the situational contributions to current dysphoric moods. In Chapter 7, we see that Andrea's depressive symptoms, although accompanied by negative cognitions, were intimately related to her oppressive situations at home and at work.

Second, the client may be acting in accordance with her understanding of family and societal expectations for her behavior. A case example here was 32-year-old Margaret, who talked seriously of suicide following the break-up of her marriage. She was convinced she was a failure as a woman, she would never find another man (who else would want her?), and if she did she would be too old to have children, and that therefore, life was no longer worth living. Rather than convince her of the irrationality of these thoughts, she was encouraged to explore messages about women's proper role (a good woman marries and has children), mandates for the successful marriage (a good wife keeps the marriage together), stereotypes about single women (an unmarried woman is an old maid), and fears about living without a partner (women are helpless and need to be taken care of). Although these gender-based messages were not the only ones driving Margaret to desperate measures, she was able to explore her acceptance of them as contributing to her sense of panic and helplessness.

In the process of a systematic situation/mood/thought pattern probe, we encourage clients to monitor their negative experiences and then to self-monitor their sex-role messages, pessimistic expectancies, negative self-talk, and detrimental attributions. Further, we may help clients to determine if they have been misinformed, uninformed, may not have taken all possibilities into consideration, may want to look further, reconsider the context in which the event occurred, etc. In this process, we assist clients in understanding that regardless of external realities, the repeated expression of negative self-evaluation and expectancies contributes to the dysphoric moods they experi-ence. The cognitive restructuring techniques of CB therapy can then be effectively implemented, without the use of pathologizing labels and client-blaming attributions. Further, these interventions are implemented without detaching the client's thought processes from the contexts in which they were initiated.

Finally, we encourage clients to consider options for implementing changes in self-situation interactions that may ameliorate the internal and external conditions that contributed to the depressive symptoms.

Focus on feelings

As we have seen, emotions have been the focus of CB and behavioral interventions in relation to the cognitive mediators that elicit and maintain unpleasant or dysfunctional mood states and their associated patterns of behavior. Thus, sadness, anxiety, and rage are viewed primarily as the result of the person's cognitive appraisal of external stressors and a negative evaluation of one's ability to cope (Lazarus & Folkman, 1984; Meichenbaum, 1977). In feminist counseling, we continue to employ CB strategies for dealing with disabling reactions of hopelessness, fearfulness, and associated avoidance behaviors, but we also explore women's responses to their angry feelings.

Traditional socialization has encouraged women to avoid direct confrontation or negative assertion with others. When individuals feel underbenefited, ignored, overworked or powerless, angry feelings are likely to be evoked. In the absence of "permission" to express these feelings directly, women are likely to be more self-critical, self-blaming, and hopeless about changing the conditions that produce their unhappiness (Major, 1987). Feelings of helplessness, self-abasement, and hoplessness are frequently those that may lead to a diagnosis of depression. In the process of sex-role analysis, we are likely to uncover situations that might elicit legitimate anger from clients, and we help them to explore their anger in a safe environment. We also encourage them to identify and express their angry feelings in ways that will benefit them without provoking alienation and violence from others. We view the appropriate expression of anger and negative assertion as important for women as they strive to gain a sense of positive self-regard and empowerment in their lives.

Social role theory

We select the broad concept of social role theory to encompass the socialized role expectations and power imbalances that influence people's lives. Adding some concepts from social role theory to CB interventions allows us to: (a) interpret current behavior in terms of gender socialization, and thus to complete a sex-role analysis (Principle I); (b) conceptualize situational behavior within a broader societal context, to perform a power analysis, and to examine the effects of patriarchy, sexism, and discrimination (Principle I);

(c) add terminology that describes aspects of role behavior, such as *role conflict*, *role strain*, and *role overload*; and (d) relabel certain concepts, such as deficit behaviors, in terms of over- or under-socialization, thus reframing pathology into woman-valuing terms (Principle III). Within a social role framework, we can then talk about *resocialization* or *reconstructing environments*, rather than remediation of deficit behavior.

Consideration of women's position within the larger societal context also enables us to encourage clients to join women's support groups, to value the female-typed traits they may possess (nurturance, caring for others, peace-making), and to value their place in society as women. Relabeling of devalued traits ("passivity," "enabler," or "codependency") in terms of women's socialization as "peace-maker and keeper of relationships" may enable clients to reframe their position more positively within their close relationships (Worell, 1988). Because the structure of CB theory is based on an interactionist approach, the merger with social role theory produces a strong union.

Re-evaluation of Cognitive-behavioral Theory

Our analysis of CB theory and its concepts and major strategies allows us to draw two conclusions. First, the theory is a viable one for feminist therapists, and its major concepts and interventions serve well within a feminist format. Second, we saw that some adjustments in terminology and conceptualization must occur if feminist insights are to be integrated effectively. We provided several examples of pathologizing concepts that require revision and added concepts that facilitate a feminist analysis and intervention. For any theory of your choice, the transformation process can be successful and heuristic, provided that it does not violate the basic structure of the theory. In the case of CB theory, the major foundations and interventions remain intact.

Psychodrama

Psychodrama is an interpersonally focused theory of psychotherapy developed by Jacob Moreno. Individuals exist in and react to their relationships with other people (Fine, 1979). Psychodrama theory regards humans as primarily social beings. Before criticizing psychodrama from a feminist theory perspective, the major concepts that form the basis of psychodrama theory will be reviewed. The theory presented here is synthesized from the works of Fine (1979), Blatner (1973), Blatner & Blatner (1988), Moreno (1985), and Moreno (1975).

Morena viewed mentally healthy people as spontaneous creators of their own lives (Fine, 1979). *Spontaneity* is the ability to respond to life situations in a novel and effective way. Spontaneity is present at birth. External environments, which include significant others (*social atoms*) and the cultural context in which one lives, can either facilitate or inhibit further development of spontaneity for the individual. Responses which at one time were spontaneous can become ritualized, patterned, and conserved if they are used repeatedly. *Conserves* are finished products or acts. They are the result of spontaneous and creative processes. *Cultural* conserves are products which are sanctioned by a given society. Examples of cultural conserves are works of art, laws, books, social rules and norms, and parameters for acceptable performance of roles. While cultural conserves contribute continuity to a social group, they also can restrict individual spontaneity and the evolution of the culture.

Moreno believed that modern society had come to worship conserves to the detriment of its own development. Thus, Moreno sought to change the culture and society as a whole, not merely to help individuals adapt to the environment. He advocated the healing of social systems. Likewise, because he believed many individual problems arise from environmental barriers of a sexual, social, economic, political, and cultural nature, he proposed that healing of the individual needed to take place in a supportive social context. He called this social healing "*sociatry*" and viewed it as a powerful source of therapeutic change.

Because the social environment is seen to play a significant role in human development, Moreno studied individuals within the structures of their intergroup relationships. These investigations into the relationships within groups is called *sociometry*. Sociometric interventions are the major tools that can be used to change society and social institutions.

Sociometric evaluations can be used to measure the attractions and repulsions between members of a group. These attractions and repulsions are influenced by two forces—*transference* and *tele*. While Moreno acknowledged the existence of transference, he believed that other therapies over-emphasized its importance. Tele is a "two-way reciprocal knowing of each other by two people" (Fine, 1979, p. 432). Tele is "one person's correct, intuitive estimate of the actualities of the other" (Moreno, 1975, p. 84). Thus, tele is different from transference, in that tele is based on the real attributes of the two people, whereas transference is one person's unreal perception of and projection of attributes onto the other.

Role-playing, role-taking and role-creating are related key concepts in psychodrama theory. The ability to respond spontaneously requires the person to have a large role repertoire (Fine, 1979). One source of pathology, i.e. lack of spontaneity, is a person having a limited role repertoire. In order for individuals to make novel and effective, i.e. spontaneous responses in a variety of life situations, they need to be able to perform, i.e. have the necessary skills, and feel free to express a wide range of behaviors (role repertoire). Individuals' role repertoires may be limited because they have had ineffective role models or because certain roles that are in their repertoires are blocked at an expressive level. Each culture has conserves which govern the acquisition and expression of roles in that culture. Blatner and Blatner (1988) point out how important it is for people to learn how to create and negotiate roles. "Roles may be assumed, modified, refined, elaborated and relinquished. This is a most liberating lesson. It invites us to re-evaluate whatever roles we play. . . ." (Blatner & Blatner, 1988, p. 32). A feminist application of conserves to sex roles allows the psychodramatist to see how sex-role conserves limit the spontaneous behavioral responses of women and men in a given culture.

Fine (1979) describes psychodrama therapy as an action method of psychotherapy that ". . . employs dramatic interactions, sociometric measurements, group dynamics, and depends on role theory to facilitate changes in individuals and groups through the development of new perceptions and behaviors and/or reorganization of old cognitive patterns" (p. 428). In therapy, clients act out their personal problems in the here-and-now moment by recreating and working through scenes from their lives. These enactments are optimally done in a group setting where group members can take the roles of significant others in each other's scenes. However, psychodramatic theory and techniques can be adapted for individual therapy.

Taking unfamiliar roles in others' enactments facilitates the role repertoire expansion for all group members. Each group member is seen as the ". . . therapeutic agent of the other; consequently, group members assist in treatment and are as important as the therapist" (Fine, 1979, p. 429). The tele between all members of the group, including the therapist, is a healing force in the group. Tele between therapist and client is a powerful source for therapeutic change. Thus, it is important for the therapist to be open with and known to the client.

The goals of psychodrama therapy are to facilitate individuals to reclaim their spontaneity, break free of cultural conserves, and expand their role repertoires. Further, psychodramatic interventions seek to create social environments that are open to change and where novelty is valued. Individuals are encouraged to explore group problems to develop social solutions.

Rationale for Psychodrama Theory

We view psychodrama theory and techniques as very compatible with a feminist therapy approach. In this section, the specifics of psychodrama's congruency with a feminist format and with feminist therapy principles is delineated.

Feminist format

Jacob Moreno began writing about psychodrama theory in the early 1920s and continuing into the late 1960s. Although Moreno developed his theory in the context of European and American cultures that sanctioned traditional sex role stereotypes for women and men, he advocated individual spontaneity and freedom from cultural conserves, including role restrictions, that inhibit individual spontaneity. His major concepts and terminology do not define females and males in differing terms, or apply differential standards of mental health to women and men. He uses non-stigmatizing labels. For example, the client in a psychodrama is called a protagonist. Thus, psychodrama is gender-free. According to psychodrama theory, an individual's behavior is a result of multiple determinants—innate spontaneity, heredity, social forces, and environmental forces. Thus, psychodrama meets the test for an interactionist theory.

Moreno believed that one's past experiences influence present behavior. Past experiences in which spontaneity was blocked give rise to "act hunger" (Blatner, 1973). These blocked responses are often repeated in present experiences. However, these previous experiences are not limited to early childhood. Adult experiences can also give rise to act hunger. Change in adulthood is seen as very possible. Indeed, psychodrama puts much emphasis on role training and spontaneity training, which are aimed at enhancing individuals' present and future effectiveness. Development is viewed as a life-long process. In summary, psychodrama meets the four feminist format requirements: gender-free, flexible, interactionist and lifespan.

Feminist therapy principles

Psychodrama fits smoothly with the three Principles of Feminist Therapy. Further, we believe that much of its theory that focuses on the role of the environment in creating problems for individuals can be a useful addition to other theoretical approaches that do not have such a component. A sample of psychodramatic techniques compatible with the three feminist principles is presented in Table 5.5.

I. The Personal Is Political.   Moreno believed that pathology could develop solely from environmental sources, and that an overly conserved environment was often the primary source of pathology. Moreno (1975) pointed out that there were people who ". . . suffer deeply from a major maladjustment, but of a collective and not a private nature" (p. 359). There are cultural conflicts in which individuals are persecuted or restricted, not because of themselves, but because of the group to which they belong.

"Pathology occurs (a) with too rigid a social structure, where the individual is unable to grow and change, or (b) when relationships are not balanced" (Fine, 1979, p. 430). The opposite of this pathology is spontaneity. Blatner and Blatner (1988) point out that creativity and spontaneity ". . . threaten the

Table 5.5.   *Psychodrama Strategies: Congruence with Feminist Therapy Principles*

Strategy	Principle	Application to feminist therapy
Sociodrama (group exploration of common social problems)	I, III	Allows women to identify common social problems and to identify personal and collective solutions to social problems
Double (person plays the role of protagonist's inner self)	I, II	Facilitates client's fuller expression of feelings, thoughts, behaviors. Clarifies unspoken sex-role rules and messages
Role-reversal (client role plays another person in order to understand other's perspective)	I, II, III	Allows client to gain appreciation of female traits and gives clients permission to practice actions and skills not usually in their repertoire. Increases empathic understanding of others
Role training (client practices new behaviors or skills in role-played scenarios)	I	Allows clients to try out new responses in a safe environment where norms are supportive of non-traditional behavior
Role-taking, role-creating (role-taking = client enacts a given role; role-creating = client creates or expands a role)	I	Helps clients learn that roles can be modified, refined, elaborated, and relinquished. Helps free clients from traditional sex-role conserves and to be creative in their expression of roles

stability and authority of the hierarchical social and religious systems" (p. 21).

Moreno sought to bring about changes at many levels. He stated frequently that his ultimate goal was to change the universe. Thus, the core of his theory embodies the notion that the personal is social. He developed techniques, such as sociograms, to assess social environments. He created sociodrama as a technique that could be used to change social environments, and he used group restructuring techniques to maximize cohesion, tele, and spontaneity and to minimize restrictive conserves in intact social groups. *Sociodrama* is a "form of psychodramatic enactment which aims at clarifying *group* themes rather than focusing on the individual's problems" (Blatner, 1973. p. 9). In sociodrama, the group chooses a common social problem to explore and for which to develop possible solutions. The aim of sociodrama is "not his (sic) own salvation, but the salvation of all members of his (sic) clan" (Moreno, 1985, p. 365). Thus, sociodrama can be used to help women explore their common life situations and search for creative, collective solutions.

There are several psychodramatic techniques that relate to role functioning. *Role-taking* is the technique of playing the collective and private parts of a given role, e.g. mother. Role-taking can help clients explore the culturally and individually conserved aspects of a role. From a feminist therapy perspective, role-taking facilitates clients' identification of sex-role messages. Through *role-creating* the individual or group is encouraged to move beyond the conserved, stereotyped role to a spontaneous, creative expansion of the role. Through this process, sex roles can be redefined and new roles created, thus expanding one's role repertoire. Practice with both role-taking and role-creating are key components in spontaneity and *role-training*. The psychodrama belief that it is important for individuals to choose spontaneously from a large role repertoire closely parallels feminist valuing of androgyny.

II. Egalitarian Relationships. One of Moreno's most important contributions to the therapy process was the change in the nature of the therapist–client relationship. The following quotations capture the essence of the collaborative client–therapist relationship that Moreno proposed:

> Therapy is a reciprocal process between the therapist and patient, and not a one-way relationship (Moreno, 1975, p. 37).

> The therapist, before he (sic) emerges as the therapeutic leader, is just another member of the group (Moreno, 1975, p. 9).

> . . . both (therapist and client) on the same level—they are equal (Moreno, 1985, p. 254).

> The initiative, the spontaneity, the decision must all arise within the subjects themselves (Moreno, 1985, p. 337).

> The personality of the therapist is the skill (Moreno, 1975, p. 39).

> . . . each patient is the therapeutic agent of the other (Fine, 1979, p. 442).

Thus, Moreno's approach calls for an egalitarian relationship between therapist and client. In fact, he believed that the tele factor between client and therapist and between all the members of the group is a major source of therapeutic change and healing. Members of the group are trusted to contribute to and heal each other. Further, the therapist must be open with and self-disclose to the client in order to maximize tele. Every psychodrama session ends with members of the group and the therapist disclosing to the protagonist exieriences from their own lives that are similar to the issues on which the protagonist has just worked. This process is called *"sharing."* Sharing allows "for group members to discover their commonality" (Fine, 1979, p. 428). Feminist therapists can borrow this technique by ending sessions with personal sharing.

Moreno also believed that individuals were self directed and self-correcting if they received accurate feedback. Moreno (1975) said that the individual was capable of ". . . meeting his (sic) own problems and patients as capable of helping one another" (p. 87). These beliefs closely parallel the feminist therapy concept regarding the client as an expert on self.

III. Valuing the Female Perspective. Psychodrama theory values many aspects of the female experience. Psychodrama theory emphasizes the importance of relationships to human beings. Tele between individuals is given a central role in therapeutic healing. The ability to *role-reverse*, to put one's self in another's role and to take the other's perspective, is considered by psychodramatists to be the most important psychodramatic technique. Both role-reversal and doubling are techniques that rely heavily on empathy. Through the technique of *doubling*, the therapist or group members become the inner voice of the protagonist helping her to express heretofore unexpressed feelings, thoughts and behaviors. Doubles must have tele with the protagonist, use intuition, and draw on the life experiences they have in common with the protagonist. Doubling can be used by feminist therapists to help clients specify and concretize the sex-role messages that influence and limit their behavior, and to give a voice to the desire to take action that violates traditional female sex-role expectations. Tele, doubling, role reversal, and viewing individuals in relational contexts all demonstrate the important roles that female values and strengths play in psychodrama. All female groups can facilitate women not only exploring their common problems, but also their common strengths.

Additional potential contributions of psychodrama to feminist therapy

Psychodrama is an action-form of therapy in which the past, present, and future can be explored on the stage. In enactments, concretization in space and action is highlighted. For example, from a feminist therapy perspective, inner struggle in a woman who wants to pursue a career, but feels that she can only be a good mother by staying home full-time, could be concretized by group members playing each side of her dilemma and actually pulling on her in different directions. Power dimensions in relationships are physically concretized in dramas by having the more powerful person stand on a chair while interacting with the less powerful person. Thus, feminist therapy power analysis can be enhanced by symbolizing and exaggerating, through high and low physical positions, the unequal power in relationships. Concepts or inanimate objects can be given form in a psychodrama or sociodrama. Thus, a feminist therapist can help a group embody a "sexist society", giving it a form and a voice. Group members can then be encouraged to engage in dialogue with that society.

Revising Psychodrama Theory to a Feminist Format

As is evident by our analysis, psychodrama theory, techniques, and therapeutic goals are congruent with Feminist Therapy Principles. However, there are several modifications that would enhance further its compatability with feminist therapy.

First, although the concept of cultural conserves obviously applies to traditional sex-roles, the psychodrama literature does not contain specific and in-depth analyses of sex-role rules as conserves. Similarly, although clients are clearly seen to be damaged by socialization and the acculturation process, more needs to be written about how sex-role messages and institutionalized sexism can be explored on the psychodrama stage.

Second, while the technique of role reversal reflects female values of empathy and understanding another's perspective, we believe that emphasizing role reversal or using it prematurely can be harmful to female clients. Premature role reversal interferes with women identifying their own needs and wants. It replicates the female socialization process of being alert to what other people want and subordinating our own needs to them. Further, role reversal into another's role makes expression of anger to that person more difficult for female clients. Thus, role reversal with female clients should be used judiciously and be carefully timed, e.g. not done prior to the expression of anger.

Third, since psychodrama as a mode of therapy was developed primarily for use with groups, and since many feminist therapists work primarily in individual sessions, adaptations need to be made in some of the techniques for their use in individual counseling. Fortunately, many psychodramatists have already made and written about these adaptations (Blatner & Blatner, 1988; Goldman & Morrison, 1984). The use of psychodrama in individual counseling is called "psychodrama-a-deux." Thus, psychodrama theory and most of the psychodramatic techniques can be and are used successfully in individual counseling.

Re-evaluation of Psychodrama Theory

Our evaluation of psychodrama theory and techniques suggests that psychodrama is very compatible with a feminist therapy approach. A psychodramatic approach does not violate any of the seven comparison criteria listed in Table 5.2. The major constructs of psychodrama remain viable throughout the transformation process. However, we did point out two revisions that would enhance psychodrama's congruence with a feminist therapy approach. Further, we have suggested that several aspects of psychodrama—its theory about the role of the external environment in individual problem development, its technique of physicalizing power differentials, and its technique of embodying or giving tangible form to abstract feminist concepts such as a "sexist society"— can make valuable feminist contributions to other therapeutic orientations.

Summary

This chapter presented a model for merging traditional theories of psychotherapy with a feminist therapy format. We first explored how the characteristics of many traditional theories may be incompatible with feminist principles. We regard a theory as gender-biased if its content and constructs are androcentric, gendercentric, ethnocentric, heterosexist, intrapsychic, or deterministic. In contrast, a feminist theory format suggests that theories of behavior change should be gender-free, flexible, interactionist, and lifespan in their structure and content. The model for transforming a theory to feminist format was further explored through the presentation of two theoretical approaches: cognitive–behavioral therapy and psychodrama. Each theoretical view was shown to be essentially compatible with feminist principles, yet lacking in certain concepts or dimensions that required revision. In the Activity below, we challenge the reader to perform a similar analysis and transformation on a selected theoretical approach.

Activity: Transforming your Theoretical Orientation

This activity builds on your responses to the Self-assessment at the beginning of this chapter. In the Self-assessment, you answered eight questions about your chosen theoretical orientation. These eight questions were designed to help you describe the basic concepts and techniques of your theory. We would now like you to use these answers as a basis for completing the transformation steps found in Table 5.2. Follow the transformation steps to help you determine how compatible your theory is with a feminist therapy perspective.

Further Readings

Blatner, H. A. (1973). *Acting-in: Practical Applications of Psychodramatic Methods*. New York: Springer.

Blatner, A., & Blatner A. (1988). *Foundations of Psychodrama: History, Theory, and Practice*. New York: Springer.

Epstein, N., Schlesinger, S. E., & Dryden (Eds.) (1988). *Cognitive–Behavioral Therapy with Families*. New York: Brunner/Mazel.

Fine, L. J. (1979). Psychodrama. In R. Corsini (Ed.) *Current Psychotherapies*. Itasca, IL: F. E. Peacock.

Jacobson, N. (1987). *Psychotherapists in Clinical Practice*. New York: Guilford Press.

Levine, F. M., & Sandeen, E. (1985). *Conceptualization in Psychotherapy: The Models Approach*. Hillsdale, NJ: Lawrence Erlbaum.

CHAPTER 6

A Feminist Approach to Assessment

Self-assessment: Assessment of Client Descriptions*

Read each of the following client descriptions. Then, answer the questions which ask you to hypothesize about the client's gender, economic status, age, race, and marital status. If you cannot make a particular judgment, leave the space blank. You can compare your answers with those of other respondents on pages 160 and 161.

Client 1

This person passively allows others to assume responsibility for major areas of his/her life because of a lack of self-confidence and an inability to function independently. This person subordinates his/her own needs to those of others on whom he/she is dependent in order to avoid any possibility of having to be self-reliant. This person leaves major decisions to others. For example, this person will typically assume a passive role and allow the spouse to decide where they should live, what kind of job he/she should have, and with which neighbors they should be friendly. This person is unwilling to make demands on the people on whom he/she depends for fear of jeopardizing the relationships and being forced to rely on him/herself. This person lacks self-confidence. This person tends to belittle his/her abilities and assets by constantly referring to him/herself as "stupid."

This person is most likely to be:
(1) Female_____   Male_____
(2) Wealthy_____   Middle class_____   Poor_____
(3) _____years old
(4) Black_____   White_____
(5) Married_____   Single_____
(6) DSM-III R diagnosis_____

---

* Reproduced from Landrine, 1989, with permission of Cambridge University Press.

Client 2

This person habitually violates the rights of others. In childhood, this person engaged in frequent lying, stealing, fighting, truancy, and resisting authority. In adolescence, this person showed unusually early or aggressive sexual behavior, excessive drinking, and use of illicit drugs. Now in adulthood, this behavior continues, with the addition of inability to maintain consistent work performance or to function as a responsible parent, and failure to obey the law. This person shows signs of personal distress, including complaints of tension, inability to tolerate boredom, and the conviction (often correct) that others are hostile toward him/her. This person is unable to sustain lasting, close, warm, and responsible relationships with family, friends, or sexual partners.

This person is most likely to be:

(1)   Female_____   Male_____
(2)   Wealthy_____   Middle class_____   Poor_____
(3)   _____years old
(4)   Black_____   White_____
(5)   Married_____   Single_____
(6)   DSM-III R diagnosis_____

Overview

The purposes of this chapter are first to summarize and criticize the uses of assessment and diagnosis in traditional approaches to therapy. The androcentric values and sex-role stereotyped bias of both processes are highlighted. Second, the values, assumptions and strategies of a feminist approach to assessment and diagnosis are explicated. More specifically, readers will be able to:

(1)   Identify the androcentric perspective that underlies most traditional approaches to assessment and diagnosis.
(2)   List the sources of sex bias in standardized testing.
(3)   Criticize standardized tests for sex bias.
(4)   Discuss the major differences between traditional and feminist approaches to assessment, diagnosis, and testing.
(5)   Understand the relationship between the sexism that women experience and the "symptoms" they develop.

Traditional Approaches to Assessment and Diagnosis

As with other therapeutic interventions, assessment and diagnoses are governed by therapists' theoretical orientations and belief/value systems. In this section, traditional approaches to assessment and diagnosis will be defined and then criticized for their possible sources of sex bias.

Assessment

Sundberg (1977) defined assessment as:

> . . . the set of processes used by a person or persons for developing impressions and images, making decisions, and checking hypotheses about another person's pattern of characteristics which determine his or her behavior in interaction with the environment. (p. 22)

A perusal of most psychological assessment books confirms that therapeutic assessment is focused primarily on measuring and describing individuals.

Assessment in psychotherapy and counseling has many possible functions (Hansen, Stevic, & Warner, 1986). Some of these functions are to:

(1) Identify the focus and goals of therapy.
(2) Identify and categorize the client's problems.
(3) Increase the client's understanding of self.
(4) Increase the counselor's understanding of the client.
(5) Identify appropriate therapeutic intervention strategies.
(6) Assess whether the therapist is competent to treat the client.
(7) Evaluate the client's progress and/or the effectiveness of therapy.

Assessment includes a wide variety of information-collection strategies such as interviewing, systematic observation, self-monitoring, life-history taking, standardized objective tests, projective tests, analysis of person–environment interactions, and biopsychological assessment. Some theorists, such as behavioral learning theorists, assert that an individual's behavior is specific to and dependent on the situation; other theorists, such as trait-factor theorists, argue that personality traits describe basic, enduring, situation-generalizable characteristics of people (Sundberg, 1977).

In general, assessment procedures, including testing and diagnosis, are sex-biased to the degree that they sex-role-stereotype females and males and discount or ignore the environmental context of clients' lives. The ways in which sexism may affect assessment procedures are detailed in the following sections on testing and diagnosis.

Sources of sex bias in testing

Tests are one kind of assessment strategy often used by therapists. Tests "provide greater standardization of stimulus conditions" and thus, are "an objective aid to observation in the diagnostic process" (Hansen, Stevic, & Warner, 1986, p. 394). As with diagnostic classification systems, tests may be sex-biased in many different ways.

In general, a test is sex-biased if it:

(1)   Causes individuals to be limited in their performance on the test on the basis of gender.
(2)   Limits individuals from considering (career) options or being eligible for opportunities on the basis of gender (Zunker, 1982).
(3)   Causes others to limit individuals from considering options or being eligible for opportunities on the basis of gender (Zunker, 1982).

Sexist assumptions and attitudes can be incorporated in tests in at least four different ways. Tests may have sex-biased items, use inappropriate norm groups for comparison of an individual's score, provide sexist interpreting information and/or use test construction concepts which reflect the sexist structure of society.

Sex-biased items.   First, sex bias in test items can occur if sexist terminology is used or if the items give a gender-based experience advantage to either females or males. An example of sexist terminology is using "policeman" instead of "police officer" on a career interest inventory. If test items are based on experiences that are more likely for males in our culture than for females, or vice versa, then the test has a gender-based experience advantage. For example, a test item on a math achievement test that asks "How many total points are scored by a football team that makes two touchdowns plus a field goal?" has a male experience advantage (i.e. playing football), while one that asks "How many ounces are in a cup of milk?" has a female experience advantage (i.e. cooking). An item may also be sex-biased if the desired response reflects an androcentric bias. For example, one item on the Minnesota Multiphasic Personality Inventory asks individuals to say whether they have ever been sorry that they were a girl. The item is scored in the pathological direction if either females or males mark it "true" for them. Thus, a female would be judged unhealthy if she said she never regretted being a female (Rosewater, 1985b)!

Inappropriate norm groups.   Secondly, tests may be sexist by using cross-gender norm groups against which to compare an individual's score. Before its revision into the Strong–Campbell Interest Inventory (SCII), the Strong–Vocational Interest Blank (SVIB) had separate tests for men and women. Many non-traditional (male-dominated) career options for women were not on the female form. If a woman wanted to know how her interests compared to those employed in male-typed fields, she had to take the man's form. Thus, her interests were compared to men working in those fields that gave her less likelihood of having "similar interests" and receiving encouragement to pursue those occupations further. While the issue of whether to use same-gender or mixed-gender norms or is a complex and debated one, there is general agreement that using cross-sexed norms on interest inventories restricts women's exploration of non-traditional careers.

Sex-biased interpretation instructions. Third, Birk (1975) proposed that if the instructions provided in the test manual do not discuss how to use the test results in a sex-fair manner, therapists will be more likely to apply the tests in a sex-biased way. She stated that for a test to be unbiased, the interpretive instructions should show counselors how to be sex-fair by using appropriate non-stereotyped (and often non-traditional) examples of how to apply test results with both women and men.

Sex-biased constructs. The fourth way that an instrument can be sex-biased is if the theoretical basis for its construction reflects the sexist structure of society. An excellent example of this problem occurs in the measurement of career interests, which can be based on one of two competing theories. One theory, the Hypothesis of Social Dominance, reflects the sexist status quo of the current social and occupational structure. The other theory, the Hypothesis of Opportunity Dominance, is based on changing the sexist status quo by broadening the individual's consideration and pursuit of non-traditional options (Coles & Hansen, 1978).

Before further explaining these two theories, it is necessary to understand the nature of career interests. Career interests measure individuals' likes and dislikes for activities, tasks, and groups of people associated with various career choices. These interests are influenced by innate factors, or genetic ability and socialization factors, or experience-with-an-activity factors. Since one's likes and dislikes are based to some extent on past experiences, one's socialization as a female or male influences the development of one's interests. For example, females have more experiences in nurturing roles and receive more direct reinforcement and modeling for nurturing roles than do males. Females are more likely to say they like nurturing activities than are males. Career interest inventories measure this sex-role socialization process.

Social dominance vs. opportunity dominance

Cole and Hanson (1978) posit two differing hypotheses about interests and subsequent satisfaction in careers. Their Hypothesis of Social Dominance states that:

> Until the areas of socially accepted interest options become broadened during a person's development, the careers in which people will be satisfied will not broaden (p. 499).

Under this theory, society and the socialization process must change before individuals' satisfactions in careers will change (Holland, 1974). The alternate Hypothesis of Opportunity Dominance states that:

> When career opportunities widen, people will find satisfaction in a wider range of careers in spite of limiting aspects of their earlier socialization (p. 499).

Under this theory, making a wider range of career opportunities available to women should come first, which will, in turn, bring about changes in society and sex-role socialization.

Cole and Hanson (1978) contend that the measurement of a person's likes and dislikes and the comparison of those preferences with people currently employed in careers supports the social dominance theory. Instruments which use cross-sex norms, or mixed-sex norms, or raw scores are compatible with the Social Dominance theory. Using instruments which predominantly measure individuals' sex-role-stereotyped socialization experiences to career-counsel women restricts their career options and perpetuates the status quo. Using instruments which de-emphasize gender socialization experiences and use same-sex norm groups for comparisons are compatible with the Opportunity Dominance theory.

Example of Social Dominance theory.   The Self-directed Search (SDS) (Holland, 1974) is an example of an interest inventory that fits the Social Dominance theory. There are five different sections on the SDS. The first section asks clients to list tentative and actual career choices they have considered and choices about which they have dreamed. The third section asks individuals to respond "yes" or "no" to competencies which they currently possess. The fifth section asks the test takers to estimate their abilities in 12 skill areas. Thus, three out of the five sections of the SDS directly assess past experiences. If a woman has in the past imagined herself being a nurse, teacher, or secretary, has been a secretary and thus possesses office skills, clerical ability (i.e. can type and take shorthand), she will score high on the conventional scale of the SDS based primarily on what she has done, rather than scoring high on scales in which she might be satisfied and successful. Further, the SDS uses raw scores and mixed-sex norm groups for determining compatible career areas.

Example of Opportunity Dominance theory. Contrastingly, Dewey (1974) developed the Non-sexist Vocational Card Sort (NSVCS) as an alternative to standardized interest inventories. The NSVCS is an Opportunity Dominance assessment strategy. The non-sexist names of a wide range of career options are on individual cards, the same set being used for both female and male clients. Individuals sort the cards into piles ranging from "would not choose" to "might choose." Then, in an interactive exchange with the counselor, clients clarify reasons for their sorting of the choices. The counselor and client collaboratively look for connecting themes and the counselor challenges sex-role-stereotyped beliefs about careers and about the client's view of self.

In summary, tests can be sexist if the types of items they contain, the terms used in items, the norm groups used, the interpretation instructions provided in the manual, and the theory underlying their construction are sexist. Biases incorporated into the test then interact with any sex-biased beliefs held by the clinician. Sex-biased tests support the Social Dominance theory and help perpetuate a sex-role-stereotyped society.

Diagnosis

Diagnosis relates specifically to three assessment functions—identification of the problem, categorization of the problem, and determination of appropriate therapeutic interventions.

> Diagnosis is the attempt to classify illness or disease in discrete, mutually exclusive categories, each of which is characterized by a common origin or cause, a common course and a common prognosis, or outcome (Hansen, Stevic, & Warner, 1986, p. 383).

The concept of diagnosis has its roots in medicine, where the focus is to identify an illness, a cause, and a prognosis (Hansen, Stevic, & Warner, 1986). In order to determine a diagnosis, a therapist must have a diagnostic classification system and strategies for identifying, measuring, and labeling of symptoms corresponding to the diagnostic classifications.

Traditional criticisms of diagnostic labels

Diagnosis has received its share of general criticism. Client-centered clinicians criticize it by suggesting that only clients can understand their behaviors and that therapists' evaluation of clients interferes with therapists' ability to be empathic (Hansen, Stevic, & Warner, 1986). Others have argued that the application of a diagnostic label can negatively influence both the client's and the therapist's perceptions that change in the client is possible. Diagnostic systems too often emphasize the pathological, i.e. client weaknesses, and too infrequently focus on health, i.e. client strengths. Another problem with diagnosis is that despite an awareness that the environment plays an important role in how individuals behave, most diagnostic classifications focus on locating the problem within the client (Hansen, Stevic, & Warner, 1986). In contrast, Sundberg (1977) asserts that ". . . assessment of a person is incomplete if it does not include assessment of context" (p. 131).

Finally, therapist misjudgment of the appropriate diagnostic category to be assigned has also been criticized. Arkes (1981) discusses five barriers to clinicians' judgment in the determination of a diagnosis. The first barrier is "covariation misjudgment", in which a symptom is linked to a particular diagnosis without acknowledgment that not everyone with the symptom has the disease, or that some people with the disease do not display the symptom. The second barrier is therapists' "preconceived ideas." Here, assumptions derived from therapists' theoretical orientations and/or personal stereotypes overpower or color the interpretation of the data collected. For example, therapists' sex-role-stereotyped beliefs may color how they view the behavior of women and men. The third barrier is therapists' "lack of awareness" of the factors that influence their evaluations. For example, many clinicians are unaware of how their internalized messages about "appropriate behavior" for women and men may affect their evaluation of pathology and assignment of a diagnosis. The fourth barrier, therapist "overconfidence", leads clinicians to discount data that do not support their initial hypotheses. The final barrier is "hindsight," or the phenomenon of being more accurate after further exposure to the client.

In summary, the therapist's theoretical approach, the diagnostic classification used, and the therapist's beliefs and prejudices interact to determine what criteria are used, what symptoms are looked for, in whom the symptoms are found, and, to some extent, how the symptoms are measured.

Feminist Critique of Assessment and Diagnostic Approaches

All of the foregoing critiques of diagnosis and barriers to accurate, appropriate diagnosis are relevant to feminists' views of assessment and diagnosis. These criticisms and barriers are also examples of the ways in which assessment and diagnosis violate the three Principles of Empowerment Feminist Therapy and/or can reflect the sex-role bias of the diagnostician/ therapist. We will present an analysis of sexism in assessment and diagnosis in psychotherapy by beginning with a summary of the ways in which sexism functions in the processes of assessment and diagnosis, and concluding with a critique of one specific and widely used diagnostic classification system, the Diagnostic and Statistical Manual (DSM-III-R) (American Psychiatric Association, 1987).

Summary of sexist dimensions in assessment and in diagnosis

Assessment and diagnostic approaches are susceptible to sex bias in four major ways. These are: (a) disregarding or minimizing the effect of the environmental context on individuals' behaviors; (b) different diagnoses being given to women and men displaying similar symptoms; (c) therapists' misjudgments in selection of diagnostic labels due to sex-role-stereotyped beliefs; and (d) using a sex-biased theoretical orientation.

Disregarding environmental context. First, assessment and diagnosis are sexist to the extent that they focus solely or primarily on the behaviors and traits of the individual without regard to the environmental context (e.g. poverty, patriarchy, and powerlessness) and the effect of the environment on the individual's response (person–environent interaction). Feminist therapists believe that when the social conditions of women's lives are minimized or ignored, misdiagnosis and blaming the victim are the results (Greenspan, 1983; Sturdivant, 1980; Walker, 1985). For example, if therapists do not perceive that women live in a society that stereotypes and discriminates against them, then the therapists are more likely to judge the woman's response to her situation as an over-reaction, or abnormal. Further, they will look for ways to explain her reactions that ignore the effects of her environment. Locating the pathology in female clients further stigmatizes and blames them for the results of their own sex-role socialization and society's oppression of them. This process reduces their self-esteem, increases depression, and increases feelings of powerlessness. For example, consider Nina, the woman in Chapter 4, who was sexually abused by her brother. She is more likely to be diagnosed as having a personality disorder if the therapist does not see her symptoms as related to possible sexual abuse and so does not assess for it, or if the therapist does uncover the sexual abuse, but does not judge it to be traumatic. For assessment strategies to be free of sexism they must incorporate an assessment of environmental factors and use diagnostic classification systems which allow for environmental stressors to be possible sources of pathology.

Differential diagnosis based on gender. Second, diagnostic approaches are sexist if the structure and definitions of their categories lead to the application of different diagnoses to female and male clients displaying similar symptoms.

This type of misdiagnosis is more likely to happen if the symptom descriptors for categories mirror traditional sex-role stereotypes. Further, the sex-role biases of therapists may interact with the sexism of the diagnostic classifications used. Diagnostic category descriptors which use traits or adjectives are more susceptible to sex bias than are behavioral descriptors, because they require more inference by the clinician. For example, a category that uses "dependent" and "submissive" as descriptors is more likely to be applied to females, because the descriptors fit the traditional female sex-role stereotype and because as adjectives they are more open to the interpretive biases of the diagnostician. Thus, clinicians are more likely to "see" the symptoms in female clients than they are in male clients. A research study by Hamilton, Rothbart, and Dawes (1986) illustrates this point. Clinicians were asked to diagnose hypothetical female and male clients. The clinicians were given identically written client descriptions with only the sex of the client varied. The client vignettes used trait descriptors consistent with a "histrionic" diagnosis. The clinicians more consistently rated the female clients as histrionic than they did the male clients.

Therapist misjudgment.   A third source of sex-role bias in diagnosis and assessment is the sex-role belief system of the diagnostician/therapist. The barriers to clinician judgment proposed by Arkes (1981), which were outlined earlier in this chapter, are useful in conceptualizing the effects of therapists' sex-role biases. Therapists' sex-role-stereotyped beliefs result in therapists having preconceived ideas about the presence of symptoms in women and men. They also have preconceived ideas about the evaluative labels applied to these symptoms. For example, dependency is more likely to be "seen" in females (i.e. believing that females are economically dependent on males) and ignored in males (i.e. failing to see that men are dependent on women for maintaining their households) (Greenspan, 1983). Further, dependency is viewed negatively, while independence is valued positively (Sturdivant, 1980). Because sex-role beliefs are accepted as norms in society, they are often applied without awareness by therapists. These preconceived sex-role beliefs which are largely out of awareness often lead clinicians to discount data that do not support their assumptions. The less that their sex bias is in their awareness, the more pervasive its influence is likely to be in their diagnostic evaluations, and the more confident of "misdiagnosis" they become.

Theoretical orientation sex bias.   Fourth, the degree of sex bias present in therapists' theoretical orientations also influences therapists' diagnostic evaluations. The theoretical orientation provides a framework for what is considered healthy and unhealthy and for explaining how individuals develop. If the theoretical orientation is sex-biased, then clinicians' conceptualizations of what symptoms are pathological, in whom they are pathological, and assessment strategies used for measurement of symptoms, are all likely to be sex-biased. In Chapter 5, we considered how sex bias can influence theoretical concepts and explanations of behavior.

Interaction of sex-biased components. A description of the interaction between components (cultural context, clinician, client) and the stages of sex bias in diagnosis is presented in Figure 6.1. Sex bias (institutionalized sexism and sex-role socialization) in the culture impacts the clinician's responses, the client's responses, and each stage of the diagnostic process. The different ways that sex bias can enter into the diagnostic process is depicted. Each source of potential sexism in the assessment and diagnostic process can occur in isolation or in combination with other sources. When more than one source is present, there is greater likelihood that a harmful, sexist, diagnostic evaluation of the client will be made.

DSM-III-R

The Diagnostic and Statistical Manual of Mental Disorders (Third Edition, revised) (DSM-III-R) is the manual for the currently most used mental disorder diagnostic classification system in the United States. Developed and published by the American Psychiatric Association (1987), the DSM-III-R is used in most United States inpatient and outpatient mental health facilities. It is also considered by many in the mental health system, especially feminist therapists, to be the most sexist of the prevailing diagnostic systems (Brown, 1987; Franks, 1986; Kaplan, 1983; Worell, 1986). The DSM-III-R diagnostic categories which have different prevalence rates for women and men are displayed in Table 6.1.

The DSM-III-R incorporates sexism in several different ways: (a) internal pathology; (b) clinician bias; and (c) use of trait descriptors.

Internal pathology. First, the DSM-III-R was developed on the medical model. It focuses primarily on diagnosing an individual's internal pathology. In fact, very few of its diagnostic categories locate the source of the problem in an environmental stressor. There is no DSM-III-R category that locates the source of the problem in everyday, "normal," life stressors. With some exceptions (e.g. rape), sex-role socialization and institutionalized sexism more often occur as everyday stressors. Thus, most sexism-based stressors are either denied or minimized in the DSM-III-R categorizations. The DSM-III-R categories assign the locus of the problem to individual pathology with little or no regard for the impact of a sexist or oppressive environment. For

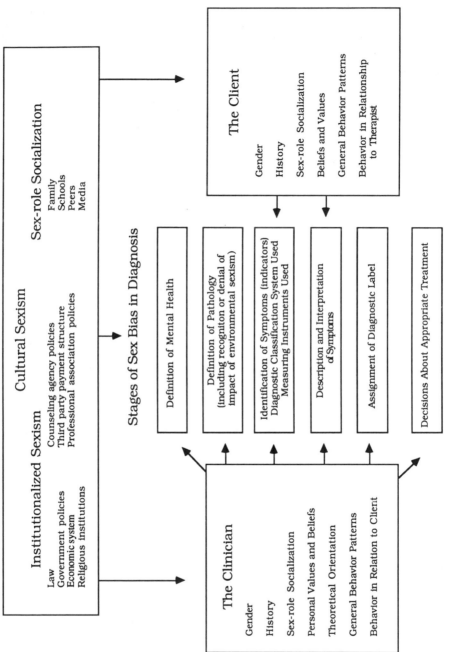

Figure 6.1. Interactional components and stages of sex bias in diagnosis

Table 6.1. *DSM-III-R Diagnostic Categories with Differential Prevalence Rates for Women and Men*

Male-prevalent disorders	Female-prevalent disorders
Pervasive developmental	Eating disorders
Specific developmental	Elective mutism
Disruptive behavior	Primary degenerative dementia of the
Gender identity	Alzheimer type
Tic	Delusional (slight)
Elimination	Induced psychotic
Stuttering	Depressive (major depression & dysthymia)
Multi-infarct dementia	Panic (with agoraphobia)
Psychoactive substance use	Agoraphobia
Social phobia	Simple phobia
Paraphilia	Somatization
Facititious	Somatoform pain
Intermittent explosive	Multiple personality
Pathological gambling	Borderline personality
Pyromania	Histrionic personality
Antisocial personality	Dependent personality
Obsessive–compulsive personality	Late-luteal phase dysphoric*
Sadistic personality*	Self-defeating personality*

* Proposed diagnostic categories needing further study

example, a woman who has a history of unstable relationships, who abuses alcohol, has short bouts of depression, has been suicidal, and who has chronic feelings of emptiness will often be diagnosed to have a Borderline Personality Disorder if her environmental context of sexual abuse is not assessed and uncovered (Briere, 1984).

In contrast, the DSM-III-R category of Post-traumatic Stress Disorder (PTSD) recognizes the impact of extraordinary, traumatic life stressors. If the external, traumatic factors of sexual abuse are assessed for the woman described above, then the more appropriate diagnosis of PTSD would be given. This moves the focus of blame attributions and treatment interventions from personality defects to traumatic events (Worell, 1986).

Clinician bias.   Russell (1986a) sees a second source of sex bias in the DSM-III-R. She points out that the way that mental disorder is defined in the DSM-III-R makes it more susceptible to clinician bias.

A mental disorder is defined as:

> . . . a clinically significant behavioral or psychological syndrome or pattern that occurs in a person and that is associated with present distress (a painful symptom) or disability (impairment in one or more important areas of functioning . . .) (American Psychiatric Association, 1987, p. xxii).

This definition requires the observation of a symptom in a person. The observor must make a judgment about the presence of a symptom and whether it constitutes impairment in functioning. The clinician must determine whether the symptoms are a maladaptive response to stress, i.e. what is a normal or abnormal reaction (Russell, 1986a). Thus, both the response and the stressor are open to interpretation. The clinician's values, biases, and theoretical orientation influence all these judgments.

Bias in therapists' diagnostic evaluations of mental health has been found in many studies (e.g. Broverman et al., 1970; Ford & Widiger, 1989; Hamilton, Rothbart, & Dawes, 1986). The classic Broverman et al. (1970) study which we described in Chapter 2 demonstrated that clinicians held a double standard of mental health for women and men. They found that trait ratings by mental health professionals for a mentally healthy woman closely paralleled traditional female stereotypes, e.g. submissive, excitable, emotional, and were seen as different from a "mentally healthy adult." These differential judgments put women in a double bind, where they may be judged mentally unhealthy both for not conforming to the traditional female stereotype and for conforming to that stereotype (Chesler, 1972).

Further, if clinicians misjudge the extent of the stressor or ignore its existence altogether, the individual's symptoms are more likely to be evaluated as pathological. An example of a DSM-III-R diagnosis which uses descriptors parallel to exaggerated traditional female traits, and which can be misapplied if the environmental stressors are minimized or ignored (e.g. being abused by one's spouse), is Self-defeating Personality Disorder (Walker, 1985).

Use of trait descriptors. A third related criticism of the DSM-III-R involves the types of descriptors used. In the DSM-III (American Psychiatric Association, 1980), several of the personality disorder categories (e.g. Histrionic Personality Disorder, Dependent Personality Disorder) that have higher prevalence rates for women (see Table 6.1) had trait or adjective descriptors which also described traditionally sex-role-socialized women (Hamilton, Rothbart, & Dawes, 1986). For example, a person with a histrionic personality disorder is described as "overly dramatic," "reactive," "often acts a role, such as 'victim' or 'princess'," "there may be a constant demand for reassurance because of feelings of helplessness and dependency" (American Psychiatric Association, 1980, p. 313). Because trait descriptors require more interpretation by the clinician in identifying them in clients, they are also more vulnerable to the sex-biased expectations of clinicians. Thus, women were more likely to be given these diagnoses (Ford & Widiger, 1989; Hamilton, Rothbart & Dawes, 1986).

Although many of these traits and adjective descriptors have been eliminated in the DSM-III-R, some female sex-role-stereotyped descripters still remain. An individual with a Histrionic Personality Disorder is still described by phrases like "excessive emotionality," "seek or demand reassurance, approval or praise from others," "are typically attractive and seductive,"and "are typically overly concerned with physical attractiveness" (American Psychiatric Association, 1987, p. 348). In contrast, all of the diagnostic categories that have a higher prevalence rate for males have clear behavioral descripters (Hamilton, Rothbart & Dawes, 1986). While the revisions of the DSM-III-R are in a positive direction, therapists judgment still plays a large role for certain categories. In the introduction to the DSM-III-R, it is stated that: "For some disorders, however, particularly the personality disorders, the criteria require much more inference on the part of the observer" (American Psychiatric Association, 1987, p. xxiii).

Prevalence rates.   The DSM-III-R reports differential prevalence rates for females and males for numerous disorders (see Table 6.1). There are divided opinions about why these differential rates exist (Franks, 1986; Kaplan, 1983; Widiger & Spitzer, 1991; Williams & Spitzer, 1983). In their defense of the DSM-III, Williams and Spitzer (1983) conclude that if the rate of certain diagnoses is higher among women it is because females have more pathology in these domains, and not that the DSM-III is sexist in structure. On the other side of the issue, Kaplan (1983) argues that:

> . . . masculine-biased assumptions about which behaviors are healthy and what behaviors are crazy are codified in diagnostic criteria and thus influence diagnosis and treatment patterns (p. 786).

Kaplan's analyses of the sexist components of two of the female-prevalent categories—Dependent Personality Disorder and Histrionic Personality Disorder—serve as a useful summary of the sexism-related problems with the DSM-III-R. She points out that there are three major assumptions underlying diagnosis which are influenced by sex bias. First is the belief that the trait or symptom is unhealthy, which is a value judgment. Second is the assumption that the symptoms are dysfunctional, rather than creative/survival strategies for coping with oppression. Third, the symptom is described in and tied to a female context, and the male context for the same symptom is exempted or ignored (e.g. dependency). Thus, Kaplan's explanation for the differential diagnostic rates in females and males for many DSM-III-R diagnostic categories is that sexism is incorporated into the DSM-III-R.

Proposed revisions.   Sexism controversy about the DSM-III-R was further generated by proposed revisions for the DSM-III-R. Women's groups within both the American Psychiatric Association and the American Psychological Association objected to several proposed new diagnostic categories: Premenstrual Dysphoric Disorder, Masochistic/Self-defeating Personality Disorder, and Paraphilic Rapism/Coercive Disorder. The criticism of the first two diagnoses were based primarily on the sexism evident in the structuring of the categories (e.g. terms and descriptors used), their tendency to blame the victim, the minimization of environmental stressors, and the lack of empirical research available to substantiate their existence and description (Walker, 1985).

The proposed DSM-III-R Paraphilic Rapism category would have linked sexual fantasies about coercive sex and actual sexual arousal and/or sexually coercive behavior, and would have labeled this association as a mental illness. The Paraphilic Rapism category was criticized on a number of grounds. First, the category could be used as the basis for an insanity plea for anyone charged with rape. Second, the diagnosis relies on self-report. Third, the diagnosis does not take into consideration the research demonstrating that sexual assaults are not linked to sexual arousal in the assaulter, but ". . . rather are manifestations of misogyny and aggression . . ." (American Psychological Association Committee on Women, 1985, p. 4). Due in part to objections from women's groups, Paraphilic Rapism was not included in the final version of DSM-III-R. However, the Premenstrual Dysphoric Disorder (renamed Late Luteal Phase Dysphoric Disorder) and Self-defeating Personality Disorder were included in the Appendix of DSM-III-R as categories needing further study. While these categories were not placed in the main body of the DSM-III-R, their inclusion in the Appendix and their assignment of numerical codes makes them available for diagnostic use.

DSM-III-R—Summary. The location of pathology in the individual, the minimization of effects of sexist environmental stressors, the use of category descriptions which parallel traditional sex-role stereotypes, the use of trait rather than behavioral descriptors, and the lack of empirical research evidence to substantiate many categories all contribute to the sex-biased structure of the DSM-III-R. Franks (1986) and Kaplan (1983) conclude that sexist assumptions about which symptoms are viewed as pathological are structured into the DSM-III-R. Franks (1986) states that therefore the ". . . concept of psychopathology is gender-determined" (p 219).

Feminist Therapy Approaches to Assessment and Diagnosis

The contrast in approaches to assessment and diagnosis between feminist and traditional therapies is rooted in their different views of the "symptoms" women exhibit. This section begins with a discussion of the feminist view of women's symptoms and concludes with a discussion of the use of assessment and diagnosis in feminist therapy.

Feminist View of Women's "Symptoms"

Feminist therapists believe that failure to acknowledge the oppressive societal context in which women live leads many mental health professionals to mislabel and misevaluate women's responses to their environment as pathological. In most instances, feminist therapists do not see these responses as pathological symptoms, but rather as creative strategies for coping with society's oppression of women. Sturdivant (1980) states that "Symptoms do not become 'symptoms', until they are labeled so by someone" (p. 117).

Feminist therapists (Franks, 1986; Greenspan 1983; Sturdivant, 1980) reinterpret women's "symptoms" or behaviors as:

(1) Behaving in accord with traditional female roles, i.e. women exhibit feminine socialized traits and then are labeled pathological (Sturdivant, 1980). Oversocialized, overdeveloped traditional female sex-role traits fit into this category. One example of this is the DSM-III-R Dependent Personality Disorder, in which individuals have ". . . a pervasive pattern of dependent and submissive behavior . . ." (American Psychiatric Association, 1987, p. 353).

(2) Representing role conflict for women. Women are often forced to choose between their own growth as individuals and their being "appropriate females," which generates internal conflict that often surfaces as anxiety (Sturdivant, 1980). For example, a woman who feels torn between being physically attractive to men and feeling angry about being primarily judged on her physical attractiveness develops a facial tic (Greenspan, 1983). Greenspan describes these reponses to being oppressed as "hidden protests" (p. 185) and Sturdivant (1980) refers to them as "survival tactics" (p. 124). Many women do not have enough safety or power to protest directly, and so must often resort to indirect, more passive modes of expressing their anger. Society's pressure to fit women into a limited sex-typed role frequently leads to "symptom" formation in the individual (Smith & Siegel, 1985).

(3) Representing a coping strategy for surving oppression, discrimination and sex-role stereotyping. Sturdivant (1980) views women's anger as a healthy response to being oppressed; ". . . pain in response to a bad situation is seen as adaptive, not pathological" (p. 165). Manipulative and passive–aggressive behavior are two examples of symptoms as coping strategies in an environment which punishes women's direct use of power.

(4)   Reflecting the result/consequence of female socialization. Greenspan (1983) summarizes this socialization factor when she says:

> The major ingredient of depression—the feelings of hopelessness, help-lessness, worthlessness, futility, and suppressed rage—are the affective components of the objective social condition of female powerlessness in male society (p. 193).

(5)   Representing societal pathological labeling of deviancy from traditional females sex-typed behavior (Sturdivant, 1980). For instance, assertive behavior in a woman is often labeled aggressive or she may be called a "bitch."

These reinterpretations do not represent distinct categories but rather are overlapping reframes of what have previously been labeled pathological symptoms in women. They are also explanations for the differential prevalence rates for women and men in many DSM-III-R diagnostic categories. Feminist therapists believe that women's "symptoms" arise for good reasons and have their etiology in the pathological environment in which women live. Greenspan (1983) believes that it is important for therapists to help women see the strength and/or health embodied in women's responses to their subordinate status in society. In accordance with Feminist Therapy Principles, these symptoms are relabeled/reframed by feminist therapists as coping strategies. Women are empowered by reframing previously labeled "manipulative" or "crazy" responses as ". . . attempts to achieve the goals of control and influence under given social constraints" (Smith & Siegel, 1985, p. 14). In therapy, the underlying goal of a given behavior (symptom) is identified, the strength represented by the behavior is acknowledged and, if desirable, a behavior which exercises more direct power may be searched for and practiced (Smith & Siegel, 1985). Further, many feminist therapists avoid using the word "symptom," substituting words such as "reaction," "coping strategy," "behavior," "sign," "indicator."

Feedback on Chapter Self-assessment: Client Descriptions

In the Self-assessment at the beginning of the chapter you were asked to predict the groups to which the client described belonged. These client descriptions were part of two studies conducted by Landrine (1989). Her premise, which was supported by the results of these studies, was that social stereotypes would match (Hypothesis of Equivalence) the client descriptions which were based on various DSM-III-R personality disorder diagnoses. Client 1 in the Self-assessment fits the DSM-III-R criteria for Dependent Personality Disorder. Respondents in Landrine's study described this person as a slightly older, married, middle-class, white woman. Client 2 in the Self-assessment fits the DSM-III-R criteria for Anti-social Personality Disorder. Landrine's respondents described this person as a young, lower-class male. She concludes that the respondents, who were college students, relied on ordinary social stereotypes to complete the identification task. We believe that this supports feminist contentions that many DSM-III-R personality disorder categories have gender stereotypes embedded in their descriptions, and that evaluators also hold those stereotypes. We hope that by examining your cognitions and answers in completing the exercise you can begin to identify the stereotypes that guide your judgments as a first step in challenging those stereotypes.

Feminist Approaches to Diagnosis

The reinterpretation of symptoms by feminist therapists challenges most of the assumptions that underlie traditional approaches to diagnosis. Indeed, feminist therapists redefine what is considered mentally healthy. Feminist therapists minimize pathologizing the individual by including appraisals of the environmental/societal contexts of women's lives in their assessments. Further, women's responses to surviving and coping with the sexist environment are frequently viewed as assets. Thus, feminist therapy requires a diagnostic approach which includes assessments of women's environments (Principle I). From a feminist therapy perspective, assessment and diagnosis should be a collaborative process between the client and counselor (Principle II). A feminist approach also incorporates reframing of many client "symptoms" as strengths (Principles II and III). Finally, the client's perspective on her own life experience is used and trusted in the diagnostic process (Principle III).

Contextual assessment of women's lives

Walker (1986) points out that therapeutic assessment procedures and diagnostic classifications often ignore the reality of women's lives. For example, women are often the victims of domestic violence, rape, and sexual abuse. Many behaviors seen in female clients are the result of the high rates of abuse and violence in women's lives. Other behaviors are the result of the "everyday" stressors of being sex-role-stereotyped, living in poverty, and living in a patriarchal society. Feminist therapists move the locus of pathology from the individual to the environment. What appear as individual or intrapersonal factors are viewed as consequences of the sex-role socialization and institutionalized sexism processes, i.e. women introject external, sexist, and sometimes abusive messages (Brown, 1987). In most cases, both individual and environmental factors are seen as contributing to clients' problems.

However, in feminist therapy it is possible that no individual/internal factors contribute to the problem; there is conceptual room to attribute the entire problem to a pathological environment. This feminist therapy concept is grounded in social psychology research that demonstrates that pathological environments can, in a very short time, produce pathology in normal, psychologically healthy people (P. Zimbardo, personal communication, 1988).

Shifting the label of pathology from the individual (i.e. personality disorder) to external factors empowers the client, as she understands that there is not something innately wrong with her (Brown, 1987). Her behaviors, viewed within the contextual reality of her life, begin to make sense as reasonable responses to her sexist and often traumatic environment. She gains a new sense of hope. More appropriate treatment interventions can be used. Further, external location of the problem makes clear the need to change environments that have such negative consequences for women. Preventive interventions at the micro- and macro-societal levels can be identified. Notice that if clients' problems are internally located, as is the case in most of our theoretical orientations, needed changes in the environment are not addressed.

Feminist therapists are knowledgable about the events that occur more often to women: rape, sexual abuse, wife-battering, job discrimination and sexual harassment. For example, about one in four women will be raped during their adult life (Russell & Howell, 1983); about one in three female children have been sexually abused (Russell, 1984); Walker (1979) estimates that 50% of all women will be battered by a male/significant other during their adult life. Feminist therapists routinely assess for the presence of these events in their clients' lives. For example, they ask clients about "unpleasant or unwanted sexual experiences." They are knowledgable about the effects on individuals of these aversive events and identify relevant client reactions as possible indicators of these experiences. The therapist's use of signs to identify abusive and oppressive client experiences is especially important with sexual abuse, since the client may not remember the events and, with subsequent spouse abuse, the client may minimize or hide the events from the therapist. In Chapter 9, we see that Clara was in counseling for 3 months before she revealed, very reluctantly, the existence of repeated and severe physical battering in her marriage.

New diagnostic categories

Routine assessment for aversive life events contrasts with most current psychological practice. While most therapists assess for suicide potential in new clients, they rarely assess for the presence of abuse experiences in clients' lives, despite the research that demonstrates a high prevalence rate of abusive events for these in women (Briere, 1984; Walker, 1986). On the contrary, many of our more traditional colleagues have chided the authors for inappropriately "seeing" sexual or spousal abuse "everywhere." Many feminist therapists have concluded that misdiagnosis is the result when women's behaviors are viewed apart from the societal context (Briere, 1984; Brown, 1987; Rosewater, 1985a; Walker, 1986). For example, Briere (1984) cites evidence that the present day reactions (symptoms) of many adult women who were sexually abused as children fit the DSM-III-R descriptions of Borderline Personality Disorder (BPD). Because many treatment approaches to BPD make little reference to the importance of sexual abuse experiences in the development of these symptoms, and because of the generally negative attitudes that clinicians have toward BPD clients, he proposes a new diagnostic classification called "Post-sexual-abuse Syndrome." This new diagnosis would more clearly feature and call for the direct treatment/healing of the sexual victimization traumas which are at the core of these clients' problems.

In a parallel fashion, Walker (1986) proposes a new diagnostic category called "Abuse Disorders" that is similar in concept to Post-traumatic Stress Disorders (PTSD, i.e. is more situationally focused than personality determined. As proposed, the Abuse Disorders category would encompass both sexual abuse and spouse abuse. She argues that PTSD is not an entirely appropriate diagnosis since it implies an extraordinary life event, whereas the high prevalence rates for violence in women's lives constitutes more of a normative experience. She is also very concerned that the Self-defeating Personality Disorder, which is included in a DSM-III-R Appendix, will give clinicians an additional category with which to mislabel environmental pathology as individual pathology in women. The descriptors for this diagnosis fit the symptoms of most women who have been abused by their spouses. Her Abuse Disorder diagnosis would focus clinicians' attention back on the situational cause of the symptoms. These "symptoms" are modified quickly when the environment is changed, i.e. when the violence is stopped or the woman leaves the violent situation (Walker, 1986).

Brown (1987) believes that feminist therapists must also account for the ". . . life-time learning experiences of living in a sexist, racist, homophobic, ageist, and otherwise oppressive cultural context" (p. 12). Thus, she asserts that everyday, continual experiences with sex-role stereotyping and institutionalized sexism can produce pathology. She suggests a new diagnosis of "Oppression Artifact Disorder" for these symptoms. She also describes a feminist therapist diagnostic process which first factors out all environmental sources of problems (e.g. trauma, sex-role stereotyping) before applying diagnostic labels which focus on individual pathology (e.g. personality disorders). A feminist analysis begins with the acknowledgment that many disorders have a higher prevalence rate in women. Then feminist therapists look at the impact of the sex-role socialization process and institutionalized sexism on that prevalence rate. The factors external to women are scrutinized for their contribution to individual pathology (Brown, 1987). The effects of a life-time of cumulative experiences in an oppressive society must be taken into account.

Environmental assessment strategies

Since the heart of a feminist therapy approach to diagnosis is environmental assessment, new strategies for this assessment are needed. Brown (1987) has developed a four-step process for evaluation of the individual's environment. First, the nature of the stressor is determined; is it interpersonal or cultural/ environmental? Second, the frequency of the experience in the woman's life is calculated. Third, the nature of the consequences (positive, mixed, negative) to the individual from the stressor are identified. Finally, the interaction of developmental stages and tasks with the stressor are conceptualized. The sex-role analysis and power analysis techniques described in Chapter 4 are also useful for evaluating women's environments.

A collaborative approach to diagnosis

In most traditional diagnostic approaches the expert therapist uses psychological test, history-taking and the clinical interview to arrive at a diagnosis. The client answers the questions without much understanding of the diagnostic process. In most cases, the diagnosis given is not shared with the client. Feminist therapists collaborate with their clients about the assessment process. If tests or other measures are used, the purpose and nature of them is explained to the client. If a diagnostic label is to be given, the label and its possible consequences are discussed with the client whenever possible. The therapist also discusses with the client the process used by the therapist to arrive at the diagnosis. Clients share in decisions about how the results will be used.

Reframing of symptoms

Once the environmental context of a client's life has been assessed, the therapist helps the woman to view her behavior in this context. What may have first appeared as dysfunctional responses or "symptoms" may now be seen to be survival strategies for coping with a negative environment, or these "symptoms" may be seen as positive and valuable socialized behaviors. Female traits such as nurturance and care-taking of others are not devalued and labeled pathological.

To diagnose or not to diagnose

Feminist therapists are divided about the use of diagnostic labels. The use of the DSM-III-R categories is seen as especially problematic. The realities of the economic marketplace in the United States render it difficult for a mental health provider to obtain third-party reimbursement from the government or private insurance company, or for clients to be reimbursed for their therapy costs if a DSM-III-R diagnosis is not used. As an alternative to personality disorders, a situational stressor diagnosis like PTSD can be used when appropriate. However, our experience with PTSD has not been free of problems. Clients who have been given a PTSD diagnosis have been later turned down for health insurance, despite our statements that the clients were now recovered. Non-sexist and feminist therapists find themselves caught between the evils of using a sexist classification system or of not having third-party reimbursement. Thus, for many middle- or low-income clients, failure to use a DSM-III-R diagnosis means that the therapist must either deny them services or provide free services.

Feminist approaches to testing

Some feminist therapists eschew the use of tests in therapy, both because the tests reflect the sexist cultural values and because the use of tests sets up the therapist in yet another expert role (Rawlings & Carter, 1977). However, other feminist therapists (Rosewater, 1985b; Walker, 1985) believe that testing can be useful if applied within feminist therapy principles. Rosewater (1985b) advocates collaboration between client and counselor in the use of test results as well as in the selection of tests. The results of tests are to be shared openly with clients and should be presented in a way that the client can understand. In accordance with treating the client as an expert on herself, she is encouraged to help make sense of the test results. Increasing clients' self-awareness and knowledge about their issues is an important empowerment strategy. Tests can be one valuable source for increasing their knowledge and self-awareness.

Rosewater (1985b) proposes using tests in non-traditional ways, i.e. to bring about social change. She says that feminist therapists armed with the knowledge of the oppression in women's lives should:

> . . . develop alternative interpretations for widely influential test instruments, interpretations that would be consistent with the philosophic base of feminism (p. 267).

For example, Rosewater used a woman's Minnesota Multiphasic Personality Inventory (MMPI) profile to substantiate that she was a battered woman, as a defense in her trial for the murder of her abusive husband. In a related vein, standardized tests can be used to research women's issues. Rosewater (1985a) gave the MMPI to battered women, schizophrenic women, and women who had been given a Borderline Personality Disorder diagnosis. This procedure allowed her to develop a differentiated profile for battered women, which can then be used to identify other battered women or to refute misdiagnosis of battered women. Battering must be considered before diagnosing a woman as schizophrenic.

Feminist therapists emphasize the use of non-sexist tests. They analyze tests for their sexist components and, based on their findings, either modify the test by deleting or revising items or discontinue its use. Feminist therapists also use non-standardized strategies for assessment, such as having clients self-monitor their own or others' behaviors. They use non-sexist assessment strategies like the Non-Sexist Vocational Card Sort (Dewey, 1974).

Alternative assessment strategies

Feminist therapists often emphasize assessment strategies that focus on collaboration between the therapist and client and which empower the client. As was discussed in the Cognitive–behavioral section of Chapter 5, self-monitoring of behaviors, thoughts, and feelings and functional analysis can increase a client's self- and situational awareness, as well as expand the therapist's knowledge of the client and her life situation. Further, a client's continuous or periodic self-assessment and self-monitoring allows her to evaluate the effectiveness of her own therapy.

Summary

We believe that feminist approaches to assessment and diagnosis are still in their infancy. Feminist therapists generally agree that sex bias enters into most traditional approaches to diagnosis and testing, and that these sexist factors must be eliminated from our assessment of clients. Beyond this basic agreement, feminist therapists have divergent approaches to assessment, falling along a continuum from avoidance of formal diagnostic and testing procedures at one end to the development of alternative methods for diagnosis and testing at the other. Our common goals are to develop and use assessment and diagnostic procedures that highlight the impact of sexism and oppression in women's lives, that make our reality visible to ourselves and others, and that validate our experiences.

Activity

Evaluating a Test for Sex Bias

Choose a standardized test with which you are familiar or with which you want to become familiar. By examining the test items and interpretive manual, evaluate the test for the existence of sex-bias along the following dimensions.

A
Test items

(1) Examine the activities present in the test items for sex-typing. Put an "M" out to the side of male-typed items and "F" out to the side of female-typed items. Put an "N" by neutral items. Count up the number of "M," "F," and "N" items. Calculate a percentage of total items for all three. Tests with a preponderance of either "M" or "F" items probably have a bias that favors that sex over the other.
(2) Look at labels used (e.g. stewardess vs. airline attendant) for evidence of sex bias.
(3) Does the test use generic "he" language or plurals (they) or a balance of "he" and "she" in the items? Use of the "generic he" violates sex-fairness in testing.
(4) Note how each item is scored. Items which label deviancy from traditional sex roles as abnormal are sex-biased.

B
Norm groups

In the test manual, read the descriptions of the norm groups against which individual scores are compared.

(1) Look for the sex composition of norm groups. Are same-sex, cross-sex or mixed-sex norm groups used?
(2) What rationale is given in the manual for the use of the chosen norm group comparison?

C
Interpretation instructions

(1) Are interpretive instructions written using the generic "he"?
(2) Examine the applied interpretation examples. Are non-traditional examples given for both females and males? Is there a balance of non-sex-typed female and male examples?

D

Theoretical constructs

Examine the theoretical constructs used to develop the test.

(1) Are these constructs sex-biased or sex-fair?
(2) Do the constructs support the "Social Dominance Hypothesis" or the
     "Opportunity Dominance Hypothesis"?

E

Summary

Based on your answers to sections A, B, C, and D, how sex-biased overall
do you evaluate this test to be? Will you continue to use this test with your
female clients? Male clients?

Further Readings

Dewey, C. R. (1974). Exploring interests: A non-sexist method. *Personnel and Guidance Journal*, **52**, 311–315.

Franks, V. (1986). Sex-stereotyping and diagnosis of psychopathology. *Women and Therapy*, **5**, 219–232.

Hamilton, S., Rothbart, M., & Dawes, R. M. (1986). Sex bias, diagnosis, and DSM–III. *Sex Roles*, **15**, 269–274.

Rosewater, L. B. (1985). Feminist interpretation of traditional testing. In L. B. Rosewater, & L. E. A. Walker (Eds.) *Handbook of Feminist Therapy: Women's Issues in Psychotherapy*. New York: Springer.

Russell, D. (1986). Psychiatric diagnosis and the oppression of women. *Women and Therapy*, **5**, 83–98.

PART 2

Lifespan Issues in Counseling Women

The issues that women bring to counseling are not easily classified into discrete categories. A presenting problem that appears to be the most salient at the time of initial contact with you may be revised, expanded, or ignored completely as therapy progresses. Some clients may be overwhelmed by emotional reactions that appear to be beyond their control, such as periods of intense anxiety, panic attacks or unexplainable feelings of sadness and hopelessness. The internal and external sources of these reactions may become clear only after careful assessment and exploration of the client's life circumstances and her perception of them.

Other clients may present a clear set of issues that they wish to address: "I want to lose weight, change my job, find a satisfying career, reconsider my marriage, keep my husband from getting angry, find a man, deal with my mastectomy, decide whether or not to have a child, confront my rape, reduce my loneliness, get along better with my mother, etc." One client may focus on a single issue, while another may detail a list of problems that complicate her life. Whatever the presenting problems may be, clients will be experiencing a range of reactions that signal personal distress. In the process of assessment, you will observe your clients' verbal and non-verbal communications of their affective states, their beliefs and attributions for their dilemmas, and the actions they have considered or attempted in their efforts to cope with their stress. The sum of these responses represents the client and her issues at any given time, and each may become a target for therapeutic intervention within the context of each woman's unique life situation.

In Part 2, we consider a selected sample of the issues that bring women to counseling. The initial chapter on depression explores one of the most frequent referrals for personal distress. The succeeding chapters explore more specific concerns that women bring to counseling: sexual assault, physical abuse, and career decision-making. The final chapter in this section discusses issues in counseling with two representative groups of multiple-risk women: lesbian and ethnic minority women. Each chapter defines the client population and the issues to be addressed, and summarizes the socialization, situational, and societal factors that may contribute to the client's personal distress. Through the presentation of case material, each chapter will suggest how the feminist therapist works within the context of a target issue to merge her theoretical viewpoint with the principles of feminist counseling and therapy.

CHAPTER 7

Dealing with Depression

Self-Assessment: Beliefs and Facts about Depression

Fact and theory about the incidence, etiology, and treatment of depression suggest divergent and sometimes conflicting interventions. The statements below represent issues that cover both fact and theory. For each statement, check the one box that best represents your understanding, belief, or knowledge about depression.

		Agree	Uncertain	Disagree
(1)	Depression is caused by faulty thinking.	___	___	___
(2)	Depressed persons overgeneralize about life's problems.	___	___	___
(3)	Depression is really anger turned inward.	___	___	___
(4)	Treatment of depression requires release of pent-up anger and rage.	___	___	___
(5)	Depression is best treated by methods that alleviate the symptoms.	___	___	___
(6)	Depressed people distort reality.	___	___	___
(7)	The "empty nest" syndrome is a major cause of depression in older women.	___	___	___
(8)	Depressive reactions are equally common in women and men.	___	___	___
(9)	Post-partum depression seldom lasts beyond a few weeks.	___	___	___

	Agree	Uncertain	Disagree
(10) Women only appear more depressed than men, because they complain more and are more likely to seek professional help.	___	___	___
(11) Depressed women tend to blame others for their problems rather than themselves.	___	___	___
(12) Depression is a genetically-based disease that is best treated with pharmacotherapy.	___	___	___
(13) Depression is inversely related to marital or partner satisfaction.	___	___	___
(14) Married women report more depressive symptoms than married men.	___	___	___
(15) Highest rates of depression occur in divorced and widowed women.	___	___	___
(16) Depressive moods in women are highly related to hormonal changes.	___	___	___
(17) A history of sexual assault predicts subsequent depression.	___	___	___
(18) There is no relationship between attributional styles and depression.			

Scoring

Statements 1–6 concern theory, and your answers may reflect your personal beliefs. The remaining items are statements of fact: 9, 13, 14, 15, and 17 are true; 7, 8, 10, 11, 12, 16, and 18 are false. Answers to these latter statements will also be found throughout the chapter.

Overview

Regardless of the specific issues that women bring to counseling, many of your clients are likely to show evidence of depression and anxiety. We believe that intervention for presenting concerns should focus on helping clients to: (a) define and explore relevant issues; (b) examine societal, sex-role, and personal factors; and (c) formulate and initiate productive solutions to current life problems. For many clients, you will also intervene to reduce intense emotional discomfort and debilitating patterns that interfere with effective functioning and personal well-being.

We consider the development of depressive reactions of women in the context of a case presentation of Andrea. We review first some data on incidence of depression, and definitions that clarify the range of feelings, beliefs, and behaviors that accompany a diagnosis of unipolar depression. We then discuss some of the factors that have been advanced to account for the disproportionate incidence of depressive reactions in women, including biological, societal, and sex-role socialization. Theories used to conceptualize Andrea's depressive episodes are related to societal sexism that produces *reinforcement deficits* for women, and sex-role socialization that encourages *learned helplessness* and *psychological entrapment*. Intervention strategies for Andrea included sex-role and power analysis, assertiveness coaching, cognitive restructuring, reattribution training, relaxation skills, stress inoculation, problem-solving, and increasing pleasant activities.

After reading Chapter 7, you should be able to:

(1) Describe biological, societal, and sex-role explanations for women's depressive reactions.
(2) Provide support and critiques for each of the variables hypothesized to precede or accompany women's depressive reactions.
(3) Suggest ways in which each of the three Principles of Feminist Therapy can be used to facilitate intervention with women's depressive reactions.

Andrea's Story: Hopelessness and Resignation

Andrea spent her entire first session in counseling weeping uncontrollably. "I don't know what's the matter with me. I cry all the time and I just can't seem to control it." In addition to periods of crying, Andrea also reported difficulty in sleeping, patterns of wakefulness at 3 and 4 am, loss of appetite and consequent weight loss, and disinterest in sexual activity with her husband. She reported feeling exhausted after work, difficulty in concentrating on her work and fear of making errors (she was an accountant in a mid-sized firm), and periods of anxiety and crying at work as well. "My life just isn't going anywhere," she explained. "I'm not performing well at work and was passed up for promotion this year, they just don't seem to like me or my work."

In discussing her marriage, Andrea appeared resigned. "That's not working out either, I can't seem to please him. He thinks I work too much and he's really not interested in my problems at work. We don't seem to have much in common any more and I can't find ways to keep this relationship alive. I feel like I'm alone all the time, even when we're together." In summing up her present life, Andrea sighed despondently, "Nothing's coming together in my life, I just feel like a total failure, what's the use of going on? It won't get any better and I can't seem to find ways to make things better . . . Lord knows I've tried. He wanted a child too, but now I'm afraid I wouldn't even make a good mother. I'm almost 34 . . . I guess I've waited too long . . . I'm probably too old anyway. He's right, it wasn't good planning on my part to put my career first before starting a family. Now I've made a mess of my career and family life too. I guess I've never been much of a success at anything . . . I don't know where to go from here."

Assessment

Andrea's initial presenting behaviors signalled that she was seriously depressed. Assessment procedures provided a lengthy interview, including present symptomatology, history of previous episodes similar to this one, and family history of depression. We asked about recent experiences of relationship termination or loss, and continuing stressors such as financial insufficiency, physical disability, and care of elderly or disabled parents. We also routinely screen for evidence of present or previous physical and sexual abuse and invite clients to raise these issues at a later time if they feel uncomfortable addressing them at the outset of counseling. In all cases, we assess for suicide risk, and we obtain an inventory of medication and substance use, both past and present. Andrea had been taking an antidepressant for about 6 months, prescribed by her family physician. She withdrew from the medication recently, saying that it did not seem to help and she feared becoming dependent on it.

We referred Andrea for a medical examination to consider psychophysiological contributions to her moods, such as hormonal imbalance, medication reactions, or evidence of other medical disorders. The medical findings in this case were negative. Responses to the Beck Depression Inventory (BDI) (Beck et al., 1961) revealed a pattern of negative self-worth, hopelessness, and somatic disturbances. Andrea's elevated score (24) was consistent with a diagnosis of moderately severe depression. Since she expressed feelings of loneliness, we used the Young Loneliness Inventory (Young, 1982) to assess for more specific areas of distress. Her high score of 26 suggested that she felt isolated and without intimate supportive relationships in her current life. Finally, since anxiety and depression often coexist, we assessed her anxiety on the State-trait Anxiety Scale (Spielberger, Gorsuch, & Luchins, 1970). Her score was elevated but within the normal range.

We then further examined the range of her attributions (perceived reasons and causes) for the present episode, as well as fully exploring her current life circumstances, especially those relating to family and work. She revealed that her husband's employment was in a neighboring town 30 miles away, and he chose to live there. This living arrangement required long hours of commuting for her and provided little time for friends or leisure activities. In response to questions about her husband's potential involvement in couples' counseling, she indicated that he had previously refused her efforts to engage him in relationship counseling, and that it was useless to attempt to gain his cooperation. We sent her home after the initial session with a mood/situation rating sheet (see Table 7.1) and asked her to gather data for us at periodic intervals each day, relating her thoughts and feelings to current situational events. The purpose of this assessment was to help both Andrea and ourselves understand the situational (what was happening) and cognitive (automatic thoughts and self-talk) correlates of her dysphoric moods.

Impression

Andrea's story is not very different from that of many other women. Her attempts to follow both traditional scripts for the "good wife" and contemporary scripts for the "successful career woman" had left her with demands from both herself and others that she perceived to be beyond her ability to accomplish. Her depressive symptoms mirrored her experiences of helplessness in the face of seemingly unsolvable problems, and hopelessness in believing that she could solve her present problems to her own satisfaction and meet the expectations of her husband at home and her supervisor at work. In both situations, she voiced responsibility and blame for her predicament, and believed that others were justified in letting her know that she was not doing her job. And as in the case of many other women, Andrea did not look beyond herself to consider the inequities in resources and power balance in her home and employment settings that contributed to her feelings of incompetence and despair.

A diagnosis of unipolar depression leads us to consider treatment plans for Andrea within the context of the extensive research literature on the conceptualization and treatment of depression. We also consider Andrea's situation from a feminist position and we explore with her how the context of her life situation, her gender-based socialization and self-expectations, the apparent sex discrimination and harassment in her work setting, the lack of parity in her marriage, her isolation from intimacy and emotional support, and her habitual methods of responding and coping have contributed to her present state. In the context of these multiple issues, we consider how

Table 7.1. *Andrea's Mood-situation Rating Form*

Day/time	Situation	I felt (rate 1–100)	I thought	I did
Thursday 8:00 a.m.	Stan complained about breakfast being cold	Clutch in my gut, fear, anxiety? (60)	I can't do it all	Told him I would cook him a hot one tomorrow
11:45 a.m.	Steve said he was going to a long lunch and if I would cover his Exigen account calls for him he'd sure appreciate it	Trapped into doing his work again, helpless, resentful (80)	He's always doing this to me, he thinks I'm his secretary or something	Covered his calls
2:45 p.m.	Steve came back, patted and hugged me, told me what a great trooper I was	Confused (90), angry (75), maybe a little pleased (20). (Rated later in session when she was better able to sort out her reactions)	Well, at least he said something nice, but why should I want to please him? I'm all confused	Smiled at him and said I was glad to help out
4:30 p.m.	Sitting at my desk, not doing anything useful	Depressed, discouraged, feeling teary (85)	I'm a mess, I can't think any more, I can't finish my own work, I always let him do a number on me—what a jerk I am	Tried to work on my own accounts but couldn't keep my mind on work, took it all home to do at night
8:00 p.m.	Finishing up dishes and Stan says his mom and sister are coming over	Clutch in my gut—resentment, fear (90)	I don't want to talk to them, I can't do my work, I can't do it all, I guess I'll have to stay up late. What a mess!	Talked to his mom and sister, stayed up late to finish accounts, didn't even answer Stan when he said "Goodnight"

Instructions given: Describe your moods when you are feeling especially high or low, happy or sad, anxious, etc., and rate them on a scale from 1–100 (least to most). Note what was happening (the situation), what you were thinking or telling yourself, then what you actually did.

Andrea helped herself to a new freedom through a reconstruction of her situation, and a series of decisions that effected changes both in herself and in her interactions with others.

Depression in Women

Incidence

Signs of depression are common in any clinical caseload. We all experience transitory periods of sadness and feeling "down," but normal depressive episodes tend to disappear and are seldom accompanied by prolonged disturbances in daily functioning. In a review of sex ratios in the epidemiology of depression across 30 different countries, Myrna Weissman and Gerald Klerman (1987) reported that women outnumbered men by about 2 to 1. These studies covered respondents from clinical settings as well as from non-clinical community surveys.

More recently, research studies have differentiated between unipolar and bipolar (manic-depressive) syndromes. Incidence ratios were equal for bipolar diagnoses, but were still skewed toward women for unipolar syndromes (Weissman & Klerman, 1987). Figure 7.1 presents relevant data from three performance sites in the United States, indicating that across all settings, women displayed higher symptomatology for unipolar depression than did men. This female–male ratio varies by age, marital status, and ethnic group. For example, it appears that younger women have shown increased rates of unipolar depression since 1950 and are being reported at an earlier age of onset (Weissman & Klerman, 1987). Likewise, divorced and widowed women have higher rates of depression than never-married or married women. Women with a history of depression are likely to have repeated depressed episodes, with mean lengths of 4–7 months in duration (Lewinsohn et al., 1984).

Definitions

Clinicians should be aware of DSM III-R criteria for the diagnosis of depression, as well as cut-off scores on major instruments for screening clients, such as the BDI and other similar measures. From an empirical approach, Lewinsohn et al. (1984) reported on factor analytic studies of depressive signs that revealed six major factors. These factors, incorporating affective, cognitive, somatic, and behavioral manifestations of depression, include the following:

(1) Dysphoric mood: feeling sad, unhappy, helpless, hopeless, worthless, and incompetent. The future appears gloomy and unlikely to improve.
(2) Reduced rates of behavior: low activity level, inefficiency, inability to complete tasks, difficulties in concentration. Daily activities become effortful and are no longer pleasurable.

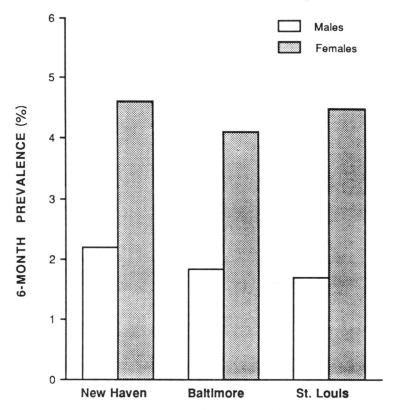

Figure 7.1   Major depression: DSM III. (Data derived from Myers et al., 1984.)

(3) Conflicted interpersonal behavior: marital distress and dissatisfaction, loneliness, social anxiety, and withdrawal.
(4) Guilt: being a burden to others, unable to perform responsibilities to family and work, self-deprecation, self-blame.
(5) Material burden: focus on external circumstances, financial problems, excessive demands by others.
(6) Somatic complaints: poor appetite, weight loss, sleep disturbances (too much or too little), headaches, fatigue, and loss of energy.

In addition to the indicators of depression listed above, we screen for suicidal ideation. Depressed women are considerably more vulnerable than other client types to attempted or completed suicides, and this risk factor should be considered in treating a client with more than two of the five syndromes outlined above. It seems clear that depression is a broad label to cover a group of related signals of personal distress and dysfunctional response patterns. Although no client is likely to manifest every response pattern, notice that Andrea displayed some indications of all the above depression factors in her presenting problems.

Issues in Women's Depression

Aside from standard criteria for diagnosing depression in your clients, a major concern is to understand the disproportionate prevalence rates for women. The literature on depression is probably more extensive than on any other clinical syndrome at the present time, and has only recently addressed questions concerning women (McGrath et al., 1990; Nolen-Hoeksema, 1987; 1990). We consider three major factors related to women's depression: biological, societal, and sex-role socialization. Since depression is conceptualized here as a complex response pattern with cognitive, affective, behavioral, and somatic attributes, we anticipate that for any individual, several factors may be implicated in its development and maintenance (see Figure 7.2 for a range of potential factors).

Biological Factors

Biological hypotheses about women's depressive episodes embrace both genetics and endocrinology. The genetic hypothesis proposes that depression is sex-linked and transmitted disproportionately to women. Although vulnerability to depression occurs in families, rates are equally distributed between women and men in first-generation relatives (Weissman, 1980). Thus, depression-proneness is inherited equally by women and men.

Hormonal factors related to levels of estrogen and progesterone are implicated in studies on premenstrual and postpartum depression. Menstruation and childbirth are both associated, in some women, with an increase in vulnerability to depressive reactions. However, both types of situations are characterized by more than simple hormonal changes.

Premenstrual depression

Periods of mild depression prior to menstruation may be influenced by increased body fatigue and bloating due to water retention, as well as to discomfort induced by intra-uterine "cramps". Further, women's attitudes toward menstruation influence both its impact and its reported frequency (Lazar, 1987; Nolen-Hoeksema, 1987). The slight increase in self-reported depression associated with the menstrual cycle is insufficient to account for women's twofold incidence rates.

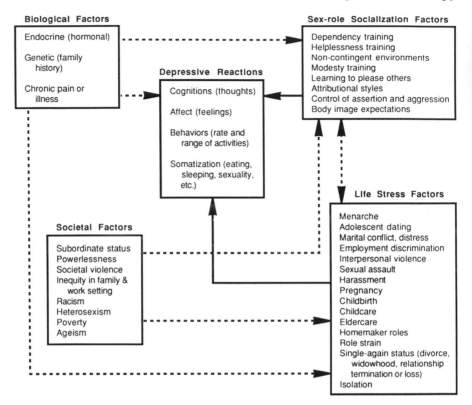

Figure 7.2   Contributions to women's depression. The multiple factors that may contribute to women's depression are divided here into categories that interact and overlap. Not all variables are discussed in the text. The heavy lines indicate direct influences on depressive reactions. The dashed lines indicate influences, which contribute to vulnerability and/or stress

Postpartum depression

Following childbirth, women commonly experience transitory depressive moods or "maternity blues" (O'Hara, 1989). Women who remain depressed after several weeks post partum, however, have been found to be already depressed prior to childbirth (Atkinson & Rickel, 1984). The risk of psychotic reactions also increases for women in the first 3 months following childbirth, but these severe reactions usually require hospitalization. Continued post-partum depression is inversely related to spousal support, and is magnified by lack of sleep, stresses of new motherhood, household responsibilities, and marital strain (Lazar, 1987).

Menopause

Finally, depression associated with menopause (formerly known as "involutional melancholia") has not been supported by recent research. In a study with 500 middle-aged women, for example, no correlation was found between depression scores and menopausal status (Amenson & Lewinsohn, 1981). Individual reactions in midlife may be related to psychosocial changes such as divorce, widowhood, death of close friends and family members, and departure of children from the home (Lazar, 1987).

Biological factors—conclusions

Although biological factors may well influence some mood fluctuations, these reactions tend to be mild and transitory (Hammen, 1982). We doubt whether they are responsible for the 2:1 discrepancy in rates of depression for women. The fact that over 70% of the prescriptions for psychotropic drugs are written for women (McBride, 1987) may reflect medical assumptions about the biological bases of women's depression and anxiety reactions. Indeed, we saw that Andrea had been prescribed an antidepressant by her physician, with little ameliorative effect. We do not reject the use of psychotropic interventions, but suggest that they be administered and monitored carefully and in the context of psychological treatment that assists clients in solving the life problems associated with the depressive episodes. Further, we note that research evidence is mixed with respect to the efficacy of pharmacotherapy in addition to psychological interventions when the depressive episode is related to situational variables (see review by Williams, 1984).

Although biological variables may interact with situational stressors in the etiology of depression, we found no evidence of a biological contribution to Andrea's current state. Instead, we turn to psychosocial factors in attempting to understand her depression. We consider two broad categories: factors descriptive of the broader culture or society, and factors that relate to women's sex-role socialization.

Societal/Situational Factors

The social status hypothesis suggests that "real social discrimination . . . (against women) . . . makes it difficult for them to achieve mastery by direct action and self-assertion" (Weissman, 1980, p. 103). We have discussed earlier the dimensions of patriarchal culture and institutionalized sexism that disadvantage women (see Chapters 2 and 3). With respect to the onset of depression, we consider those factors that suppress women's sense of mastery and control over their lives, and that relegate women to positions of diminished status, resources, and interpersonal power. For Andrea, two factors seemed salient: the quality of her marital relationship and circumstances in her workplace.

For other clients, differing societal factors might be important to consider. The acceptance and prevalence of violence toward women is a prime example. Note (see above) that we screen all clients for evidence of physical or sexual abuse, because these events have high probability levels in the lives of women, and are correlated with evidence of depression. For example, in a sample of college students, Witt and Worell (1988) found that levels of depression on the BDI were significantly elevated for those who reported past or present physical abuse in a romantic relationship. Likewise, in a large probability sample of 3132 community residents, sexual assault during some time in the respondents' lives (16.7% of the women) predicted later major depressive episodes, as well as substance abuse and a variety of anxiety disorders (Burnam et al., 1988).

Marriage

Marital distress has been consistently related to depressive disorders (Barnett & Gotlib, 1988; Gotlib & Hooley, 1988). Although earlier research provided evidence that marriage was a risk factor for women but a protective factor against depression for men, recent data indicate that this discrepancy is narrowing (Lazar, 1987). However, in a survey of over 1000 community residents who were both married and employed, women reported more depressive symptoms than did men. This relationship did not hold for employed but unmarried respondents, pointing to a risk factor for married employed women (Aneshensel, Frerichs, & Clark, 1981).

The research literature is unclear on whether women's satisfaction with work external to the home may serve as a barrier to the experience of depression in women. For the most part, multiple roles have contributed positively to women's self-esteem (Crosby, 1991), but this relationship is contingent on several factors, including satisfaction with work, and support and equity within the marriage. When marital arrangements are inequitable in terms of power and decision-making, and household workloads are unevenly distributed, women continue to be disadvantaged. Adding "worker" to "homemaker" with little modification in the "wife" role leads to role overload and role strain. Andrea reported that, despite her career and child-free status, her marital arrangement was relatively "traditional" in terms of demands for her activities at home and the expectations that she place her husband's wishes, such as where they lived, ahead of her own. She felt that her efforts to communicate her needs to him were fruitless and that he continued to "manage" the marriage to his own image. Both her husband and his family indicated their displeasure with her continued childlessness and thought she should "settle down" and be a good wife and mother.

In contrast to Andrea's situation, a full-time homemaker client who presents similar depressive signs would suggest a different scenario. Radloff (1975) reported that wives who did not work outside the home were more depressed than wives who were externally employed. Since the home-maker role may be unrewarding to some women (see Chapter 2), we would explore the dimensions of her satisfaction and discontent with her household activities, as well as with her marital and community relationships. It is particularly important that psychotherapists who work with depressed women be cautious about viewing the resumption or "improvement" of their clients' traditional household roles as a sign of recovery. For example, some structured programs for depression assign such tasks as housecleaning, shopping, laundry, ironing, cooking, making beds, use of cosmetics, stylish clothing, and hair-care as therapeutic strategies for women but not for men (cf. Liberman & Roberts, 1976). Evaluation of improvement, in this case, consists of reshaping the woman back into the role of the good wife. When working with prescribed social role behaviors, it is crucial that therapists explore carefully what activities are rewarding and satisfying to women apart from societal expectations for their roles.

Work

We saw in Chapter 2 that employment conditions for women are generally characterized by job segregation into low-paying and low status positions that offer little opportunity for advancement and self-determination. For women in male-dominated professions, the picture is somewhat different. The societal expectations for women in non-traditional employment settings contain conflicting messages. Women are expected to be hard-working and competent at their jobs (performance level), but are frequently not expected to achieve the same position as men (accomplishment level). They are reminded of their status as women and are frequently given little support for advancement despite their professional training and expertise.

As an accountant in a mid-sized firm, Andrea was the first and only woman to be employed in her unit in other than a secretarial position. Her supervisor and co-workers expressed support and desire to increase their staff of women in the accounting division, but made no moves to hire others. Although she had more years of experience than he did, her office-mate made frequent suggestions about how she could improve her work, and questioned why she used certain procedures. On weekends, he occasionally left early and commented that she could finish up, since she had no children to look after at home. Further, he made sexually suggestive remarks to her and made it clear that he was interested in her as a woman rather than as a colleague.

In discussing these issues with her supervisor, she was told that the co-worker was "just trying to be friendly and helpful" and that she "shouldn't take things so seriously." In division staff meetings, she felt that her suggestions were not considered or implemented and that she seemed to have little impact on office procedures and decisions. The final blow was the recent promotion of her office-mate in preference to her as first-line supervisor, a position she had expected to be offered to herself. Andrea knew that he had frequent lunches with their supervisor, but believed it was friendship rather than business. Looking back at it, she commented that her supervisor had never invited her to lunch.

In Andrea's work situation, we see at least three elements of employment discrimination; isolation, sexual harassment, and devaluation of her competence. It appeared that her firm was satisfied to hire a token woman, but then expected her to remain "in her place". She was not accorded a pathway to administrative connections (socializing with the supervisor) and her complaints about sexual harassment and co-worker interference were minimized and disregarded. Her position in staff meetings was typical for that of a woman in a male-majority group, in that her comments were ignored and her contributions were overlooked.

Reinforcement deficit theory

The social status hypothesis of women's depression is compatible with formulations by Peter Lewinsohn and his associates that reinforcement deficits may function to precipitate and maintain depressive reactions (Lewinsohn, Youngren, & Grosscup, 1979). That is, depression is related to an unfavorable ratio between positive and negative person-environment outcomes. The low rate of positive outcomes is assumed to result in increasingly passive behavior and dysphoric mood, as the individual feels incapable of reaching personal goals and reacts with withdrawal and despair. These researchers do not specifically address the gender-driven societal aspects of oppression as a reinforcement deficit in the lives of women. However, their theory is compatible with a feminist position, since it considers environmental contributions to the development of depression. Although reinforcement deficit theory recommends adding pleasurable activities to balance the reinforcement ratio, we believe that it is also necessary to effect a change in the individual's power position in interpersonal transactions.

In Andrea's situation, the failure of both her family and her supervisor to respond favorably to her requests for parity in the marriage and recognition at work set the stage for her feelings of impotence and powerlessness. In addition, the theory suggests that individual skill deficits may contribute to depressive reactions by reducing the probability that the person is able to obtain reinforcing events or to reduce negative ones. We see that Andrea's strategies for modifying conditions both at home and work were ineffective in producing desirable changes; thus, she attributed her failures to her own lack of ability. We shall consider the individual outcomes of sex-role conditioning in the next section.

Societal/situational factors—conclusions

In summarizing the societal contributions to Andrea's current reactions, it seems clear that socialized expectations about her roles and behaviors were communicated clearly to her by both family and the workplace. Although the research literature provides inconsistent support for the hypothesis that women experience more general life stress than do men, we believe that this question has not been sufficiently addressed. Women's stressors may differ in quality, content, and duration. Women's stressors may be more likely to leave women feeling helpless, incompetent, and out of control of their lives. The issue for understanding and treatment of women's depression is not whether women have more stressors than men, but to consider and explore the nature of societal events, images, and expectations for each client that produce continuing stress in her life.

Sex-role Socialization Factors

The societal expectations, rules, images, and messages that women receive throughout their lives become internalized and translated into individual modes of habitual reacting. Women are frequently unaware of how their automatic thoughts and behaviors are shaped and maintained by the gender-driven expectations of others. Some of the primary signs of depression, although demonstrated by men as well as by women, appear to be correlates of societal socialization for womanhood: passivity, unassertiveness, feelings of incompetence, self-blame, crying, expectations below ability and achievement levels, and dysfunctional attributional patterns.

Learned helplessness/hopelessness

The most frequently-proposed hypothesis to account for these signs of depression is the learned helplessness/hopelessness model. The original model of learned helplessness (Seligman, 1975) proposed that as a result of repeated exposure to uncontrollable aversive outcomes, individuals may come to believe that their behaviors have no effect on external events. Therefore, outcomes are believed to be uncontrollable. The cognitive, affective, and behavioral correlates of this belief are consistent with those of depression, including passivity and lowered self-esteem. A reformulation of the learned helplessness model to account for individual differences proposed that the person's attributions for the uncontrollable events were the primary determinant of the helplessness/hopelessness response pattern (summarized by Seligman, 1981).

The pattern of attributions for greatest risk (we call this the hopelessness triad) is characterized by attributions of negative events to internal, stable, and global causes, and the attribution of positive outcomes to external, unstable, and specific causes. A recent meta-analysis of 104 studies on the relationship of attributional styles to depression found that the more people attributed negative events in their lives to internal, stable, and global causes, the more likely they were to evidence depressive symptoms (Sweeney, Anderson, & Bailey, 1986).

Thus, people like Andrea who blame themselves for bad events (since I didn't get promoted, I must be a poor manager) will experience a loss of self-esteem. Attributing bad events to stable causes that are unlikely to change (I'm probably not fit to be in the business world) leads to feelings of incompetence over time in coping with future situations. And generalizing to many situations (I can't seem to make it anywhere in my life) results in chronic feelings of helplessness and hopelessness, and inability to cope effectively with stress. In contrast, when such individuals experience positive outcomes, they discount these by attributing their occurrence to an external unstable factor such as luck or chance (I'm lucky even to have this job, because they needed a woman; I shouldn't complain), once more diminishing their self-efficacy. Finally, the importance of the situation to the individual influences the severity and intensity of depressive symptoms. Thus, for Andrea, the two areas of her life with most value, her marriage and work, were the focus of her feelings of uncontrollability and failure.

There is considerable evidence that women and girls, more than men and boys, may use attributions that depress their performance and inhibit positive and assertive efforts to overcome adversity. However, we believe that there are additional socialization factors, reviewed in Chapter 3, that for many women produce lower expectancies for success in male-typed tasks, low risk-taking tendencies, and increased "compliance" and attempts to please authority. Together with the learned helplessness hypothesis, the accumulated effects of these sex-role socialization factors appear to contribute substantially to the depressive syndromes more frequently observed in women.

Sex-role socialization factors—conclusions

It was evident in Andrea's dialogue that her reactions to her situation were characterized by pervasive negative cognitions, but we can also see that there were many factors in both home and work situations to induce such beliefs. There is considerable research to support the view that the negative cognitions of depressed individuals reflect their actual life circumstances and the reactions of significant others (Krantz, 1985). Rather than presume that her dysphoric moods resulted from distorted thinking patterns or selective recall of negative events, we proceeded to explore further the details of her home and work situations, and the specific interactions that left her feeling incompetent and out of control of her life.

Interventions for Andrea were planned in the context of the real and oppressive situations that confronted her at home and in the workplace, the societal messages that she had internalized and accepted as her own, the socialized behaviors she tended to use in interpersonal situations, and the attributions she made for the outcomes of her interactions.

Intervention Strategies

A Four-phase Model

In counseling sessions with Andrea, her therapist Ellen used a modified cognitive–behavioral approach. Plans for counseling followed a four-phase procedure: (a) assessment and goal-setting; (b) exploration of behaviors, thoughts, and feelings within the context of both societal messages and Andrea's situational patterns of reacting; (c) initiation of problem-solving strategies, experiments to test out hypotheses, implementing new insights into Andrea's work and home settings; and finally (d) planning of maintenance and generalization strategies to help strengthen Andrea's revised view of herself and her environment and to provide support for further change.

Phase 1

In phase 1, Feminist Therapy Principle II was addressed first. Ellen discussed the general procedures to be followed, shared her own views on how behavior change occurs, and provided feedback to Andrea on the results of the assessment. Together they developed a set of goals and a contract that would be re-evaluated at the end of 3 months.

Principle II: egalitarian relationship

Ellen set the stage for implementing Principle II by pointing out that as a trained psychologist she possessed knowledge of behavior change, but that Andrea was the expert on herself. Counseling would be both a teaching and a learning process, in which each member of the dyad assumed the roles of teacher and learner. Together, they composed a team with equal but differing contributions to the change process.

Andrea initially rejected responsibility for her own progress, stating that she didn't know how she could be of any use because she was obviously a failure in solving her problems. Ellen countered these objections with questions about Andrea's feelings and perceptions (Principle III), validating them as "real" data that provided a unique perspective on Andrea. Ellen was careful to avoid labeling any of Andrea's reactions as "distorted", "faulty", or "irrational", since these labels tend to lower self-esteem, and further convince the client that she is out of control of her thoughts as well as of her life.

Principle I: the personal is political

Ellen then brought Principle I into play by helping Andrea to reframe some of her statements from self-blame (I'm a failure at keeping my marriage together) to social messages (I'm feeling responsible for keeping my marriage together because I was taught that relationships are supposed to be the woman's job). Through careful questions posed by Ellen, Andrea was able to see that marriage is a shared partner responsibility and that the "failure", if any, was not hers alone. Ellen shared some information on factors that contribute to women's relationship satisfaction, including intimacy, emotional support, and equity in the distribution of power (Lange & Worell, 1990; Worell, 1988).

In a similar vein, her attributions for her problems at work were reframed in a manner that suggested the possible roles of sexism, isolation, discrimination, and sexual harassment in her employment setting. Ellen provided Andrea with some information about women in male-dominant work-settings, and the effects of the solo woman on men's behavior in groups. These insights into societal contributions to her dilemmas were both confusing (now I'm not sure what to believe) and exciting (maybe it's really not all my fault?), and she felt challenged to explore them further.

Goal selection

In developing therapeutic goals, Ellen helped Andrea to narrow her focus from general affect (I want to feel better) to prioritizing more specific behavioral goals (I want to feel better about my progress at work). Andrea decided that her marital concerns were complicated by her husband's non-participation and the demands of his family, so that these issues were set aside temporarily. She chose instead to work on her sleep and somatic problems, and to explore her sense of failure and incompetence in relation to the work setting. In helping Andrea to set specific behavioral goals, Ellen was providing the foundation for a situational view of stress that removed the pathology from her (I must be going crazy, I'm so mixed up) and focused instead on the specifics of her interpersonal transactions and her perceptions of them. Ellen was also concerned about Andrea's decision to side-step her marital difficulties, but determined that Andrea needed to set her own priorities and would consider the marriage when she was ready to do so.

Phases 2 and 3

In practice, phases 2 and 3 tended to merge. A range of cognitive–behavioral and feminist strategies were used: progressive relaxation, increasing pleasant activities (self-nurturing), stress inoculation, sex-role and power analysis, cognitive restructuring, bibliotherapy, self-disclosure by Ellen, reattribution coaching, homework agreements, problem-solving, role-playing, and assertiveness practice. We summarize these procedures briefly.

Relaxation, stress inoculation, pleasant activities

Ellen suggested that Andrea might be better able to cope with daily hassles at home and work if she were getting more sleep and could learn to relax. Ellen recommended a book that included relaxation instructions as well as other information about depression (*Control Your Depression*, Lewinsohn et al., 1978). Progressive muscle relaxation was taught as a first strategy for helping Andrea to "read" her body signals and to exert more control over her experiences of tension. Andrea was given an audiotape with Ellen's spoken relaxation instructions, which Andrea then used to help herself to sleep at night as well as to return to sleep during periods of insomnia. Ellen showed Andrea how to use her self-monitoring data on sleep periods and ruminative thoughts to evaluate her progress.

Andrea was also coached on how to use coping self-statements in real-life situations (stress inoculation) to strengthen her ability to cope with situational stress (Meichenbaum, 1986). Together they role-played some alternative ways that Andrea could deal with work-related problems. Andrea took to this approach quickly and found it effective in helping her at work to reduce body tension (I can breathe deeply and relax my shoulders) as well as to confront and handle stressors (I can deal with this situation) that interfered with daytime performance. Andrea was pleased with her new competencies and encouraged by early progress in self-managing some of her debilitating patterns.

In addition to working with stress-produced tension and negative self-statements, Ellen recommended that Andrea begin to self-nurture, with time set aside for things that she wanted to do just for herself. Andrea objected at first, saying that she had no time for anything else in her life. Ellen directed her to the *Control Your Depression* workbook (Lewinsohn et al., 1978), and suggested that she begin to monitor her day for those activities that were very enjoyable to her. She was to monitor her mood at those times as well.

Andrea also completed a list of potentially pleasurable activities that were currently absent in her life.

The process of activating Andrea to consider her personal needs and desires each day resulted in her realization of how little pleasure she allowed herself. As a first step, she decided on a project she had been wanting to do "forever", to join a health club and work out every day. Although Ellen suggested taking small steps at first, such as daily walks, Andrea set larger goals for herself. She decided to investigate health clubs near both home and work, and made a commitment to join one and work-out 3 days weekly. This commitment had to be renegotiated several times before Andrea was able to convince herself that she had the time and the energy to carry it through.

Sex-role and power analysis

Andrea and Ellen further explored the work environment, focusing on the characteristics of employment in a male-dominant setting (power analysis) and the messages that women in such situations give themselves (sex-role analysis). Ellen recommended a book on organizational risks for women, *Games Your Mother Never Taught You* (Harrigan, 1977), to help Andrea view her work-related problems in a different light. Andrea was a cooperative client (good girl?) and completed the book in 2 days. She began to see how her isolation from supportive relationships at work, the overbearing, competitive, and seductive behavior of her office-mate, and the discriminatory attitude of her supervisor were contributing to her feelings of incompetence and failure.

For each situational factor, Ellen and Andrea explored together how she was feeling, what she was telling herself (attributions and automatic thoughts), and how her self-talk matched with the realities of these situations. Ellen spoke briefly about how negative thoughts can influence feeling badly about oneself, and that then, feeling incompetent might reciprocally influence her subsequent performance and interactions. Ellen supported Andrea's perceptions of the real power games that existed, but challenged her self-blame (I just stood there and let them do that to me, what a dope I was) and her low sense of self-efficacy for change (I'll never be able to make it in the business world). Andrea was encouraged to perform small "experiments" at work, testing out her hypotheses against the daily events and her responses to them.

At this point, Ellen shared some of her own experience in being the only woman in an all-male department (self-disclosure), and that she also reacted by withdrawing and feeling incompetent, and said nothing to her supervisor when she did not receive a raise her first year when others (all men) did. Andrea was able to reframe her attributions accordingly, and together they explored alternative ways to account for the events at work. Andrea was encouraged then to use her new perceptions to re-evaluate the situation and to view her behavior and outcomes at work in a more positive and self-affirming manner (cognitive restructuring and reattribution).

Problem-solving, role playing, assertiveness

Once Andrea began to determine that her issues at work were related to real discriminatory practices, her anger at what had transpired became overwhelming to her. In her sessions, she alternately wept and raged at the "injustice of the system" and swore to even the score with her office-mate and supervisor. Ellen supported her feelings of rage as legitimate, and helped Andrea consider how she could turn rage into energy for effective action— "How can you deal effectively with what has happened to you and what do you want to do about it now?" Ellen's shared goal was to help empower Andrea to initiate some changes in herself and in her work relationships to increase her positive experiences.

In considering alternatives and how to implement them, Ellen was careful to support Andrea in her personal values that work relationships should be friendly, cooperative, and supportive (Principle III: Valuing the Female Perspective). Although one of Andrea's solutions was to revise her values (I'll just have to become like them—scheming, aggressive, and self-serving), she realized that these traits were alien to her sense of fairness and equity. Ellen pointed out the differences between aggressive and assertive behavior, suggesting that Andrea could choose both positive and negative assertive strategies to improve her work environment.

Ellen and Andrea role-played a range of strategies for altering the situation at work, including asking for a new office-mate, asking for a raise, reporting her office-mate's harassment to a higher administrator, confronting her supervisor on her failure to be promoted, and so on. Each solution was role-played and evaluated for its possible outcomes. Andrea also decided to consider employment in another firm, as she realized that each strategy in her present environment might be useless in changing things. Her decision to look at other job possibilities freed her immensely in being able to try new behaviors at work. When she confronted her supervisor, she was surprised and pleased to find that he agreed to give her a new office. However, the promotion issue was not resolved, and she became more "depressed" with the failure of her new assertiveness to get everything she wanted. For a while she regressed, stopped her exercise program, and said she felt once more like a failure. Earlier cognitive and behavioral strategies were reinstated and Andrea was supported for the progress she had been accomplishing. Depressed women may need continuing support to acknowledge and take credit for their progress (Kaslow, 1989). Toward the end of the counseling sessions, however, Andrea finally found a position as first-line supervisor in another firm. She was ecstatic as she reported on her new horizon, and on her termination session with her own company, in which she confronted them with the reasons why she was leaving. She began to see that the changes in herself enabled her to make effective changes in others. Although she never knew the outcomes of her confrontation with her original firm, she felt very powerful indeed at having been able to tell them what she had experienced. She hoped her information would help other women in that firm, but she was not willing to stay there under present conditions.

Phase 4

The outcome of Phases 1, 2, and 3 was a new sense of self-efficacy for Andrea, as she began to view her problems in a different light, and to take positive action toward change. She felt ready to terminate counseling for a while, even though she had barely touched her marital issues. Ellen supported Andrea's decision to set the marital relationship aside temporarily, giving Andrea time and space to try out a new set of perceptions and behaviors. She left the path open for Andrea to return in the future, suggesting that over time, the marital difficulties might sabotage her new strategies for combating depression (Jacobson, Holtzworth-Munroe, & Schmaling, 1989). Further sessions might involve support and feedback on how Andrea was functioning in the new job, or they might begin to focus on the marriage situation, as Andrea became more prepared to deal with it.

The final issues for Ellen to raise with Andrea concerned maintaining new skills and insights, coping with new situations, and finding a support system. Recall that Andrea scored high on the Young Loneliness Scale and indicated a lack of intimate support in her life. Her post-therapy score was reduced from baseline, but remained uncomfortably high. Since the marital relationship was on hold, Ellen discussed women's support groups and together they explored the possibilities for finding other professional women with similar professional issues (Principle III). Ellen suggested several women's groups in Andrea's work city, and encouraged Andrea to join one. A follow-up telephone call 1 month later revealed that Andrea had joined a Professional Women's Forum, finding three other woman accountants there, and was enjoying the social and professional contacts. She decided to take an evening once a week for herself to meet and socialize with these new friends.

Intervention Strategies—Conclusions

The counseling sessions with Andrea covered a period of 6 months. Although she did not resolve all her presenting problems, particularly with respect to her marriage, her final evaluation (BDI = 9) indicated success in decreasing the depressive symptoms. She was sleeping fairly well, had gained some needed weight, no longer felt sad and hopeless, and was making many positive statements about her life. She felt apprehensive but optimistic about her new job situation, was taking time to renew and nurture herself, and felt a welcome sense of her personal competence and ability to deal with problems as they arose. She no longer believed that her life was a failure, and even viewed her marriage differently (there are some definite problems but perhaps I can work them out—we'll see). We view the combination of cognitive–behavioral and feminist strategies as particularly effective in working with this client.

Summary

An overview of the signs of depression in women included a summary of primary symptoms, the epidemiology of depression, and major hypotheses for the higher incidence of unipolar depression in women as compared to men. Three factors were discussed in relation to women's depression: biological, societal/situational, and sex-role socialization. The case of Andrea was presented as an example of a woman whose depressive symptoms reflected a reaction to her feelings of powerlessness and failure both at home and at work.

Cognitive-behavioral and feminist strategies were combined, using a four-phase model of intervention. The addition of feminist principles and strategies to the more established cognitive-behavioral techniques enabled the client to consider her depressive reactions within the context of societal, situational, and sex-role socialization factors. The outcomes of this time-limited therapy included reduction in symptoms of depression, an increase in self-reported efficacy, a new awareness of work-related variables that serve as barriers to women's achievement, and a more positive and self-affirming style of attribution. Self-initiated changes in the client's work, home, and social situations provided new opportunities for personal development and a renewed sense of control in her life.

Activities

A
Self-assessment: beliefs and facts about depression
After reading this chapter, retake the Self-assessment at the beginning of this chapter to determine if you have revised any of your beliefs or have gained new information.

B
Practicing a feminist case analysis
Assume now that you are Andrea's therapist and that she has returned to
you for a re-examination of her marriage. Once more, her husband will not
join the counseling sessions. Review the four-phase model presented in this
chapter, and the strategies that were used to assist Andrea with her work-
related issues. List and discuss briefly:

(1)   What issues should be addressed now with Andrea.
(2)   How Feminist Principles would enter the therapy process now.
(3)   Which cognitive–behavioral procedures appear relevant.

How can you be of help to Andrea if her husband is a non-participant?
    Pair yourself with a partner and role-play one session with "Andrea",
addressing the issues outlined above. Reverse roles and see if your partner
would confront it differently.

Further Readings

In order to further your understanding of cognitive and behavioral approaches to the
treatment of depression, you may want to read the following resources. Please note,
however, that each approach contains strategies that may need to be modified in
order to increase its compatibility with feminist principles.

Beck, A. T., & Young, J. E. (1985). Depression. In D. H. Barlow (Ed.) *Clinical
    Handbook of Psychological Disorders: A Step-by-step Treatment Manual* (pp.
    206–244). New York: Guilford.
Lewinsohn, P. M., Antonuccio, D. O., Steinmetz, J. L., & Teri, L. (1984). *The
    Coping with Depression Course: A Psychoeducational Treatment for Unipolar
    Depression.* Eugene, OR: Castalia.
Nolen-Hoeksema, S. (1990). *Sex Differences in Depression.* Stanford, CA: Stanford
    University Press.
Williams, M. G. (1984). *The Psychological Treatment of Depression.* New York: The
    Free Press.

CHAPTER 8

Surviving Sexual Assault

Self-assessment: Beliefs About Rape

The beliefs and knowledge you possess about rape influence how you respond therapeutically to clients who are rape survivors. For each statement below, check the space that best represents your belief about rape.

		Agree	Uncertain	Disagree
(1)	Women often say they have been raped in order to protect their reputation.	⎯	⎯	⎯
(2)	Only young and beautiful women are raped.	⎯	⎯	⎯
(3)	Women cannot always prevent being raped by resisting their attackers.	⎯	⎯	⎯
(4)	Men rape because they experience uncontrollable sexual urges.	⎯	⎯	⎯
(5)	Most reported sexual assaults are true.	⎯	⎯	⎯
(6)	Most women secretly desire to be raped.	⎯	⎯	⎯
(7)	Most rapes are not reported to the police.	⎯	⎯	⎯
(8)	Most women who are raped are raped by someone they know.	⎯	⎯	⎯
(9)	Sexually experienced women are not really damaged by rape.	⎯	⎯	⎯

	Agree	Uncertain	Disagree
(10) Women who dress in a sexually seductive way provoke rape.	____	____	____
(11) Sexual assaults usually occur away from a woman's home—in isolated or dark areas.	____	____	____
(12) A rapist cannot be identified by his appearance and general behavior.	____	____	____

Scoring

Statements 1, 2, 4, 6, 9, 10, and 11 represent common myths about rape. If you marked "Disagree" to these seven items and agree to statements 3, 5, 7, 8, and 12 (which represent facts about rape), then you possess accurate and non-victim-blaming beliefs and knowledge about rape. These 12 statements are discussed in further detail on pages 199 and 200.

Overview

The negative consequences of sex-role stereotyping of both women and men and of institutionalized sexism are most clearly reflected in the violence against women which is so prevalent in our society. Increasing numbers of our clients come to us directly or indirectly because they have been victims of adult rape, childhood sexual abuse and/or spouse abuse. Feminist therapists must be knowledgeable about the occurrences of violence in women's lives, the impact of those traumas on women, and therapeutic strategies that facilitate healing from these traumas. In Chapter 4, we briefly overviewed feminist therapy interventions with an adult survivor of incest, and in Chapter 9 we will discuss feminist interventions with victims of spouse abuse. In this chapter, we describe an Empowerment Feminist Therapy approach to working with Susan, a survivor of an adult rape. In addition, we discuss the prevalence of rape, rape myths, and assessment procedures for identifying sexual assault survivors. Intervention strategies for Susan include sex-role analysis, cultural (power) analysis of rape, cognitive restructuring, desensitization, emotional catharsis, and behavioral management of fears, flashbacks and triggers.

The purpose of this chapter is to help readers:

(1) Understand the cultural context of rape.
(2) Distinguish between rape myths and facts.
(3) Develop a definition of rape compatible with a feminist therapy approach.
(4) Recognize the symptoms associated with rape trauma.
(5) Become familiar with the stages of recovery from rape trauma.
(6) Become familiar with an Empowerment Feminist Therapy model for counseling rape survivors.

Susan's Story: Delayed Post-traumatic (Rape) Reaction

Susan, a 30-year-old married teacher, was referred by the local rape crisis center for therapy. She had called them because she began having nightmares about a forced sexual encounter she had while on a date in college. She reported waking up and feeling very anxious.

> I wake up three or four mornings a week in a state of terror. My heart races and it's hard for me to move. My last dream reminded me of a bad experience I had in college when my date drove to an isolated part of town, held me down and threatened to beat me up unless I had sex with him. I tried to get away, but couldn't. I gave up fighting. But my reactions don't make sense. That experience was 10 years ago and I didn't react much at the time. I felt lucky not to have been physically hurt and I felt pretty stupid to have gotten myself in such a predicament. I didn't tell anyone until last week when I called the crisis line. I feel like I'm going crazy. I just don't get this overpowered by things.

During the first session, Susan revealed that although she and her husband have a happy marriage, recently she had started feeling irritated with him in the middle of making love—"for no reason".

In addition to the nightmares, Susan began having flashbacks about her rape where she would see the rape happening over and over again and would feel like she was back in it. She also reported feeling "different" from others and isolated from them. At first, Susan had great difficulty in talking about her traumatic experience. Eventually she was able to relate the details of her experience to Amy, her therapist. She gave the following description:

> A male friend of mine suggested that I go on a blind date with a friend of his who was coming to visit for the weekend. This guy, Brian, was a "big-man-on campus" at a neighboring university, so I agreed to go. We went out for dinner and then went to a fraternity party. Brian was a charming companion and I was flattered by his interest in me. Over the course of the evening, Brian and I had a couple of drinks, but towards the end of the evening Brian began drinking a lot. I wanted to walk back to my dormitory, but he insisted that he was sober enough to drive.
>
> Instead of going directly to my dorm, he turned toward the west side of town

where there were a number of small farms. When I questioned him, he said he wanted to show me a beautiful view of the night sky. He pulled off onto a private road and stopped the car in an isolated meadow. He began to kiss me and put his hands on my breasts. I did not want to have sex with him. I was a virgin. I pushed him away and told him that I wanted to go back to my dorm. He responded very coldly that he was not going to take "no" for an answer. Suddenly he was very different from the charmer he had been all evening.

He ripped open my blouse and I struggled to get free, but he was just too strong. He let me know that one way or another we were going to have sex, that we could do it with or without my being hurt. I felt paralyzed and numb. He took off my skirt and underwear easily because I stopped struggling. He dropped his trousers. While he held me down by my wrists, he ordered me to put his penis in my mouth. The whole idea nauseated me, but I complied. I remember thinking that if he would just ejaculate, everything would be over. Instead, after he came, he put his mouth on my genitals and tried to stimulate me. I felt so invaded and I was terrified that he would never let me go. I left my body at some point and became an observer. I don't remember many more details. Somehow I got my clothes on and he took me back to the dorm. He warned me not to tell anyone, saying no one would believe that I hadn't consented. Besides, he would tell everybody that I was a tramp. I went into the dorm, took a long shower, and said nothing to anyone.

Assessment

Susan's nightmares, flashbacks, feelings of fear, and negative reactions during sex are consistent with a delayed post-traumatic stress (PTSD) reaction to her rape experience. Although the details of Susan's nightmares allowed her to connect them with her earlier rape, many survivors experience symptoms which are not as clearly related to their rapes. Thus, feminist therapists must be knowledgeable about typical symptoms/reactions connected with sexual trauma. These reactions include depression, sleep disturbance, nightmares, flashbacks, anxiety or fear reactions, inability to concentrate, sexual dysfunction, interpersonal conflicts, guilt and shame, anger and rage, lowered self-esteem, loss of trust in self and others, and disturbance in typical eating patterns. Therapists who encounter clients displaying several of these symptoms should ask them about previous unwanted or unpleasant sexual experiences. Further, Russell (1986b) found that 65% of incest survivors in her survey study had been raped as adults, whereas 35% of non-incest survivors had been raped as adults. Thus, any client who has been raped as an adult should be assessed for possible childhood sexual abuse.

Since depression is a common long-term reaction to rape, instruments like the Beck Depression Inventory (BDI) (Beck et al., 1961) are often useful diagnostic tools with rape survivors. They can also help assess for suicide risk. Susan was given the BDI at several points in her therapy. In addition, she was given the Impact of Event Scale (IES) (Horowitz, Wilner, & Alvarez, 1979) to assess the frequency of her avoidance and intrusive responses, both of which are common to trauma survivors. While the IES has been used primarily in trauma research rather than therapeutically, we believe that it can provide useful clinical information. Susan also completed a life history questionnaire which inquired about her developmental history, her current functioning in a variety of areas, and her use of various drugs, including alcohol. At the beginning of therapy, Susan's IES Intrusion score was high and her Avoidance score was in the moderate range, indicating that the memories of her rape were intruding psychologically, and that in part she was trying to cope by avoiding them. Her BDI score indicated that she was not clinically depressed initially, although she did become mildly depressed at several points in therapy. Her life history questionnaire seemed to indicate a relatively happy childhood, although she did grow up feeling less physically attractive than her older sister. Nothing else was remarkable on the questionnaire. Susan and her therapist decided to focus therapeutically on the experience with Brian and its traumatic after-effects.

The duration and intensity of rape-related reactions vary depending on situational circumstances, what recovery stage the survivor is in, and how the symptoms are reacted to by others. Both delayed reactions and long-term, on-going symptoms have been found in rape survivors (Burgess & Holmstrom, 1979; Sutherland & Scherl, 1970; Zollicoffer, 1989).

Cultural Analysis of Rape

Rape occurs in a social context. Rape cannot be understood apart from that context, and the woman who has been raped cannot be treated effectively without understanding that context. A cultural analysis of Western societies shows that we live in a society that often condones rape, misdefines it, blames victims for its occurrence, sets up women to be raped and men to be rapists, and offers inadequate services to aid survivors in their long-term recovery. The existence of rape and trauma from rape is strongly influenced by what a society teaches about rape, how it sex-role-socializes women and men, and by the power differentials that exist between women and men (Sanday, 1981). Thus, a *cultural analysis* of rape includes an *analysis of rape myths*, a *sex-role analysis*, and a *power analysis*. In the next sections, we present a brief overview of these three areas.

Rape Myths

At the beginning of this chapter you responded to 12 statements which reflected rape myths and facts. Facts about rape often directly contradict the cultural myths about rape perpetuated by our society. For instance, most rapes occur not in "dark alleys" but in familiar locations, especially in victim's homes. In addition, at least 50% of rapes are committed by a person who is known to the victim, i.e. acquaintance rapes (Zollicoffer, 1989). Women of all ages and of all physical statures have been raped. Women do not unconsciously desire to be raped, neither do they provoke rape by their appearance or actions. Women cannot always stop a rape attempt by fighting back. In some cases, physical resistance may stop a rape; in others, it may lead to escalation of violence and greater physical injury in the victim.

Rapes are rarely reported to the police. In contrast to the myth that a woman "cries rape" to protect her reputation or to seek revenge, the truth is that many women who are raped do not report the incident. Victims of acquaintance rape are less likely to report the rape to authorities and are more likely to tell no one about their rape (Koss, 1985). Because acquaintance rapes differ markedly from society's definition of rape, many acquaintance rape survivors do not even label their forced sexual experience as "rape" (Koss, 1985). For example, Susan did not refer to her experience as "rape" until she had been in therapy for a while. By learning about rape myths and facts in counseling through a cultural analysis of rape, Susan was able to acknowledge that she had been raped. Further, rapists do not commit rape because of uncontrollable sexual urges. Research indicates that the primary motives for rape are aggression and need to control/subjugate (Groth, Burgess, & Holmstrom, 1977). That is, rape is a violent and aggressive act which is accomplished through sexual behavior. Rapists cannot be identified by their appearance, socioeconomic status, or educational level. Many rapists are married or have regular sexual partners.

Belief in rape myths contributes to people "blaming the victim" for being raped and excusing the rapist's acts.

Sex-role Analysis

The incidence of rape in a society is related both to sex-role socialization of women and men and to a hierarchical power distribution in which women are dominated by men (Sanday, 1981). Through a cross-cultural analysis of 95 societies, Sanday was able to categorize about half of these as "rape-free" societies, where sexual assault did not occur or occurred infrequently. The other half were labeled "rape-present" or rape-prone societies. Rape-prone societies were characterized by a tolerance for violence; encouragement of men to be aggressive; isolation of the sexes; devaluation of female traits and activities, especially nurturance and childcare; non-involvement of men in childcare; and promotion of male dominance over females. She concluded that the way a society sex-role-socializes its females and males determines whether it will be a rape-free or rape-prone society.

Sex-role prescriptions for women

Weis and Borges (1977) discuss how sex-role socialization and dating rituals in Western society contribute to the prevalence of rape. The following sex-role prescriptions for women set them up to be victims.

(1)   Women are property of men.
(2)   Women are responsible for controlling men's sexual behavior.
(3)   Women need to be protected by men.
(4)   Women should be kind, gentle, and physically non-aggressive.
(5)   Women should not be physically strong.
(6)   Women should always be polite.
(7)   Women should be dependent on men, passive and child-like.

Weis and Borges (1977) conclude that women are socialized to ". . . internalize the psychological characteristics of defenseless victims who have not learned or cannot apply the techniques of self-defense and so must rely upon the protection of others" (p. 47). In an acquaintance rape, their protector is often the rapist.

Sex-role prescriptions for men

Men are socialized to be sexually assertive and/or sexually aggressive by the following sex-role messages:

(1)   Men should be physically aggressive, powerful and controlling.
(2)   Sex is to be viewed as a conquest. Women who say "no" really mean "maybe".
(3)   Men should pay for dates and women should "reimburse" them sexually.
(4)   Women are the possessions of the men who protect them.
(5)   Women are sexual objects.
(6)   Men should initiate sex and dominate women.
(7)   Men should be the boss and women should obey men.

Thus, many males are socialized to be sexually aggressive, to view women as sexual objects, and to expect to be obeyed. These messages help set the stage for sexually aggressive behavior by some men. These lessons also help blur the distinction between seduction and rape for these men. For example, Remer and Witten (1988) found that men perceive more commonality between rape and seduction than do women, who see more commonality between rape and assault. Additionally, over-identification with the "macho" role may lead some men to adopt a rapist attitude. Such men may validate their masculinity by intimidating women and sexually aggressing against them. Malamuth (1981) found that 35% of college male subjects indicated a likelihood of raping a woman if they believed they would not get caught and punished.

Power Analysis

As a group, men have more economic, physical, role, resource, and political power than most women. In relation to rape, a man can use his more powerful position to coerce a woman into sexual acts or can use his physical power (or threats) to overcome a woman's resistance. His role and economic power make it harder for her to report a rape. Her lower social value makes it less likely that she will be believed and more likely that she will be blamed for the rape (Weis & Borges, 1977).

Interaction Effects

Sex-role messages interact with male power dominance and with rape myths to produce a *rape victimization* process. Weis and Borges (1977) define *victimization* as " . . . the social process that before, during, and after the event simultaneously renders the victim defenseless and even partly responsible for it" (p. 35). Thus, our society teaches women to accept responsibility for victimizing events that befall them, and teaches men to legitimize their sexual aggression against women. Further, this process makes it less likely that women will report or even talk about their sexual assault experiences because they are likely to be blamed for them: "Led to believe that she is responsible for any sexual outcome and faced with an unsupportive social environment . . ., the woman experiences herself as having only the choice of responsibility and self-blame, or denial" (Koss & Burkhart, 1989, p. 35). Thus, most women live in fear of being raped and rape survivors become stigmatized and isolated.

Definition and Prevalence of Rape

Definition of Rape

A variety of definitions can and are applied to the word "rape". Although legal definitions vary from state to state in the United States, the most common legal definition of rape involves sexual intercourse by forcible compulsion with a woman who is not one's wife. This definition is not compatible with feminist counseling because it is so narrow, e.g. sexual acts other than penile penetration of a vagina, rape of a woman by her husband,

and rape of a male are excluded. Legal definitions of rape exclude the experience of many rape survivors. A clinical definition of rape needs to be more encompassing of our clients' rape experiences.

The definition of rape that therapists use is influenced by their attitudes and experiences and, in turn, influences their reactions to clients who have been raped. As we discuss throughout this book, feminist therapists examine carefully their attitudes and values in relation to their clients' issues and are open with their clients about these views. Feminist therapists who work with sexual assault survivors need to be aware of their own rape myths and sex-role stereotyping and work to change those attitudes and beliefs that will revictimize their clients. Feminist therapists use definitions of rape which are encompassing of a wide variety of rape experiences and which do not "blame the victim".

A definition of rape is difficult to agree upon, even for feminist therapists. As we wrote this chapter, we wrestled with finding a definition with which we both could live. One of us felt that defining rape very broadly, i.e. "any sexual activity imposed on one person by another", was crucial so as to be comprehensive and inclusive. The other felt that a definition of rape needed to be specific enough, i.e. "any coerced sexual activity in which a part of the body is penetrated", so that rape was distinct from other terms, e.g. sexual harassment. We both wanted a definition that: (a) included various kinds of sexual activity, not just penile penetration of a vagina; (b) included various kinds of force or threat of force; and (c) included coerced sexual activity to a variety of victims.

In a research study by Koss (1985), sexual victimization was operationalized along four levels: highly sexually victimized, moderately sexually victimized, low sexually victimized, and not sexually victimized (see Table 8.1 for her definitions). We have included her definitions as well as both of ours so that you can arrive at your own definition of rape and/or sexual victimization.

Prevalence of Rape

Estimates about the prevalence or incidence rates for rape vary according to the definition of rape used and the methods for gathering the data. Further, the number of unreported and unacknowledged rapes makes accurate tabulations of rape incidences difficult.

Russell and Howell (1983) found that 46% of women in their prevalence study had experienced a rape or attempted rape during their adult lives. In Koss's (1985) study of college women, 12.7% of the respondents fell into the highly sexually victimized group, 24% into the moderately sexually victimized group, 17.9% into the low sexually victimized group and 37.6% met the criteria for the not sexually victimized group. Thus, 62.4% of the women in her study had experienced some kind of sexual victimization.

Table 8.1. *Koss's (1985) Categories of Sexual Victimization*

Category	Definition	Respondents in group (%)	Group members who indicated they had been raped (%)
Highly sexually victimized	Experienced ". . . at any time in the past, oral, anal or vaginal intercourse against their will through the use of force or threat of force" (p. 196)	12.7	57
Moderately sexually victimized	"Experienced sexual contact (fondling, kissing) or attempted sexual intercourse against their consent through the use of force or threat of force" (p. 196)	24.0	0
Low sexually victimized	Experienced "sexual intercourse when they did not desire it subsequent to the use of extreme verbal coercion, insistent arguments, false promises, or threats to end the relationship . . ." (p. 196)	17.9	0
Not sexually victimized	Did not experience any of the above	37.6	0

Koss (1985) also asked all respondents if they had been raped. Of those who were highly sexually victimized ($n = 256$), only 57% said they had been raped. Koss called this subgroup *acknowledged rape victims*. Thirty-one per cent of these acknowledged rape victims were romantically involved with the perpetrator, and 48% had not told anyone about their rape. Forty-three per cent who were highly sexually victimized said that they had not been raped, even though they met the legal definition of rape. Koss called this subgroup *unacknowledged rape victims*. In the unacknowledged group, more than 50% had not told anyone. One hundred per cent had not reported to the police, a hospital or a rape crisis center, and 76% were romantically involved with the perpetrator. Thus, even when a woman experiences an event that meets the legal definition of rape, she may not self-define that event as rape, and this unacknowledgement of the rape is more likely when the victim and perpetrator are romantically involved, e.g. date rape.

Far from being a rare occurrence, rape is a common happening in many women's lives. The "usual" figure for adult rapes is that one in four women will be raped at least once during their adult lives. Note that this figure does not even include sexual assault experiences that occur in childhood.

Stages of Coping with Rape

Before describing the therapeutic interventions used to facilitate Susan's resolution of her trauma, it is important to understand the reactions that rape victims have to being raped. Weis and Borges (1977) describe rape as ". . . a total attack against the whole person, affecting the victim's physical, psychological, and social identity" (p. 72). Rape victims experience loss of control, fear for their lives, and physical violation of their bodies. "Directed, focused, intentional harm involving the most intimate interpersonal act—that is the nature of rape" (Koss & Burkhart, 1989, p. 31).

Models of Coping

Several writers have proposed rape response stage models for understanding victims' short and long-term reactions to rape. Burgess and Holmstrom (1979) suggested a two-stage model which they labeled Rape Trauma Syndrome. Their first stage is the *acute stage*, which encompasses the immediate crisis period following the rape. This is a period of disorganization, intense fear, and shock and exhaustion. Their second stage is called *long-term reorganization*, which covers the remainder of the recovery period, lasting months or even years. Sutherland and Scherl (1970) proposed a three-stage model. Their first stage, *acute reaction*, is similar to Burgess and Holmstrom's first stage. Their second stage, *outward adjustment*, is a time during which the victim attempts to get her life back together and, in so doing, often denies or suppresses thoughts of the rape and of its negative consequences on her life. Their third stage, *integration and resolution*, begins as the survivor's denial breaks down. During this stage, victims become depressed and begin re-experiencing the rape through nightmares and flashbacks. Those victims who successfully navigate this stage resolve their feelings about having been raped.

An Empowerment Model for Counseling Rape Survivors

Remer (1986) developed a feminist-oriented stage model which is an elaboration of Sutherland and Scherl's (1970) stages. This model also delineates client needs and counseling strategies for each stage. Remer's model provided the underlying structure for Susan's therapy.

Stage One: pre-rape

Since rape occurs in a social context of cultural norms and myths that misdefine rape and blame victims, Stage One of the Remer model, *the pre-rape stage*, includes all of the life experiences, sex-role socialization and all the societal depictions of rape myths that a woman has had prior to being raped. The woman's learning at this stage influences how she will feel and behave during and after the rape, and even whether she defines her forced sexual activity as "rape."

Stage One also includes all women living with the constant fear of being raped. Within this stage many feminist therapists work politically and preventively to bring about changes in people's attitudes toward rape, in laws related to rape, and in the services and support available to rape survivors. Inclusion of this stage in the model underscores Feminist Therapy Principle I, The Personal Is Political. Stage One emphasizes that sexism is institutionalized in our rape laws, court procedures, and blaming of rape victims, and that sex-role stereotyping and institutionalized sexism contribute to the prevalence of rape.

During Susan's counseling, she and her therapist did a cultural analysis of rape in general, and more specifically of Susan's pre-rape personal learning about rape, so that Susan could understand more clearly her reactions during and after the rape. This analysis was a crucial factor in Susan's ability to stop blaming herself for her rape and in coming to define the event as rape.

Stage Two: rape event

Stage Two, the *rape event*, includes all the events immediately preceding, during, and following the rape. The rapist's behavior, the situation, and the victim's reactions are important details for the client to share with the therapist. Figley (1985) suggests that therapists' knowledge of the trauma details enables them to refute clients' erroneous self-blaming.

The events immediately preceding the rape often influence whether the potential victim senses danger. For example, if the assailant is an acquaintance whom she trusts, she will interpret his actions leading up to the rape in the context of that trust and is unlikely to realize she is in danger. Further, whatever the circumstances, the victim initially may deny the reality of what is happening to her. The more "time lag" there is in realizing the danger, the less likely it is that the victim will be able to escape (Weis & Borges, 1977). The awareness of danger often begins vaguely and increases. The awareness depends on actual cues present and on the victim's prior learning. Victims often report feeling confused (Zollicoffer, 1989).

Once the reality of the rape is acknowledged, victims use a range of coping strategies. In a study of 88 rape survivors, Zollicoffer (1989) found that survivors reasoned with the rapist (54.5%), struggled (44.3%), remained motionless and quiet (43.2%), pleaded (40.9%), numbed out (36.8%), cried (35.2%), and screamed (18.2%). Victims experience a wide range of emotions during the rape. The survivors in Zollicoffer's study reported feeling afraid (81.8%), helpless (80.7%), overwhelmed (65.9%), confused

(60.2%), fear for their lives (59.1%), disgusted (46.6%), angry (38.6%), guilty (35.2%), and physical pain (33%). In Zollicoffer's study, rapists were reported to use various forms of coercion. Rapists physically entrapped victims (75%), made verbal threats (56.8%), physically restrained victims (56.8%), threatened physical harm (54.5%), shoved and hit victims (40.9%), and displayed a weapon (37.5%). In this study, 87.5% of the assaults involved vaginal sexual violations, 40.9% involved oral sexual violations, and 9.1% involved anal sexual violations.

Victims' needs during Stage Two are first to escape being raped. When they fail to escape, they focus on getting through the rape alive and on minimizing physical and psychological damage. Victims dissociating from their physical bodies and perceiving time distortion are common.

Feminist therapists who work with sexual abuse survivors must be clear within themselves that the rape victim is never to blame for the rape. As we hear the details of a client's rape events, we need to listen for how the client's actions were influenced by her own myths about rape and by her sex-role-socialization process. Two examples help illustrate this point. First, a rape victim who has been taught that rape is committed by strangers in dark alleys is less likely to perceive that she is in danger of being raped by someone she knows early enough in the encounter to enable her to prevent the assault or escape. Second, for most rape survivors there is a point in the rape in which they realize that they are unable to escape being raped. Their behavior changes from trying to stop the rape to trying to get through the rape. In retrospect, these victims may blame themselves for not being able to see the danger and escape, or for not being able to fight off the attack. By examining their own misconceptions about rape contribute to their self-blame, they can lessen their shame and guilt, and begin to appreciate what they did to survive. Susan reported that sharing the details of her rape with her non-blaming counselor, while difficult, helped her to feel less isolated and alone as well as to feel less guilty.

Stage Three: crisis and disorganization

Stage Three, crisis and disorganization, encompasses the crisis period immediately following the rape. Victims are often in a state of shock, feel helpless and out of control, and feel ashamed, confused, and guilty. Their feeling reactions may vary from numbness to hysterical crying. This stage may vary in length from a few hours to a year, depending on the choices the survivor makes (e.g. whether to prosecute) and the coping strategies she uses. During this stage she is especially vulnerable to negative, blaming reactions by others. Negative reactions revictimize the survivor. These "second wounds" (Brickman et al., 1982) become part of the rape trauma that needs to be healed.

Women may contact rape crisis centers during this stage. A therapist counseling a recent survivor may benefit from consultation with a rape crisis center, if one is available. The victim's needs during this stage include regaining a sense of control over self, making decisions about reporting, medical care and disclosure to others, being accepted and understood, and not being revictimized. Decisions about reporting and disclosure are especially conflictual, as victims often accurately fear that others will blame them for being raped. Useful counseling strategies at this stage include information-giving about legal and medical procedures and about community support services available, teaching decision-making skills, open-ended questions, primary empathy, and supporting the victim as she implements her decisions. Therapists must be careful to allow and/or encourage survivors to make their own decisions about disclosures and pursuing medical and legal services. Attempts to steer clients in a particular direction take away their control yet another time and thus, revictimize them.

Stage Four: outward satisfactory adjustment and denial

Survivors attempt to get their life back to normal in Stage Four. To accomplish this they attempt to avoid thinking about the rape through various uses of denial, suppression, and minimization. These avoidance strategies can include forgetting they were raped, not defining what happened to them as rape, denying there were any negative consequences to them from the rape, believing they have "made up" their memories of being raped, minimizing the impact of their rape by seeing themselves as "less hurt" than other survivors, and repressing some details of the rape. While this stage is often a useful resting place and a time in which survivors regain some sense of control over their lives, there are often negative impacts of the rape, e.g. nightmares or unexplained depression, which they may or may not connect to their rapes. Some survivors move on to Stage Five in a matter of months. Others, like Susan, may stay in the denial stage for many years. Many women never move beyond Stage Four. A survivor's needs in Stage Four are to have a sense of control over her life and to be allowed to cope with the rape memories as she is able. Therapists need to respect the client's coping strategies as well as to help the client begin to see connections between the symptoms she is having and her rape. This is a tight-rope walk for the therapist.

Stage Five: reliving and working through

The victim's denial gradually or suddenly lifts in Stage Five. She often begins to have intrusive nightmares and flashbacks about the rape, reliving vividly the rape events. In many ways, her reactions are similar to those of the crisis stage and, in fact, many survivors report feeling as if they had been raped "yesterday" instead of years earlier. Susan reported that she did not understand having such strong, delayed emotional reactions and wondered whether she was going crazy. Her therapist, Amy, assured her that her reactions were normal and were typical responses to traumatization. The negative effects of the rape must be worked through in order for the survivor to move to Stage Six.

Stage Six: resolution and integration

The survivor positively integrates the rape into her life in Stage Six, making it an undenied part of her identity. She has worked through most of the negative consequences of the rape and comes to accept the rape as a part of her life. This process involves making existential sense of the meaning of having been raped. (See Table 8.3 for examples of changes in existential beliefs.) She enhances her existing coping skills. In addition, she comes to a fuller appreciation of the strengths that helped her survive the rape. She moves from being a Victim to being a Survivor. She does not "recover" from the rape, but rather "integrates" it. Additionally, survivors often get involved in bringing about societal changes regarding rape or in helping other rape victims. Many of these societal changes worked for by survivors during Stage Six cycle back to become preventive strategies for Stage One. In writing about her own rape, Katz (1984) captures the essence of this coming back full circle: "It is only through shared experience, understanding and action that we can create change. That is the purpose of this testimony. For I am a survivor and the role of the survivor is to testify" (p. 102). Stages Five and Six will be described in more detail as Susan's therapy is summarized.

Susan's Story: A Therapeutic Journey

The Empowerment Feminist Therapy approach to counseling Susan, which we present here, is firmly built on the three Feminist Therapy Principles. First, in accordance with Principle I, The Personal Is Political, the societal context of rape is explored with the client. The rapist is held fully responsible for his actions and the victim is never blamed. The victim is helped to see that the rape was not her fault and to challenge others' negative reactions to her. In relation to Principles II and III, Egalitarian Relationships and Valuing the Female Perspective, the client is treated as an expert on her own experience by being believed and not blamed, and by being encouraged to trust her perceptions of what happened during the rape, even though they do not fit society's views of rape. She is helped to develop a definition of rape that encompasses her own experience. The client's coping strategies are redefined as positive and as survival-oriented. The client is a full, collaborative partner in setting therapy goals. She is encouraged to take back control of her life. The therapist teaches the client about the trauma recovery process and helps her to see how her reactions are normal given the trauma she has survived (Scurfield, 1985). She is not pathologized. The therapist self-discloses appropriately. She shares her own related experiences to living in our rape-prone culture. If she is a survivor herself, she shares relevant aspects of her rape and of her reactions. Clients are encouraged to join a rape therapy or support group in order to reduce their isolation and stigmatization.

Susan was in Stage Five, *Reliving and Working Through*, when she sought out therapy. We chose to focus on Susan's case because it is during Stage Five that many women seek out counseling, and very little is written about therapeutic interventions for Stages Five and Six. Space will not allow us to present a comprehensive therapeutic plan for working with Susan. Rather we will highlight the aspects of her therapy that emphasize Feminist Therapy Principles. Susan's therapist, Amy, is a feminist therapist and a psycho-dramatist. Although we described Stages Five and Six earlier, we will discuss them more specifically as we explore Susan's therapy.

Stage Five: Reliving and Working Through

Behavioral, cognitive, and affective counseling techniques facilitate a survivor's resolution of rape trauma. Since the trauma usually taxes the victim's coping skills, survivors often need to learn additional coping skills, especially strategies for managing flashbacks. Previous beliefs about self, the world, and rape often need to be restructured in order to incorporate and resolve the trauma. Feelings related to the rape and its aftermath need to be expressed, accepted, and validated. Thus, Susan's counseling included behavioral, cognitive, and affective focused interventions.

Normalizing responses to trauma

After building a trust relationship with Susan, her therapist began to give Susan information about the trauma recovery process so that Susan could see the normality of her reactions. Amy shared the six stages of the Remer model with Susan, encouraging Susan to comment on how the model fitted or did not fit with her experience. Amy's therapeutic approach was in part based on the trauma stress models proposed by Figley (1985) and Scurfield (1985). These models emphasize common "normal" reactions to trauma experiences, as opposed to describing survivors' reactions/symptoms as pathological. Amy showed her Scurfield's (1985) six educational statements about trauma reactions. These include the ideas that trauma can produce symptoms in anyone, that flashbacks etc. are expected and normal, and that healing from trauma is possible. Susan was relieved to learn that her reactions were normal and to have both a map and hope for her recovery.

Identifying and sharing the traumatic events

Since Amy was a rape survivor herself, she self-disclosed to Susan relevant aspects of her own history and feelings. Susan was encouraged to share the details of her rape at her own pace. Amy facilitated this process by asking Susan to be as specific as possible and by psychodramatically doubling Susan's feelings. Psychodramatic enactment of parts of the rape helped Susan reclaim some pieces of the rape event that she had forgotten, as well as to begin to express the feelings she had not been able to express during and after the rape. Feelings which many rape survivors need to express include fear and powerlessness, rage, anger, sadness, shame, guilt, and isolation. Expression of feelings associated with the rape and its aftermath in the presence of non-blaming, supportive others facilitates healing. Re-experiencing feelings associated with the rape helps confront cognitions which have minimized the severity of the rape and its aftermath. For example, Susan initially stated that, "My rape wasn't too bad. I got off lucky because he didn't force me to have intercourse." After sharing her rape event details with Amy and expressing her anguish and rage, Susan said, "I was very traumatized by my rape. I felt paralyzed with fear and was so invaded by him. He robbed me of my relaxed enjoyment of sex even before I got to know much about it. I feel so angry with him."

Recapitulation of the details of the trauma and the accompanying feelings also facilitates desensitization to the trauma. Amy's knowledge of the details of Susan's rape was also crucial to helping Susan refute her self-blame and to helping her identify the triggers for her flashbacks. (Therapeutic strategies for coping with flashbacks are presented in a subsequent section.)

Making the personal political

Susan and Amy did a cultural analysis of rape which followed the format we presented previously. Information-giving by Amy and self-analysis by Susan were the foundation of this analysis. Susan discovered that she had learned and internalized that rapists were always strangers who jumped their victims in dark alleys, that women should be able to fight off rape attacks, that it is the woman's fault if she allows herself to get in a dangerous situation, and that forced types of sexual activity that were not vaginal–penile intercourse were not rape. She had not classified her experience with Brian as "rape" because it did not match any of her learned messages about rape. As a female who was raised to be polite, to trust male acquaintances as her protectors, and not to be physically aggressive, Susan had a difficult time

Table 8.2. *Susan's Restructured Cognitions*

Self-blame cognitions	Restructured cognitions
"I should have been able to see that he was dangerous"	"He deliberately portrayed himself as trustworthy and hid his dangerousness from me" "Society misled me to believe that only strangers commit rape"
"I should have prosecuted"	"Given the laws at the time and the circumstances of my rape, he probably would not have been convicted and I probably would have been traumatized further. I made a good decision"
"I should have fought harder and longer"	"He was larger and stronger than I. If I had fought more, I might have been more physically hurt and I probably still wouldn't have been able to avoid being raped"
"The rape was my fault"	"I did nothing for which I deserved to be raped. Brian is fully responsible for having raped me"

perceiving that she was in danger and in physically defending herself. She also believed that she should have been able to identify that Brian was dangerous. Amy shared facts about rape with Susan, e.g. that about 60% of rapes are acquaintance rapes, that rapists generally are *not* crazy men who are readily identifiable. Further, she explained that acquaintance rapists often deliberately behave in a trustworthy manner so as to gain the intended victim's trust in order to set her up. Thus, Susan was able to see that she did not have clear signals to let her know she was in danger.

Processing all of this analysis and information helped Susan change her self-blame attributions and reduce her guilt. (See Table 8.2 for examples of cognition changes Susan made as a part of her healing process.) Further, her actions during and after the rape began to make more sense to her. She began to appreciate that by stopping her struggling, she protected herself from further physical damage. She began to understand that her decision not to report the rape or tell anyone about it were typical responses for an acquaintance rape victim. Her silence may have shielded her from probable blame and stigmatization. Thus, she also began to perceive that many of her responses during and after the rape, rather than being inadequate, were actually effective coping strategies.

Restructuring self-blame

Rape survivors often feel ashamed and guilty about having been raped (Veronen, Kilpatrick, & Resick, 1979; Wortman, 1983). The shame and guilt may result from self-blame, blame from others, stigmatization, societal rape myths, and shattered assumptions about the self and the world. Self-blame has been found by researchers to have differential effects on the long-term recovery process. For example, Janoff-Bulman (1979) pointed out that in attributing the responsibility for the rape to an external agent, e.g. the rapist or society, the survivor gives up a sense of personal control. In a study designed to assess the role of self-blame in recovery, Janoff-Bulman divided self-blame into two sub-categories. Survivors who blame their enduring personality characteristics, e.g. "I was raped because I am a slut," were classified as using "characterological self-blame." Survivors who blamed their behaviors, e.g. "I should have locked the window," were classified as using "behavioral self-blame". Janoff-Bulman found that characterological self-blame was associated with depression, and that behavioral self-blame was associated with more positive coping outcomes. Janoff-Bulman (1985) concluded that: "While the behavioral self-blamer is concerned with the future and the avoidability of misfortune, the characterological self-blamer focuses on the past and the question of deservedness, rather than avoidability" (p. 29).

In contrast to Janoff-Bulman's findings, Meyer and Taylor (1986) identified three kinds of blame attributions: (a) judgment or behavioral self-blame; (b) victim type or characterological self-blame; and (c) societal factors or non-self-blame. In general, rape survivors in their study who used behavioral or characterological self-blame displayed more negative adjustment than did survivors who attributed blame to societal factors. Their findings suggest that therapists should work at helping clients change both kinds of internal, self-blame attributions to external blame ones. Moving the focus of blame to external causes, e.g. society or the rapist, is compatible with Feminist Therapy Principle I, The Personal Is Political.

Through both the cultural analysis and event detailing, Susan developed her own definition of rape that encompassed what had happened to her. Her definition, "sexual intimacy forced on one person by another", included being attacked by a date and having forced oral sexual activity instead of intercourse. She began to use the word "rape" in reference to herself. Amy was careful to respect Susan's own labeling and so did not use the word rape to refer to Brian's behavior until Susan did.

Clarifying flashbacks

Understanding Susan's nightmares and flashbacks was another important aspect of her therapy. Horowitz (1979) theorized that survivors respond to the trauma by cycling between *avoidance*, i.e. denial of and emotional numbing to the rape, and *intrusion*, i.e. unwanted recall of the rape. The avoidance responses, which include numbing of emotional responses to the rape, denial or suppression of memories of the rape, and minimization of the trauma of the rape, allow the survivor to ward off psychologically the reality of the rape. Avoidance responses can offer respite for the survivor from being overwhelmed by the rape trauma and allow her time to build the resources needed to deal with its reality.

The intrusion of the rape into conscious thought usually occurs through nightmares, flashbacks, and unwanted thoughts. Flashbacks are an intense re-experiencing of the trauma while awake. In a flashback, survivors begin to react emotionally as if they were actually in the trauma; they may see, hear, or feel the trauma happening. Flashbacks and nightmares are upsetting because of the intense feelings that usually accompany them, and because they often represent involuntary recall of the traumatic events (Figley, 1985). Flashbacks are often triggered by present-day events in the survivor's life that are reminiscent of or associated with the trauma. By voluntarily or involuntarily recalling the traumatic events, survivors appear to be trying to make sense of and gain control of the events (Figley, 1985). As they deal with each intrusion phase of the cycle, survivors can build more coping ability.

Horowitz (1979) and Figley (1985) believe that this cycling between avoidance and intrusion represents a normal response for coping with trauma. Horowitz (1979) sees these cycles of avoidance and intrusion as being part of a natural "completion tendency", a "predisposition to integrate reality and schemata . . ." (p. 249). The cycle will continue until the survivor has integrated the trauma emotionally and cognitively. This cognitive integration process is discussed more specifically in Stage Six.

Amy shared information about the avoidance and intrusion cycle with Susan. Understanding that these responses were normal reactions to trauma, and that they were part of a healthy organismic tendency to heal, helped Susan feel less out of control and crazy. With this new knowledge, Susan decided to learn strategies for coping with the intrusions, made a commitment to change her use of avoidance responses, and agreed to work in therapy on cognitively integrating her rape.

Coping with flashbacks

Although Susan's nightmares and flashbacks eventually diminished, she initially needed to learn ways to gain some control of them. First, Amy told Susan that flashbacks and nightmares, while painful to experience, are often indicators of where to focus in counseling. From this perspective and in accordance with Principle II, Amy suggested that Susan trust these intrusions (and herself) as road signs to guide them. Second, Susan learned that her flashbacks were often triggered by present stimuli in her life that were similar to stimuli present during her rape. For example, during her rape the rapist held her down by her wrists. One evening her husband playfully tugged on her right wrist. Susan felt trapped and angry and snapped at her husband. Understanding how her strong reaction got triggered helped Susan feel less out of control and to trust herself more. With Amy's encouragement she was able to talk with her husband about how he had triggered her and he avoided touching her in that way again.

In Chapter 7 we introduced you to the "mood ratings sheets." These sheets can help identify the rape-related triggers for a survivor's strong emotional reactions or for her flashbacks. Once triggers are identified they can be anticipated, modified, and/or avoided. For example, by asking her husband not to grab her wrists, Susan created a way for her to *avoid* that trigger. Susan was able to *anticipate* that driving down a gravel road to a friend's farm house might be triggering. She *modified* this potential trigger by using relaxation techniques while approaching the road and by focusing on the wild flowers in the field instead of on the sound of the tires on the gravel.

Coping with fear

Rape victims usually score higher on fear measures, especially on rape-specific fear measures, than do non-raped women (Kilpatrick, Resik, & Veronen, 1981). From a feminist perspective, working with a rape survivor's fear responses is tricky business. On the one hand, it is important to reduce the client's fear responses, e.g. panic attacks, so that she can function in her daily life and not feel continually overwhelmed. Relaxation and desensitization techniques are two ways to accomplish this. On the other hand, women who have not been raped tend to live in denial about the prevalence of rape and of their risk to being raped. Thus, a woman who has been raped may have a more realistic appraisal of the need to be fearful about rape. Acknowledging this accurate appraisal is important, because it can be another occasion for the survivor to rebuild her trust in her own reactions. This appraisal can also be motivation for getting politically involved to bring about societal changes related to rape. For example, Susan began to work with other women from the local rape crisis center to change the state law to include marital rape as a criminal act of violence.

Enhancing social support

Amy knew that healing from rape can be facilitated by supportive environments, while blaming environments may retard recovery and revictimize the survivor. Significant others are especially important. Thus, Amy suggested that Susan's husband, David, be included in several sessions throughout the course of therapy. She gave David information about the rape recovery process and about how to be supportive of Susan. She also taught David about potentially destructive responses. Two examples of destructive responses to rape survivors are "You shouldn't have gone out with him" and "You should be over this by now."

Survivors move out of Stage Five when they have alleviated most of the negative consequences of the rape. They may move back and forth between Stages Five and Six as new issues emerge.

Stage Six: Resolution and Integration

Confronting existential beliefs

An important aspect of Stage Six, *Resolution and Integration*, is for the survivor to make sense of having been raped. Pre-rape existential beliefs about the world and about oneself are often shattered by the reality of being raped (Janoff-Bulman, 1985). These pre-rape beliefs may include viewing the world as benign, orderly, and just; believing oneself to be invulnerable to harm; and having a positive view of self. When these beliefs are shattered by the rape, survivors develop strategies to reduce or resolve the dissonance.

Survivors may avoid acknowledging the reality of the trauma, find ways to incorporate the trauma into the pre-rape schemas, or develop new beliefs or schemas about self and the world (Horowitz, 1986). Cognitive processing of the event will continue until the perception of the trauma matches the schema (McCann, Sakheim, & Abrahamson, 1988). Many survivors need to restructure their pre-rape beliefs in order to integrate the rape. Survivors often become anxious and fearful during this restructuring process.

Susan has always felt in control of what happened to her. She believed that she was a "good person" and that the world was basically a good place. She believed that rape was something that happened to other women who were careless or promiscuous. Her rape disrupted her existential view of herself and of her world. As she learned more about the prevalence of rape and talked with other rape survivors, she began to change her existing cognitive schemas. She still saw herself as a good person, but came to see that bad things can happen to good people. She grieved over the loss of the part of herself that had believed that she could prevent bad things from happening.

This schematic integration of the trauma is a highly individualized process for each survivor. (See Table 8.3 for examples of Susan's changes in beliefs.) Treating the individual as an expert on herself is especially important to this process. This integration occurs over a long period of time, encompassing both Stages Five and Six. For a more detailed explanation of cognitively integrating the trauma, see McCann, Sakheim, and Abrahamson (1988).

Positively integrating the trauma

Positive integration of the rape experience into their lives is the major goal of Stage Six for survivors. This positive integration can take many forms. It may include identifying strengths and coping strategies used to survive and to resolve the rape, becoming involved in bringing about social or legal changes related to rape, helping another survivor, self-disclosing to others

Table 8.3. *Pre-rape, Post-rape and Reconstructed Existential Beliefs for Susan*

Pre-rape existential beliefs (pre-rape assumptions that are shattered)	Post-rape existential beliefs	Reconstructed existential beliefs
"The world is positive, and ordered"	"The world is negative and chaotic"	"The world is somewhat ordered and somewhat chaotic. It is made up of positive and negative elements"
"The world is just: good things happen to good people, bad things to bad people"	"A bad thing happened to me, so I am a bad person"	"The world is not just. Bad things can happen to good people. I am still a good person"

about the rape, confronting others who perpetuate rape myths, developing a self-enhancing, non-self-blaming perspective on the rape, and finding positive meaning for the rape. Figley (1985) refers to this process as one of moving from being a victim to becoming a survivor.

Part of moving from being a victim to a survivor is finding positive meaning in the rape. In discovering positive meanings for the rape, survivors make sense of the trauma, gain mastery, and increase self-esteem. Scurfield (1985) proposed that positive outcomes of a trauma may include a healthy reassessment about the direction of one's life, appreciation of one's ability to cope with adverse circumstances, and sensitization to human trauma and dehumanization. Susan's involvement as a volunteer at a local rape crisis center, and her political involvement in working to change the state's rape laws, were two strategies she used to find positive meaning from her rape. Survivors often come to new insights about themselves by working on their rapes. For example, Susan realized that she rarely allowed others to support her during trying times. Because she felt so overwhelmed by feelings in Stage Five, she learned to reach out, ask for, and take in support from others. Because of this experience, she was able to balance her autonomy and self-sufficiency with interpersonal connectedness.

Recovery and Resolution

We believe that resolving one's rape experience is an ongoing, lifelong process. The meaning of recovery and resolution is best individually determined by each survivor (Figley, 1985). In a study by Zollicoffer and Remer (1989), rape survivors were asked what recovery, resolution, and healing meant to them. Their qualitative answers give insight into possible definitions for these terms and into the process of working through a rape.

First, 20% of the respondents indicated that they did not believe that one ever fully recovered from rape. Second, while there were commonalities among survivors' responses, there were also many individual differences. Resolution and healing seem to be multidimensional processes. The following categories represent some of the commonalities among survivors' responses to what constituted recovery, healing, and resolution for them.

(1)   *Working through feelings* so that one is no longer overwhelmed by rape-related emotions.
(2)   *Integrating the rape* into their lives so that the rape was no longer controlling their lives.
(3)   *Accepting the reality of the rape*, including acknowledging that one was raped and that it was a traumatic experience.
(4)   *Helping others* by counseling and supporting others who have been raped.
(5)   *Perceiving support from others* as the survivors shared their feelings and thoughts about the rape. If they could share and not be blamed or judged, and be listened to empathically, then survivors felt validated and less isolated and stigmatized.
(6)   *Loving, appreciating, and forgiving oneself*, e.g. learning to trust oneself to perceive accurately and to make good decisions and judgments.

One other finding from this study sheds further light on the meanings of recovery and resolution. Some participants who rated themselves as high on resolution also had moderate or high Avoidance and Intrusion scores on the Impact of Event Scale. Thus, among survivors who perceived themselves to be resolved, some continued to experience rape-related effects.

We believe that a woman does not go back to being the same person she was before the rape. She is changed by it. Resolution involves both finding ways to alleviate the negative consequences of the rape and finding positive meaning from the rape in her life.

Conclusions

Susan was in therapy weekly for about 9 months. Although some sessions focused on areas of her life not directly related to her rape, the majority of her sessions did focus on rape-related issues. In addition, Susan attended an 8-week, time-limited group for rape survivors. At the end of therapy, Susan assessed that she had accomplished many goals. She had:

(1)   Defined herself as having been raped and had acknowledged the traumatization she had experienced.

(2) Expressed her feelings related to the rape.
(3) Come to feel less stigmatized and isolated.
(4) Replaced self-blame statements with external blame ones.
(5) Perceived her post-rape reactions as normal and as a validation of her victimization.
(6) Decreased her flashbacks and nightmares.
(7) Grieved the loss of her pre-rape self.
(8) Identified and learned to appreciate the strengths that she used to survive the rape and to work through the resolution process.
(9) Increased her self-esteem and trust in herself.
(10) Revised her existential beliefs to incorporate her rape.
(11) Identified positive meanings from her rape.
(12) Increased her behavioral repertoire of coping skills.

She continued to deal with several rape-related issues, including struggling with how to respond to people who tell jokes about rape, and deciding whom to tell about her rape. She summed up her progress by saying, "As a result of my having survived my rape and having worked to resolve it, I feel stronger than I did before I was raped. I am a survivor!"

Summary

The Empowerment Feminist Therapy approach to counseling rape survivors begins with a feminist analysis of the cultural context in which rape exists. Rape myths, sex-role socialization, and power differentials between women and men all contribute to the prevalence of rape. Feminist therapists empower rape survivors by validating their experience, educating them about trauma, confronting client's internalization of societal rape myths, and identifying and appreciating client strengths in coping with the rape.

Counseling sexual assault survivors is both a challenge and a privilege. In our work with survivors, we have felt challenged to confront our own biases, myths, and need to believe that we are invulnerable to any future victimization. We have felt challenged to apply the Feminist Therapy Principles and rewarded when we succeeded. Indeed, in our work with sexual assault survivors we have been able to see most clearly the effects of societal oppression of women, of institutionalized sexism, and of sex-role-stereotyping. More importantly, we appreciate the privilege of counseling survivors. We appreciate the trust they place in us by being vulnerable as they share their stories and feelings with us. Finally, we are awed by the courage and inner strength of these survivors—testimonies to the strength and courage of all women.

Activities

With a friend or in small classroom groups, complete one or more of the following exercises.

A

Remember and share joking comments about rape that you have heard, admonitions about protecting yourself from rape that you have been given, and the portrayal of rape in movies you have seen. Discuss how the jokes, movies, and admonitions reflect various rape myths and facts.

B

Identify what things you do or do not do currently that are precautions against being raped, e.g. not going out at night alone. Be aware of how much the threat of being raped influences your actions. If you are a male, identify how your life has been influenced by women living in fear of rape.

C

The threat of the possibility of rape is a part of women's lives. Remember and share any of the following:

(1)   A time you were alone and began to worry about being raped.
(2)   Having someone you were dating become overly sexually aggressive and not listening to/discounting your wants not to be sexually involved.
(3)   Sexual and verbal abuses you have encountered on the street, at parties, at work, etc. that make you feel sexually violated.
(4)   Physical sexual abuses (even "minor" ones) that made you feel sexually violated.
(5)   Any situation you have been in where you became afraid you might be raped.

Further Readings

Colao, F., & Hunt, M. (1983). Therapists coping with sexual assault. *Women and Therapy*, **2**, 205–214.

Figley, C. R. (1985). *Trauma and its Wake: The Study and Treatment of Post-traumatic Stress Disorder, Volume I*. New York: Brunner/Mazel.

Katz, J. H. (1984). *No Fairy Godmothers, No Magic Wands: The Healing Process After Rape*. Saratoga, CA: R&E Publishers.

McCann, I. L., Sakheim, D. K., & Abrahamson, D. S. (1988). Trauma and victimization: A model of psychological adaptation. *The Counseling Psychologist*, **16**, 531–594.

CHAPTER 9

Confronting Abuse

Self-assessment: Beliefs about Abuse in Close Relationships

Common beliefs about the causes and consequences of interpersonal abuse are frequently used by the victim, the abuser, friends, and family, as well as the law enforcement and legal systems, to excuse and maintain the abuse. For each of the following statements, determine whether you believe it is true (T) or false (F) by circling the appropriate letter on the right.

(1)	The abuser is seldom pathological or mentally ill.	T	F
(2)	Physical abuse occurs in families from all socioeconomic levels.	T	F
(3)	The victim could leave if she really wanted to.	T	F
(4)	Women who are in abusive relationships are masochistic and secretly enjoy being dominated.	T	F
(5)	Women frequently provoke abuse by nagging and being overly critical.	T	F
(6)	Since the abuser is only after the wife, the children are safe.	T	F
(7)	The legal system will protect her from further abuse if she will only report it.	T	F
(8)	Once a battered woman leaves her home, she is safe.	T	F
(9)	Neighbors and friends would help her if they knew about the abuse.	T	F
(10)	A wife can avoid getting her husband angry and violent by her own reactions.	T	F
(11)	The abuser is not responsible for his violent behavior if he has been drinking.	T	F

(12)   Abusers are usually unemployed or under exteme personal
       stress.   T   F

(13)   Abused women grew up in abusive homes and are therefore
       predisposed to accept further abuse.   T   F

(14)   The abused wife stays only for the sake of the children.   T   F

(15)   The abuser will change when he is under less stress.   T   F

(16)   A woman who earns more than her spouse threatens his self-
       esteem and thus provokes the abuse.   T   F

(17)   The abuser may slap his spouse occasionally but seldom
       causes serious injury.   T   F

(18)   Wife battering occurs in 20–50% of American families.   T   F

(19)   Victims who seek shelter in a safe house frequently return
       home to the abuser.   T   F

(20)   Children who observe or experience family violence are at
       risk for cognitive, emotional, and behavioral problems.   T   F

Scoring

Of the above statements, only the following are true: 1, 2, 18, 19, and 20. The remaining statements are false, but reflect commonly held myths about wife abuse. Refer to the chapter text and to Tables 9.1 and 9.2, and Figures 9.1 and 9.2 for further information on items you may have missed.

Overview

Estimates of woman abuse suggest that over half of the clients who seek counseling have experienced interpersonal violence in a close relationship. Many clients, however, shield the facts of battering behind other presenting issues. We suggest that all initial assessments with women clients should include screening for possible violence and abuse. In this chapter, we discuss the dimensions of battering in close relationships, including definitions of abuse, incidence rates, and psychological effects on the victim. We present a model of abuse in close relationships that includes societal, situational, and maintaining factors in the initiation and persistence of woman battering.

Once the existence of current abuse is revealed, intervention is focused on: (a) ensuring the safety of the woman, and exploring the dimensions of her current situation and her responses to her victimization; (b) assisting in the decision-making process by helping her to consider possible alternatives and their probable outcomes; and (c) restructuring her situation and planning for action.

We consider the story of Clara, who came to us initially to seek career counseling and to deal with her "weight problem." We focus the intervention with Clara on the phases following the session in which she revealed a history of severe physical abuse by her husband. Intervention strategies for Clara included responding to crisis, ensuring safety, power and sex-role analysis, bibliotherapy, cognitive restructuring, assertiveness coaching, reattribution training, problem-solving, career exploration, contact with police and community agencies, legal consultation, and entrance into a spouse abuse support group,

After reading this chapter, you should be able to:

(1)   Identify the characteristics of the Battered Woman Syndrome.
(2)   List and describe external factors that support abusive relationships.
(3)   Explain the theory and effects of entrapment.
(4)   Outline a plan for enabling women to terminate abuse in their close relationships.

Clara's Story

The Struggle Toward Freedom From Abuse

Denying abuse

Clara's request for counseling was typical for many women who are living in abusive relationships. Experiencing terror, abuse, and alternating attacks of anxiety and depression, she wanted to change something about herself. "I think I need some help in deciding what to do about my job. I'm also much too fat and I'd like some help in losing weight." At that point, she was unable (or unwilling?) to locate the source of her dissatisfaction within the home situation. In searching for the causes of her distress, she decided that: (a) she was "too fat," which was associated with periodic depressive episodes; and (b) that her job required too much evening and overtime work (she was the credit manager in a large discount store), and she was finding it increasingly difficult to concentrate on her work.

In the course of assessment and some exploratory sessions, Clara's two presenting issues were accepted as initial counseling goals. We had some reservations about her weight reduction goal. However, for many women, the excessive concern about weight can become the focus of therapeutic intervention in itself. Clara's reasons for wanting to lose weight, her current and past strategies for approaching the "problem", and the underlying self-concept that her weight-related concerns reflected, were all topics of relevance to her situation. Preliminary steps in the assessment and counseling of career decision-making comprised the second set of counseling strategies (see Chapter 10 for more details on career counseling).

During the first 2 months of counseling, Clara began to drop hints about her relationship with her husband (Drake) that led her therapist to "listen with a third ear." Clara gradually revealed that her feelings of dissatisfaction with her appearance and her job were related to Drake's reactions. It became clear that Drake was saying she was too fat. Drake was also "annoyed" with her night work. He wanted her home when he came home and objected to having to "baby-sit" himself or leaving their 6-year-old daughter with a sitter at night. Clara periodically dieted in attempting to lose weight, and finally agreed with Drake that her job, which required her to stay until 11 pm on weekends, was the source of many of their problems.

The multiple cues about Clara's investment in pleasing Drake led her therapist, Terry, to probe further for evidences of psychological intimidation and the possibilities of more serious abuse. Clara's response was to defend Drake, providing "good reasons" for his concern about her and the welfare of their daughter Sherry. Clara believed that Drake's love for her and Sherry led him to be concerned with how she looked and with having her safely home at night whether he was there or not (he also spent many late evenings at medical school, where he was a fourth-year student). She also viewed his jealousy of one of her co-workers as further indication of his love. Drake started asking her about this man frequently, and monitored her telephone calls carefully ("Who was that you were just talking to on the phone?"). Clara assured Drake that the man was "just a friend" but Drake accused her of having an affair. The new piece of information concerning Drake's jealousy further alerted Terry, who then kept an open ear for evidences of abuse.

Eight weeks into counseling, Clara came in one day wearing dark glasses in session. Behind the camouflage, Terry could detect obvious lacerations on the side of Clara's forehead and what appeared to be evidence of a "black eye." It required very little probing to break through Clara's mask of a happy marriage and to encourage Clara to share the burden of her misery.

Uncovering abuse

Clara and Drake were married shortly before he applied to medical school. After Sherry was born, Clara continued to work as a credit manager and was the major source of their limited income during Drake's medical training. She recalls that over time, Drake became withdrawn and irritable and began to shout obscenities at her for "small mistakes." Since she knew that medical school was difficult and demanding, she attributed these abusive reactions to his stressful situation. He grew increasingly critical of her, attacking her appearance, habits, housekeeping, mothering, cooking, family, and the conditions of her job. He became demanding of sex, frequently waking her up late at night to insist that she engage in various sexual practices with him, some of which she found painful or unpleasant. He became angry if she declined, telling her she was a "cold fish," and he would coerce her into satisfying his demands. With each new source of dissatisfaction, she attempted to appease and please him. "Things seemed to go smoothly as long as I could figure out ways to keep him from getting angry," she said.

But over time, Clara's efforts to placate Drake failed to control his outbursts of anger. A heated argument over her late work hours one evening ended in his pushing her violently across the room, hitting and seriously cutting her head on the corner of a table. Clara recalls that "Drake was really scared, 'cause I was bleeding real bad and Sherry woke up and saw me like that and she was crying. He picked me up and hugged me and told me to go in and clean it with water. The whole next week he was real good to me and things went along just fine."

The next physical battering incident occurred almost 3 months later, when they were arguing about her telephone calls to friends in the evening.

> Drake just hated me to talk to my friends when he was home, and he kept trying to pull the phone away from me but I wouldn't let him, so when I didn't get off the phone right away, he just ripped it off the wall and threw the whole thing at me. I was so mad, him tearing up the phone like that, I started screaming at him and he hit me in the mouth and told me to shut up, and some other foul things too, and then threw me down on the floor and kicked me over and over in the stomach and on my breasts. I was crying so hard by then, and screaming too, I knew I had lost a tooth or something, but he just picked up and left the house, yelling at me through the door.

As she told this story, Clara began to sob, raising her voice as she described the violence of the scene. Having been able to disclose these early acts of violence toward her, Clara could not seem to stop, and began repeating the details of each subsequent abusive incident, enacting her fears, escalating terror, and feelings of hopelessness. She was beginning to realize that she could not find ways to escape the increasingly angry outbursts, threats of violence, destruction of household objects (throwing dishes, lamps, etc.) and periodic slapping, kicking, hitting, and sexual coercion. Her reasons for entering counseling were thus to improve the situation by making herself more attractive to Drake, so that "he would want to be loving with me again."

Confronting abuse

Now, the focus of counseling shifted. Terry communicated her concern for Clara's safety, as well as for Sherry's, and suggested that they renegotiate their counseling goals. Clara's reaction was to deny that the abuse was the major problem. She retreated into a defense of Drake, his difficult childhood, their economic insufficiencies, and his stress in medical school. She denied that he ever hit Sherry except to "discipline" her. She was certain that something could be done to help him, as well as to continue her efforts to modify her own behaviors. "I just want to make it easier for both of us, I know he'll come around when he's finished with school and he's under less stress", she insisted. "Please help me to make it better now."

The uncovering of serious and possibly lethal abuse to both Clara and Sherry triggered a major change in the direction of counseling. Terry immediately communicated her concern for Clara's safety and initiated a discussion of how she might take precautions to reduce the risk of physical endangerment. Clara listened politely, but remained unconvinced that she or Sherry were in danger of serious harm. However, she did agree to complete an abuse index to "prove" she was not at risk.

Assessment

We introduced the assessment with a modification of the Center for Social Research (CSR) Abuse Index (Stacey & Shupe, 1983), which provided Clara with objective feedback on Drake's behavior in the context of abusive relationships. Table 9.1 presents the items included in this revised index. Clara was visibly shaken by her score on the CSR (81), which indicated a seriously abusive situation, and she agreed to the need for further assessment and a change in the direction of the counseling sessions.

Precautions in assessment

Precautions are important in the assessment and record-keeping procedures when a client's issues might involve future court proceedings. In Clara's case, the issue of custody for Sherry could be influenced by our "diagnosis" of Clara and the implications of pathology for her future "fitness" as a parent. The similarities of the Minnesota Multiphasic Personality Inventory (MMPI) profiles of abused women with schizophrenic and borderline patients has been documented (Rosewater, 1988). The interpretation of these data has been that the observed pathology (increased anger, confusion, depression, and paranoia) is the outcome of a history of abuse rather than representing pre-existing psychological conditions.

We used a structured interview procedure in evaluating for the presence of the Battered Woman Syndrome (Douglas, 1987; Walker, 1984), and for the symptoms of physical, psychological, and sexual abuse. Douglas (1987) defined the Battered Woman Syndrome (BWS) in terms of the effects of physical abuse that reduce the woman's ability to respond proactively to

Table 9.1. *Revised CSR Abuse Index. (From* The Family Secret *by A. Stacey & A. Shupe. Copyright © 1983 by W. A. Stacey & A. Shupe. Reprinted by permission of Beacon Press.)*

Questions 1–14
3 = Frequently   2 = Sometimes   1 = Rarely   0 = Never

---

(1)   Does he continually monitor your time and make you account for every minute (when you run errands, visit friends, commute to work, etc.)?   _____

(2)   Does he ever accuse you of having affairs with other men or act suspiciously of you?   _____

(3)   Is he ever rude to your friends?   _____

(4)   Does he ever discourage you from starting friendships with other women?   _____

(5)   Is he ever critical of things such as your cooking, clothes, or appearance?   _____

(6)   Does he demand a strict account of how you spend money?   _____

(7)   Do his moods change radically, from very calm to very angry, or vice versa?   _____

(8)   Is he disturbed by your working?   _____

(9)   Does he become angry more easily when he drinks?   _____

(10) Does he pressure you for sex much more often than you like?   _____

(11) Does he become angry if you do not want to go along with his requests for sex?   _____

(12) Do you and your partner quarrel much over financial matters?   _____

(13) Do you quarrel much about having children or raising them?   _____

(14) Does he ever strike you with his hands or feet (slap, punch, etc.)?   _____

Questions 15–26
6 = Frequently   5 = Sometimes   4 = Rarely   0 = Never

---

(15) Does he ever strike you with an object?   _____

(16) Does he ever threaten you with an object or weapon?   _____

(17) Has he ever threatened to kill either you or himself?   _____

(18) Does he ever give you visible injuries (such as welts, bruises, cuts, etc.)?   _____

(19) Have you ever had to treat any injuries from his violence with first aid?   _____

(20) Have you ever had to seek professional aid for any injury at a medical clinic, doctor's office, or hospital emergency room?   _____

(21) Has he ever hurt you sexually or made you have intercourse against your will?   _____

(22) Is he ever violent toward the children?   _____

(23) Is he ever violent toward other people outside your home and family?   _____

(24) Does he ever throw objects or break things when he is angry?   _____

(25) Has he ever been in trouble with the police?   _____

(26) Have you ever called the police, or tried to call them, because you felt you or members of your family were in danger?   _____

Total   _____

To score responses simply add up the points for each question. This sum is your Abuse Index Score. To get some idea of how abusive your relationship is, compare your Index score with the following:

120–92	Dangerously abusive	34–13	Moderately abusive
91–35	Seriously abusive	12–0	Non-abusive

violence against her. The BWS includes three categories of response: (a) the effects of trauma; (b) learned helplessness deficits; and (c) self-destructive coping responses to violence. We explore these characteristics in the following sections within the context of Clara's experiences.

Goals of assessment

Goals of the assessment were to:

(1)   Obtain the history, frequency, and extent of abuse to both Clara and Sherry.
(2)   Evaluate the medical status of the client with respect to past physical injury.
(3)   Uncover Clara's cognitive reactions to the situation (attributions, self-blame, locus of control, minimization).
(4)   Evaluate her psychological status (depression, anxiety, anger, and hopelessness).
(5)   Assess the range and outcomes of her previous coping strategies and efforts to end the abuse (leaving home, contacting others, calling police).
(6)   Assess the risk of serious self-injury or suicide, and of homicidal ideation or intention with respect to Drake.
(7)   Assess the range of her personal strengths (self-esteem and self-efficacy).
(8)   Evaluate her social support network and economic resources.

Assessment outcomes

Each of these assessment goals was designed to provide information to Clara, as well as to Terry, about the potential for serious outcomes for herself and Sherry, and to assist in further intervention plans. Terry believed that normative feedback on her situation might motivate Clara to adopt safety precautions and arrive at difficult decisions. Clara was certain that Sherry was not being harmed physically and did not want to involve her daughter at this time. Clara was referred for a medical evaluation for evidence of persisting injury. The structured interview questions revealed evidence of moderate depression, anxiety, low trust of others, and intermittent anger and hopelessness. Further questions uncovered her *minimization* of the abuse (he's really a good man under stress), *denial* (I don't think he'd really hurt me seriously; sometimes he can be so sweet and loving), and some evidence of global *self-blame* (I guess I'll never be all the things he wants a wife to be). On the other hand, she did not take responsibility for the abuse (I know he shouldn't act like that, he's got to realize he's wrong about me), and she asserted her determination to change the relationship (I don't want to live like this). The outcome of this assessment procedure was to move Clara to a new stage of counseling, in which she was able to self-identify as a battered woman, to begin to come to terms with that realization, and to agree to work on the abuse as her primary issue.

Impression

Clara's story is one that is repeated, in different forms, in many intimate relationships. The early part of her marriage was generally a satisfying experience for Clara. During their last year of college, Drake had courted her with intensity and persistence, convincing her to marry before he entered medical school, so that they would "belong to each other forever." Clara felt attractive and loved, reflected in the eyes of the man who had chosen her.

When the first abusive incident occurred, she found it difficult to believe that this was the "real Drake," and discounted his behavior as due to external circumstances (stress), the facts of his childhood (early neglect), and her own failure to meet his needs (self-blame). Rather than being afraid for her safety, her initial reaction was to intensify her commitment to Drake in an effort to "help him be a happier person." Over time, her perception that Drake frequently followed his violent outbursts with remorse and renewed demonstrations of affection (usually sexual), maintained her belief in the viability of the marriage and strengthened her determination to improve their relationship and to keep the family together.

To the external observer, this increased commitment by Clara may appear to be a "masochistic reaction," suggesting that she really enjoyed the abuse and needed to experience pain in relationships. The use of masochism to explain women's apparent attachment to an abusive relationship is another example of a victim-blaming attribution, and serves to excuse and condone the behavior of the abuser, rather than to confront him with his responsibility for the violence (refer to Chapter 6 on diagnosis for further discussion of woman-blaming categories).

As the abuse escalated, Clara continued to believe that she was somehow at fault (reinforced by Drake's criticism) and she reciprocally escalated her efforts to please him and to avoid conflict. These efforts took the form of increased silence and withdrawal at home, eliminating calls to family and friends in the evenings (further isolating her from sources of potential support), agreeing to have him take her to work and pick her up at night so that she lost access to her own car, and her obsessive dieting to lose weight.

Clara's investment in keeping the relationship viable, in being a good partner for Drake and providing a stable home for Sherry, and her embarrassment and shame about the abusive events, all kept her from sharing her unhappy situation with family and friends. She once revealed a violent incident to her minister, when she thought she was pregnant again and Drake threw her down and kicked her in the stomach ("Whose baby is that?"). The minister advised her to try to be a better wife and to smooth it over and put up with his "irritability" until he graduated; "He'll feel better when he's the wage-earner and you can stay home with Sherry" (see Alsdurf, 1985, for research on pastoral advice in wife battering). Supported by her own desires for a happy marriage, Clara wanted to believe her minister, and never again sought help from others until she entered conseling.

The outcomes for Clara were both physical and psychological entrapment (see Figure 9.2). The more she invested in maintaining the relationship, the greater was her loss of freedom of movement and sense of competence and independence. As she responded to verbal intimidation and physical violence with increased compliance, isolation, and withdrawal, her self-confidence was eroded. She increasingly doubted her perceptions of reality and her ability to make clear decisions. The tactics that she adopted for personal survival became the very ones that consolidated her entrapment.

Facts About the Abuse of Women

Incidence

You are more likely to be physically assaulted, beaten, and killed in your own home at the hands of a loved one than any place else, or by anyone else in our society" (Gelles & Strauss, 1988, p. 18).

Although most of us are taught to fear danger and assault from strangers in the streets, documented violence to a woman is most likely to be inflicted by someone she knows and frequently loves.

Estimates of abuse and violence in close heterosexual relationships depend upon the populations surveyed and the kinds of questions that are asked. An early telephone survey with nearly 2000 women in Kentucky was conducted by the Harris Poll for the Kentucky Commission on Women (1979). Twenty-one per cent of the women respondents had been physically abused by a husband or partner, and over two-thirds of those who had been separated or divorced the previous year experienced physical violence in that relationship.

Marital abuse

In a large national survey in the United States conducted in 1976 (reported in Strauss, Gelles, & Steinmetz, 1980), an estimated 1.8 million American wives were being beaten by their husbands each year. Using the Conflict

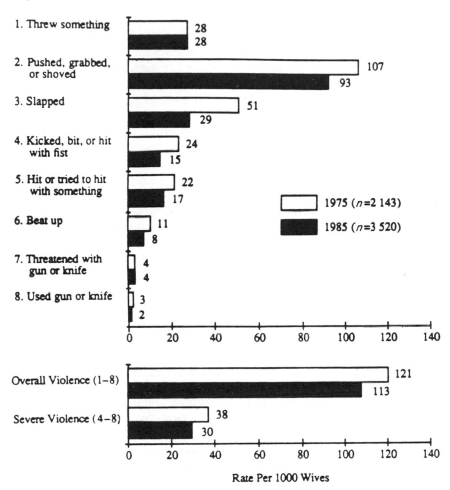

Figure 9.1.   Husband-to-wife violence: comparison of rates in 1975 and 1985. (From Gelles & Straus, 1988. Copyright © 1988 by R. J. Gelles & M. A. Straus. Reprinted by permission of Simon & Schuster, Inc.)

Tactics Scale (CTS), these researchers conducted face-to-face interviews with over 2000 randomly selected families. Their data indicated that one in six wives had been struck by her husband during the course of their marriage, and the "average battered wife is attacked three times each year" (Gelles & Strauss, 1988, p. 104).

Ten years later, Gelles and Strauss (1988) conducted a telephone survey with over 6000 respondents, finding similar rates of violence toward wives. Figure 9.1 displays the collapsed CTS rates for eight types of violence toward wives for the two surveys.

In evaluating these reported incidence rates, we note at least five problems with the use of the CTS. First, the CTS documents only single instances of physical violence, and therefore may underestimate the frequency of violence to wives and may overestimate the frequency of violence by wives toward their partners (Dobash & Dobash, 1988). Their finding of relatively "equal" violence by wives ignores the evidence that most of the aggression used by women is in the service of their own defense (Yllo, 1988). Second, since the CTS does not include degree of injury to the victim, it omits documentation of severe injury such as broken bones, teeth knocked out, and need for extensive surgey and restoration. Women are more likely than men to be severely injured by physical conflict. Third, the CTS is limited by its omission of the multiple forms of violence reported by battered women: hair-pulling, smothering, burning, attempts to drown, throwing her across the room or down the stairs, stomping or jumping on her, twisting her arms and legs, forcing her to crawl on the floor, throwing her out of a moving car, and sexual assault or genital mutilation (Walker, 1984). Fourth, the CTS fails to assess many aspects of coercion and intimidation, such as bondage, locking the woman in the car or closet, surveillance of her activities when away from home, destruction of her property, and threats of violence or death to her, the children, pets, or other loved ones. Finally, limiting these rates of violence to currently married women underestimates the total extent of woman abuse.

The incidence of sexual abuse in marriage has been seriously under-reported. In a survey of 900 community women, Russell (1982) found that 12% of the women reported marital rape. Within samples of battered women, the incidence of sexual abuse is high, ranging from 29% (Gondolph, 1988) to 59% (Walker, 1984). Similarly to reports of physical violence, the variation in reported sexual abuse across samples is probably due in part to differences in how the women defined sexual abuse and how the researchers presented the questions to repondents.

Premarital abuse

Premarital or dating abuse has been reported mainly for college populations, probably because they are easily available to researchers. Across a range of studies, interpersonal violence occurs in 20–60% of dating couples, depending upon whether only physical abuse is considered, or verbal and sexual abuse are also included (Cate et al., 1982; Laner & Thompson, 1982; Makepeace, 1981; Witt & Worell, 1986, 1988).

We have little information about the extent of abuse and violence toward women from diverse groups: socioeconomic, age, and ethnic groups, as well as from lesbian couples. In these more invisible relationships, the limited research does not provide stable data.

The last resort

Survey research does not tell us about the most violent form of woman abuse—murder. In a historic study, Jones (1980) reported that four out of five women who are killed by men are murdered at home, and three-quarters of all murdered women are killed by husbands or lovers. Danger exists also to the men in these relationships as the woman turns to a last desperate move for freedom from terror: about 10% of all homicides in the United States are perpetrated by women, many of whose victims were former husbands or lovers (Thyfault, Browne, & Walker, 1987). The therapist who sees a battered woman must consider that her life is always in danger, whether she is at home with the abuser, or has followed through with her decision to leave. Although most violent conflicts occur in the home, many women are killed once they leave the abusive situation (Walker, 1989). The documented danger to a battered woman's life is essential to remember when helping the woman to consider the stay-or-leave decision.

The relatively high incidence of abuse and violence in close interpersonal relationships suggests that therapists should routinely screen for such abuse with all female clients. We confess that in our initial intake procedures with Clara, abuse screening was omitted because the issue appeared to be one of career counseling. Although we have no indication that she would have admitted to the violence at an earlier stage of counseling before sufficient trust had been established, the screening questions can frequently set the stage for client self-disclosure. Once the disclosure of violence occurs, further screening for life-threatening danger is essential.

Defining Abuse and Violence

We are using the concept of "abuse" here in a broad sense to include any threats or acts of coercion (controlling another's behavior), aggression (intent to cause harm to another), or violence (perpetration of damage or injury to another or to their belongings and property) that are unwanted by the victim. We thus include three factors of coercive control, intention to harm, and injury outcome, as well as physical, emotional, and sexual categories of abuse.

Definitions of abuse exist in all state legislative regulations in the United States with respect to children, but only a few States have attempted to define wife abuse as an illegal or criminal act. There is further inconsistency in defining threats and abuse to wives and partners as either misdemeanors (mild infractions of the law) or as a felony (more serious criminal behavior). There is also considerable controversy over how to define abuse for either children or adults, especially with respect to (a) intentionality to harm, and (b) demonstrated injury (Gelles & Strauss, 1988). We believe that both intent and injury are important to consider, since neither one may cover all instances of interpersonal abuse. In addition, we include the concept of control, since many abusive behaviors include holding the other person against her will, locking her in or out of spaces, following her wherever she goes, removing her car keys so that she cannot drive, tearing out the telephone, and otherwise restricting her freedom of movement and access to communication with others. These control behaviors inflict harm on the victim by relegating her to the status of a prisoner or hostage within her own life space.

Gelles and Strauss (1988) contend that the concept of "abuse" is political rather than scientific, reflecting the values and norms of a particular society at a particular time. We concur with this view, noting that, at the time of writing this book, laws regarding violence toward women are still uneven across legislatures and communities. Thus, behavior regarded as criminally violent in some communities, such as wife rape, is both legal and sanctioned in other regions. Likewise, the prosecution of violence toward women is frequently colored by the legal relationship between the woman and her abuser (Erez, 1986). Violence perpetrated by a stranger is likely to be taken more seriously by police, for example, than "domestic violence," which is frequently believed to be within the private domain of the home. Incidents of violence toward women or wives is not routinely reported in most communities, so that the true epidemiology of violence toward women is currently unknown and probably underestimated.

Issues in the Abuse of Women

Few issues in counseling women generate as much concern, consternation, and coordination of resources as wife abuse. First, intervention with partners of violent men always involves risk. There is an over-riding issue of danger—not only to the woman, but often to her partner, and potentially to the therapist or other help-givers as well. Second, because a large proportion of abused women remain with or return to their battering partners (Walker, 1989), help-givers often feel frustrated and ineffective. A common reaction here is to blame the woman for undermining her own counseling by "allowing" herself to continue the abusive relationship. Third, the decision to leave an abusive relationship frequently requires a concerted organization of economic, social, and physical resources that many clinicians believe are beyond their scope and experience. These three factors combine to create a unique challenge to the professional who works with abused and battered women.

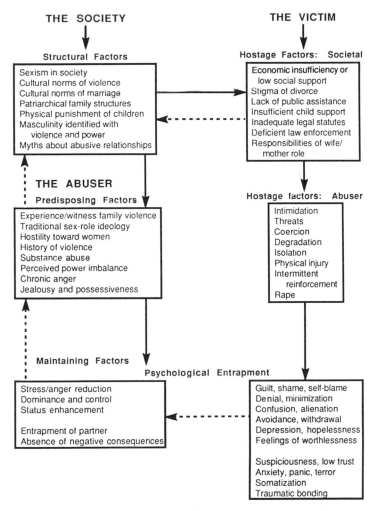

Figure 9.2.   A model of violence toward women

A Model of Abuse Toward Women

We have conceptualized the abusive process as a three-part model, involving the society at large, the violence-prone abuser, and the female victim of abuse. Figure 9.2 displays the hypothesized relationship among the three variables, in which the straight lines represent a direct influence of one factor on another. The dotted lines signify a feedback loop in which the consequences of the societal and abuser factors provide reinforcement and repetition of the violence and oppression. The hypothesized outcomes of the model, if not attenuated at some juncture, provide for a continuation of violence to women. In the following sections, we offer a brief description of each factor.

Societal Support of Male Violence

The societal factor includes cultural norms of violence, norms of inequality between women and men, and general institutionalized sexism that promotes the dominance of men and devalues and subordinates women (Dobash & Dobash, 1981; Resick, 1983; Strauss, Gelles, & Steinmetz, 1980; Walker, 1986). Rather than asking why Drake batters Clara, we ask first why men in general use violence against women (Principle I). How does this violence serve to maintain traditional family and societal structures by keeping women in relatively powerless and subordinate positions? (Bograd, 1988).

We examine the cultural norms of marriage, which generally provide for male-advantaged arrangements and the sanctity of the home. We take the position that abuse is a matter of public concern, not private privilege. The control of women and children through physical punishment is widely accepted in most cultures, and the identification of masculinity with the use of force further supports this view of the right to control. In a study with 300 college students, Finn (1986) reported a correlation of 0.65 between traditional sex-role beliefs and endorsement of violence toward wives. In a study of 1000 battered women, Bowker, Arbitell, and McFerron (1988) found that in 70% of the families with children present, men who beat their wives also physically abused their children.

These sociocultural variables work together to: (a) increase the potential for violent, dominant, and controlling behavior by males who grow up in a violence-prone and patriarchical culture; and (b) keep women intimidated, powerless, economically insufficient, and lacking in community and legal recourse and police protection in the face of violence.

A View of the Abuser

The abuser in Figure 9.2 is conceptualized by: (a) the range of characteristics that have been reported in the literature on wife-battering, not all of which will apply to a particular individual (for example, see Bowker, 1982; Gondolph, 1988; Ganley, 1987; Ptacek, 1988; Sonkin, Martin, & Walker, 1985; and (b) the variables that appear to maintain his abusive behavior. Men with a history of family and personal violence, traditional ideology about the position of women and the rights of men to dominate through the use of physical force, and a sensitization to minimal cues of male–female power imbalance, may be prone to resort to violence in the effort to control their women.

Table 9.2. *Cluster Behaviors of Sociopathic (I), Antisocial (II), Chronic (III), and Sporadic (IV) Abusers. (Reprinted with the permission of Lexington Books, an imprint of Macmillan, Inc., from* Battered Women as Survivors: An Alternative to Treating Learned Helplessness *by E. W. Gondolf & E. R. Fisher. Copyright © 1988 by Lexington Books.)*

| | Cluster | | | | |
	I	II	III	IV	Total
Cluster of sample	5%	32%	30%	33%	100%
Length of relationship (more than 5 years)**	36	38	45	28	37
Weekly abuse*	68	50	49	35	46
Kicked*	46	96	56	32	61
Weapon used*	36	80	26	17	43
Sexual abuse*	59	36	34	20	31
Child abuse*	46	26	24	17	23
Threaten or blame (in response to abuse)*	91	62	76	9	50
Broken bones*	46	23	7	5	13
Drug abuse*	60	37	28	22	30
Non-family violence*	68	54	43	25	42
Arrest for non-family violence*	64	23	15	13	19

$n = 550$; * $P < 0.0001$; ** $P < 0.01$; *** Not significant.

Gondolph (1988), reporting on a cluster analysis of the characteristics of 500 male batterers, divided these men into four groups, based on their history of arrests and patterns of violence within and outside the relationship. These types include the sociopath, the antisocial batterer, the chronic batterer, and the sporadic batterer. Table 9.2 displays these four types and their frequencies of battering behaviors. It can be seen that the sociopathic group represents only 5% of the sample. The sporadic batterer, however, is the only type that is likely to be remorseful and to benefit from counseling. Gondolph maintains that "the pursuit of a unitary batterer profile is in vain" (p. 74). Since Drake was not directly our client, we have insufficient information with which to understand his particular pattern of violence. However, he fits many aspects of the profile of abusers who use intimidation, force, and coercion to maintain their power.

What maintains the violence once it is initiated? Lenore Walker (1979) proposed a "cycle of violence" theory, in which each successive round of violence is followed by (a) remorse and apologies by the batterer, and (b) a "honeymoon" period in which the wife believes that he loves her and that things will improve. This intermittent reinforcement functions to maintain her hopes and to keep her attached in the relationship. Her compliance with his demands also reinforces the male in believing that he can be successful in deploying violence in the future as a means of control. Gondolph (1988) questions the cycle theory, suggesting that only a small proportion of male batterers, the sporadic group, express remorse for their actions, and that those who do may be over-represented in research because they are more receptive to counseling.

Social exchange theory uses a cost–benefit analysis, predicting that a balance of reward over punishment will encourage the behavior to continue. The "normal" or typical survival strategies of battered women include increased compliance and submission to abuser demands, and hypervigilence to avoid displeasing him. Once the abuser uses violence successfully to establish dominance and control with no negative contingencies, the reinforcement of his power and the absence of negative consequences ensures that further violence will follow.

In support of a social exchange view, Edna Erez (1986) reviewed all "domestic incident" reports filed with a county prosecutor's office for 1 year, a total of 3021 reports. Across all female–male intimate relationships, the frequency of arrest of the assaultive party did not exceed 13%! Police intervention with "domestic violence" in all communities has been notoriously deficient, and police responses to women who are personally violated frequently increases the woman's distress (Wyatt, Notgrass, & Newcomb, 1990). In contrast, a pilot project in Minnesota (Sherman & Berk, 1984) found that immediate arrest of the batterer, with a minimum of 24 hours' incarceration, reduced subsequent violence in these men by 50%. As long as the rewards of power and control outweigh the costs of perpetrating abuse, violence against women will not abate.

The Victim's Dilemma

The victim in Figure 9.2 is viewed in the context of the "hostage syndrome," which leads to a psychological state we call "entrapment." The hostage syndrome, originally developed to explain the paradoxical attachment of hostages to their captors, has been applied to the situation experienced by battered women (Dutton & Painter, 1981; Graham, Rawlings, & Rimini, 1988; Resick, 1983). The "hostage effect" is created by both society and the individual abuser.

As a hostage of society, the battered woman is unable to leave her abuser when external circumstances deny her access to resources that would enable her to escape the violence and to live independently. These external variables include norms of marriage and motherhood, low social support from community and family, lack of economic equity that enables her to subsist independently, and inadequate legal and police protection against the batterer.

In Clara's case, she received little support from the one person to whom she revealed the abuse, her minister. The minister's advice for her to stay with Drake was traditional in its alliance with the continuation of marriage and the wife/mother role. Clara felt guilty for wanting to deny her daughter's need for a father, and for not being patient with Drake under his medical school pressures. She rationalized his violence as a "natural" reaction to stress, thus buying into the cultural norms of justification for male violence. Further, she had internalized the sex-role belief that women are primarily responsible for the success of marital relationships: "I will be a failure as a woman if this relationship does not succeed" (Worell, 1988).

As a hostage to the abuser, the battered woman is alternately intimidated, terrorized, isolated, violated, and injured. Intermittently, her abuser encourages her to stay by providing some affection, attention, and promises to reform. According to the hostage syndrome theory, the victim responds to this life-threatening relationship by reactions that (a) ensure her safety and survival, and (b) increase her commitment to her abuser (traumatic bonding). As hostage to the abuser, she feels unable to leave him when she fears for her life and that of her children, and she believes as well that she "loves" him (Graham, Rawlings, & Rimini, 1988). She may be grateful to her abuser for not harming her more than he did ("At least I'm still alive"). In denying the real danger to herself and her children she can still believe that she has some control over his violence in a situation in which she really has no control at all (Resick, 1983).

Clara was clearly intimidated and terrorized by Drake's unpredictable outbursts of anger, humiliating remarks, and periodic violence. He was able to control her movements, to whom she spoke, and access to her car and friends. She was also clearly attached to Drake and wanted to continue the marriage. She believed that under all the abuse, he loved her and would return to his former self when medical school was behind them.

The outcome for the victim of this dual hostage situation is the psychological state we call *entrapment* (for a fuller discussion of entrapment theory, see Brockner & Rubin, 1985; Strube, 1989). In psychological entrapment, the individual feels committed to a course of action, and escalates attempts to improve the situation as goal attainment fails. In abusive marriages, sex-role messages encourage the woman to feel it is her

> . . . responsibility to make the relationship run smoothly, and that if the relationship is failing, she must not be trying hard enough. The more time and effort the woman invests, the harder it is to give up without success and the less likely that a battered woman will leave the relationship (Strube, 1989).

Perceived personal responsibility, and the belief that alternatives are risky or unavailable, serve to strengthen her commitment and increase her inability to leave.

The entrapped victim of repeated abuse experiences a variety of internal negative states, including shame, guilt, self-blame, and worthlessness. She may use withdrawal and avoidance strategies to reduce the abusive incidents,

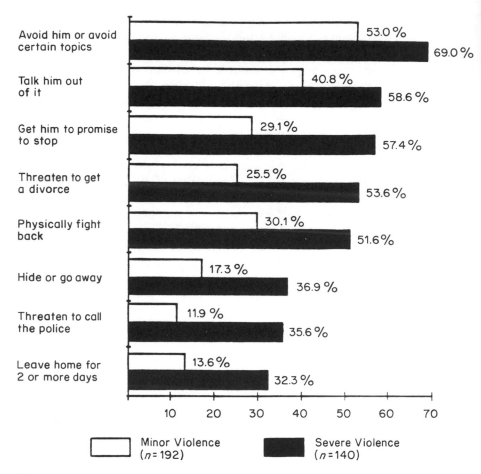

Figure 9.3.   Strategies used by women to end violence. (From Gelles & Straus, 1988. Copyright © 1988 by R. J. Gelles & M. A. Straus. Reprinted by permission of Simon & Schuster, Inc.)

but she experiences periodic attacks of anxiety and panic when violence threatens to erupt. Figure 9.3 displays the strategies used by the battered women in the Gelles and Strauss (1988) sample. We use the term "entrapment" to point out that the psychological outcomes of repeated abuse and the lack of resources for escape convince her that she is unable to leave. In addition, the strategies she uses in her desperate attempt at survival and safety are the same ones that reinforce the batterer and further reduce her personal power. The model of hostage and entrapment are clearly appropriate to our understanding of Clara's dilemma.

Intervention Strategies

As we suggested earlier, treatment with violently abused women can be problematic for many help-givers. Those who work with abused women require specific training that is designed to develop skills in competent, effective, and ethical practice with battered clients.

Counseling Competencies

The competent counselor of women in battering relationships requires: (a) knowledge about abuse in close relationships; (b) attitudes that contribute to, rather than deter from, the process of therapy; and (c) skills in assisting the process of decision-making and in coordinating personal and community resources (Walker, 1978).

Knowledge

The model presented in Figure 9.2 provides a summary of information that is minimally important in understanding the issues in the abuse of women. Each topic in the model encompasses a background of theory, research, and clinical data with which the therapist should become familiar. In particular, you should know the facts that challenge the validity of the myths listed in the Self-assessment section (see pp. 221–2) and be able to present these facts to your clients. In accordance with Principle I, you should be able to untangle the political from the personal in the individual lives of each client, thus assisting clients to see their situation as a relatively "normal" extension of societal structure and attitudes, as well as involving their responsibility for change.

Attitudes

Dealing with violence and anger is emotionally draining and frequently frightening. As a competent counselor, you should be able to:

(1) Listen empathically to extended stories of horror, bloodshed, and violence, and allow the client to recount full details without premature foreclosure.

(2) Confront and deal with your own fears of violence and be willing to share and self-disclose where appropriate (especially for the counselor who was herself violently abused) (Principle II).

(3) Allow the client to work through her issues without pushing her to arrive at decisions you feel she should make (Principle II).

(4) View the woman's "pathology" as the probable outcome of her abuse and not the cause of it (Principle I).

(5)   Accept and encourage the client's expression of anger and rage.
(6)   View the client's reactions as normal survival strategies to cope with terrorizing and life-threatening events (Principles I and III).
(7)   Advocate actively for the client and avoid blaming her for "provoking" the abuse. Share with her your conviction that violence is always inflicted, not provoked (Principles I and III).
(8)   Avoid reacting with annoyance and frustration if the client decides to remain or return to the abusive relationship (Principle II).
(9)   Respect and affirm the client's power to arrive at decisions that are appropriate for her life at this time (Principles II and III).
(10) Support and validate her capacity for change (Principles II and III).

Skills

In addition to the broad range of skills required for all feminist counseling, working with battered women will also challenge you to:

(1)   Be knowledgeable about state and community laws regarding spouse abuse and the procedures for obtaining police protection.
(2)   Maintain contact with legal service resources and be willing to assist your client in following through with legal procedures to protect her safety.
(3)   Maintain contacts with other community professionals who deal with battered women, especially woman shelter personnel.
(4)   Be competent in collaborating with a variety of other professionals and lay persons in planning for your clients' future well-being.
(5)   Develop a network of community resources for childcare, financial and living assistance, and whatever else is required to assist your client to live apart from her abuser should she choose to do so.
(6)   Maintain resources for spouse abuser survivor groups or couples counseling if the client wishes to explore these options.
(7)   Develop and maintain a personal support group with whom you can discuss and validate your intervention strategies and concerns with abused clients.
(8)   Diversify your client load so that abused women are interspersed with clients presenting other issues.
(9)   Establish careful assessment data and record-keeping that anticipate the possibility of legal actions and child custody litigation.

These three areas of knowledge, attitudes, and skills related to working with abused women form the basis of your intervention plans. In the remainder of our discussion, we briefly summarize how Terry helped Clara through the process of confronting her abuse and coming to some decisions about the future directions of her life.

A Three-phase Model

Once the violence in the marriage became the focal point in Clara's counseling, new goals were considered. In the negotiation and implementation of new goals, Terry followed a three-phase model for intervention with battered women (Douglas, 1987): (a) crisis intervention; (b) exploration and decision-making; and (c) resolution and restructuring. In practice, the three phases may overlap or merge, as the client moves at a pace that is comfortable and non-threatening to her. The three Principles of Feminist Therapy were used liberally throughout the sessions. We believe you are now sufficiently skilled to detect the use of each principle and to be able to support the context in which it appears.

Crisis intervention

When violence to the client is present, crisis intervention procedures become paramount. In crisis intervention with Clara, Terry had three major goals: (a) increasing her safety; (b) documenting the violence; and (c) providing information and support.

Increasing safety. Terry's first concern for Clara was to ensure her safety as well as that of her daughter, Sherry. Although she had previously denied injury to Sherry, the data on the high frequency of child abuse by battering men was presented to her as a cautionary measure. In assessing the risks, Terry pointed out to Clara that Drake had seriously injured her in the past, had access to guns and knives, and sometimes appeared to be "out of control" of his anger. We do not subscribe to the myth that battering men are "unable to control" their violence, since they exhibit violent behavior only under certain circumstances and toward their wives and children rather than toward more powerful others. However, it was important to affirm for Clara that nothing she could do would necessarily be effective in controlling Drake's future violence.

Terry also asked Clara for a written suicide/homicide contract, in which she agreed not to inflict lethal harm on either herself or Drake during the course of our sessions with her. Although our assessment for suicide risk was minimal, Clara expressed intense rage at this point and indicated her wish to see Drake "burn in H----." Terry interpreted this statement as a wish rather than a threat, but Terry knew that predictions of dangerousness are unreliable. In response to Clara's insistence that she could control Drake's outbursts, Terry kept repeating "I'm afraid for your safety. If Sherry were my daughter, I would be afraid for her too." Terry also validated Clara's anger toward Drake, saying "I feel very angry that he did that to you."

Clara was helped to develop a plan of escape should the violence reoccur.

She found a place to hide a set of car keys, memorized the number of the local women's shelter hot-line, and agreed to explore the possibilities of calling her mother or younger sister. Clara was encouraged to consider how to deal with the next violent episode, including calling the police ("Assault is a crime," said Terry), visiting the hospital to document injury, and swearing out a warrant for Drake's arrest. Clara was unwilling at this point either to leave the home or to ask Drake to leave.

Documenting the violence.   The process of uncovering the abuse and detailing the violence had begun prior to crisis intervention. Now, we encouraged Clara to tell her entire story in detail, having her describe each incident of violence and everything she could recall about it. Her ability to recall and recount the incidents of abuse, sexual coercion, and violence increased with each session and she had difficulty in stopping at the end of the hour. Terry took copious notes of the violence and, with Clara's permission, included them in her clinic records. The documentation of violence provided information to the therapist, but also served as a therapeutic step in helping Clara to break through her denial and to confront the realities of her situation.

The process of documenting the violence is a painful one for both client and counselor. Terry was mindful of asking clarifying questions, but also of focusing on Clara's feelings of anger, shame, guilt, terror, and reactions of denial and minimization. She noted where Clara made excuses for Drake and carefully labeled Drake as the batterer and Clara as a battered women. The process of documentation, then, will lead naturally into an educative and supportive phase.

Information and support.   Here, Terry used all three Feminist Therapy Principles. She gave Clara a "fact sheet" that provided facts to challenge the myths of wife battering, and offered more short reading materials when Clara was ready to address them. Clara was encouraged to keep these materials at work until the battering issues were brought out openly with Drake. Clara was amazed to discover how the incidence and details of wife abuse matched her own situation. This information led into some discussions of Clara's anxiety, panic attacks, and depressive episodes, and together they developed some strategies to help Clara relax (see Chapter 7 for strategies with anxiety and depression). In particular, Terry modeled some cognitive stress inoculation techniques that Clara could use to affirm her determination to take care of herself and Sherry and to reduce her self-blame ("This wasn't my fault," "I can take care of myself," "I'm not to blame for his anger," etc.).

Terry invoked Principles II and III by affirming Clara's caring and supportive approach to Sherry and Drake, pointing to her attempts to maintain the family as a woman-valued approach. She also supported Clara's ambivalence about leaving the relationship, but reminded Clara that she was strong and competent (hadn't she coped effectively until now?) and that she had many career and interpersonal skills which would enable her to live independently should she choose to do so.

Terry then self-disclosed that she was a formerly abused wife. Clara was surprised and wanted to hear more details. Terry gave a brief account of her experiences, how difficult it was for her either to remain or to leave a long-term marriage, and how she had filed twice for divorce before she found the strength and determination to go through with it. She also modeled the successful outcome of her independent living, but cautioned Clara that each person must arrive at her own individual solution that fits her situation and her values. This discussion led naturally into the second phase, exploration and decision-making.

Exploration and decision-making

The self-disclosure of personal history of violence in marriage by Terry certainly served as a catalyst for Clara. However, for therapists without such a personal history, self-involving responses of personal feelings about the violence can be quite effective ("I am afraid for your safety," etc.). For the first time, Clara seriously considered the option of separation. Terry pointed out that separation, even if temporary, is a desirable interim step if further violence is anticipated (and it certainly was in this case). Temporary separation while the woman (and possibly the man) explores the situation and options can send a clear message to the batterer that his violent behavior will not be tolerated. It also increases the woman's safety (although in some instances the batterer follows and continues to harass the woman) and provides her with psychological space in which to arrive at rational decisions. A separation was explored here but rejected by Clara, who feared that it was too final and that she would "lose" Drake. She was still interested in helping him and wanted him to seek counseling.

Feminist therapists are generally opposed to couples counseling with battering men, unless the woman has had sufficient time and assistance to arrive at firm decisions for herself. We are particularly concerned about the use of a traditional family systems approach, which places equal responsibility on both partners for the abuse, or which locates the causes of the abuse solely within the transactions between the partners. Couples therapy that is aimed at re-establishing homeostasis, and that ignores the dynamics of unequal power in the relationship, will be detrimental to the woman (Bograd, 1986). More recent advocates of feminist family therapy have revised these traditional formats, enabling them to employ a systems approach that remains sensitive to gender imbalances (Goldner, 1985; Goodrich et al, 1988).

Terry judged that couples therapy would not be advisable for Clara and Drake at this time for the following reasons:

(1) The power imbalance between them could make it difficult for Clara to assert her ideas and true feelings.
(2) The disclosure of violence by Clara could trigger more violence and retaliation by Drake.
(3) Terrorizing at home by Drake could then reduce Clara's disclosure in session.
(4) Couples counseling sends a message to both that the goal for Clara is to remain in and repair the marriage before she has had the opportunity to complete a careful decision-making process.
(5) Drake's anticipated criticisms of her behavior may encourage her to further attempts to placate him.
(6) Couples counseling would require a new therapist, possibly co-therapists, and would remove an important source of personal support for Clara unless she also continued with individual counseling.

Terry advised Clara of her approach, suggesting that once she had come to a fuller understanding of her situation, and felt strong enough (and safe enough) to confront Drake openly, couples counseling might be a option. In the interim, Terry suggested that Clara join a spouse abuser survivor group, in which 6–8 women survivors shared experiences and provided mutual support. There, she would meet other women like herself, some of whom had remained with their abusers and some who had left. In this context, she would have exposure to different kinds of solutions and strategies. In the group, she could receive validation and support for her own situation, as well as being in a position to view the choices made by other women. Terry also proposed an abuser group for Drake. Clara was eager for a group experience, but Drake scoffed at her suggestion and said it was all Clara's problem, not his.

In the remainder of the decision-making phase, Clara and Terry explored possible options and her accumulated feelings of helplessness, ambivalence, depression, and intermittent rage. Clara needed time and opportunity to mourn the ideal marriage she never had, and began to look more realistically at what positive qualities remained of the relationship between Drake and herself. Together, they examined Clara's cognitions about blame, abuse, guilt, and denial. They reviewed cognitions related to Clara's self-efficacy and self-esteem and the probability that Clara could either (a) forgive Drake and live with him amicably if the abuse terminated, or (b) live independently as a single parent. Neither choice became attractive to Clara.

Terry showed Clara how to complete a cost–benefit analysis according to a social exchange paradigm (Rusbult, 1983), looking at each option and its possible outcomes. Clara determined that her job was indeed a good one and that she did not need any more career counseling. She also decided that her income, with child support, would suffice for both herself and Sherry should she decide to make a break. They covered some aspects of assertiveness, so that Clara could feel more competent in expressing her position and eventual decision to Drake. They explored community resources for childcare, costs of apartments, etc. Clara continued to monitor Drake's behavior to document physical, sexual, and psychological abuse, and one day she came into session with new bruises on her head and arms.

Resolution and restructuring

Now the sessions moved to a new level. Clara repeated her earlier statement "I've had enough, I'm not going to take any more of this," and returned home to demand a separation. In the final phase of Clara's counseling she became very task-orientated and proactive. She refused to file assault charges against Drake, but asked him to leave the house. She obtained a restraining order which required that Drake remain away from the home for a predetermined period of time. He was furious and threatened to sue for custody of Sherry. For many women, this step in restraining the man from access to his home triggers increased violence and anger. Clara was made aware of this, but Drake suddenly reacted with compliance and even agreed to attend an abuser's group in order to reinstate their relationship.

The remainder of Phase 3 was concerned with developing Clara's self-confidence and self-sufficiency. She had many skills in dealing with others and in independent living that required only that she believe in herself and agreed to attempt new behaviors. Counseling at this point was concentrated on helping Clara to identify herself as a caring and competent woman who could make rational and wise choices, either to remain with Drake or to leave and live on her own. Since she had submerged her needs and desires so heavily with his in the past few years, time was devoted to helping Clara nurture herself by attending a sports clinic, and going to dinner and theater with friends. As she continued her survivor group attendance, she found new friends and a new view of herself that belied the incompetent and unattractive woman that Drake tried to fashion for her.

At the end of 6 months, Clara announced that she was ready to take Drake back. She wanted one more chance to mend the relationship and to make her marriage work (she confronted Terry: "You did that too, didn't you?"). Clara decided to terminate her counseling and to recontact Terry if she needed further support. She did agree to remain in the survivor group, but our information was that she dropped out shortly afterwards.

Conclusions

Clara's story is one that is told over and over in many counseling experiences. During the 6 months she was with Terry, she gained considerable insight into the dynamics of her battering relationship with Drake and was no longer in a state of denial. She labeled him as a batterer, and warned him at the reunion that she would not tolerate another episode or it would be truly the end of the marriage. Her view of herself had changed dramatically, from a frightened and self-effacing "fat person who needed a new job" to a relatively self-confident professional woman who could rehearse her strong points and who liked the way she looked and the career she had originally chosen. However, she decided to return to the marriage with the hopes that Drake would change. For Clara and Sherry's sake, Terry hoped so also. However, research with battering men, even following group therapy, suggests that the battering will continue in a majority of cases (Gondolph, 1988; Snyder & Fruchtman, 1981). This was information that Clara had to determine for herself. We believed that, armed with her new view of herself and with a background of information and support from the counseling sessions, she would make a wise choice if the battering did repeat itself.

Summary

The abuse of women in close relationships is sufficiently frequent to be viewed as normative in Western society. In this chapter, we reviewed the incidence and theories about violence toward women. A three-part model of violence and entrapment was presented that includes the larger society, the male batterer, and the abused victim. In this model, the violence and sexism of society and the abuser combine to create a hostage situation for the woman. As hostage to terror and violence, she escalates her attempts to placate and please, and in doing so she increases her powerlessness and becomes psychologically and physically entrapped in a relationship from which she feels unable to extricate herself.

We presented the case of Clara, who was physically, psychologically, and sexually abused by her husband, and applied the theory of hostage and entrapment to her situation. The counseling followed a three-phase model of crisis intervention, exploration and decision-making, and resolution and restructuring. Terry combined these phases with Feminist Therapy Principles and cognitive–behavioral strategies to support and validate Clara as a strong and worthwhile individual, and to assist her in the process of decision-making about the course of her life. At the end of 6 months, Clara decided to give her marriage another try, and Terry lost contact with her. We judged that, at the end of this period, her depression and anxiety were decreased and her self-efficacy and self-esteem were much higher. She had learned to provide herself with non-blaming self-statements, and was determined not to live with abuse again. Terry wished her well and hoped for a positive outcome. She did not return for further counseling.

Activities

A

Review the three phases of counseling with Clara. For each phase, identify one procedure or topic that represents a Feminist Therapy Principle. List the principle and explain how it was used here in the counseling process.

B

(1) With a partner, role-play a session in which you are Clara and have decided to stay in the relationship with Drake at the termination of counseling. Although he has been violent once more, you have decided that the rewards are higher than the anticipated costs of leaving. You want your therapist to help you now in managing this relationship. Then reverse roles and play the therapist.

(2) With a partner, role-play Clara. You have returned to counseling because Drake has continued to be violent and you want help in the decision about whether to leave him. Then reverse roles.

(3) For each part you played above, what were your affective reactions (feelings)? What were your thoughts?

C

(4) Challenging myths. For each myth (false statement) in the Self-assessment at the beginning of the chapter, prepare a response you would give to a client (female or male) who believed the myth to be true. Role-play your challenges with a partner and be prepared to deal with counter-challenges.

Further Readings

There are many good books on battering relationships. Read at least one of the following in order to expand your understanding:

Gelles, R. J., & Strauss, M. A. (1988). *Intimate Violence: The Causes and Conse-quences of Abuse in American Families*. New York: Simon and Schuster.
Sonkin, D. J. (Ed.) (1987). *Domestic Violence on Trial*. New York: Springer.
Walker, L. E. A. (1979). *The Battered Woman*. New York: Harper & Row.
Yllo, K., & Bograd, M. (Eds.) (1988). *Feminist Perspectives on Wife Abuse*. Newbury Park: Sage.

CHAPTER 10

Choosing a Career Path

Self-assessment: Analyzing Your Career Development

Using the age-line given below, you are going to create a chart of the important events in, and influences on, your own career development. In following the step-by-step instructions, enter each indicated experience or influence on the time line at the age or ages where it occurred. The left half of the page will be for entering career-related events; the right half will be for entering career choices you have fantasized, considered or chosen at various ages.

(1) To the *left* of the line, enter your major educational experiences, e.g. elementary school, graduate school.

(2) To the *left* of the line, enter some of your major life events, e.g. marriage, partnering, divorce, birth of children, illnesses, etc.

(3) To the *right* of the line, enter all the careers you fantasized about, considered, and/or actually chose at various ages.

(4) For the ages you have not yet reached, enter to the *right* of the line the career choices or positions you hope to have at future points in time.

(5) As you look across your career dreams and choices, note how your choices have been affected by your being a woman or a man. Enter to the right of the line in red ink any critical turning points related to your gender and your career choices.

Personal Career Development Chart

Life Events		*Career Choices*
	Birth	
	5 Years	
	10 Years	
	15 Years	
	20 Years	
	25 Years	
	30 Years	
	35 Years	
	40 Years	
	45 Years	
	50 Years	
	55 Years	
	60 Years	
	65 Years	
	70 Years	
	75 Years	
	80 Years	
	85 Years	
	+	

Overview

The negative impact on women's lives of sex-role stereotyping and institution-alized sexism is clearly visible in yet another area—women's career develop-ment and choice processes. Women earn less than two-thirds of what men earn (United States Department of Labor, 1983) and continue to be employed in low-paying, lower status occupations. The high precentage of women with household incomes below the poverty level is reflected in the phrase "feminization of poverty."

While the career development process for women is complex and difficult to capture in a simple theoretical model, in this chapter we present a sociocultural perspective for understanding women's career development and a change agency–feminist approach to meeting the career counseling needs of women. In this chapter, we meet Marie, who sought career counseling because she wanted to return to work after the birth of her two children, but was uncertain whether she wanted to go back to her nursing career. In counseling, Marie explores how her career development has been affected by her sex-role socialization, and begins to challenge these beliefs and to choose a career path more in line with her potential.

Marie's Story: Stereotypical Career Choice

Marie, a 29-year-old woman, was self-referred for career counseling. She reported feeling slightly depressed and confused about her life direction.

> I have had an uneasy feeling in the pit of my stomach for the past 6 months every time I think about my next (30th) birthday. I feel restless, yet guilty. I have a wonderful husband and two beautiful children. Jamie, aged 5, and Laura, aged 3, are still young so I don't think that I should go back to work yet. In fact, my husband, Louis, is a successful attorney. As he points out, we really don't need the money. I know I should be happy as a clam; I have everything a woman could want. Yet, I still feel down and kind of at loose-ends. To make matters more confusing, I don't even know what I would want to do if I do go back to work. I have my BS degree in nursing and worked as a nurse for 4 years while my husband completed his law degree. I was good at my hospital nursing supervisor job, but I don't think that I want to go back to nursing. To tell you the truth, I was relieved when I left right before Jamie was born. As you can see, I'm a real mess. I'm not even sure I want to leave my kids to go to work, and even if I was sure, I don't know what I want to do.

When Marie's therapist, Holly, inquired about Marie's personal and educational history, she discovered that Marie had been in honors classes through junior high and high school. Marie remembered being tested by someone in junior high and thought that he had told her that her IQ was over 140. Marie knew she had done well in school, but was surprised when Holly used the word "gifted." Marie and Holly contracted for ten career counseling sessions over a 4-month period. At that point they agreed they would re-evaluate and contract for additional sessions if they were needed. They decided to focus on two major areas: clarifying Marie's long-term career goals, and resolving her immediate conflict over whether to return to work at this time. Holly informed Marie she was a feminist therapist and explained to Marie what that meant. Holly noted that Marie was a gifted woman who seemed to have made a career choice below her potential. Holly shared with Marie that she felt it was important for them to explore the impact of sex-role messages on Marie's past and current career choices, in order for Marie to make choices that were self-fulfilling. They also agreed to use a decision-making model to guide their work together.

Definitions

Marie's case can be understood within the general context of women's career development. We will examine this context, first by defining career and career development, and second, by overviewing some of the factors that may influence women's career development.

The study of factors affecting women's career choices is directly linked to the ways in which career and career development are defined. Typical definitions of career found in the literature vary from broad and encompassing of all life activities to more narrow definitions that focus solely on paid work activities. An example of a broader conceptualization comes from Super (1976), who defines career as ". . . the sequence of occupations and other life roles which combine to express one's commitment to work in his or her total pattern of development" (p. 4). Similarly, McDaniel's (1978) definition of career includes both work and leisure activities. Hansen and Keierleber (1978) propose a definition of career in which work, education, and family are related. An example from the narrower end of the continuum is provided by Zunker (1986). He defines career as ". . . the activities and positions involved in vocations, occupations, and jobs as well as related activities associated with an individual's lifetime of work" (p. 3).

Most theories of women's career development focus on the interaction between paid work and family responsibilities for women. From this perspective, broader definitions of career, like the one offered by Super (1976), would seem to be the most compatible with a feminist therapy approach. However, Fitzgerald and Crites (1980) argue for a more narrow definition of career. They define career as ". . . the developmental sequence of full-time, gainful employment engaged in by the individual during the course of his or her working life" (p. 45). Although they acknowledge that pursuing homemaking activities is an important factor affecting the career choice process, they do not consider homemaking to qualify as a career choice. Fitzgerald and Crites argue the importance of financial compensation for careers. They assert that women will not achieve equity with men until they are no longer dependent economically on others. Thus, from this perspective, a more narrow definition of career is compatible with a feminist therapy approach.

We agree with Fitzgerald and Crites that economic independence for women is crucial to achieving full equality. However, we also believe that to exclude homemaking, volunteer, and leisure activities from a definition of career denies not only the centrality of these activities in women's lives, but also the career-related skills that women develop as a result of participation in these activities. Thus, we define career as the developmental sequence of all life experiences (including education, paid employment, leisure, homemaking, volunteer work) that affect one's commitment to work.

Career development is affected strongly by environmental factors. These external factors include sex-role socialization, social class, economic class, ethnic/racial identity, economic, political, and educational structures. Thus, we use Herr and Cramer's (1988) definition of career development: "The total constellation of psychological, sociological, educational, physical, economic, and chance factors that combine to shape the career of any individual" (p. 17). To their "constellation," we add sex-role socialization and institutionalized sexism.

Factors Affecting Women's Career Development

Our definition of career development reflects the variety of factors influencing women's career paths. In the following sections, we overview these factors. Further, we explore the inter-relationships among these factors and the ways in which women's sex-role socialization and experiences with institutionalized sexism inhibit their career achievement. We begin our overview by reviewing the problems with current theories of and research on women's career development.

Most of the widely-used career development theories (e.g. Holland, 1966; Super, 1957) have been based primarily or entirely on the research studies of white, middle-class males. Despite the fact that these theories have limited applicability for women, women's career development is often compared to these male-based norms. Further, the career development process for women is complex, and thus, is difficult to predict and to capture in a theory. The complexity of women's career development processes is reflected in the plethora of research studies in the past 15 years related to women's career development, their career choice processes, and their achievement motivation.

Research on the variables affecting women's career development has produced some conflicting results. Frequently the factors that are significant contributors to women's career achievement in some studies are not found in others. Research methodology, variance in how the factors are measured, population sample used, and which factors are included all contribute to the inconsistency of outcomes across studies. Synthesizing this literature is beyond the scope of this chapter. Rather we have chosen to focus on the internal and external factors most often theorized to enhance or inhibit women's career achievement. Further, we are emphasizing those factors which are impacted by or due to sex-role socialization and institutionalized sexism.

Internal and external influences on women's career achievements have been conceptualized here in the context of gender bias. Gender bias includes any factor which limits one's career choices or career development solely on the basis of being female or male (Zunker, 1986). The wheel shown in Figure 10.1 illustrates the enormous impact of gender bias on women's career choices and career development, and how gender bias often results in women choosing careers below their potential.

The outer part of the wheel depicts external, environmental factors affecting women's career development. These social, economic, educational, and political forces can generally be viewed as embedded in sex-role socialization and institutionalized sexism processes. We believe that all women's career development and career choices are embedded in this gender-biased, external context. In turn, these environmental forces impact on, and interact with, factors internal to each of us. The wheel illustrates that what were originally environmental variables, external to women, become internalized. Thus, it is important to remember that even factors appearing as internalized on the wheel largely began as externally induced factors.

As you read the following sections on external and internalized factors, consider which of these factors fit for your own career development experiences. Return to the Self-assessment exercise that you completed at the beginning of the chapter. Enter in red ink on your career-line any additional sex-role, sexism-related experiences that have affected your career development.

External Factors: Sex-role Socialization and Institutionalized Sexism

Discrimination against women is evident in many sectors of society. Gender-based discrimination is institutionalized in our political, economic, educational, occupational, and religious systems. Astin's (1984) theory of career development contains two elements dealing with external influences: sex-role socialization, and the structure of opportunity. Sex-role socialization is accomplished in families, at school, at work, and in play. Astin's "structure of opportunity" includes the distribution of jobs, sex-typing of jobs, job

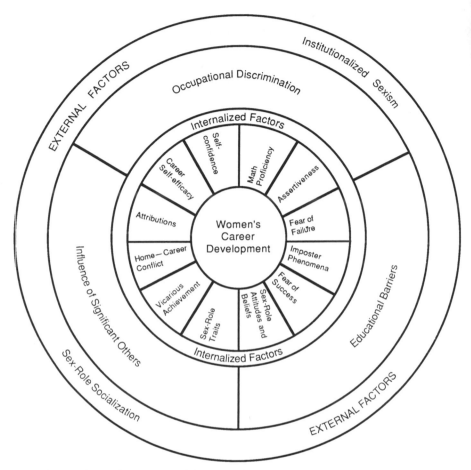

Figure 10.1.   Gender-based factors affecting women's career development

requirements, discrimination, the economy, family structure, and reproductive technology. A diagram of Astin's model is presented in Figure 10.2. Many of these external factors were discussed in Chapters 2, 3, and 4. For our discussion here, we have chosen to highlight three external influences— occupational discrimination, educational discrimination, and influence of significant others. In each of these areas, there is an interplay between sex-role socialization and institutionalized sexism.

Occupational discrimination

Sex-stereotyped beliefs about appropriate roles for women and men exert a major influence on employment opportunities and barriers experienced by

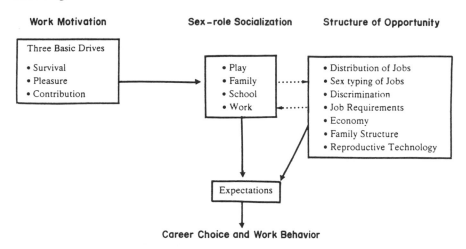

Figure 10.2. Astin's career development model: a need-based sociopsychological model of career choice and work behavior. (Reproduced from Astin, 1984, with permission of Sage Publications, Inc.)

each sex. The traits and behaviors stereotypically viewed as appropriately possessed by men, e.g. competitiveness and logical, initiating behaviors, lead people to see men as suited for certain occupations, especially ones involving leadership and professional or technical skills. On the other hand, stereotyped traits and behavior seen as appropriate for women, e.g. nurturing ability, cooperation, gentleness, are associated with a more narrow range of occupations, clustered into caretaking, lower-status, and lower-paying careers. Foxley (1979) concludes that women are societally channeled into preparing themselves primarily to be wives and mothers; if they do work outside the home, they are expected to choose careers that are an extension of their domestic roles.

Sex-role stereotyping of occupations refers to beliefs about the appropriateness of particular occupations for women and for men (Shinar, 1975). That this sex-typing of occupations exists is demonstrated by: (a) the sex-typed labels applied, e.g. policeman, fireman, stewardess; (b) the uneven distribution of females and males in various careers; and (c) the inequitable economic compensation given to female-dominated and male-dominated careers.

Although women have increasingly entered the paid labor force and have increasingly chosen non-traditional careers, they continue to be clustered in lower-paying, lower-status, traditionally sex-typed occupations. For example, in 1982 women in the United States accounted for 96.8% of nurses, 83.6% of elementary school teachers, and 80.5% of clerical workers, but accounted for only 4% of engineers, architects, and dentists and 13.7% of physicians (United States Department of Labor, 1983). The statistics for career preparation are slightly better. In 1982, Unites States university women comprised 76% of education majors, 94% of home economic majors, 13% of engineering majors, and 27% of medical school students (Chronicle of Higher Education, 1988). Given these distributional inequalities across occupations, Seager and Olson (1986) conclude:

> And, in every country and every region of the world, there are jobs that are specifically defined as "women's work." They are usually considered beneath men's station . . . (p. 45). Men's jobs, on the other hand, are often well-paid and highly respected, and women have a very hard time breaking into their ranks (p. 109).

The traditionally sex-typed occupations for women typically have lower pay than those occupations traditionally sex-typed for men. There is some support for the status and pay being directly linked to the distribution of females and males in a given career. For example, when research participants are told that women will soon comprise more than 50% of people in a career, they rate that occupation lower in status than if they are told that men will continue to dominate that career (Touhey, 1974).

The perceived desirability of a career is affected by the distribution of females and males in that career and by the perceived accessibility of that career. For example, people's interest in a career can be influenced by information about female or male domination in that career. Collin, Reardon, and Waters (1980) reported that men's interest in being a lawyer decreased when they were informed that women would soon comprise more than 50% of all lawyers. Further, Bridges and Bower (1985) found the perceived job availability affected women's likelihood of pursuing male-dominated occupations. Female respondents showed the greatest interest in pursuing occupations that were described as having good opportunities for women.

Wage-earning statistics illustrate the effects of sex discrimination in the workplace, as well as demonstrating the negative consequences to women of that discrimination. Black women have the lowest average income and the highest unemployment rates of all groups (United States Department of Labor, 1983). The unemployment rate for women with a doctoral degree is two to five times higher than for men with similar degrees (Reis, 1987). Women workers with 4 or more years of college earn the same as male workers with 1–3 years of high school (United States Department of Labor, 1983; see Table 10.1 for additional international statistics).

In a United States-based study conducted in the State of Kentucky, Straus and Zoe (1989) provide evidence that men's work is more highly valued than women's work. These researchers found that in one school district, substitute janitors, positions which require little education, are paid more than substi-

Table 10.1. *Women's Earnings Compared with Men's: some Cross-nation Comparisons. (From Seager, & Olson, 1986, with permission of Pluto Press.)*

Country	Women's earnings when compared to men's earnings (%)
Norway	80+
USSR	70–79
Australia	
United States	70–79
United Kingdom	60–69
Peru	60–69
Brazil	50–59
	40–49

tute teachers. In the United States, women and children under 18 years comprise 78% of all people living in poverty, and this trend is increasing (Seager & Olson, 1986). Basing their conclusions on international data, Seager and Olson (1986) state:

> Women are ghettoized into low-paying jobs and are often denied promotions, and commonly face outright wage discrimination . . . and form the bulk of part-time workers. As a result women everywhere earn less than men . . . The earnings gap is universal and growing, in spite of equal pay laws which exist in a great number of countries . . . Women's relative underpayment in work is a major factor in the growing feminization of poverty (p. 47).

Examining commonly held myths about female workers is helpful in understanding one way in which stereotyped beliefs about appropriate roles for women and men are applied in the world of work. A few of these *myths* are: (a) women do not work out of economic need; (b) women quit their jobs more often than men; (c) women are too emotional for certain kinds of work and responsibilities; and (d) women do not make good bosses. Although these statements are consistent with sex-role stereotypes, research reviewed by Herr and Cramer (1988) has demonstrated the inaccuracy of these myths. The extent to which employers believe gender-based myths guides their treatment of female workers.

These myths about female and male workers, and beliefs about appropriate roles for women and men, are formally and informally institutionalized into many employment structures. Although overt sex discrimination in employment practices is prohibited by law in the United States, such practices still overtly and covertly exist. In fact, after a review of the relevant literature, Hamilton et al. (1987) conclude that, "Employment discrimination is a prevalent and serious stressor in the lives of women" (p. 178).

The structure of our occupational institutions is often based on male values, e.g. competition and aggressiveness, and on norms of male experiences, e.g. men being primarily the "bread-winners." This male-normed bias poses additional problems for women in the workplace. For example, Herr and Cramer (1988) point out that childbearing and rearing are a major source of disruption in women's employment. Seager and Olson (1986) conclude that lack of childcare facilities is a handicap to women in the workplace, and that inadequate maternity policies leave women with little or no job protection.

As we reviewed in Chapter 3, employment discrimination is an institutionalized form of sexism. It is manifested in many ways: hiring and firing practices, differential working conditions, work assignments, promotions, salary, and sexual harassment. Among these various forms, sexual harassment has been one of the most studied, probably because it is easily identifiable (Hamilton et al., 1987).

Sexual harassment, unwanted sexual advances, requests or denegration, includes ". . . pressure for dates, sexually suggestive words or gestures and sexual remarks, deliberate touching, pressure for sexual favors, letters and calls, and actual or attempted rape or assault" (p. 156). Studies of sexual harassment differ in their estimates of incidence, ranging between 40% and 90% of all working women (Hamilton et al., 1987).

Employment discrimination, like other forms of gender-based discrimination such as rape, spouse abuse, and incest, has pervasive effects on working women. Among these effects are:

(1) Women leave their jobs or are driven out.
(2) Increased negative working conditions.
(3) Deceased opportunity for advancement.
(4) Loss of income.
(5) Loss of seniority.
(6) Disrupted work history.
(7) Emotional stress, including loss of self-esteem, self-doubt, depression, and fear.

These consequences reinforce traditional sex-role messages and serve as a threat to those who deviate from these norms (Hamilton et al., 1987). Further, for those women who are making career choices, they serve as a deterrent to entering the workplace, especially to entering non-traditional careers.

Educational barriers

Most of us spend about half of our waking hours in school during the most formative years of our career development. As we discussed in detail in Chapter 3, gender-based discrimination in our educational systems has been well documented and is manifested in several ways.

First, many studies have shown that teachers, counselors, and administrators respond differentially to boys and girls in ways that reflect traditional sex-role stereotyping.

Second, textbooks, instructional materials, and tests have been demonstrated to be sex-biased (Sadker & Sadker, 1982). These educational materials often show women and men in sex-stereotyped activities and occupations, use more male than female pronouns, under-represent female contributions in all fields and, in general, depict males more often than females. In addition, girls and women are often portrayed as incompetent, afraid, and unable to take effective action on their own behalf. Sex bias in textbooks exists at all grade levels from kindergarten through graduate school. Although there have been improvements in recent years, sexism is still present in educational materials.

Third, the administrative hierarchy of our educational institutions also reflects sex-role bias. While the majority of elementary teachers are female, the percentage of female faculty and female administrators dramatically decreases as grade level increases. For example, less than 2% of public school superintendents are female. Only 26% of higher education faculties are female, and these women are concentrated at the instructor and assistant professor levels (Reis, 1987).

Fourth, school personnel often encourage females and males to enroll in sex-stereotyped courses and to pursue sex-stereotyped careers. Lack of encouragement or active discouragement of non-traditional pursuits inhibits women from breaking from traditional sex-role socialization.

Thus, through the sex-biased attitudes and behaviors of school personnel, lack of non-traditional role models, sex bias in educational materials, sexism in the administrative hierarchy, and differential patterns of encouragement for achievement, our educational systems are a major source of sex-role stereotyping and institutionalized sexism. All these factors impact directly and indirectly on women's career development.

Influence of significant others

The role of significant others, including parents, peers, husbands, teachers, mentors, etc., demonstrates the influence of role models, or encouragers and rewards, and of discouragers—lack of reinforcement or punishment. In general, women who choose non-traditional careers are more likely to have had direct encouragement for, and role-modeling of, non-traditional careers. For example, non-traditional career-choosing women, as compared to traditional choosers, are more likely to have: (a) mothers and fathers with higher levels of education; (2) mothers who were employed outside the home; (3) parents who did not encourage stereotypical behavior (Sandburg et al., 1987); and (4) career encouragement from parents, teachers, peers, and counselors (Lunneborg, 1982; Stake & Levitz, 1974).

Summary of external factors

The messages sent to women from sexist, environmental barriers have a three-fold impact. First, they convey that women are not as valuable or as competent as men, especially in traditional male sex-typed arenas, i.e. that "women can't." Second, they suggest that it is not appropriate for women to pursue traditional male careers, i.e. that "women shouldn't" (Terlau, 1991). Third, they suggest that, even when women are competent and do pursue a non-traditional career, they will not be rewarded appropriately and may even be punished. When women realistically perceive these barriers, they are less likely to choose non-traditional paths. These overt and covert structural barriers discourage women from considering, choosing, and persisting in non-traditional majors and careers.

Internalized Factors

In the following sections, we will explore the more specific ways in which these external negative messages and structural barriers impact women's perceptions of themselves and their environment, and how these internalized perceptions influence their career-related choice behaviors. External sexist messages and barriers impinge on women so pervasively that the messages are no longer perceived as external, but rather as something wrong or deficient in the women themselves (Washor-Leihaber, 1982). The large number of internal factors on the career wheel demonstrates the myriad of ways in which each woman may internalize her external experiences. Also, for any particular woman, any number of these factors may be working in combination. The whole impact is greater than the sum of the individual factors.

Attributions

When males experience success, they are more likely to attribute their success to their ability, whereas women are more likely to attribute their successes to luck or effort. Males are more likely to attribute their failures to chance or lack of effort, whereas females are more likely to attribute their failures to their lack of ability (Dweck, Davidson, Nelson, & Enna, 1978). Female attributions of success to external sources and of failure to internal sources, contributes to women having less self-confidence and to their avoidance of some achievement situations. While this gender difference may seem to have a psychological foundation, there is evidence that attribution-making is a socialized phenomenon. Yee and Eccles (1983) found that adults were more likely to tell task-succeeding girls that they were lucky than task-succeeding boys that they did well because they were smart. The adults attributed the boys' task failures to lack of effort and the girls' task failures to lack of ability.

Career self-efficacy

Career self-efficacy is a specific form of self-efficacy which refers to people's beliefs that they can successfully perform job activities that are part of specific occupations (Betz & Hackett, 1981). In general, Betz and Hackett have found that females report higher self-efficacy for traditionally female occupations than for non-traditional occupations. Betz and Hackett view career self-efficacy as a mediating variable of career choice, in that, if individuals believe that they cannot perform the tasks required in a career, they will not aspire to that career. Career self-efficacy is not global, but rather refers to expectations for performance in specific situations.

Betz and Hackett theorize that women are lower in self-efficacy for non-traditional occupations because of traditional sex-role socialization. With respect to non-traditional careers, women have lower self-efficacy because they have less direct experience with non-traditional tasks, they lack same-sex role models, they receive less encouragement from others that they can perform the non-traditional tasks, and they experience higher anxiety in relation to the tasks. For the opposite reasons, women develop high self-efficacy for traditional occupations. Betz and Hackett conclude that traditional sex-role socialization directly affects development of specific career self-efficacies; career self-efficacy, in turn, directly affects women's traditionality of occupational choice. Hackett and Betz (1981) have found high non-traditional career self-efficacy of women to be positively related to the range of non-traditional careers considered; Nevill and Schlecker (1988) found that women who were high in generalized career self-efficacy were more willing to engage in non-traditional occupational activities.

Self-confidence and self-esteem

In general, males tend to overestimate their abilities, while females underestimate theirs (Maccoby & Jacklin, 1974). Both estimates are inaccurate, but the male perceptual error has a positive effect on performance and self-esteem, while the female error has detrimental effects. For example, Dweck (1986) found that girls are less confident of their intellectual abilities, despite having equivalent abilities. The underestimation by females contributes to fear of failure, i.e. "I don't have the ability, thus I am likely to fail," and to lower self-esteem. For example, Marie lacked confidence in herself in general and she consistently underestimated her intelligence.

Math proficiency

Males tend to excel at higher level math courses, are more likely to enroll in higher level math courses, and score higher on Math on the Scholastic Aptitude Test. The issue of what accounts for the female–male differences has never been fully resolved. While some argue for biological differences, others argue that the differences in math performance are tied to sex-role socialization and institutionalized sexism. The latter is compatible with a feminist therapy approach. Fenema and Sherman (1977) reviewed the literature and concluded that sex-role socialization and the sex-typing of math as a male domain were major factors in the math performance difference. For example, Yee and Eccles (1983) found that boys' parents tended to attribute their male child's math success to talent, wheras girls' parents tend to attribute their child's math success to effort. In a study of gifted mathematicians, three times as many women as men reported discrimination by teachers and advisors, receiving stereotyped messages, being given fewer job offers, and being offered lower salaries (Luchins & Luchins, 1980).

Math is a "critical filter in the job market" (Sherman, 1982) because math skills are crucial to so many fields and because math-related fields, such as engineering and accounting, are higher-paying and are male-dominated. Rekdal (1984) found that only 12% of women at the University of California had the high school math prerequisites to qualify for 80% of the undergraduate majors offered. Thus, possession of math skills is a critical factor in the restricted range of career options open to women.

Marie had always been good at math and had received reinforcement for her math abilities from several of her teachers. She took several extra math courses in college beyond those required for her nursing degree. Thus, proficiency in math was a facilitating force in Marie's career choice process.

Insufficient assertiveness

Assertiveness has been cited as a major internal barrier to women's career development (Epstein, 1970). Assertiveness skills are not typically taught to girls and traditionally are not sanctioned for women. Non-assertion restricts women from expressing the abilities they have. Assertiveness skills are especially important for confronting and persisting in the face of discrimination barriers in educational and occupational systems. For example, Nieva and Gutek (1981) found that individuals who apply for non-traditional sex-role jobs are more likely to be turned down. Women who are higher in assertiveness are more willing to engage in career activities of non-traditional occupations (Nevil & Schlecker, 1988).

Marie was appropriately assertive with most females and had used these skills well as a nurse supervisor. However, she had difficulty being assertive with most men. Holly and Marie explored the sex-role messages underlying Marie's difficulty with assertiveness with men, role-played situations requiring assertiveness, and contracted for behavioral changes related to assertiveness, especially related to interactions between Marie and her husband.

Fear of failure

Fear of failure is an expectancy that one will not be able to attain a particular goal (Sherman, 1987). When individuals experience fear of failure, they are more likely either to not attempt to reach the goal or to become handicapped by anxiety while attempting to attain the goal. While both women and men may experience fear of failure, Sherman (1987) and Clance and O'Toole (1987) assert that, because men are generally more confident and receive more encouragement than women, fear of failure has more negative impact for women. Fear of failure has been found to be related to lack of confidence, low self-esteem, low risk-taking and fear of success (Sherman, 1987).

Imposter phenomenon

The imposter phenomenon is a term used by Clance and Imes (1978) to describe a feeling of phoniness by high achievers. Individuals who have attained a level of success, but feel like imposters, assess that they do not deserve the achievement and expect to be "found out." "Imposters" do not enjoy their accomplishments, and negate external evidence of their abilities (Clance & O'Toole, 1987). Many of the characteristics of "imposters" demonstrate the close ties between attributions, fear of success, fear of failure, self-confidence, and sex-role messages. "Imposters" tend to be anxious about failure when faced with evaluation or a new task, feel guilty or ashamed about their success and ambitions, have difficulty internalizing positive feedback, underestimate their own abilities, attribute their successes to luck and hard work, may avoid some accomplishments, and set goals below their potential (Clance & O'Toole, 1987). Kerr (1985) believes the imposter phenomenon for women is related to the internalized effects of sex-role stereotyping. Women need to explain away their accomplishments, e.g. "I didn't deserve it," because success at difficult tasks that require competence is inconsistent with both societal expectations for women and with many women's self-concepts.

Marie consistently discounted positive feedback and tended to down-play all of her accomplishments. With the exception of her math ability, Marie especially discounted skills and assets which stereotypically fall in the male domain. For example, although she possessed and used many leadership skills, she had been surprised when she was promoted to the supervisor position at the hospital. She was sure they had made a mistake. Once she assumed the supervisor position, she worried that the hospital would discover her incompetencies.

Fear of success

Horner (1972) characterized fear of success (FOS) as a motivation to avoid success which she believed was a key factor accounting for differences in female and male motivation. She assessed for the presence of FOS by giving college students a story to complete. Women were given a "successful situation" scenario about Anne, who is at the top of her medical school class; men were given the same scenario except that the main character's name was John. If the story endings denied the success or the character's responsibility for the success, or described conflict about the success, or contained inappropriate responses, the person was said to have FOS. A low percentage of males and a high percentage of women were found to have FOS. Horner believed that FOS was a stable personality trait that developed early in childhood and was related to sex-role identity development. She believed that as long as achievement and being "feminine" were societally defined as conflicting, women would internalize these conflicts.

Horner's original findings have had mixed substantiation by subsequent researchers. In particular, the context of the successful situation, e.g. success in a female- or a male-dominated occupation, success in a competitive or cooperative situation, changes individuals' FOS scores. Thus, many researchers have concluded that FOS is not a stable personality trait (Condry & Dyer, 1976; Paludi, 1984; Tresemer, 1976). Rather, FOS is seen as a realistic appraisal by women of societal rewards and punishments for women who conform to, or deviate from, sex-role-stereotyped norms in achievement situations. Women, especially high-achieving women, perceive not only the positive rewards that come from high achievement in careers, but also the negative consequences of being seen as "unfeminine." Women who experience FOS appraise that they are likely to suffer negative consequences for non-traditional achievement, i.e. for deviant behavior. Thus, FOS is not a personality trait, but rather a manifestation of the cultural restrictions of women.

When "success" carries with it a high price, including chastisement for lack of femininity, withdrawal of support, increased external barriers to performance, and isolation, women may choose other alternatives that are perceived to have more positive outcomes. Or they may still choose the non-traditional option, yet experience increased conflict. Yuen and Depper (1987) concluded that fear of success is really a fear of failure, i.e. being successful at a career, but risking relationship loss.

Sex-role attitudes and beliefs

A variety of non-tradititional sex-role beliefs have been found to be associated with women who choose, or are employed in, non-traditional careers. Non-traditional occupation choosers, as compared to traditional choosers, (a) view their career as being equally important to that of their husbands and believe that husbands should help with household tasks (Nagely, 1971); (b) choose fewer sex-role-stereotyped occupations (Crawford, 1978); and (c) attain more liberal scores on the Attitudes Toward Women Scale (Crawford, 1978). Thus, there is evidence that holding liberal attitudes toward sex roles allows women to choose careers based on their interests and abilities, rather than on cultural norms.

Sex-role traits

In general, women who pursue non-traditional careers have been found to be high in masculinity, as measured by the Bem Sex-role Inventory (Strange & Rhea, 1983; Williams & McCullers, 1983). Positive correlations have also been found between high androgyny scores and non-traditional career choice (Clarey & Sanford, 1982). Since possession of masculine traits is common to both high masculine scores and high androgyny scores, instrumental traits appear to be crucial for non-traditional occupation choice.

Vicarious achievement

Vicarious achievers find personal fulfillment and satisfaction through a relationship with a directly achieving person with whom they identify (Lipman-Blumen & Leavitt, 1978), and they take pleasure both from the accomplishments of the other person and from their relationship with this person. Some degree of identification of the vicarious achiever with this other person is necessary; to some degree, vicarious achievers take as their own the goals, values, and interests of this person (Lipman-Blumen & Leavitt, 1978). In contrast, direct achievers derive pleasure by using self as a means to goals.

Lipman-Blumen and Leavitt believe that traditional sex-role socialization contributes to the development of vicarious achievement patterns in females, and of direct achievement patterns in males. They point out that girls are socialized to seek help from others, develop close affiliation ties, and not to master their environments directly. In their study of married women, they found that vicariously achieving women had lower expectations for continuing their education, and were more likely to subscribe to traditional sex-role stereotypes, than were the direct achievers. They conclude that vicarious achievement is congruent with traditional roles for women, i.e. the vicarious achiever tends to choose marital and maternal roles and/or occupational roles that are nurturant. Women with a vicarious achievement orientation will often fulfill their achievement needs through their spouse's and/or children's accomplishments.

Home–career conflict

Traditional sex-role socialization emphasizes the nurturing role for women. When a woman chooses a career, she usually expects herself, and is expected by others, to carry the majority of home maintenance and childcare responsibilities. She often believes that her career achievement is acceptable only if she is first successful with her home responsibilities (Clance & O'Toole, 1987). She often feels guilty about not giving 100% to each and pushes herself to be perfect at both—a "superwoman." Other women may resolve the home–career conflict by pursuing only one arena, to be wife and mother *or* to have a career. No matter which of these paths is taken, for many women, the home–career conflict has a significant impact on career development, at decision points as well as on a daily basis. Because sex-role socialization varies across minority groups, minority women experience the home–career conflict with various degrees of intensity.

During the course of counseling, Marie became aware that part of the confusion she felt at the beginning of counseling was related to her internal conflict between wanting to achieve and wanting to be a good wife and mother. Although Marie was not completely satisfied with her home-bound role, she believed that she should be happy since she had "everything a woman could want." She felt "inadequate" and "unfeminine" because she was not satisfied. She felt guilty about even thinking of returning to work.

Internalized factors—summary

Most women can identify one or more of these internalized factors as having inhibited their career development. Identifying these internal barriers, tracing them to their external sources, and challenging and changing both external and internal barriers forms the foundation of a feminist therapy approach to facilitating women's career development.

A Change Agent Career Counseling Model

In Chapter 5, we presented four conditions that must be met in order for a counseling theoretical approach to be compatible with feminist therapy. In addition to meeting these four conditions, a feminist career counseling approach should address external factors affecting career development as well as internal ones, and include strategies for bringing about changes in economic and occupational structures (Principle I). A feminist career counseling approach should account for the interaction between the individual's choices and environmental opportunities and barriers, as well as allowing for changes in both (Astin, 1984). The model should challenge the restrictions placed on women's potential by sex-role socialization, internalized sexism, and racism. In line with Principles II and III, a feminist career counseling approach needs to enhance self-exploration of sex-role variables, facilitate the woman's trust in herself, and empower her.

"Agency," the "tendency of the individual to respond proactively to situations representing educational and career opportunities" (Betz & Hackett, 1987, p. 299), is an important empowerment strategy. Agency includes creating opportunities and being assertive. Agency has been found to be a crucial behavioral competency for professional women (Betz & Hackett, 1987). Holly, Marie's counselor, used a career counseling approach with Marie that directly incorporates teaching clients agency skills, and encourages clients to use these agency competencies to challenge past, present, and anticipated career barriers. Holly's approach was based on a change agent career decision-making model called "Career Optimization through Change Agency" (COCA), developed by Remer and O'Neill (1978).

COCA is a 13-step decision-making model that focuses on teaching clients to be active agents in overcoming obstacles in the path of their most desired career choices. Approaching career choice in the context of total life planning, and highlighting the developmental nature of career choices, are also included in the COCA approach. Clients are taught to identify internal and external barriers to obtaining highly prized career goals, and to perceive these barriers as problems that can be changed. Research on the use of the COCA model with undergraduate, undecided majors who took a semester-long course based on the model, indicated that students became significantly more rational and less intuitive (i.e. impulsive) and dependent in their decision-making styles, more certain about their choices of an occupation, more crystallized in their vocational self-concept, and had fewer vocationally-related identity problems. Further, they engaged in more career information-seeking and were more likely to endorse change agent strategies for solving career problems that involved barriers (Remer, O'Neill, & Gohs, 1984).

The 13 steps of the COCA model are overviewed in Table 10.2. We will highlight several of COCA's 13 steps as we summarize Holly's counseling of Marie. However, it is beyond the scope of this chapter to present a complete description of the COCA model. See Remer and O'Neill (1980) for a detailed explanation.

Table 10.2.   *Overview of "Career Optimization Through Change Agency" Decision-making steps*

Step

1   Admit I am confused or uncertain about my career decisions
2   Commit myself to learning the decision-making process and to applying that process to my specific career-decision problem
3   Collect information about myself
4   Generate a list of career alternatives
5   Collect information about my career alternatives
6   Eliminate any career alternatives that are obviously most incompatible with myself
7   Compare the self-evaluation with the career alternatives analysis
8   Assess the advantages and disadvantages of each alternative
9   Attempt to improve my chances in any alternative
10 Weigh (assign priority to) ordering the alternatives of career alternatives
11 Implement my decision
12 Evaluate my decision
13 Generalize what I have learned about how to make a decision

Marie's Counseling: Discovering and Valuing Potential

Contracting for Counseling Goals

During the initial phase of counseling at Steps 1 and 2 of the COCA model, Holly and Marie clarified mutual expectations for counseling and began building a collaborative counseling relationship. In addition to suggesting that Marie explore the impact of sex-role messages on her career choices, Holly recommended that Marie learn a change agent approach to identifying and overcoming barriers that prevent Marie from reaching her full personal potential. Holly overviewed the COCA model for Marie and taught her about the change agent approach. Their contracted goals were described earlier in the chapter.

Assessing for Career Potential

At Step 3, Holly and Marie engaged in a major career-related assessment of Marie. In addition to the usual career assessment of client's abilities, career interests, personality factors, and work values, Marie and Holly explored Marie's typical decision-making style, her sex-role orientation and beliefs, and her life goals. When useful and relevant they chose standardized assessment measures, but were careful to supplement with other less-traditional assessment strategies that were less prone to sex bias and social-dominance bias (see Chapter 6).

Abilities

Because Marie viewed herself as over-achieving rather than as gifted, Holly suggested that she take an individual intelligence test. Marie's score of 135 fell in the superior, gifted range. Marie continued to express surprise, saying that she believed that she had obtained high grades in school only because she had worked so hard. She had previously given graduate school only passing consideration, since she believed that hard work would not be enough to succeed. Holly taught Marie about women's typical attributions about their successes and failures, and about the imposter phenomenon. Marie was able to see how her attributions of her successes to effort, and her belief that she was not deserving of her previous promotion to nurse supervisor, were linked to her socialization as a female. Holly suggested that Marie complete a variety of abilities identification exercises. For example, Marie identified her most significant life achievements and did an analysis of the specific abilities she used in each of these achievements. These abilities were stated as non-career-content-bound *functional skills* (Figler, 1979), so that they could be applied easily across various career alternatives. Functional skills analysis is a particularly useful career counseling tool with women who have never been in, or have periods being out of, the paid work force because these women can analyze their volunteer, home-related, and leisure activities/ achievements for the skills they possess. These identified skills can then be translated into the abilities needed for various careers.

These exercises helped Marie begin to "own" her abilities and challenge her attributions of her successes to effort and luck. She also became aware of how she had often down-played her accomplishments in order not to "threaten" the men in her life, and in order to preserve her own sense of femaleness. Marie also read research articles about gifted women and learned that her conflicts between wanting to achieve and wanting to be seen as feminine are often heightened for gifted women.

Interests

Marie's performance on the Strong–Campbell Interest Inventory showed high basic interests in science and math, and high similarity scores to nurses, physicians, biologists, and lawyers. Holly gave Marie the Non-sexist Vocational Card Sort (Dewey, 1974) that we reviewed in Chapter 6. Through the card sorting process, through a sex-role analysis, and with challenging from Holly, Marie became aware that she held several sex-role beliefs that were barriers to her considering careers that were in line with her potential (see Table 10.3 for a list of Marie's sex-role beliefs). First, she realized that her original choice of nursing was partially based on her learned belief that women should be helpmates to men, rather than achieving directly, and that

Table 10.3.   *Marie's Sex-role Analysis Chart*

Women should	Women shouldn't
Be polite and nice	Be a leader
Be a wife and mother	Be aggressive
Be supportive of her husband	Be too smart
Achieve through contributions to the family	Be angry
Be a caretaker	Do 'male things'
Have primary responsibility for the rearing of children	Achieve
	Be competitive

women should be in subordinate roles to men. She admitted that her current stay-at-home, vicarious achievement arrangement was not fulfilling to her.

Second, she became aware that she was rejecting otherwise desirable career alternatives if they required a high degree of responsibility or leadership skills. For example, while doing the card sort, she initially put "physician" in the "would not choose" pile because of "the responsibility physicians have to take." When Holly asked for clarification, Marie answered, "Women shouldn't be in leadership positions and can't handle life-and-death responsibilities." As Marie began to challenge her sex-role beliefs, she was able to acknowledge that she had already held leadership positions as a nurse supervisor and had made daily life-and-death decisions as a nurse. Further, she shared with Holly that she had sometimes fantasized about being a physician, but had never seriously pursued the option because she could not see how to combine it with being a wife and a mother. Holly encouraged Marie to talk with some female physicians who had combined career and family. In so doing, Marie not only collected information about being a physician, but also gained contact with non-traditional role models and potential mentors.

This exploration by Marie and Holly illustrates applying change agency strategies to the career choice process. Marie's sex-role beliefs were not treated as immutable facts to which Marie needed to adjust. Rather, they were treated as mutable barriers to be challenged and possibly eliminated or reduced. As a result of this challenging process, Marie began to restructure her sex-role beliefs. She moved the career alternative of "physician" to her "probably would choose" pile.

Values

Marie and Holly explored Marie's life and work values through a series of values clarification exercises. One advantage of this experiential approach, as compared to use of standardized tests, is that it gives clients practice with being experts on themselves. An especially helpful exercise for Marie was

Table 10.4. *Marie's Brainstormed List of Career Alternatives*

Housewife	Public relations person
Physician	Hospital administrator
Nurse administrator	Musician
Chemist	Veterinarian
Pharmacist	Travel agent
Nurse	Lawyer
Biologist	Physicist
Psychologist	Dentist
Statistician	Homemaker

writing a newspaper article about herself 20 years from now. Marie wrote about being recognized for a significant professional contribution she had made and for which she was to receive an award. In the article, she also mentioned having the support of her husband and grown children. Thus, she saw clearly that both achievement outside of the home and close family ties were very important to her. Her initial counseling sense of "something missing from my life" was emerging as need for direct achievement outside the family. Marie and Holly completed Step 3 by doing the exercise presented at the beginning of this chapter.

Generating Alternatives and Collecting Information

At Step 4, Holly encouraged Marie to brainstorm a quantity of possible career alternatives for herself. Brainstorming, with critical judgment suspended, is an especially useful technique for women whose range of alternatives has been limited by sex-role messages and institutionalized sexism. Marie and Holly collaborated in the brainstorming process. Marie's list of brainstormed alternatives can be found in Table 10.4.

At Steps 5 and 6, Holly contracted for Marie to collect some information about all of her brainstormed alternatives. The amount and variety of information varied according to how much information Marie already posessed. Some alternatives that were grossly incompatible with Marie were eliminated as Marie collected information. Holly challenged Marie when she thought Marie was eliminating alternatives prematurely, or on the sole basis of a barrier that could be changed. By the end of Step 6, Marie had narrowed her alternative list to five: PhD in administrative nursing, physician, PhD in biology, nurse supervisor, and college nursing professor.

Analyzing the Alternatives

In Steps 7 and 8, Marie applied a systematic process for identifying the short- and long-term advantages and disadvantages of each of her alternatives.

During these steps, Holly also focused Marie on her intuitive and emotional responses to each of her alternatives through imagery work. While in a relaxed state, Marie imaged or fantasized herself in a typical day working at each of her alternatives. Marie's feelings and the symbols that emerged in the imagery work were explored. In accordance with Principles II and III, Holly encouraged Marie to trust her feeling reactions as an additional source to the rational approach they had been using.

Identifying Change Agent Strategies

Holly and Marie used a problem-solving approach to Marie's internal and external career barriers that were encountered throughout the decision-making process. The disadvantages identified for each alternative at Step 8 can also be viewed as barriers that can be changed. Reducing or eliminating a disadvantage improves the desirability and probability of that alternative. Thus, at Step 9, Holly and Marie reviewed the disadvantages of Marie's alternatives. "Too much time commitment" was listed for four of the alternatives. When questioned further, Marie indicated that she expected her husband to be unsupportive of any of her alternatives that required years of additional schooling and a strong energy commitment by Marie. After more discussion, Marie decided to request of her husband that they seek marriage counseling to clarify expectations and work on this potential conflict. Marie delayed completing Step 10 until after they received couples counseling. As a result of this change agent intervention aimed at external environment change, Marie and her husband were able to negotiate some changes in their relationship which, in turn, reduced the "too much time" barrier for Marie.

Choosing and Implementing

At Step 10, Marie ranked ordered her alternatives from most to least desirable as: Professor of Nursing, PhD-level Biologist, Physician, PhD in Nursing Administration, Nurse Administrator. With Holly's help, Marie developed a plan for implementing her first-ranked choice. The implementation plan included change agent strategies relevant to this choice. Marie was pleased with her 1350 total Graduate Record Examination (GRE) scores and acknowledged without qualification that she was indeed an intelligent woman! Marie was admitted to the PhD program in nursing at a nearby university.

Summary

Marie's journey toward reaching her full potential was facilitated by a combined feminist therapy and change agent counseling approach. Marie had confronted and worked to change several internal and external barriers that had limited her previous career development. She had an appreciation about how being a woman had affected her choices. She expanded the number and range of alternatives she was considering. She learned a decision-making process that she could apply to other life decisions, and a problem-solving approach for challenging barriers to her desired goals. Further, she began to own and appreciate her intellectual and personal power.

Marie's career journey represents only one type of career development problem encountered by women. Indeed, she had many financial, educational, and intellectual resources that many of our clients do not have. Her counseling needs would be very different were she a single, divorced mother who had no labor force experience and whose husband was not paying child support. Daily survival needs would then take precedence over career–self actualization needs (Harmon, 1978). As we will discuss in Chapter 11, minority women will often be encountering racial bias in addition to sexism barriers.

In this chapter we have presented an overview of the many gender-based external and internal factors affecting women's career development. We have asked you to identify how these factors have influenced your own career development and we have illustrated the interplay among some of those factors for Marie. The challenge to feminist career counselors is at least two-fold. In addition to using our knowledge and awareness at an individual level to unyoke ourselves and our clients from the restraints of our socialization and discrimination as women, we are challenged to change the social, economic, educational, and occupational structures that limit the career achievement of all women.

Activities

A

Make a list of the sex-role messages that have influenced your career-related decisions. Underline those messages that are currently restraining you from reaching your full potential. Choose one of these messages and identify possible change agent strategies for changing/restructuring this message.

B

Complete the following imagery exercise in a quiet place and after relaxing yourself. Imagine that you were born male (if you are a woman) or female (if you are a man). Slowly see yourself growing up as this gender. Imagine what activities you would choose and what messages you would hear. Now imagine yourself fantasizing about trying out, and choosing career paths throughout your life. When you are finished with the imagery, note how your choices were different as this other gender.

Further Readings

Astin, H. S. (1984). The meaning of work in women's lives: A sociopsychological model of career choice and work behavior. *The Counseling Psychologist*, **12**, 117–126.

Fitzgerald, L. F., & Crites, J. O. (1980). Toward a career psychology of women: What do we know? What do we need to know? *Journal of Counseling Psychology*, **27**, 44–62.

Kerr, B. (1985). *Smart Girls, Gifted Women*. Columbus, OH: Ohio Psychology.

Remer, P., & O'Neill, C. D. (1980). Clients as change agents: What color could your parachute be? *Personnel and Guidance Journal*, **58**, 425–429.

CHAPTER 11

Dealing with Multiple Risks: Lesbian and Ethnic Minority Women

Self-assessment: Cross-cultural Counseling Skills

Each time you are confronted with a client whose major life experiences differ from yours (age, life-stage, cultural identity, affectional preferences, gender, race, nationality, socioeconomic status, etc.), you will need to access and use your cross-cultural counseling skills. For both of the following clients, answer the questions below:

(A)   Jeanne, a 34-year-old woman whose female lover has just decided to "come out" to her family of origin.

(B)   Anise, an African-American woman who is the only black person working in the trust department of a major bank.

---

(1)   List three personal issues that might be important for this client;
(2)   Share your list with a partner and compare your responses.

Did you agree on any or all of them? The issues and cases described in Chapter 11 will be useful in determining for yourself how well you answered these questions. Please refer also to Table 11.1, which displays a model set of cross-cultural counseling skills.

Overview

Each client who seeks help in redesigning her life situation is a unique person. Her individual life pattern and experiences are matched by no other person. However, each client is also a member of multiple groups that can be defined by categories such as age, life-stage, affectional preference, ethnic origin, cultural identity, religious or spiritual orientation, family constellation, employment status, educational attainment, physical or mental disability, or socioeconomic level. Membership in any of these groups (as well as other groups not listed above) are accompanied by implicit or explicit norms and standards that may define and structure the client's beliefs, attitudes, values, expectations, and interpersonal transactions.

Some group memberships also place the individual at personal risk for categorical assignment to low social status, destructive cultural stereotypes, and pervasive societal discrimination. As a result, individuals from these groups may experience powerlessness, social stigma, and systematic exclusion (Kinloch, 1979). Some of your clients will identify with several high-risk groups, bringing with them issues that are common across groups as well as some concerns that are unique to each individual. One client, for example, may be an African–American lesbian woman, a single mother, currently unemployed, and under economic stress. Although she may have contacted you initially for help in managing her three young children, her group membership issues are likely to be inter-related with the problems she is experiencing with childcare. Her particular group memberships place her in additional jeopardy for continuing exposure to societal oppression and exclusion, and may have important implications for her effective functioning and personal well-being.

Members of high-risk or minority groups face the additional stigma of being blamed for their social conditions, such that their "innate" characteristics, rather than societal oppression, are seen as the causes of their problems (Atkinson & Hackett, 1988). Thus, poverty is attributed to lack of motivation, singleness to a breakdown in family structure, and childcare difficulties to the absence of a male in the home. These "blaming the victim" attributions further stigmatize the individual and increase her difficulties in receiving social services.

For each client, both acknowledged and unacknowledged identification with high-risk groups will function to shape many of the expectations, attitudes, and behaviors that the client brings to the counseling relationship. Similarly, your own group memberships and experiences will have shaped your personal biases, attitudes, values, and expectations about others. Both client's and therapist's cultural identities, then, will influence the course of therapist–client interactions.

We believe that an awareness and understanding of the client's important group identities is essential to the practice of ethical and effective counseling. In this chapter, we present an identity-development model originally constructed for Black Americans that can be applied both to lesbian and minority-group clients. In Chapter 13 we apply a similar model to the development of feminist identity. Therapists and counselors who work with clients that differ from themselves in functionally important ways (age,

Table 11.1. *Characteristics of the Culturally Skilled Feminist Therapist. (Adapted from Atkinson, Morten, & Sue, 1979.)*

Knowledge	Has a good understanding of the sociopolitical system's operation in the dominant culture with respect to its treatment of minorities.
	Possesses specific knowledge and information about the particular group she/he is working with.
	Is aware of institutional barriers that prevent minorities from using mental health services.
Attitudes	Is aware and sensitive to her/his cultural heritage and to valuing and respecting differences.
	Is aware of her/his own values and biases and how they may affect minority clients.
	Is comfortable with differences that exist between self and client in terms of ethnicity, age, race, affectional preferences, socioeconomic status (SES), and beliefs.
	Is sensitive to circumstances (personal biases, sociopolitical influences, etc.) that may suggest referral of the minority client to a member of her own reference group.
Skills	Can generate a wide variety of verbal and non-verbal responses.
	Can send and receive both verbal and non-verbal responses accurately and appropriately.
	Is able to exercise institutional intervention skills on behalf of her/his client.

ethnicity, affectional preference, etc.) need to develop multiple skills that will enable them to approach each client with empathy and sensitivity to her particular group identities, as well as to her individual issues (Sue, 1983).

The sets of skills for working with clients who differ from the therapist in important ways have been described as cross-cultural skills. For the feminist therapist, it is particularly critical to recognize the implicit power imbalance that occurs when the client's important identities lie with culturally-oppressed groups. Cross-cultural counseling skills assist the therapist in identifying those attitudes and behaviors that communicate inequality and distance to the client. Table 11.1 displays a set of cross-cultural skills that we have adapted to the framework of feminist therapy.

In this chapter, we select two representative groups for discussion: lesbian women and ethnic minority women. Clients from each of these groups may experience a dual risk of discrimination, both as a woman and as a member of a group that is associated with low status and widespread societal stigma and/or exclusion. For each group, we discuss: (a) major client issues; (b) client–therapist concerns; and (c) management of the counseling processes. A final section ties the practice of feminist therapy to the concerns of multiple risk women.

Table 11.2. *Rates of Depression in Women over 65. (From Gardner, 1989, with permission.)*

Group		Prevalence (%)
Total sample	(N = 972)	10.8
Whites	(N = 529)	11.5
Blacks	(N = 48)	20.8
Low income Whites	(N = 183)	14.8
Low income Blacks	(N = 25)	24.0

Ethnic Minorities: Individuals or Stereotypes?

Who are the ethnic minority women? We include here any defined ethnic group that (a) is identified by self or others as physically or culturally different, and (b) experiences low social status, pervasive discrimination, and powerlessness within the dominant culture. Here, the term *ethnic* refers to inclusion in a group through a common nationality, cultural heritage, or race (Axelson, 1985). We use the term *ethnocultural* to denote the combined cultural meanings and standards of the person's identified ethnic group (Comas-Diaz, 1988). The concept of *minority* refers not to relative numbers, but to relative degree of oppression and powerlessness within a dominant culture (Atkinson, Morten, & Sue, 1979).

In the United States, these ethnic minority groups include Blacks (both African–Americans and Blacks from Caribbean and other backgrounds), Hispanic/Latinos, Asians, and Native American Indians. Other ethnic groups, such as native Arabs and Pakistanis and other middle-eastern cultures, may also fit the definition of ethnic minority. As a group, ethnic minority women experience frustration, powerlessness, and alienation, and are at particular risk for stress-related illness (Olmedo & Parron, 1981). Across ethnic groups, "minority women exhibit significantly higher distress, depression, and mental health service utilization than minority men, mirroring white women's patterns" (Thoits, 1987, p. 92). For Black individuals, however, recent community prevalence studies suggest that these data reflect an interaction between race and socioeconomic status, such that Black and White differ in mental health status mainly at the lower income levels (Kessler & Neighbors, 1986). For women over 65, for example, Bonny Gardner (1989) reported that income was a better indicator of depression on the Center for Epidemiological Studies–Depression Scale (CES-D) (see Chapter 7) than race. Black women with low incomes, however, had the highest rates of subclinical depression (Table 11.2).

For each minority group client, individual ethnocultural backgrounds must be explored if client and therapist are to communicate effectively. Ethnocultural world views, values, and sex-role expectations will vary considerably across groups (as between Hispanic and Black women), as well as within groups (as between Puerto Rican and Mexican women). Acculturation to the dominant culture will be vastly different for the recent Hispanic immigrant than for the Black woman whose great-grandparents were slaves (Comas-Diaz, 1988). The competent cross-cultural counselor should become knowledgeable about the culture of each particular group with which her client is identified, and in particular, the gender relationships and sex-role standards of her subculture.

Example: Counseling Black Women

For the purposes of this chapter, we center on African–American Black women to exemplify some of the issues that arise in cross-cultural counseling situations. Although each situation is unique, you should be knowledgeable about three major issues for Black women: (a) ethnocultural identity; (b) stresses arising from lifespan experiences of racism and discrimination; and (c) gender and sex-role concerns. The combination of risk factors for Black women multiplies their total life stressors, and places them at additional jeopardy for illness and hospitalization. In contrast to her vulnerabilities to stress, however, you will also look at the strengths of your Black client, the sources of her pride and personal empowerment, and the effective coping strategies that have faciliated her survival.

Ethnocultural identity

Differences in cultural identity describe the extent to which minority group members adopt the values and behaviors of the majority population, or become immersed in the norms and ways of their ethnic group. Several models of cultural identity have been proposed; we focus on the model of Black identity development described by Cross (1980), which can be applied to other ethnic and minority groups as well. A modified form of this model is displayed in Table 11.3, which compares with the stages of lesbian identity development (see Table 11.5). These stages represent a continuum rather than discrete locations in life experience.

The original model proposed by Cross (1980) describes five sequential positions that define the manner in which the person mediates the self between two contrasting cultural orientations. Your understanding of the client's current placement along this identity continuum may be helpful in understanding her attitudes and behaviors, with respect to both her own ethnic heritage and the dominant majority culture. The five stages include

(1) Pre-encounter, in which the individual attempts to assimilate herself into the dominant culture, with the consequent reflected negative self-evaluation.

Table 11.3. *Stages of Black Identity Development. (Adapted from Cross, 1980 and Parham & Helms, 1985)*

Pre-encounter
   The unaware person. Acceptance of oppression as justified. Values assimilation
      into majority culture. Negative self-concept.
   "I believe that to be Black is not necessarily good."

Encounter
   Profound events increase awareness, rejection of oppression, and feelings of guilt
      and anger.
   "I am determined to find my Black identity."

Immersion
   Withdrawal from dominant culture. Immersion in one's heritage, hostility towards
      Whites. Pride emerges.
   "I believe the world should be interpreted from a Black perspective."

Internalization
   Development of an integrated and more positive self.
   Adopting a pluralistic and non-racist perspective.
   "I feel good about being Black, but I do not limit myself to Black activities."

---

(2)   Encounter, in which she becomes acutely aware of and angry toward
      her cultural oppression.
(3)   Immersion, in which she becomes immersed and prideful in her ethnicity
      and hostile toward the dominant culture.
(4)   Internalization, in which she integrates the two perspectives.
(5)   Internalization/commitment, in which she invests herself in action
      toward positive community change.

The advantages of exploring a minority woman's stage of identity development are three-fold: (a) it assists you in destereotyping the client and in considering her individual integration of her ethnicity; (b) it may enable you to enter her world with a lens that more clearly matches her own; and (c) it may assist you in looking at the sources of her strengths as well as her problems. For example, Parham and Helms (1985) developed a Racial Identity Scale based on the five stages. They reported that the Pre-encounter stage was associated with high anxiety and low self-esteem, while Encounter attitudes correlated with low anxiety and high self-esteem. More recently, Wilkinson (1990) explored the relationship between the Racial Identity Scale and measures of personal well-being in professional Black women. She found that measures of depression, anxiety, and life satisfaction were differentially correlated with stages of racial identity, as well as with perceived discrimination and personal coping skills.

Depending upon the level of integration of dominant culture with Black subculture, the Black woman may have differing attitudes toward having a Black vs. a White counselor, and differing attitudes and values related to self-esteem, sex roles, achievement, family, religion, and feminism. For minority women in general, integration of their ethnocultural heritage and attachment to a supportive community are important sources of self-awareness, self-esteem, individual and group pride, and resiliency in the face of stress (Olmedo & Parron, 1981).

Experiences of racism and discrimination

We define *racism* here as systematic policies of oppression directed toward people of color (Lykes, 1983). Although no Black woman is immune to racism and discrimination, individual clients will perceive, interpret, and cope with these experiences in differing ways. Some of these reactions are related to the individual's cultural identity cognitions and the manner in which she interprets and integrates experiences that disconfirm and negate the positive aspects of herself (Wilkinson, 1990).

In the United States, institutionalized racism toward Black people has been embedded within the history of slavery and the assumption of White supremacy and Black inferiority (Boyd-Franklin, 1989). However, contemporary racism is also "routinely acted out by people who may not consciously accept racist views" (Greene, 1986, p. 46). The general bias toward White superiority has supported economic, social, political, and educational discrimination toward people of color, as well as toward other minority groups.

Despite the introduction of Civil Rights legislation and affirmative action programs designed to promote social justice, systematic discrimination toward minorities continues to take its toll. On the basis of extensive research, Taylor and Smitherman-Donaldson (1989) conclude that "A national descriptive overview of Black women reveals minimal penetration into mainstream institutional life and virtually no power in these institutions. Economic, social, and educational institutions reveal similar patterns in their resistance to change" (pp. 10–11). Continuing racism has resulted in restricted access to privileges and opportunities for most Black women, and consequently has limited their level of education (McCombs, 1989), employment and salary (Woody, 1989), health care, and choice of residence (Leigh, 1989). For most occupations, Black women have salary levels below that of White women as well as below that of all employed men, regardless of ethnicity (Woody, 1989). The experience of racism in its many forms and manifestations provides a continuing source of lifespan stress for Black women (Wilkinson, 1990).

Gender and sex-role concerns

Black women experience double discrimination. That is, Black women are isolated from other groups by the existence of dual discrimination, both as a woman and as a Black (Reid, 1988; Taylor & Smitherman-Donaldson, 1989; Trotman, 1984). As Reid (1988) points out, "Conflicts for Black women arising from their interactions with White women, White men, and Black men present unique sets of problems and issues" (p. 218). As a result, "Black women are left to decide where they should stand" (p. 213).

When faced with exclusion, derogation, or any form of discrimination, does the Black woman attribute it to race, to gender, or to both? How does the literature on sex roles accommodate to the realities of more egalitarian gender arrangements in the Black community? How do professional Black women, faced with being both the only woman and the only Black in an administrative unit, cope with isolation, exclusion, racism, and sexism? How do Black women integrate their feminist views with the realities of their loyalties to Black men and their awareness of patriarchy at all levels? And how do Black women, embracing both feminism and an ethnocultural identity imperative, integrate these two ideologies? Although you may not know now how to respond to such questions, these are the kinds of issues that may concern your client.

More recently, the gender-related issue of "Black beauty" has received attention in the research literature. In contrast to men, women of all cultures are exposed to greater pressures to be attractive, and are more likely to be negatively affected by dominant cultural norms of beauty that do not match their own characteristics. For Black women in particular, Anglo norms of fair skin, straight nose, and silky hair can have a negative impact on Black women's ". . . central feelings related to self-worth, intelligence, success, and attractiveness" (Neal, 1989, p. 324). In a detailed review of the role of physical attractiveness as a therapeutic issue, Neal (1989) proposes that skin color and features are a common topic for Black women, and may be associated with feelings of anger, resentment, guilt, and shame. In addition to therapeutic attention to the positive reframing of women's physical self, Neal recommends bibliotherapy for such clients, using books that affirm their cultural heritage and their beauty as Blacks.

These questions, and many others, are real issues for many Black women who are in the process of self-definition and personal empowerment. Although your client may present her issues as child management, depression, family conflict, or employment decisions, questions of ethnocultural identity, racism, gender, and sex roles may need to be addressed.

Client–counselor Issues

Let's assume that you, as the counselor, are White and your client is Black. What concerns are likely to confront each of you?

Client issues

The immediate issue for your client is ethnicity (Block, 1984; Hunt, 1987). Although broad reviews of ethnicity as a variable in psychotherapy with minorities do not support differences in measured outcomes of well-being for same or cross-cultural therapy dyads (Sue, 1988), disagreements persist in the research and therapeutic community. In Black client–White therapist dyads, as compared to Black–Black dyads, research suggests earlier termination from counseling (Terrell & Terrell, 1984), and less client self-disclosure (Ridley, 1984).

Frances Trotman (1984) asserts that a Black–Black female dyad results in more therapeutic gain because the therapist will be less likely to label culturally modal behaviors as pathological. Thus, distrust of police and other authorities, transmission of meanings through particular language structures, self-disclosure, and expressions of anger and rage—will all be expressed more openly and will receive more acceptance within an ethnically matched dyad. Trotman points out that the Black therapist is also an effective role model for the Black client by communicating love and demystifying Black success.

In a contrasting view, Beverly Greene (1986) assumes that cross-cultural dyads will occur due to the scarcity of Black mental health professionals, and she provides guidelines for therapists who work with Black clients. She confirms the Black client's initial anxiety, mistrust, hesitancy, and tendency to "test" the therapist on acceptance of herself as an individual. Greene emphasizes the responsibility of the therapist to be familiar with Black culture and experience, as well as to be aware of her own feelings and attitudes about working with Black clients. Hunt (1987) suggests some useful guidelines for supervision of trainees who work with cross-cultural clients.

Counselor issues

As with all cross-cultural counseling, the development of attitudes, knowledge, and skills in working with Black clients is essential to an effective relationship (see Table 11.1).

With respect to attitudes, Greene (1986) lists three major pitfalls that may confront the White therapist: bigotry, color-blindness, and paternalism. Bigotry may be either conscious or unacknowledged, and is likely to be reflected in attention to ethnic deficits rather than ethnocultural strengths. Your assumption of ethnic deficits might guide you to perceive pathology in normal coping strategies, and might further lead you to blame your client for the unemployment, poverty, or her difficulties with relationships. You might interpret her sense of inner strength, for example, as "matriarchal dominance," thereby misinterpreting her family structure.

Color-blindness, on the other hand, denies the client's freedom to explore her experiences of racism. If you are color-blind to the facts of racism, you may incorrectly interpret your client's perceptions of discrimination as cognitive distortions. Thus, you may impede her opportunity to confront her issues and to develop effective coping strategies.

Finally, the stance of paternalism reflects a condescending approach that places responsibility on you for redressing all previous grievances. Greene (1986) suggests that paternalism may stem from the therapist's collective sense of guilt and her eagerness to prove that she is not like other Whites. Paternalism tends to assign all the client's problem to the racist social order, and may impede both client and counselor from encouraging more personal explorations of self in context.

Managing the Counseling Process

For the feminist therapist, the process of counseling with minority women incorporates the Principles of Feminist Therapy with a multicultural perspective. Lillian Comas-Diaz (1987, p. 469) describes a feminist model that empowers minority women by helping them to:

(1) Acknowledge the deleterious effects of sexism and racism.
(2) Deal with feelings of anger and self-degradation imposed by their status of ethnic minorities.
(3) Perceive themselves as causal agents in achieving solutions to their problems.
(4) Understand the interplay between the external environment and their reality.
(5) Perceive opportunities to change the responses from the wider society.
(6) Integrate ethnic, gender, and racial components into their identity.

Lesbian Women

Definition

A lesbian woman is:

A-woman-identified-woman whose lifestyle is centered around women (Loewenstein, 1980).

A-woman-loving-woman (Zollicoffer, 1984).

. . . a woman whose primary emotional, psychological, social and sexual interests are directed toward other women (Kingdon, 1979, p. 44).

Table 11.4.   *Continua for Assessment of Sexual Preference*

Kinsey's Heterosexual–Homosexual Rating Scale. (Adapted from Kinsey et al., 1953.)

0   Completely heterosexual
1   Largely heterosexual with incident(s) of same-sex relationships
2   Largely heterosexual with a distinct history of same-sex relationships
3   Equally heterosexual and homosexual
4   Largely homosexual with a distinct history of cross-sex relationships
5   Largely homosexual with an incidental history of cross-sex relationships
6   Entirely homosexual

Moses and Hawkins' Sexual Orientation/Sexual Preference Components. (Adapted from Moses & Hawkins, 1982.)

Past history of sexual activity and relationships
Current history of sexual activity and relationships
Past history of affectional relationships
Current history of affectional relationships
Past history of fantasy
Current history of fantasy

A woman who has affectional preferences for women (Orzek, 1989).

A homosexual woman.

The above descriptions are just some of the ways in which "lesbian" is defined. The lesbian lifestyle encompasses not only a sexual preference for women, but also a commitment to a woman-centered lifestyle that has personal, political, social, and cultural components.

Most of us tend to dichotomize people into two or three groups, i.e. people are either heterosexual, bisexual, or homosexual. However, thinking about sexual preference along a continuum more closely describes how people actually behave. Kinsey et al. (1953) proposed a seven-point continuum ranging from completely heterosexual to entirely homosexual. Moses and Hawkins (1982) used a six-point assessment by kinds of activity continuum. These two continua are presented in Table 11.4. These continua demonstrate the complexity of defining and assessing for sexual preference.

Although lesbian women share the commonality of affectional preference for women and a women-centred lifestyle, they are a diverse group of women in terms of personality characteristics, lifestyle variables, and philosophy (Sophie, 1982). Based on an extensive review of the literature, Sophie concludes that lesbian women and heterosexual women are quite similar on a variety of mental health criteria.

Discrimination and Oppression of Lesbian Women

Lesbian women and gay men have historically been targets for pervasive societal discrimination and oppression. Kingdon (1979) suggested that a common and central problem for lesbians is learning to live in a homophobic and heterosexist culture.

Homophobia

Homophobia is fear, dislike, or hatred of gay men and lesbian women. Homophobia, which is rooted in our culture, includes institutional discrimination and negative personal responses of people. External homophobia includes legal, political, economic, religious, and psychological discrimination. Internalized homophobia is manifested in non-gay individuals' negative reactions to, jokes about, violence toward, and fear of gay people. Internalized homophobia is manifested in lesbian or gay individuals by low self-esteem, guilt, fear, self-hatred, and secrecy about lesbian identity (Zollicoffer, 1984).

Heterosexism

Heterosexism is the belief that heterosexuality is inherently better than or more normal than homosexuality. Gartrell (1984) suggested that lesbians are a direct threat to patriarchy and its compulsory heterosexuality. Heterosexism is demonstrated by institutional or personal devaluing of the lesbian lifestyle and of lesbian women, by sexualizing the lesbian life-style choice, by making the lesbian life-style invisible, by trying to convert lesbians to a heterosexual orientation, and by searching for underlying causes of being lesbian (Zollicoffer, 1984).

Myths about lesbian women

The effects of homophobia and heterosexism on societal beliefs about lesbian women is reflected in the following *myths* about lesbian women:

(1) Lesbian women are less psychologically healthy than are heterosexual women.
(2) Growing up in a lesbian family is detrimental for children.
(3) Childrearing practices determine sexual orientation.
(4) Lesbianism is a developmental disorder.
(5) Lesbian women are all masculine in appearance and behavior.
(6) All lesbian women hate men.
(7) Lesbians do not form long-term relationships.

Both lesbian women and non-lesbian individuals may believe these socialized myths. These myths, homophobia, and heterosexism are a great source of stress for lesbian women and often aggravate any problems that they may be experiencing. In other words, being lesbian is not the disease, but rather the disease is a homophobic, heterosexist society (Martin & Lyon, 1984).

Homophobia, heterosexism, and myths also affect the practice of psychology. Mental health professionals have been found to hold negative attitudes about gay men and lesbian women and to be uneducated about gay and lesbian life-styles (Graham et al., 1984). A feminist therapist approach to counseling lesbian women requires above all else that the counselor be not homophobic or heterosexist, in order to provide a supportive and validating therapeutic environment.

Counselor Issues

Counselors of lesbian clients need to be non-judgmental and knowledgeable about lesbian issues. A non-judgemental therapist response allows lesbian clients to explore their issues in a safe environment. A knowledgeable therapist is able to counteract client myths about lesbians and to help clients analyze the effects of living in an oppressive society. Mental health counselors may have a heterosexual or homosexual sexual orientation themselves. We will next explore the issues involved if (a) the counselor is a lesbian and (b) the counselor is heterosexual.

Lesbian therapists

Gartrell (1984) advocates that lesbian clients should be counseled by lesbian therapists. She cites a number of advantages that lesbian therapists can provide. First, research has found that when clients and counselors are matched on sexual orientation, therapy has more positive outcomes (Liljestrand, Gerling, & Saliba, 1978). Further, lesbian therapists can: (a) have empathy for both the pain of living in a homophobic, heterosexist culture and the strengths needed to survive those experiences; (b) be knowledgeable about societal myths about lesbians; and (c) be a positive role model. Gartrell emphasizes the importance of the lesbian therapist's "being out" as a lesbian. "Being out" means that the individual does not conceal her lesbian identity. Gartrell believes that the therapist's secrecy in her life may reflect unresolved homophobia and heterosexism and that "being out is necessary for a healthy adaptation to lesbian life" (p. 23). Lesbian therapists must have worked through their own internalized homophobia and heterosexism.

Heterosexual therapists

The small number of lesbian therapists alone necessitates a practical consideration of heterosexual therapists working with lesbian clients. Therapists counseling lesbian clients must above all else have confronted and worked through their own heterosexist and homophobic biases. Therapists must be active in and diligent throughout this process. The desire of a therapist to be free of lesbian biases and myths does not automatically lead to the elimination of those attitudes and feelings (Gartrell, 1984).

Effects of counselor bias on therapy with lesbian clients

If counselors (heterosexual, lesbian, or gay) hold negative attitudes about and have little knowledge about the lesbian life-style, they are likely to revictimize the lesbian client. This revictimization in counseling can take several forms. First, counselors may look for the source of the woman's lesbian life-style choice, and they may view a client's lesbian identity as a symptom of some other underlying problem. Their assumptions here are that being lesbian is pathological in some way and that it will be "cured" if the underlying problem is resolved (Kingdon, 1979). Second, therapists may try to convert or change the lesbian to a heterosexual orientation. Third, counselors may minimize the effects of homophobia and heterosexism on the client. This attitude will lead to "blaming the victim" by attributing all client problems to internal sources. Fourth, therapists may attribute all of a client's problem to her lesbian identity.

Basic therapist conditions for working with lesbian clients

As we have stated previously, counselors of lesbian clients must be non-judgmental and knowledgeable about lesbian issues. In addition, feminist therapists believe that society, not just the individual, needs to change. Feminist therapists need ". . . to be educated about the personal, political, social, and cultural ramifications of homophobia" (Gartrell, 1984, p. 21).

Zollicoffer (1984, pp. 28–31) proposed that therapists who counsel lesbian clients follow four principles:

(1)   Acknowledge the existence of and work through external and internalized homophobic and heterosexist messages.
(2)   Maintain empathy by learning about and understanding lesbian identities and needs of lesbians.
(3)   Affirm lesbian women and lesbian life-styles as viable and legitimate alternative life-choices for women.
(4)   Validate lesbian women by acting as change agents with clients, peers,

colleagues, and traditional and non-traditional institutions for social and political change.

A variety of strategies can be used to eliminate bias and enhance therapist knowledge about lesbian issues. Awareness and self-confrontation of myths, stereotypes, and biases, values clarification exercises, bibliotherapy, individual therapy for the counselor, interactions with lesbian women and lesbian therapists, careful listening to lesbian clients, working through a devalued feeling of being a woman and not fitting male norms of society, imagining oneself to be lesbian, sex-role analysis, power analysis, and learning about lesbian history and culture have all been suggested as strategies that can be used to reduce therapist bias and increase therapist knowledge of lesbian issues (Siegel, 1985; Zollicoffer, 1984).

Client Issues

Because lesbian women are a diverse group of women, the issues that bring them to therapy also vary. Due to their sex-role socialization as women, they share many of the same experiences and concerns as heterosexual women. However, because Western culture devalues and oppresses lesbian women, they have a double set of discriminations with which to cope. One of the major tasks with which lesbian women must deal is the development of their lesbian identity. In fact, "coming out" issues may complicate all other concerns.

The coming out process

The process of developing a lesbian identity is called "coming out." This process of identifying oneself as lesbian has two major components, coming out to oneself, and coming out to others. Table 11.5 presents one generalized developmental model for the lesbian coming out process (Sophie, 1985/6).

As is demonstrated in this model, the lesbian woman becomes aware of being different or confused about her identity, moves through a period of self-examination and of learning more about lesbianism, and finally ideally accepts and is proud of her lesbian identity. The cultural climate, i.e. acceptance or rejection of the lesbian life-style, has a central impact on the coming out process. For example, Sophie (1985/6) compared lesbian women's description of their coming out experiences to six models of coming out proposed in the literature. She found that many of the women had not experienced a strong anger or a negative view of their lesbian identity. She hypothesized that this change may reflect recent historical changes toward a slight improvement in society's views of lesbians and the increased availability of social support from the lesbian community. External and internalized

Table 11.5.   *General Stages of Lesbian Development.* (*Adapted from Sophie, 1985/6, and Cass, 1979.*)

Stage 1: First awareness
  Awareness of lesbian feelings prior to contact with lesbians.
  Non-disclosure of these feelings to others.
  Possible alienation from oneself and others.
  Confusion about identity.

  Who am I?   Am I lesbian?

Stage 2: Testing, exploration
  Exploration of lesbian culture and community.
  Testing precedes acceptance of lesbian identity.
  Disclosure to heterosexuals may or may not occur.
  Alienation from heterosexuals may occur.
  First lesbian relationship may occur.

  Am I lesbian? Am I bisexual?   I may be lesbian.

Stage 3: Identity acceptance
  Preference for lesbian social contact.
  Individual may or may not go through negative lesbian identity stage.
  Development of a positive view of lesbianism; usually precedes self-labeling.
  Acting in accordance with lesbian identity.
  Expansion of contact with lesbian community.
  Self-disclosure to others varies.

  I may be lesbian.   I am lesbian.

Stage 4: Identity integration
  Has pride in lesbian identity and anger at oppression.
  Has positive lesbian identity.
  May dichotomize world into lesbian and heterosexual.
  Integrates lesbian identity into sense of self.
  Disclosure to many people.
  Increased difficulty or unwillingness to change one's lesbian identity.

  I am a lesbian woman.   I am proud of being lesbian.

---

homophobia and heterosexism contribute to the need to hide one's lesbian identity.

Although coming out models are helpful for understanding common experiences in coming out, it is important to remember that each woman will have a unique experience. Sophie (1985/6) also points out additional problems with stage models. First, they impose a linear description on what in reality is not a linear process, i.e. women will move back and forth between the steps. Second, some women do not develop a fixed, never-changing, view of their sexual identity, but rather may move between heterosexual, bisexual, and lesbian identities and thus, display a more flexible identity. And third, women begin the process at different places. For example, some women may have always been attracted to women, while others may have had sexual relationships with men and only become aware of a possible lesbian identity when they become attracted to, or have an adult sexual experience with, another woman.

One of the more dangerous, and thus difficult, parts of the coming out process is for the individual to self-disclose about her lesbian identity to others. Self-disclosure makes her vulnerable to second wounds from significant others, loss of employment, and loss of custody of her children. In fact, custody fights are the major legal problems for lesbians (Sophie, 1982). Because of the vulnerability involved in self-disclosure, it is critical that therapists respond in an accepting, non-judgmental manner when clients come out to them. Sophie (1982) and Gartrell (1984) point out the disadvantages of not coming out to others. Hiding one's lesbian identity requires a lot of energy to monitor constantly what one is saying and doing, interferes with being intimate with others, leads to lowered self-esteem, and can result in use of harmful denial strategies, such as alcohol or drug abuse. Self-disclosure issues recur across the lifespan each time a lesbian woman must decide whether to tell someone about her life-style. Clients need to assess the advantages and disadvantages of coming out and reach their own decisions.

Therapeutic Strategies and Goals

Therapists can facilitate the coming out process by being accepting and by helping clients distinguish between gender, sex-role orientation, and sexual preference. They can help clients identify resources about lesbian life-styles, build a lesbian social support network, and reassure the client about the normality of her coming out process. Confronting and correcting clients' myths, teaching clients how to cognitively restructure internalized homophobia and heterosexist messages, and role-playing are additional effective strategies. Helping the client identify and own the strengths they possess, and the positive coping strategies they have used in surviving in an oppressive environment, is also very important.

Desirable outcomes for counseling women through the coming out process vary with the woman's stage and are reflected in the following possible counseling goals:

(1) Developing a positive lesbian identity.
(2) Reducing identity confusion.
(3) Increasing self-esteem.
(4) Enhancing interpersonal relationships.
(5) Increasing knowledge about lesbian women and their life-styles.
(6) Decreasing myths about lesbian women.

(7)   Decreasing internalized homophobia and heterosexism.
(8)   Developing strategies for coping with oppressive environments.
(9)   Learning change agent strategies for bringing about environmental change.
(10) Changing institutionalized homophobia and heterosexism.

Lesbian Women—Summary

Therapy with lesbian clients presents many issues that challenge the feminist therapist. First, feminist therapists are challenged to become knowledgeable about homophobia, heterosexism, myths about the lesbian life-style, and society's oppression of lesbian women. Second, they are challenged to identify and work through their own biases. Third, they need to perceive the lesbian life-style as viable and legitimate. Feminist therapists also work toward changing societal practices which are harmful to lesbian women. Finally, feminist therapists are challenged to facilitate the healing of lesbian women from society's double oppression of them both as women and as lesbians.

Summary and Applications to Feminist Counseling

In this chapter, we have addressed the issues and needs of two groups of women at multiple risk: lesbians, and minority (specifically, Black) women. An identity-development model was applied to the understanding of each of these two groups. Counseling approaches were considered within a cross-cultural model, in which knowledge, attitudes, and skills related to each special group were briefly reviewed. For both groups of women clients, we view the cross-cultural model as compatible with our Feminist Therapy approach. However, the application to clients in either of these groups of your own theoretical model, a cross-cultural approach, and a feminist therapy structure, may appear overwhelming to manage. Here, we summarize some of the ways in which Feminist Therapy Principles can be applied to women from multiple-risk groups.

Principle I: The Personal Is Political stands out as the primary consideration. For women who are the particular targets of societal demands, discrimination, negative stereotyping, and exclusion, liberation from internalization and self-blame is critical. Clients from either of the two groups considered here will benefit from a careful examination of the ways in which the dominant culture has stigmatized them and reduced their power and control over their lives, thereby restricting their freedom to seek rewarding life goals. Each multiple-risk woman deserves the opportunity to explore the external sources of her pain and confusion, and to integrate this understanding with the need to take control of her own life.

Principle II: egalitarian relationships is particularly critical for groups who are doubly negated by social attitudes and subordinate status. When clients come to you with expectations that you may also place yourself in a superior position to them, the task of establishing trust and developing equality between you is magnified. Simply stating your desire to meet your client on an equal basis may not be sufficient to break through her wariness and suspicion, generalization from other situations, denial that you could possibly understand her, and willingness to make herself vulnerable through self-disclosure and self-exploration. Thus, your task in establishing an equal footing may require more effort, skill, patience, and time than with many other clients. In accomplishing the goals of Principle II, your credibility and effectiveness with each client will depend, to a great extent, on your ability to set aside your stereotypes, expectations, and cultural blind-spots. Competent supervision of your efforts here will be a helpful asset in meeting the spirit and practice of egalitarianism.

Principle III: valuing the female perspective requires your flexibility in determining each client's personal and group-identified concepts of femininity and womanhood. For the minority or lesbian client, for example, we cannot assume that White, middle class, heterosexual concepts of feminity, women's roles, and relationship structures are necessarily applicable to this client. Unless you are familiar with her culture and background, you may have to explore this dimension carefully with her. What is her ideal woman, what qualities does she value, how does her reference group view these values, and how does she integrate her values with theirs? Her cognitive schemas about woman-messages may need to become explicit between you, if you are successfully to implement Principle III.

Activity

Consider the two clients described in the Self-assessment. Review your answer to the self-assessment question concerning their issues in counseling. After reading Chapter 11, would you change or add to these responses? Pair off with a partner and share your thoughts.

Now, stay with these two clients and respond to the following:

(1) Describe three cross-cultural counseling skills you will need to deal with each client.
(2) Describe the possible situational or cultural contexts of each client's life space (e.g. sexism, homophobia, racism).

Further Readings

Berzon, B. (1988). *Permanent Partners: Building Gay and Lesbian Relationships that Last*. New York: Dutton.

Greene, B. A. (1986). When the therapist is White and the patient is Black: Considerations for psychotherapy in the feminist heterosexual and lesbian communities. In D. Howard (Ed.), *The Dynamics of Feminist Therapy*. New York: Haworth.

Lykes, M. B. (1983). Discrimination and coping in the lives of Black women: Analysis of oral history data. *Journal of Social Issues*, **39**, 79–100.

Rothblum, E. D., & Cole, E. (Eds.) (1988). Lesbianism: Affirming non-traditional roles. *Women and Therapy*, **9**, 112.

Trotman, F. K. (1984). Psychotherapy of Black women and the dual effects of racism and sexism. In C. M. Brody (Ed.), *Women Therapists Working with Women: New Theory and Process of Feminist Therapy*. New York: Springer.

PART 3

Becoming a Feminist Therapist

Becoming a feminist therapist is a life-long, challenging process. One of our goals in writing this book has been to give you a structure for learning about, and applying a feminist therapy perspective to women's counseling issues. Once you have learned the basic theory, principles, and techniques of feminist therapy covered in Part 1, you are ready to apply these perspectives to various issues women bring to therapy. In Part 2, we provided samples of this application process. In Chapter 12, we explore additional challenges in applying a feminist therapy perspective. First, we address ethical guidelines for practice congruent with a feminist therapy value system. Second, we explore the impact of gender and power on client–counselor relationships. Finally, we discuss professional labels and conflicting client and counselor goals. In Chapter 13, we propose a model for training feminist therapists, a model for enhancing the process of developing attitudes, knowledge, and skills needed to become a feminist therapist.

As we end our part of your journey to becoming a feminist therapist, we are keenly aware of the topics we have been unable to include in this book. For example, we did not have the space to address the application of a feminist therapy perspective to marriage and family therapy, eating disorders, body image, women's groups, older women, substance abuse, and agoraphobia, as well as to a variety of women's health issues such as menarche, menopause, mastectomy, infertility, and unwanted pregnancy. You will want to become more informed about each of these areas. In addition, you will benefit from expanded reading on the sex bias often present in traditional approaches to research and alternative models for research congruent with a feminist perspective.

We realize our book can be only a part of your journey to becoming a feminist therapist. We hope we have given you a different set of lenses with which to view yourself, the world, and the issues your clients bring to counseling. We encourage you to continue your journey through further reading, discussions with colleagues, and attending workshops and classes. If our professional paths should cross, we shall be interested in hearing about your journey. Bon voyage!

CHAPTER 12

Ethical and Practice Issues

Self-assessment: Ethical Issues

For the client case given below: (a) identify possible or potential ethical violations using the standard of the ethical guidelines of your profession; (b) review the three Principles of Feminist Therapy; and (c) identify possible or potential violations of the three Feminist Therapy Principles. What would be the advantages and disadvantages for the client if the client's second therapist is a female? A male? If possible, discuss your answers with a colleague or in small groups in class.

Client case

You have had eight counseling sessions with an adult survivor of childhood sexual abuse. In her last session, she disclosed having had a sexual experience with her previous therapist while in therapy with him. She felt uncomfortable with the experience and terminated counseling. She feels guilty and responsible about the encounter, saying she didn't physically resist, and must have sent him "come on" signals. She has disclosed to you because she didn't want to be secretive, but she doesn't want to pursue the matter with an ethics board.

Overview

In this chapter, we are going to explore some of the issues associated with practicing feminist therapy. We begin by focusing on ethical issues. Several feminist therapy guidelines/ethical principles adopted by various professional organizations are presented, and we summarize the commonalities in these guidelines. Next, we discuss ethical and practice issues that have special relevance for feminist therapists. In these latter sections, our approach is to raise tough questions and review a variety of perspectives on these issues. Our goal is to stimulate your thinking about these issues and to facilitate you in reaching your own conclusions. More specifically, we hope that as a result of reading this chapter, readers will:

(1)   Become acquainted with several feminist and non-sexist guidelines for counseling women.
(2)   Incorporate a feminist therapy perspective into their own professional code of ethics.
(3)   Understand the debilitating effects on clients of therapists' sexual misconduct.
(4)   Be able to analyze the potential problems that may accompany dual relationships with clients.
(5)   Recognize the influences of gender power on the counseling relationship.
(6)   Reach their own decisions about difficult practice issues, such as dual relationships, self-identifying professional labels, and conflicts between client and counselor therapy goals.

The structure, perspective, and resources we bring to this chapter are tied to our training and practice as psychologists. For example, several of the guidelines we present come from psychological organizations. Our basic understanding of professional ethics is rooted in the Ethical Principles of the American Psychological Assocation (APA) (1981).[1] However, we realize that many of our readers will be from different mental health professions. We have decided to stay within the limits of our competence/expertise by offering these psychologist-oriented materials and perspectives as samples of ways to approach the questions explored in this chapter. We encourage our readers to review their own code of professional ethics, to evaluate the strengths and weaknesses of those documents from a feminist therapy viewpoint, and to integrate the Feminist Therapy Principles into their own applications of their profession's ethical code.

Guidelines for Counseling Women

Several professional groups have adopted guidelines for competent and ethical non-sexist or feminist counseling. We begin by presenting some of these guidelines and then we summarize their commonalities. Whenever

---

[1]We are using the 1981 APA Ethical Principles, which, as we go to press, are in the process of being revised.

possible, we have added in brackets which feminist therapy principles are relevant to specific parts of each guideline.

Sex-fair Guidelines

In 1982, the Kentucky Psychological Association (KPA) adopted the 10 sex-fair guidelines displayed in Table 12.1. To our knowledge, Kentucky is one of only two states to have added gender-fair ethical guidelines to the APA Ethical Principles. The guidelines are adaptations of the "Guidelines for Therapy with Women" which were developed by the American Psychological Association Task Force on Sex Bias and Sex-role Stereotyping in Psychotherapeutic Practice (1978). The development of the KPA Sex-fair Guidelines was a joint effort of the KPA Ethics Committee and the KPA Women's Committee. As members of those committees at that time, we had a unique opportunity to impact our state's practice of psychology. Adoption of the guidelines by the KPA Executive Board required consciousness-raising of board members, patience, and lobbying, all of which demonstrate the political nature of professional ethical documents.

One of the strengths of these guidelines is the use of sex-fair and gender-inclusive language, i.e. the guidelines apply to both women and men. A second strength is that each of the 10 guidelines was anchored to specific relevant APA Ethical Principles (American Psychological Association, 1981) as indicated by the Principle numbers in parentheses following each guideline. We have also added in brackets the Feminist Therapy Principles which pertain to each guideline.

American Psychological Association's Principles Concerning the Counseling and Psychotherapy of Women

The Division of Counseling Psychology of the American Psychological Association adopted the 13 Principles Concerning the Counseling/Psychotherapy of Women in 1978 (Fitzgerald & Nutt, 1986). These principles can be found in Table 12.2. In brackets following each of the 13 principles, we have added the numbers of the Feminist Therapy Principles which pertain.

These 13 principles stress the importance of therapists being knowledgeable about the effects of sexism on female clients and on the therapeutic relationship, and of being aware of one's own values and personal functioning.

Feminist Therapy Network Code of Ethics

The introductory section of the Feminist Therapy Network's Code of Ethics (1988) can be found in Table 12.3. In addition to this introduction, we

Table 12.1.   *Sex-fair Guidelines**

It is the intention of the Kentucky Psychological Association's Ethics Committee and Committee on Women to increase the awareness of KPA members about maintaining professional standards of ethical behavior. These sex-fair guidelines which have been adopted by KPA are not intended to be an exhaustive list of regulations in the area of sexism. They are viewed as an essential minimum frame of reference for all professional activity. They are to be used as an addition to the established APA Ethical Principles of Psychologists.

Each sex-fair ethical guideline will be presented. The number and letter of relevant parts of the APA Ethical Principles which also pertain are given in parentheses.

(1)   The conduct of therapy should be free of constrictions based solely on gender-defined roles, and the options explored between client and practitioner should not be constrained by sex-role stereotypes. The therapy should not aim to maintain or reinforce client behavior based solely on gender-related stereotypes. (APA Ethical Principles 2C, 2D, 3C, 1F, 6A: Feminist Therapy Principle I.)

(2)   The theoretical concepts employed by the psychologist should not impose sex bias and sex-role stereotypes on the client. (APA Ethical Principles 1F, 2C, 2D: Feminist Therapy Principle I.)

(3)   The psychologist should demonstrate acceptance of women and men as equals by refraining from using derogatory labels based on sex-role stereotypes. (APA Ethical Principles 1F, 2C, 2D: Feminist Therapy Principles I, II, III.)

(4)   Psychologists should avoid emphasizing only personal factors in client problems and should emphasize situational or cultural factors whenever appropriate. (APA Ethical Principles 1A, 1F, 2D: Feminist Therapy Principle I.)

(5)   Psychologists should be cognizant of the reality, variety and implications of sex-discriminatory practices in society and should not constrain the client's examination of options in dealing with such practices. The client's assertive behaviors should be respected. (APA Ethical principles 2C, 2D, 3C, 7C: Feminist Therapy Principles I, II.)

(6)   The psychologist should strive to be knowledgeable about current empirical findings and theoretical views on sex roles, sexism, and individual differences resulting from individual's gender-defined identity. (APA Ethical Principles 2C, 2D: Feminist therapy Principles I, III.)

(7)   The psychologist should avoid imposing sex-role stereotypes on clients' expressions of their sexuality. (APA Ethical Principles 1F, 2C, 2D: Feminist Therapy Principles, I, III.)

(8)   The psychologist whose client is subjected to violence in the form of physical abuse or rape should recognize and acknowledge that the client is the victim of an illegal act. (APA Ethical Principles 2C, 3C: Feminist Therapy Principles I, II.)

(9)   Sexual intimacies between client and therapist, dual relationships between client and psychologist, and sexual harassment of the client by the psychologist are prohibited. (APA Ethical Principles 6A, 7D, 7C: Feminist Therapy Principles I, II.)

(10) Psychologists should be aware of current professional ethical codes and avoid deviations based on the client's sex. (Feminist Therapy Principles I, II, III.)

* These guidelines were passed at the February 5, 1982, Executive Council Meeting. They will serve as guidelines for KPA's Ethics Committee in addition to the APA Ethical Principles.

Table 12.2. *American Psychological Association's Principles Concerning the Counseling/Psychotherapy of Women*

Principle I   Counselors/therapists should be knowledgeable about women, particularly with regard to biological, psychological, and social issues which have impact on women in general or on particular groups of women in our society. (Feminist Therapy Principles I, III.)

Principle II   Counselors/therapists are aware that the assumptions and precepts of theories relevant to their practice may apply differently to men and women. Counselors/therapists are aware of those theories and models that prescribe or limit the potential of women clients, as well as those that may have particular usefulness for women clients. (Feminist Therapy Principles I, II, III.)

Principle III   After formal training, counselors/therapists continue to explore and learn of issues related to women, including the special problems of female subgroups, throughout their professional careers. (Feminist Therapy Principles I, II, III.)

Principle IV   Counselors/therapists recognize and are aware of all forms of oppression and how these interact with sexism. (Feminist Therapy Principle I.)

Principle V   Counselors/therapists are knowledgeable and aware of verbal and nonverbal process variables (particularly with regard to power in the relationship) as these affect women in counseling/therapy so that the counselor/therapist interactions are not adversely affected. The need for shared responsibility between clients and counselors/therapists is acknowledged and implemented. (Feminist Therapy Principles I, II.)

Principle VI   Counselors/therapists have the capability of utilizing skills that are particularly facilitative to women in general and to particular subgroups of women. (Feminist Therapy Principles I, II, III.)

Principle VII   Counselors/therapists ascribe no preconceived limitations on the direction or nature of potential changes or goals in counseling/therapy for women. (Feminist Therapy Principles I, II, III.)

Principle VIII   Counselors/therapists are sensitive to circumstances where it is more desirable for a woman client to be seen by a female or male counselor/therapist. (Feminist Therapy Principles I, II, III.)

Principle IX   Counselors/therapists use non-sexist language in counseling/therapy, supervision, teaching, and journal publication. (Feminist Therapy Principles I, III.)

Principle X   Counselors/therapists do not engage in sexual activity with their women clients under any circumstances. (Feminist Therapy Principles I, II.)

Principle XI   Counselors/therapists are aware of and continually review their own values and biases and the effects of these on their women clients. Counselors/therapists understand the effects of sex-role socialization upon their own development and functioning and the consequent values and attitudes they hold for themselves and others. They recognize that behaviors and roles need not be sex-based. (Feminist Therapy Principles I, II.)

Principle XII   Counselors/therapists are aware of how their personal functioning may influence their effectiveness in counseling/therapy with women clients. They monitor their functioning through consultation, supervision, or therapy so that it does not adversely affect their work with women clients. (Feminist Therapy Principles I, II.)

Table 12.2.   (*Continued*)

Principle XIII   Counselors/therapists support the elimination of sex bias within institutions and individuals. (Feminist Therapy Principle I.)

Adapted from Fitzgerald & Nutt (1986).

have included a summary of four subsequent specific issues which their code addresses.

Feminist Therapy Institute Code of Ethics

The Feminist Therapy Code of Ethics, developed by the Feminist Therapy Institute (1987), consists of a preamble and five ethical guidelines for feminist therapy practice. The preamble stresses the importance of applying feminist analyses of the effects of sexism on client issues, and of understanding both the internal and external aspects of client issues. The five ethical guidelines address cultural diversities and oppressions, power differentials, overlapping relationships, therapist accountability, and social change. These five guidelines can be found in Table 12.4.

Commonalities Among Ethical Guidelines for Counseling Women

The four sets of ethical guidelines for counseling women which we have presented here have several similarities. First, all of them incorporate aspects of the three Feminist Therapy Principles. Indeed, they seem to be ways to integrate the Feminist Therapy Principles into an ethical code. The presented guidelines give specific feminist/non-sexist definitions to the more general professional ethical principles of competence, confidentiality, client welfare, and counselor responsibility. Second, all of the presented guidelines focus on the importance of acquiring special knowledge and skills related to counseling women. Third, most of the guidelines address the importance of therapists knowing themselves, resolving their own personal issues which may harm female clients, and being aware of and open about their value systems.

However, the guidelines presented here also have several differences. These approaches vary in the level of specificity of the issues addressed and in whether they are gender-inclusive. The KPA Sex-fair Guidelines and the Counseling Psychology Principles are designed to apply to all licensed psychologists, while the Feminist Therapy Network Code and the Feminist Therapy Institute Principles govern the practice of feminist therapists who belong to those organizations.

Table 12.3. *Feminist Therapy Network Code of Ethics (Adapted from* Feminist Therapy Network Code of Ethics, *1988*)

I Introductory section
(1) The name of the organization is the Feminist Therapy Network.
(2) A Feminist Therapy Network member is expected to adhere to the Code of Ethics of whichever professional societies she is a member. As feminist therapists we assume the following principles in therapy practice with clients:
    (a) Feminist therapy is directed toward growth, self-actualization and self-empowerment. (Feminist Therapy Principles I, II, III.)
    (b) Feminist therapy affirms the importance of the process of dealing with the following issues: ageism, sexism, heterosexism, racism, and classism. (Feminist Therapy Principle I.)
(3) Feminist therapy emphasizes the importance of sharing of common experiences among women and among men, to contribute to the changing dialogue between women, between men and between sexes. (Feminist Therapy Principles II, III.)
(4) Feminist therapy supports the formation of non-exploitive relationships which are more equal and respectful, including those with children, parents, partners, and friends. (Feminist Therapy Principle II.)
(5) Feminist therapy values and requires a relationship between client and therapist which is non-authoritarian and in which the therapist serves as facilitator, advocate and educator. (Feminist Therapy Principles I, II, III.)

II Summary of specific issues
(1) *Friendship and boundaries.* The differences between friend and therapy relationships are noted. Therapists are prohibited from doing therapy with a friend and are warned of the complexities of post-therapy friendships.
(2) *Sexuality in and out of therapy.* Therapists are prohibited from engaging in sexual contact in therapy and are cautioned about the problems associated with post-therapy sexual relationships. It is recommended that *at least* 6 months elapse between the end of therapy and the beginning of a sexual relationship.
(3) *Touching.* The healing power of and potential problems with touch are discussed. The importance of respect for the client is stressed. They suggest using discussions of appropriate touching, exploration of boundary issues for both client and therapist, getting permission for physical contact, and stopping any kind of self-abusive behavior.
(4) *Business ethics: barter guidelines.* The use of barter in psychotherapy is opposed.

Challenging Special Issues

We are devoting the remainder of the chapter to exploring difficult issues related to the practice of feminist therapy. We begin with some issues raised by the ethical codes reviewed above; and conclude with several issues that are less related to ethics, but are, nevertheless, very challenging concerns for feminist therapists.

Table 12.4. *Feminist Therapy Code of Ethics—Ethical Guidelines for Feminist Therapists.* (*From Feminist Therapy Institute, 1987, with permission.*)*

I   Cultural diversities and oppressions (Feminist Therapy Principles I, II)

(1)   A feminist therapist increases her accessibility to and for a wide range of clients from her own and other identified groups through flexible delivery of services. When appropriate, the feminist therapist assists clients in accessing other services.

(2)   A feminist therapist is aware of the meaning and impact of her own ethnic and cultural background, gender, class, and sexual orientation, and actively attempts to become knowledgeable about alternatives from sources other than her clients. The therapist's goal is to uncover and respect cultural and experiential differences.

(3)   A feminist therapist evaluates her ongoing interactions with her clientele for any evidence of the therapist's biases or discriminatory attitudes and practice. The feminist therapist accepts responsibility for taking action to confront and change any interfering or oppressing biases she has.

II   Power differentials (Feminist Therapy Principle II)

(1)   A feminist therapist acknowledges the inherent power differentials between client and therapist, and models effective use of personal power. In using the power differential to the benefit of the client, she does not take control of power which rightfully belongs to her client.

(2)   A feminist therapist discloses information to the client which facilitates the therapeutic process. The therapist is responsible for using self-disclosure with purpose and discretion in the interests of the client.

(3)   A feminist therapist negotiates and renegotiates formal and/or informal contacts with clients in an ongoing mutual process.

(4)   A feminist therapist educates her clients regarding their rights as consumers of therapy, including procedures for resolving differences and filing grievances.

III   Overlapping relationships (Feminist Therapy Principles I, II)

(1)   A feminist therapist recognizes the complexity and conflicting priorities inherent in multiple or overlapping relationships. The therapist accepts responsibility for monitoring such relationships to prevent potential abuse of or harm to the client.

(2)   A feminist therapist is actively involved in her community. As a result, she is especially sensitive about confidentiality. Recognizing that her client's concerns and general well-being are primary, she self-monitors both public and private statements and comments.

(3)   A feminist therapist does not engage in sexual intimacies nor any overtly or covertly sexualized behaviors with a client or former client.

IV   Therapist accountability (Feminist Therapy Principles I, II, III)

(1)   A feminist therapist works only with those issues and clients within the realm of her competencies.

(2)   A feminist therapist recognizes her personal and professional needs, and utilizes ongoing self-evaluation, peer support, consultation, supervision, continuing education, and/or personal therapy to evaluate, maintain, and improve her work with clients, her competencies, and her emotional well-being.

Table 12.4. (*Continued*)

---

(3) A feminist therapist continually re-evaluates her training, theoretical
     background, and research to include developments in feminist knowledge. She
     integrates feminism into psychological theory, receives ongoing therapy
     training, and acknowledges the limits of her competencies.
(4) A feminist therapist engages in self-care activities in an ongoing manner. She
     acknowledges her own vulnerabilities and seeks to care for herself outside of
     the therapy setting. She models for the ability and willingness to self-nuture in
     appropriate and self-empowering ways

V   Social change (Feminist Therapy Principle I)
(1) A feminist therapist actively questions other therapeutic practices in her
     community that appear abusive to clients or therapists, and when possible,
     intervenes as early as appropriate or feasible, or assists clients in intervening
     when it is facilitative to their growth.
(2) A feminist therapist seeks multiple avenues for impacting change, including
     public education and advocacy within professional organizations, lobbying for
     legislative actions, and other appropriate activities.

---

* © 1987 The Feminist Therapy Institute, Inc. Corporate Office: 50 South Steele, #850
Denver, CO 80209, USA.

Dual and Overlapping Relationships

Conflicting roles and relationships with clients are an important area of
concern for all therapists. However, because feminist therapists are sensitive
to the lower power status of women, feminist therapists assert that these dual
or overlapping relationships may be particularly detrimental to female clients.
Berman (1985) uses the term "overlapping relationships" to describe counselors having more than one role or relationship with a client, i.e. an
overlapping of personal, professional, and social roles. There are many kinds
of overlapping relationships, some of which are more problematic than
others.

Sexual misconduct with clients

Almost all mental health professional ethical codes have prohibitions against
sexual contact between counselors and clients. Prohibitions against sexual
contact are relatively new to most of these codes and have usually been
added at the urging and lobbying of women's committees within these
organizations. In addition, several American states have established sexual
contact with a client by a therapist as illegal. State of California law, for
example, defines sexual contact and sexual misconduct in clear and under-
standable terms. This definition is displayed in Table 12.5. The California
law also mandates that therapists must provide a standard, informational
pamphlet to any client who reveals sexual contact with a former therapist.

Table 12.5. *State of California: Legal Definitions of Sexual Contact and Sexual Misconduct. (Adapted from Quinn, undated, California Office of State Printing, with permission.)*

According to California laws:

Any kind of sexual contact, asking for sexual contact, or sexual misconduct by a psychotherapist with a client is illegal, as well as unethical. (Business and Professions Code sections 726 and 4982k.)

"Sexual contact" means the touching of an intimate part (sexual organ, anus, buttocks, groin, or breast) of another person. "Touching" means physical contact with another person either through the person's clothes or directly with the person's skin. (Business and Professions Code section 728.)

Sexual contact can include sexual intercourse, fondling, and any other kind of sexual touching. *Sexual misconduct* covers an even broader range such as nudity, kissing, spanking, and sexual suggestions or innuendos. This kind of sexual behavior by a therapist with a client is sexual exploitation. It is unethical, unprofessional, and illegal.

Actual Statement by client who was sexually abused by therapist:

He started to tell me his troubles and the burden was heavy. Then he made me feel like I had to comfort him. I was the one who needed help. I have more problems now than when I started.

Clients are in a very vulnerable role and therapists who engage in sexual relationships with clients obscure their therapeutic objectivity and take advantage of their clients' vulnerability. For example, sexual abuse survivors have a greater likelihood of revictimization by authority figures (Russell 1986b; Whetsell, 1990). Whetsell (1990) found that 20% of the adult survivors of sexual abuse in her study had been sexually abused by at least one therapist. Further, these women identified sexual involvement with their therapists as traumatic. In a national survey of 1320 psychologists, Pope and Vetter (in press) found that half of the respondents reported assessing or treating at least one client who had had sexual involvement with a previous therapist. Ninety per cent of these cases involved harm to the client as a result of the sexual misconduct by the former therapists.

While most mental health professional codes prohibit sexual contact with a current client, there is debate about what time limits should be placed on the therapeutic relationship. For example, if the therapeutic relationship is terminated on one day, can the therapist ethically be sexual with the "former" client the next day? Or, given that clients may want to return to therapy at another time in the future, does the therapeutic relationship last for life? The Feminist Therapy Network Code of Ethics recommends an elapse of at least 6 months between the termination of therapy and the initiation of sexual activity between a counselor and a former client. On the other hand, many psychologists believe "once a client, always a client." This perspective has been incorporated into the proposed revision of the APA Ethical Principles. Until these debates are formally resolved, therapists must define their own time limits. Several questions seem important to address in making this decision. Can the power imbalance in the therapeutic relationship ever be overcome, even in post-therapy relationships? How may the particular issues a client brings to therapy, e.g. resolving sexual trauma, affect the former client's susceptibility and reaction to sexual involvement with the therapist? What is the qualitative and quantitative nature of the therapist's social network? Might the counselor terminate therapy in order to establish a sexual relationship, thereby doubly disadvantaging the client?

Non-sexual dual relationships

Other examples of overlapping relationships with clients include friendships, social network contact, business relationships, social action involvement, and having two or more clients involved in relationships with each other. In these situations, the client may feel uncomfortable or violated by the dual relationship, the counselor may feel caught between the roles and even feel triangulated, or the client may suffer negative consequences as a result of the overlap. To the above list of dual relationships, Brown (1991) adds several potential boundary violations by therapists:

(1) Inappropriate use of self-disclosure, e.g. counselor talks about own problems for first 15 minutes of each session.
(2) Routine or ritualistic touch.
(3) Using clients' skill or resources for counselor benefit.
(4) Being too available to clients, e.g. encouraging clients to call whenever they experience discomfort.
(5) Fostering client dependency.
(6) Inappropriate disclosure of client information (professional gossiping).
(7) Encouraging the client to worship the counselor.

Most of these examples apply primarily to ongoing therapeutic relationships; however, some of them may pertain to post-therapy relationships as well. For example, if the counselor is or becomes the employer of a current client, the dual relationships put the client at risk professionally and therapeutically. If the counselor becomes the employer of a former client, the client may still be at risk, yet the complications of the dual relationship are not as clear. Many of these concerns about dual relationships may apply to professional situations other than client–counselor, e.g. student–teacher, supervisee–supervisor.

These overlapping roles are diverse and complex. Many of these overlapping relationships and boundary issues cannot be avoided completely. Therapists who work in small communities have an especially difficult time avoiding these overlaps. Lesbian therapists who counsel lesbian clients often find their personal and professional roles overlapping. Feminist Therapy Principles and techniques may increase the likelihood of occurrence of several of these situations (Brown, 1991). For example, as feminist therapists join social action groups, they find themselves working side-by-side with current and former clients whom they have encouraged to work for institutional change. Further, because feminist therapists may publicly declare or own their value systems, individuals who have existing relationships with therapists (friend, colleague, business associate) may actively seek them out as therapists because of their values (Berman, 1985).

Resolving boundary dilemmas

Simple "do and don't" rules for therapists are inadequate to addressing the complexities of overlapping relationships and boundary violations. Thus, feminist therapists must weigh and resolve these issues for themselves. They must assess the consequences of the issues individually within the context of each unique situation. Brown (1991) outlines a three-step process for approaching these role and boundary issues. First, therapists need to acknowledge the existence of and potential problems with the overlapping relationship. Second, in a planned manner, therapists must assess the risks and benefits of the overlapping relationships for the client, for the counselor, and for the client–counselor relationship. Third, therapists must have effective ways to take care of themselves in order to maintain their own mental health and not depend on relationships with clients to meet their needs.

Within the framework of Brown's steps, we propose that feminist therapists consider the following five areas in reaching effective decisions about overlapping relationships. Under each of the five areas, we have posed a series of relevant questions.

(1) *The nature of the therapeutic relationship.* What is the status of the client's mental health? What is the focus of therapy? How long did the therapy relationship last or how long is it anticipated to last? Is the client in individual or group therapy? How egalitarian is the therapy relationship? In general, the more vulnerable the client is, the more important it is to avoid overlapping relationships.

(2) *The nature of the overlapping relationship.* Does the overlapping relationship involve a power differential? What negative consequences might accrue to the client and/or counselor as a result of the dual relationship? In general, if the overlapping relationship involves a

substantial power differential, e.g. employer–employee, teacher–student, then a therapy relationship should not be initiated. On the other hand, while a friend-to-friend relationship does not involve a power differential, there are many potential problems with counselors being friends with clients.

(3) *Health of therapist.* What is the mental health status of the therapist? How effectively does the therapist take care of self? Therapists who are psychologically impaired or who are not getting their personal needs met outside the therapeutic relationship are more likely to engage in practices which are damaging to their clients.

(4) *Context variables.* What is the nature of the community shared by the counselor and client? What is the size of the community? What are the norms of the community and how might they contribute to problems with the overlapping relationships? Because of the small size of most lesbian communities and because of the importance of the shared values and support in the lesbian community, lesbian therapists often find themselves making tough decisions about overlaps.

(5) *Therapist theoretical orientation.* What assumptions or important constructs, e.g. transference, of the therapist's theoretical orientation are violated or complicated by the overlapping relationship?

In this assessment and decision process, priority must be given to the impact of all decisions on the client. The more vulnerable status of the client must be kept in mind. Therapists must acknowledge and own their special power and status and must ensure that they do not abuse that power and their client's trust.

Client–counselor Gender Issues

The general societal power imbalances between women and men affect the more specific dynamics of the therapy relationship as well. "The social construction of appropriate gender roles affects both the ways women and men behave and the ways others perceive them" (Warburton, Newberry, & Alexander, 1989, p. 156). Whether the counselor is female or male and whether the client is female or male have potentially different impacts on the outcome of therapy. The impact of gender power on the process and outcome of therapy is especially important in feminist therapy because of its emphasis on egalitarian counseling relationships. In this section, we highlight the role of gender power in counseling and analyze the costs and benefits of same- and cross-gender counseling relationships.

In Chapter 13, we cite the findings of a literature review by Beutler, Crago, and Arizmendi (1986) which indicates that same-sex therapeutic dyads resulted in greater client satisfaction and improvement than cross-sex dyads.

Thus, there is general, although not conclusive, evidence that matched sex dyads are therapeutically more effective. However, this research does not assess directly how outcomes related to the three Feminist Therapy Principles are affected by same- and cross-sex therapeutic dyads. Even if same-sex counseling dyads are found to be superior in all dimensions, it is unlikely that cross-sex dyads would cease to exist.

In Chapter 4, we posited several reasons for the importance feminist therapists give to building egalitarian relationships with clients. First, egalitarian relationships reduce the social control aspects of therapy, whereby therapists misuse their power to get clients to comply and adapt to a sexist society. In egalitarian relationships, therapists have less of a power base from which to push their values on clients. Second and most importantly, feminist therapists believe that the therapy relationship should not recreate the power imbalance women experience in society. Client–counselor relationships should be models for egalitarian relationships in general. Because of the central role that power plays in these reasons for egalitarian therapeutic relationships, it is important to understand the power differentials between clients and therapists in same-sex and cross-sex relationships.

Power imbalances in therapeutic relationships

Mary Ann Douglas (1985) defines different kinds of power present in the therapist role and points out the ramifications of these power sources in four different therapy dyads. Douglas notes that although feminist therapists strive to build egalitarian relationships with clients, they still retain greater power than clients because clients are dependent on receiving something from therapists. Acknowledgement and owning of this power differential by therapists is important in order for therapists to minimize the misuse/abuse of their power. Reward, coercive, informational, expert, legitimate, and referent powers are either inherent to the therapist role or are available sources of power for therapists. To these six sources of power, Douglas adds gender power, reflecting the general greater power status of men vis-à-vis women in our society. The power dynamics of any heterosexual relationship exist ". . . within a context of permanent inequality between the sexes" (Douglas, 1985, p. 244). The interactive effect of therapist role power and gender power is summarized in Douglas' model, presented in Table 12.6.

Although a feminist therapy approach seeks to build egalitarian relationships, the degree to which therapist role power and gender power can actually be reduced in the therapy relationship needs to be investigated empirically. At present, a feminist therapist analysis of advantages and disadvantages of same- and cross-sex therapy dyads must take into account these power differentials.

Table 12.6. *Relative Power of Therapist vis-à-vis the Client, Based on Therapist and Gender Roles. (Reproduced from Douglas, 1985, Relative Power of the Therapist. Copyright © 1985 by Springer Publishing Company, Inc., New York 10012. Used by permission.)*

Sources of power	Female therapist		Male therapist	
	Female client	Male client	Female client	Male client
Therapist role	GT	GT	GT	GT
Gender role	EQ	GC	GT	EQ
Total relative power of therapist vis-à-vis client	GT	?	GT	GT

Key: GT = greater therapist power; GC = greater client power; EQ = equal client/ therapist power.

Cost–benefit analysis

Same-sex therapeutic dyads. The potential advantages to a female client–female counselor pairing are: (a) increased empathy for the client due to similarities in life experiences; (b) the therapist can serve as an effective non-stereotyped role model with whom the client can identify; (c) an egalitarian therapeutic relationship is easier to develop since the gender power is equal; and (d) some female clients may feel more comfortable disclosing about sensitive topics to a female therapist. Potential disadvantages are (1) the possible lack of clear distinctions between therapist and client issues, and (2) the therapist may fail to clarify the meaning of a client's statement because she assumes their experiences are the same. In the male–counselor and male client dyad, there are advantages similar to the female matched pair: (a) the male therapist can be an effective non-traditional male role model, (b) there may be increased empathy due to a common life experience base, and (c) an egalitarian therapy relationship may be easier to establish. Reluctance of the male client and counselor to express sadness and fear in the presence of another man is an important potential disadvantage. Further, similarly to the matched female dyad, the male counselor in the matched male dyad may erroneously assume similarity between him and his client, obscuring actual differences.

Cross-sex therapeutic dyads. The cross-sex pairings generally have more potential problems than same-sex pairings. When the client is female and the counselor is male, one potential advantage is that the therapist can be an effective non-stereotyped male role model, thus providing the client with a positive experience relating to a man. However, an egalitarian relationship is more difficult to achieve because of the gender power imbalance. Power inequality is heightened by the male therapist–female client dyad (Fitzgerald

& Nutt, 1986). Female clients may feel intimidated by and unsafe with a male counselor and may fall into a female stereotypic behavior pattern of acquiescence. Further, there are specific issues or life experiences that the female client may have that make it difficult or impossible for her to trust a male therapist, no matter how sensitive and empathic the therapist is. Women who have been raped, sexually abused, or have been a victim of spouse abuse frequently request a female therapist. As the female client's consciousness is raised as a result of counseling, she may become angry with the men in her life, including her male therapist. If the therapist fails to validate that anger because of his own defensiveness, the client's progress may be hindered. Male counselors must be aware of their non-verbal messages, especially ones that convey dominant–subordinate power status (Fitzgerald & Nutt, 1986).

When the client is male and the counselor is female, there are several potential advantages: (a) the client will learn to appreciate and relate to a non-stereotyped woman; and (b) male clients may find it easier to express feelings in the presence of a female therapist than with a male therapist. As is indicated in Douglas' (1985) chart in Table 12.5, the overall power balance of this dyad is unknown or may vary depending on the specific individuals involved. Potential disadvantages to this pairing are: (a) the male client may discount or devalue the female counselor herself and/or her interventions; and (b) the female counselor may feel intimidated by the male client and fail to confront or challenge him.

Gender and mutliple clients

Issues emerging out of same and cross-sex counseling pairings become even more complex in couple and family counseling. For example, in studies of female and male family therapist trainees, Warburton, Newberry, and Alexander (1989) found that both female and male trainees "can expect pulls for affiliation with the same-sex parent and defensiveness from the opposite-sex parent" (p. 153). However, the female trainee is likely to experience more defensiveness from the father than the male trainee is from the mother. Gender power imbalances may be present not only between the counselor and each family member, but are also present among family members.

From a feminist perspective, all sources of power imbalances must be acknowledged and worked with if therapy is to be effective and is not to be harmful to the women in the family (Bograd, 1986; Hare-Mustin, 1978). The effect of whether the family therapist is a woman, a man, or even a female–male co-therapist team will have similar, although more complex, benefits and costs to those previously discussed for each dyad pairing. While female–male co-therapist teams have the potential to model an egalitarian cross-sex partnership that may transcend some of the costs, the co-therapists must be careful to have an egalitarian relationship in which both counselors model androgynous, non-stereotyped behaviors and skills.

Summary of gender issues

An analysis of the costs and benefits of cross-sex counseling dyads demonstrates the cross-cultural nature of these relationships. Female and male feminist therapists who want to minimize or overcome the disadvantages of the cross-sex pairings must work especially hard at increasing self-awareness of their own sex-role messages, their stereotypic responses, and their non-verbal behaviors. It is especially important and difficult to put themselves in the shoes of the other sex and to understand their perspective and experiences. Supervision by a feminist therapist can be crucial to identifying and dealing with the cross-sex dyad disadvantages. In addition, we believe that priority and respect must be given to clients' gender preferences for a counselor whenever possible.

Pre-assessment Exercise Update

Now that we have discussed dual relationships and client–counselor gender issues, we want to return to the client case we presented at the beginning of this chapter. At this point, you are probably very aware that the first therapist's sexual involvement with the client was unethical and was a revictimization of the client, in that many of the dynamics of the client's childhood sexual abuse experiences were recreated by the therapist's sexual exploitation of her. Feminist Therapy Principles I and II have been violated by the therapist's misuse of both his professional and gender power. In addition to the harm done to this particular client, this therapist may be likely to violate other clients as well. Since the client does not want to pursue the issue further, several other ethical issues are raised. Because of the client privilege of confidentiality, the second therapist cannot confront the first therapist without the client's permission.[2] One possible goal for therapy with this client is to help her restructure her self-blaming cognitions about the encounter to cognitions that hold the therapist responsible for his behavior. Sex-role analysis, power analysis, and confrontation of sexual abuse myths may help empower this client to be able to confront her former therapist and/or to take her case to an ethics review board. Her current therapist must be careful to support her in her decision-making, as undue pressure to take action will revictimize the client.

---

[2]In some states, client sexual abuse requires mandatory reporting. Thus, in this mandatory reporting situation, confidentiality may be broken.

"I am a Feminist Therapist"

If you decide to embrace the three Feminist Therapy Principles, you will need to decide how to label yourself in relation to these values. There is a continuum of choices: (a) labeling yourself as a feminist therapist; (b) listing yourself as a therapist specializing in women's issues; (c) calling yourself a non-sexist therapist; (d) not labeling yourself, but stating your feminist therapy values to clients. You will need to decide how to label yourself not only to clients, but also to colleagues and to yourself.

Many feminist therapists believe that using the label "feminist therapist" most accurately reflects their value system and allows clients to make a more informed decision about the choice of a therapist. Others argue that the label "feminist therapist" can be both a negative red flag and mistakenly interpreted by potential clients. For instance, any negative associations that people have to "feminist" may be attributed to the feminist therapist label. Thus, the feminist therapist label may unnecessarily restrict potential clients from choosing therapists who could be very effective with them. The feminist therapist in private practice will also need to consider the financial implications of the label they choose. A "specialist in women's issues" designation may exclude male clients unnecessarily. The label "non-sexist therapist" also has interpretation problems by potential consumers. As we discussed in Chapter 4, the label "non-sexist therapist" can mean many things to both therapists and clients.

A recent study by Enns and Hackett (1990) provides data to support positive outcomes associated with feminist therapist value orientation and therapists' explicit disclosures about their values. Using an analogue study format, in which college women viewed videotaped counseling vignettes of a female client and female counselor, Enns and Hackett (1990) investigated the differential effects of non-sexist, liberal, feminist, and radical feminist counseling approaches. The vignettes were varied by counseling orientation and by the explicitness of the counselors' value statements. Participants were grouped into a feminist or non-feminist stance, based on their responses to the Attitudes Toward Feminism Scale developed by the authors. All participants (feminist and non-feminist) preferred to see the two feminist counselors for career and sexual assault concerns; no differences were found for personal–interpersonal concerns. Counselors who made explicit value statements were seen as more helpful than any counselor in the implicit value condition. Both types of feminist counselors were seen as significantly more helpful, expert, and trustworthy than was the non-sexist therapist. Thus, these findings suggest that both feminist and non-feminist clients may perceive feminist therapists more favorably and that the "red flag" worries about the feminist therapist label may be unfounded.

Your labeling decision may fit currently, but may change over time and with your experience. The following questions may help you decide what to call yourself. How closely do your beliefs and values match the three Principles of Feminist Therapy? What does being a "feminist therapist" mean to you? Will each of the labels that you are considering attract or repel the clients with whom you want to work? Which label will contribute most to your effectiveness in your professional work? Which label will contribute most to your professional identity?

Conflicting Client–Counselor Goals

Throughout this book, we have addressed the importance of client self-determination and collaborative goal setting by the client and counselor. Collaborative goal setting is a relatively easy process when the client and counselor agree on the direction of therapy. However, major difficulties can arise when our clients want to achieve therapy goals which violate our personal and feminist values.

We will use an example to illustrate the dilemma of conflicting goals. A woman comes to you for therapy, saying she wants to stop criticizing her husband and to stop arguing with him. In the initial assessment phase of therapy, you discover that: (a) she and her husband have a traditional he-dominant, she-submissive relationship; (b) he has been physically abusive to her; and (c) she feels responsible for provoking his attacks on her. Your desired goals for her are to increase her self-esteem, decrease her economic dependency, increase her self-assertion, and for her to take steps to ensure her physical safety. Given this situation, how would you answer the following question? At what point, if any, in the therapy process would you disclose your goals for her? How would you go about resolving the goal discrepancies? If the conflict cannot be resolved, would you counsel her in working toward her goals? Your goals? Would you begin by working toward her goals with the hope of convincing her of the importance of your goals? Would you refer her to another counselor, and if so, at what point? You may want to review the case of Clara in Chapter 9 as an example of how a similar dilemma was resolved.

Summary

Having a feminist therapy perspective of ethical practices permits us to behave more congruently with our chosen value system. We have ". . . added to the definition of ethics the concept that sexist, racist, homophobic, or other discriminatory attitudes on the part of the therapist could be evidence of unethical behavior" (Brown, 1991). Feminist therapy ethical guidelines give additional protection to clients, especially female clients, from the possible misuse of power by therapists.

Being a feminist therapist has many unique challenges. How will we define our relationships to our clients both inside and outside of the therapy relationship? How will we own and positively use our professional power to facilitate our clients' growth? How will we cope with gender and our own sex-role socialization in our roles as therapists? What shall we call ourselves? How shall we respond when our goals and values do not match those of our clients? We each must answer these questions for ourselves within our own understanding and application of the three Feminist Therapy Principles. In our answers to these questions, we each define more specifically, not only our relationships to our present and potential clients, but also our relationships to ourselves and to our communities.

Activities

Think about and/or discuss with others the following questions:

A
How do you relate differently in your female and male relationships?

B
Given the person that you are and the professional attitudes and skills which you possess, what do you see as the strengths and weaknesses you bring to your work with female clients? With male clients?

C
How do the various ethical code models presented in this chapter fit with your own profession's ethical code? What problems would you anticipate in trying to have a non-sexist or feminist therapy set of ethical principles added to your profession's existing ethical code?

Further Readings

Douglas, M. A. (1985). The role of power in feminist therapy: A reformulation. In L. B. Rosewater & L. E. A. Walker (Eds.), *Handbook of Feminist Therapy*. New York: Springer.

Fitzgerald, L. F., & Nutt, R. (1986). The Division 17 principles concerning the counseling/psychotherapy of women: Rationale and implementation. *The Counseling Psychologist*, **14**, 180–216.

CHAPTER 13

Toward a Model of Training

Self-assessment: Evaluating Current Educational Programs

Consider both your undergraduate and graduate education in responding to the following questions:

(1) How was the psychology of sex roles, gender, or women included or integrated into your regular college curriculum?
(2) Identify the ways in which your undergraduate and graduate education reflected sexist practices with regard to students, faculty, resources, curriculum, clinical practice, research, and interpersonal relationships.

As you read this chapter, determine whether your answers to these two questions should be expanded, reconsidered, or revised.

Overview

This chapter considers the process of becoming a feminist in terms of personal values, cognitions, interpersonal behavior, community action, and clinical practice. We suggest that an educational agenda with respect to feminist counseling requires attention to all these variables. First, we explore some of the history and contemporary meanings of feminism in psychology. We then introduce a model of feminist identity development and its application to educational practice. Next, we propose a four-factor model of training that promotes coordination of student, faculty, departmental, university, and community resources. The model emphasizes a broad band of interventions across the student's educational experiences that integrates attitudes, knowledge, and skills toward the implementation of a feminist counseling perspective.

Developing a Feminist Perspective

The process of becoming a feminist therapist requires that you first develop an understanding, acceptance, and integration of a general feminist perspective. The application of this perspective to the client–counselor process then follows a clear rationale. How does the process of feminist identity occur and how can we encourage a feminist view of psychology within graduate educational programs?

We know that learning can occur in many ways and under diverse learning conditions (Worell & Stilwell, 1981). Many of the professionals who currently identify themselves as feminist psychologists, therapists, or counselors were educated and trained in traditional psychology programs. Most of us had few or no women faculty or mentors, no texts or research literature on women and their issues, and we were trained and supervised with traditional practices in research, assessment, and psychological intervention.

For most of its 100 years' existence, academic psychology had little to say about women or their life experiences (Walsh, 1985). If we were aware of sex discrimination, sexual harassment, or the contributions of societal structures and practices to women's mental health problems, we were unable to articulate this awareness into a cohesive theory or to translate it into action. How did we revise our thinking to become active as feminist psychologists, as competent in developing a new field of the Psychology of Women? Do we need new programs to prepare psychologists to meet the feminist agenda?

Early Awakenings

Influences of the Women's Movement

The introduction of feminist theory and practice into mainstream psychology occurred in the late 1960s and early 1970s, with the advent of the revitalized Women's Movement. Awareness and consciousness-raising crept upon some of us slowly, with a gradual integration of disparate but conceptually similar experiences. For others, the feminist awakening shattered our lives with sudden cognitive clashes and emotional drama, as previous beliefs gave way to new understandings. These new understandings stimulated much self-questioning. How could we have so misperceived all that we had experienced but had not understood? How could we have failed to confront the machinery of patriarchy and subordination that governed the structure of our lives? As Ellen Kimmel (1989) so aptly expressed it:

> What the women's movement did for me was to cure my schizophrenia. It provided a corpus callosum for making connections. Feminism was an integrating force joining diverse roles played, traits held, and experiences I'd had into one identity. The splits between wife and parent, scientist and professional,

masculinity and femininity, and southern lady and political activist, healed or learned to live together in harmony. My experience of . . . "otherness" was replaced by new feelings of both community and agency (p. 134).

Response of the psychological community

The articulation of a revisionist approach to women's roles and place in the social structure began to appear in the psychological literature, thus furthering our opportunities to explore new paradigms. In 1970, the now-famous study by Broverman et al. broke new ground in questioning the current conceptualizations of the mentally healthy woman as more passive and less assertive than the healthy man (see Chapters 2 and 4 for further discussion of this work). That same year, a fiery flag for feminism was raised by Robin Morgan's (1970) book *Sisterhood is Powerful*, and women began to reconsider the implications of patriarchal power structures as well as the strength that lies in women's collective action. One of the earliest books on the Psychology of Women appeared in 1971 (Sherman, 1971), and 2 years later the *Counseling Psychologist* (1973) published its first issue specifically devoted to counseling women.

A new strand of thinking was stimulated by Sandra Bem's (1974) publication of her Sex-role Inventory (BSRI), which challenged current beliefs about the mental health advantages of traditional sex-role traits. Bem's concept and measurement of psychological androgyny became a flag around which many developing feminists rallied in their search for new social roles that would move them closer to the ideal of equality between the sexes.

As new measures of androgyny appeared in the literature, some critical reviews cautioned us to take a closer look at the complex issues in measuring these concepts, and the evidence of negative as well as the positive outcomes of androgyny (Kelly & Worell, 1977; Worell, 1978). Further commentary on the androgyny concept argued that "it continues to link behavior with gender, and to label certain attributes as characteristic of women, and others as characteristic of men, with little regard for the abundance of within-gender variability" (Lott, 1981). Despite these reservations, the emphasis in androgyny theory on women's agency and autonomy, as well as their communal and expressive traits, remains as a foreground of concern in counseling with women (see Chapter 3).

New perspectives: the Psychology of Women

The emerging field of the Psychology of Women was recognized officially by the American Psychological Association in 1973, which voted to establish a new Division (35) devoted to furthering theory, research, and practice related to women. The Division established a new journal in 1976, *Psychology of*

Women Quarterly, dedicated to these same goals. The *Annual Review of Psychology*, certainly a mainstream publication, published its first chapter on the Psychology of Women (Mednick & Weissman, 1975), further "legitimizing" the study of women as a scholarly field. We were beginning to come of age.

The study of women is not necessarily feminist in its content and process (Wallston, 1981, 1986; Worell, 1991). Feminist perspectives are advanced, however, by the academic recognition given to research and theory written by and about women within a scientific discipline that had been mainly "womanless" (Crawford & Marecek, 1989; Worell, in press). In the psychological literature, women were becoming less invisible, and research began to reflect "woman-valued" topics that were previously ignored. Several early books on feminist therapy further awakened the professional community to new possibilities: Franks and Burtle's (1974) *Women in Therapy*, Rawlings and Carter's (1977) *Psychotherapy for Women*, and Brodsky and Hare-Mustin's (1980) *Women and Psychotherapy* contributed to the evolving definitions of the field.

The list of influential writing is barely touched upon here; for each signal work, dozens more appeared in print. As researchers and scholars, we could hardly ignore, or fail to be influenced by, the rising "tide in the affairs of women" (Westerveldt, 1978, p. 1). By 1985, over 13 000 publications on women appeared in the psychological literature. A new discipline and a new identity had been formed (Walsh, 1985; Worell, 1980).

Recognition of an emerging feminist identity among women raised questions in many quarters about what kinds of women were these who dared to confront traditional values, to challenge the scientific establishment, and to ask for an equal place in the social order? In a large-scale study on 979 female and male university students, Judith Worell and Leonard Worell (1977) reported that certain personality traits did differentiate those who supported or opposed the Women's Movement. Supporting women (emergent feminists?) differed from college female norms on only one trait: they described themselves as more independent and autonomous. In contrast, opposing women scored as more autocratic and dogmatic, more concerned with external sources of approval, more conventional, less rational, and more cautious in risky-choice situations. These characteristics tend to suggest that opposers were individuals who were generally resistant to new ideas and to social change. These early results were encouraging to those of us who thought of ourselves as supporters of equal status for women, and who were still in the process of creating a personal feminist identity. A subsequent review of relevant research by Lucia Gilbert (1980) found feminists, in contrast to non-feminists, to be more politically liberal and active, achieving, self-confident, autonomous, self-actualizing and higher in self-esteem. From diverse sequences of research, theory-building, and organizational structures, gradual images of a feminist perspective emerged.

Feminist Identity Development

In Chapter 1, we defined feminism in terms of advocating political, social, and economic equality between women and men. We expanded this definition with the addition of five major tenets:

(1) Recognition of the politics of gender and the oppression of women in most societies.
(2) Insistence on equal status in all situations, not only for women but for under-represented minority groups.
(3) Valuing and trusting women's experience.
(4) Realization that all science involves values that should be publicly stated.
(5) Commitment to action for social change.

We recognized that not all women (and men) who consider themselves feminist subscribe to these goals, and that many persons who support one or more goals do not identify themselves as feminists. How can we then understand the differing positions of individuals with respect to feminist goals?

A model of feminist identity development

A format for conceptualizing feminist identity development, patterned after that constructed for Black minorities (see Chapter 11 for a display of this model), was proposed by Nancy Downing and Kristin Roush (1984). Table 13.1 displays the five stages of the model, which coincide with the stages of Black identity development defined by Cross (1980). These stages are elaborated below.

Stage I: Passive Acceptance "describes the woman who is either unaware of or denies the individual, institutional, and cultural prejudice and discrimination against her (Downing & Roush, 1984, p. 669). She is likely to accept her subordinate position with respect to men, and appears to enjoy traditional sex-role arrangements.

Stage II: Revelation is precipitated by consciousness-raising experiences that invalidate her previous perceptions. These experiences may include personal discrimination, loss of a relationship, or contact with feminist ideas. At this stage, she becomes angry at the realization of her oppression and guilty for her own role in having collaborated with patriarchal power

Table 13.1. *Parallels Between the Identity Development Stages for Women and Blacks.* (*From Downing & Roush, 1984, with permission of Sage Publications, Inc.*)

Stages for Women

Passive acceptance	Revelation	Embeddedness–emanation	Synthesis	Active commitment
Passive acceptance of traditional sex roles and discrimination; belief that traditional roles are advantageous; men are considered superior	Catalyzed by a series of crises, resulting in open questioning of self and roles and feelings of anger and guilt; dualistic thinking; men are perceived as negative	Characterized by connectedness with other select women, affirmation and strengthening of new identity. Eventually more relativistic thinking and cautious interaction with men	Development of an authentic and positive feminist identity; sex-role transcendence; "flexible truce" with the world; evaluate men on an individual basis	Consolidation of feminist identity; commitment to meaningful action, to a non-sexist world. Actions are personalized and rational. Men are considered equal but not the same as women

Stages for Blacks

Pre-encounter	Encounter	Immersion–emersion	Internalization	Internalization–commitment
The unaware person; acceptance of oppression as justified; values assimilation into majority culture; negative self-concept	Catalyzed by profound event(s) resulting in increased awareness, rejection of oppression, and feelings of guilt and anger	Initially characterized by withdrawal from the dominant culture, immersion in one's heritage and hostility toward Whites. Eventually greater cognitive flexibility and pride emerge	Development of an integrated, more positive self-image; adoption of a pluralistic, non-racist perspective	Commitment of the new self to meaningful action for the benefit of the minority community

structures. She is likely to polarize gender by valuing all women and devaluing all men.

Stage III: Embeddedness–Emanation describes the woman who immerses herself in women's culture and increases her social and emotional connections with other women. The authors point out that the immersion process is more difficult for most women than for minorities, since social structures prevent them from avoiding male contact entirely. If she is married or has male children, she may see herself as imprisoned with her oppressor. As women emanate from this stage, they relinquish their polarized position and begin to reintegrate themselves into a new personhood.

In *Stage IV: Synthesis* the woman has arrived at a flexible and positive feminist identity, and increasingly values her female self. She is still aware of societal oppression, but is "able to transcend traditional sex roles, make choices . . . based on well-defined personal values, and evaluate men on an individual, rather than a stereotypic, basis" (Downing & Roush, 1984, p. 702).

Finally, *Stage V* describes a position of *active commitment to social change*. The woman becomes involved in working for Women's Rights and "in creating a future in which sex-role transcendence is a valued and encouraged goal" (Downing & Roush, 1984, p. 702).

The authors point out that most women will alternately advance and then retreat to earlier stages, as they progressively encounter new situations and develop new skills. Thus, feminist identity becomes a process through which we evolve gradually and within which we continually seek new perspectives. In a recent study of feminist identity development in psychology graduate students (Worell, Stilwell, & Robinson, 1991), the stage model appeared to be replaced by a dimensional model, in which individual scores varied across dimensions of feminist commitment but did not follow a step-up progression.

As a cautionary note, however, we recognize that the model does not take into account individual differences in feminist orientations due to ethnocultural group, affectional preferences, age, socioeconomic class, or male gender. A model of feminist identity development for men, for example, remains to be explored. Arnold Kahn (1984), a self-identified feminist, has pointed out that for many men, the possession of power—in society and over women—is central to their self-definition, self-esteem, and concept of masculinity. In order to acknowledge and advocate women's equality, such men will have to relinquish the goal of power and to find sources of identity and self-esteem in ways that are independent of their gender. Thus, men's feminist identity development may require a stage that includes consideration of power and its potential loss. To the extent that a range of variables enters into the feminist identity process, modifications in the format and measurement of the model should be considered.

Applying the model

An initial approach to evaluating the feminist identity model was taken by Adena Bargad and Janet Hyde (1991). These authors constructed the 39-item Feminist Identity Development Scale (FIDS) to test the application of the model to evaluation of the effects of college courses centering on women's studies. They administered the FIDS to women in three different classes pre- and post-completion of these courses, comparing their responses with those of a control group who did not enroll in a women's studies course. The overall goals of the courses were to raise student consciousness of feminist perspectives and to empower students through increased self-awareness.

The pre–post scores of the groups on each of the five stages of feminist identity are displayed in Figure 13.1. At pretest, the control group did not differ from the three women's studies groups, and at post-test, the controls did not differ from their own pretest scores. In contrast, the experimental groups changed on all five stage measures, supporting the effectiveness of a university course curriculum in promoting a feminist perspective. This interesting study supports previous research that reported changes in student attitudes and values following a course related to gender and women (Brush, Gold, & White, 1978; Kahn & Theurer, 1985; Ruble et al., 1975; Scott, Richards, & Wade, 1977; Stake & Gerner, 1987; Vedavato & Vaughter, 1980).

The effectiveness of training and exposure to feminist concepts was further explored in a recent study with psychology graduate students (Worell, Stilwell, & Robinson, 1991). These authors found that field and program exposure to content and issues related to women were significantly related to students' personal epistomology (Unger, 1985/6), performance self-esteem (Stake, 1979), endorsement of feminist therapy goals (Robinson & Worell, 1991), and stages of feminist identity on a revised version of the FIDS (Bargad & Hyde, 1991).

We reviewed these studies in some detail to highlight the effectiveness of university courses with a feminist perspective on changes in student self-awareness and endorsement of feminist principles. These research findings also suggest that a curriculum which incorporates gender and feminist perspectives across a range of attitudes, knowledge, and skill areas should be effective in promoting the goals of a feminist counseling training program.

A Feminist Training Model

The foregoing studies suggest strongly that exposure to theory and research on gender and feminist perspectives can influence student awareness and attitudes. Michelle Harway (1979), Worell (1980, 1987), and Worell and

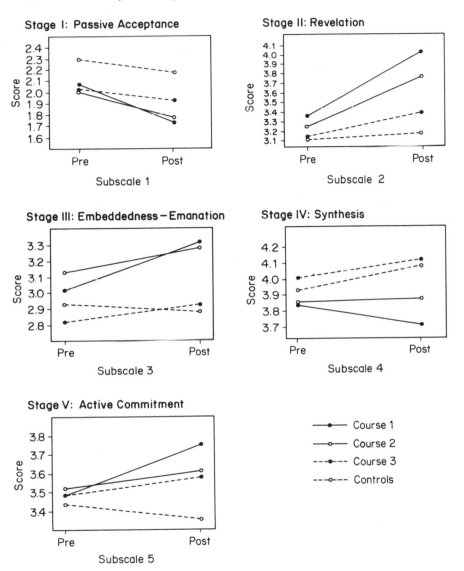

Figure 13.1. Mean subscale scores by course at pre- and post-tests. (From Bargad & Hyde, 1991, with permission of Cambridge University Press.)

Remer (1979) have proposed models of feminist training in Counseling Psychology that contain similar components. The models are designed to enable students to gain the knowledge, attitudes, and skills that will facilitate their effective functioning in feminist-oriented research and practice. In addition, the training models focus on issues of personal identity, autonomy, and growth for all students and faculty involved.

Patricia Faunce (1985) has added important process variables to pedagogy in this area that contribute to the feminist focus. She pointed out that feminist pedagogy is an integral component of an effective training program, such that the classroom becomes "a laboratory of feminist principles . . . based on cooperation, mutual respect, and interdependence. The instructor/therapist and student/client are both learner and expert; they teach each other, and knowledge, information, and experience are shared." In particular, she emphasized power dissemination and reciprocal influence in the teaching–learning process. "When power is shared it increases, regenerates, and expands. This is also true with ideas: If they are freely given and exchanged, ideas change and expand constantly, remaining alive and fresh" (Faunce, 1985, pp. 311–312).

Here, we propose a graduate program that encompasses four major components:

(1)   Attitudes and values.
(2)   Structures.
(3)   Resources.
(4)   Outreach.

These four factors are displayed in Figure 13.2.

Attitudes and Values

Feminist values and belief-orientations are clear prerequisites for initiating a feminist training program. Relevant attitudes may be held by only one or two faculty members. These faculty members disseminate information to relevant others (students, faculty, administration) in a consciousness-raising effort to encourage interest and motivation for change. Soliciting interested women faculty to teach a course on gender or sex-role issues is a viable way to increase awareness in an interested but uncommitted faculty member. Walsh (1985) reported that faculty who teach modules or courses on gender become more knowledgeable and demonstrate significant attitude changes as a result of their preparations for the course. Remaining departmental faculty and some administrators, while not initially interested, need to be informed and integrated toward a common effort so that new courses can be added to existing programs.

   Strategies for accomplishing the task of modifying attitudes vary with institutional structures, and may be more difficult in some situations than in others. Circulation of brief readings, invited speakers, volunteering to present guest lectures in their classes, personal confrontation, and persistence may be necessary to convince an otherwise negative faculty of the legitimacy of the program. When one of the authors proposed a new course on sex-role

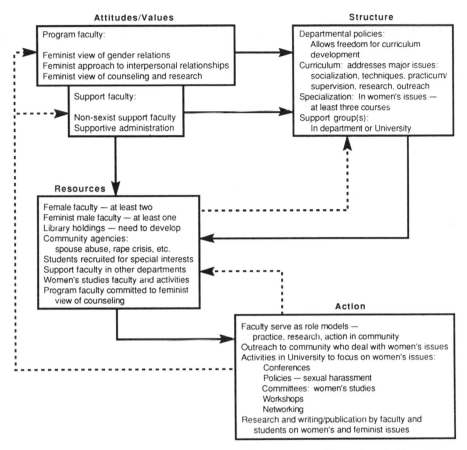

Figure 13.2.   Components of a feminist training program. Heavy lines indicate direct influence. Dotted lines propose recursive feedback loops and subsequent influences

development in her academic department, a statistics faculty member commented: "Can't you just integrate that material as a lecture or module into your Social Development course?" In response, he was asked: "You teach multivariate analysis as a semester course; can't you just integrate that content into a seminar in your ANOVA class?" The point was clear; the new course was approved and implemented.

Structure

When there are at least two committed faculty (and some interested and supportive students as well), policies and curriculum can be set into place. Evidence on the experiences of lone or isolated female faculty, especially those with feminist values, suggests strongly that there should be support and strength in numbers (Makowsky & Paludi, 1990). Many decisions require planning and contact with others: about what courses to develop, appropriate breadth and depth for an adequate curriculum, and strategies for implementing the revised curriculum. Factors that require attention include: (a) departmental and university policies; (b) curriculum development; (c) research activities; (d) practice, supervision, and internships; (e) social support; and (f) outreach.

Policies

Departmental and university policies may need revision toward modifying current practices. First, a move toward increasing female faculty is essential. Although women contribute 38% of the membership of the American Psychological Association, for example, fewer than 25% of the faculty of professional training programs are women. Further, current student body distribution suggests that women are entering the field of professional counseling and clinical psychology at a higher rate than are men, so that women students are unrepresented by the insufficient proportions of female faculty (Ostertag & McNemara, 1991).

Second, departmental and university policies need to address issues of persisting sexism in language, allocation of funding resources, and incidence of sexual harassment of students by faculty. A departmental policy on use of non-sexist language in all student writing and faculty documents and memos, for example, is essential. Despite the prohibition of sex-biased language by official publication guidelines (American Psychological Association, 1983), the use of the generic "he" is still in evidence in student papers as well as in more scholarly scientific writings (Worell, 1991). For example, in a recent review of research that is frequently assigned for graduate student reading on the effectiveness of psychotherapy (Lambert, Shapiro, & Bergin, 1985), the therapist is still referred to as "he" (p. 161 ff).

As a second concern, funding resources need to be monitored continually to ensure that women faculty and students receive their share of financial assistance and research support. Finally, sexual harassment of women faculty and students is a problem on college campuses (Dzeich & Weiner, 1984; Fitzgerald et al., 1988; Malovich & Stake, 1990), and needs to be monitored, exposed and censured. At the university at which the authors teach, no sexual harassment policy was in place until one of the authors pioneered a university policy that, despite considerable administrative protest that it was unnecessary, finally made its way into the student, staff, and faculty codes.

A convincing factor in the modification of university policies regarding sex and gender has been the growing awareness by administrations of federal laws that might be violated in the absence of such policies. Although policies and guidelines do not preclude continued sex-biased behavior, they form the basis for student, faculty, and administrative awareness and provide a resource for action and appeal procedures.

Curriculum

Cecelia Foxley (1979) suggested a minimum of four courses for developing an adequate curriculum in non-sexist counseling. The basic courses for a feminist training curriculum include gender and sex-role development, gender analysis of contemporary society, issues and techniques in counseling and therapy with women, and practicum with feminist supervision of cases. Specific topics within these courses may vary, but fundamental principles of feminist theory, therapy, and research would permeate all elements of the curriculum. Excellent sources are now available for developing courses in the Psychology of Women (see Golub & Freedman, 1987; Paludi, 1989).

In addition to specialized coursework, program faculty can be encouraged to infuse their other courses, such as the standard career development course, with modules or content that focus on gender and women's issues (Harway, 1980). Faculty in related areas, such as human development, history and systems, psychopathology, or assessment, can be persuaded to remedy sex-biased or womanless readings and texts, and to introduce modules into existing courses that emphasize non-sexist or gender-sensitive content. Recent studies on textbooks used in psychology programs have documented the need for mainstreaming the new information on the Psychology of Women into traditional texts. Florence Denmark (1983), reporting on a sample of 16 introductory psychology textbooks, found sex-typed examples and illustrations throughout the texts, and the overwhelming majority of research and professional exemplars were male. Similar findings were reported for a sample of abnormal psychology textbooks (Bristow, Frieman, & Dickson, 1984; Harris & Lightner, 1980).

Although there is still controversy about whether the new scholarship on women should be segregated in separate courses or should be infused into mainstream academia (Makowsky & Paludi, 1990; Walsh, 1985), we take sides with both positions. Specialized coursework can explore important gender-related issues with both breadth and depth, and infusion into mainstream curriculum can expand these findings to related topics. Students in all areas will benefit from a balanced view of human behavior that takes into consideration the full range of human experience.

Research activities

Feminist scholars have pointed to the ways in which our science has been sex-biased and androcentric in its content and methods, and have called for

Table 13.2.   *Emergent Feminist Research Criteria.* (*From Worell, (in press), with permission.*)

---

1. *Challenges traditional views of women.* Presents women in a range of roles, free of prescribed sex-role constraints.
2. *Uses alternative methods of inquiry.* Expands the boundaries of accepted methodology to explore the personal lives of women.
3. *Looks at meaningful contexts.* Considers women in the natural settings in which they function.
4. *Collaborates with research participants.* Enters into a partnership with participants to explore personally relevant variables.
5. *Solicits diverse samples.* Looks at women who vary by age, socioeconomic class, partner preference, minority or ethnic group, etc.
6. *Compares women and men contextually.* Replaces 'sex differences' research with meaningful sex comparisons.
7. *Avoids blaming victims of violence and injustice.* Considers victim behavior in the context of power imbalance and gender-related expectations.
8. *Empowers women and minorities.* Looks at the positive characteristics and contributions.
9. *Examines structure and power hierarchies.* Considers women's behavior in the context of social structure and patriarchy.
10. *Includes implications for social change.* Is proactive.

---

revisions in the manner in which research is conceptualized, conducted, and taught (Crawford & Marecek, 1989; Grady, 1981; McHugh, Koeske, & Frieze, 1986; Unger, 1981; 1982; 1983; Wallston, 1981). Feminist scholars have also provided new conceptions of the research agenda and have given us revised visions of possibilities for enriching the field (Lott, 1985a; Peplau & Conrad, 1989). Emergent views of research that reflect a feminist agenda are displayed in Table 13.2.

The 10 criteria are "emergent" in the sense that we are still in the process of shaping and refining them. They serve as goals or guideposts rather than as fixed principles. The criteria affirm the study of women as a legitimate activity, focus on the social construction of gender, insist on attention to societal and power issues, open the selection of research participants to broad populations, engage participants in a collaborative activity, resist blaming women for their vulnerabilities, and openly declare the role of social change in designing and implementing psychological research (Worell, 1990; in press).

Within graduate education programs, feminist research can review and renew the study of human behavior and the process of behavior change. In a feminist framework, new views of research are built onto the foundations of traditional psychological knowledge, to expand our understanding and interventions. Students are introduced to feminist and gender-related journals, and are encouraged to build their own models of research using revised criteria for seeking topics and methods appropriate to their interests. Students are encouraged to explore their own experiences in the search for appropriate research questions, thus uncovering the ideographic and moving it into the realm of common experience. The research that is produced by graduate trainees will thus reflect a reconstructed conception of women's and men's lives, and will feed back in a recursive process into the furthering of new knowledge about human existence.

Practice issues

Practice in feminist theory and process is encouraged through four broad procedures: (a) assignment of cases that provide opportunities for practicing a feminist approach; (b) supervision that is feminist in focus; (c) placement in agencies that specialize in women's issues (women's shelters, rape crisis centers, women's health centers, eating disorders and reproductive planning clinics, etc.); and (d) monitoring of predoctoral internship sites to facilitate a feminist or gender-sensitive placement. Qualifying examinations can contribute to this unfolding process, by written or oral questions for the student on how her or his theoretical orientation is compatible with feminist counseling theory and practice. As an example of feminist process in practice training, we center on supervision.

Supervision. Contrasting models of clinical supervision tend to differ in terms of their emphasis on process, procedures, relationships, or didactics (Hess, 1980). Feminist supervision may include aspects of all these models, but also includes unique characteristics. In particular, feminist supervision is sensitive to power differentials between trainee and supervisor, as well as to broadly valued philosophical goals (Porter, 1985).

Feminist supervision can consist of direct observation or co-therapy, audiotape and/or videotape review, case conference, and case analysis. We believe that group supervision is particularly appropriate because it is relatively efficient in faculty resource allocation, it exposes a larger number of students to the process of feminist analysis, and provides for peer, as well as faculty, feedback. Within any feminist model, each of the following components should be included:

(1) Attention to process (between counselor and client, and between trainee and faculty) to facilitate egalitarian, open, and flexible interactions.
(2) Gender and sex-role analysis with trainee with respect to interactions with female and male clients; issues of empathy, warmth, power, and

     self-disclosure with cross-sex clients (such as in marital or family counseling).

(3)   Exploration of how trainee's currently-held theoretical orientation matches with feminist goals.

(4)   Examination of contracted therapy goals in terms of client–counselor collaboration; analysis of problematic goals for client (such as client's goal to avoid making her husband angry).

(5)   Redefining health and pathology; attention to assessment and diagnosis to monitor potentially damaging labels and procedures; (such as the tendency to describe women in relationships as nagging or co-dependent, mothers as controlling and enmeshed, and ambivalent clients as passive–aggressive).

(6)   Focus on external as well as internal sources of client problems; looking at how current issues trace back to institutionalized sexism and internalized sex-role messages.

(7)   Evaluation of progress that provides continuous and constructive feedback to client and emphasizes her strengths; focusing the process of change toward personal autonomy and empowerment.

(8)   Assistance in designing and developing specialized women's groups, workshops, and educational formats for reaching a wider range of public consumers. Emphasis on prevention as well as on remediation.

(9)   Respect and validation for the strengths and strategies of the trainee; assisting trainee to trust own experience.

Social support

Support groups for students with a feminist counseling focus are important for: (a) dealing with personal issues related to being a woman and/or a developing feminist; (b) continued consciousness-raising for applications of their program to personal and professional issues; and (c) personal support for surviving in a non-feminist environment. A women's group becomes a useful mechanism for meeting these needs and can be a vehicle for introducing newer students to the possibilities of the program.

    Modifications in social support grouping might be necessary for programs in which one or more men have decided to become feminist in their orientation, and wish to join a support group. Women's groups frequently reject the inclusion of men due to their experiences with mixed-sex groups and consequent difficulties in interactions. We know of no evidence, however, of mixed-sex groups for feminist counselors, a model that is potentially useful and might increase awareness for both sexes.

    Scholars in teaching the Psychology of Women, however, recommend that even in mixed-sex groups, women and men should be provided with the opportunity to meet separately for periods of time in same-sex groupings in order to facilitate open and uninhibited self-disclosure (Paludi, 1990).

Resources

Resources can be minimal or lavish, but certain basic prerequisites need to be in place before a fully functioning program can operate. These resources include at least two feminist female faculty members, one or more supportive male faculty, departmental support with respect to allocation of coursework responsibilities, support faculty in other university departments for committee participation, students recruited for specific interest in the program, adequate library holdings including gender-focused periodicals, cooperating community agencies, and professional contacts with other feminist professional psychologists. The process of developing, acquiring, and conserving current resources is typically gradual and continuous.

Finally, the departmental program is enriched if other curriculum and faculty resources are available within the university. Gender-related coursework can include offerings from perspectives other than psychology: sociology, anthropology, education, women's studies, etc. Students are encouraged to attend cross-departmental and external seminars, colloquia, and workshops. Early in their program, students are encouraged to expand their professional commitment through membership and participation in relevant organizations that provide professional contacts related to women's issues.

Outreach

A fully functioning psychology graduate program for training feminist therapists will require concerted activism and outreach on the part of both faculty and students. First, faculty serve as role models, not only for their research and practice approaches, but for their visibility in local, regional, and national activities. Feminist faculty join and take active steps in organizations that articulate and facilitate their goals, and they make students aware of these activities. Faculty serve on boards and committees in the community that further feminist goals, such as a rape crisis or spouse abuse center or a teenage mothers' project. Feminist faculty may organize or become part of other local professional groups that are working for women's equity and professional advancement. All of these activities are communicated to students, who are encouraged to participate as well.

Feminist faculty also become active in university affairs dealing with women. They participate on committees that investigate women faculty salaries, tenure procedures, policies affecting women (such as sexual harassment), and employment of female faculty. They initiate or cooperate in developing workshops, seminars, and conferences relevant to women. They volunteer time to speak to other classes, thereby helping to infuse women's content into mainstream academia. And feminist faculty focus on networking with other university, community, national, and international women who can serve as resources and support systems for the program and its participants.

Addendum

If this training program seems ambitious and demanding of time, effort, and dedication, the implications for expansion are clear. In the absence of considerable personal commitment, networking with other feminist professionals, and support from the home university, such programs will be difficult to implement and maintain. The few women faculty can become overburdened with more responsibilities than are possible to fulfill, especially those related to outreach and social action. The program outlined here represents more of an ideal than a reality until women faculty are no longer a minority in academia.

Evaluating Outcomes

We envision multiple outcomes of a training program in feminist counseling. Worell and Remer (1979) proposed a cascade model which depicts a triad of training outcomes in terms of: (a) types of service provided (educational, preventative or remedial); (b) populations served (many to few); and (c) ratio of intervention cost to size of populations served. Within these dimensions, the attitudes, knowledge, and skills produced by the training program are integrated within each service-provider function: researcher/ scholar, educator, consultant, change agent, or direct counseling practice. Graduates are prepared to function effectively in any of these areas, but in practice will probably select a few areas for personal commitment. The cascade model is displayed in Figure 13.3.

At the broadest level of intervention, the researcher/scholar function produces new knowledge about women, men, and their social environments that is disseminated through research reports and written documentation. This information becomes available nationally as well as internationally, and survives over time to influence the development of the discipline. At the narrowest level, personal counseling is provided for individual clients in a clinical practice or agency. Across the functions within the model, the training program aims to produce a cadre of specialists in the psychology and life-career development of women who will interface with organizations, community agencies, and individuals to create a collaborative network for implementing social change.

Evaluation of the model and of training program outcomes is accomplished

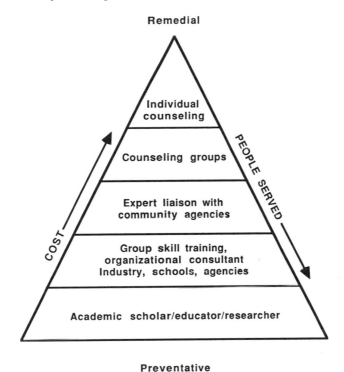

Figure 13.3. A cascade model of intervention for social change

by means of within-program assessment of attitudes, knowledge, and skills, and periodic follow-up of graduates to determine the implementation and distribution of their skills and activities (Worell, Stilwell, & Robinson, 1991). Evaluation of the therapeutic outcomes of feminist counseling and psychotherapy is a separate and more complex issue.

Evaluating Counseling and Psychotherapy Outcomes

Research on the effectiveness of psychotherapy generally suggests that a variety of methods may be helpful to clients with a variety of problems (Lambert, Shapiro, & Bergin, 1986; Orlinsky & Howard, 1986). Not all clients benefit equally, of course, and some may not be helped at all or may become worse following certain interventions. Garfield (1986) points out that evaluating the outcomes of psychotherapy is complicated by the existence of over 200 kinds of psychotherapy. Further, many variables enter into the therapeutic process and may be objects of evaluation. For feminist approaches, the complexity in evaluating outcomes is compounded by the addition of feminist principles to the existing set of variables to be considered.

Comparing Traditional and Feminist Goals

A major difference between evaluation of traditional interventions and feminist approaches can be found in the definition of desirable outcomes. For traditional psychotherapies, goals are generally divided into three categories: (a) remission of pathological symptoms and behaviors; (b) ratings of the client's behaviors by others as "normal"; and (c) evidence of interpersonal or community social competence (maintaining a household, holding a job, going to school, etc.).

Although any of these goals might be used in feminist approaches, they represent only one side of the picture. The traditional side is focused on remission of pathology and readjustment to society in its present form and within its current norms of behavior. Adjustment, defined as behavior that falls within accepted definitions of social norms, is a broad goal.

In contrast, the broad goal of feminist therapy is to assist women in achieving social, political, and economic equality within society (Rawlings & Carter, 1977). Feminist therapy goals emphasize empowerment, egalitarianism, and change, both for one's self and for one's effective environment. Adjustment to oppressive environments is not a valued outcome. Clients who return to pretreatment levels are less likely to be viewed as examples of successful outcomes than those who effect a change toward autonomy in decision-making, self-efficacy, and flexibility in problem-solution. Thus, evaluation research that looks mainly at remission of symptoms taps only a part of the feminist counseling agenda.

Research on feminist psychotherapy

Research on feminist approaches to therapy is sparse. Most of it has been in the form of analog studies, which have looked at college student attitudes toward working with a feminist counselor (cf. Enns & Hackett, 1990). Such studies present a problem in terms of validity for real clients who are experiencing genuine anxiety, pain or confusion. Other groups of studies are reported according to particular areas of distress, such as recovery from sexual assault, agoraphobia, depression, or family concerns. Although many feminist therapists work within these areas, outcome studies across differing topical areas and discrepant theoretical orientations are difficult to compare.

Applying Traditional Research Outcomes

We can extrapolate from research on traditional therapy by selecting those results that match with feminist therapy goals. In Chapter 4, the three major

Principles of Feminist Therapy are followed by specific goal statements that translate the Principles into desirable outcomes for clients. Please refer to these goals in the process of understanding how we apply traditional research outcomes to these goals.

Orlinsky & Howard (1986) have summarized in detail the outcome research for process in psychotherapy across 1100 studies. They draw general conclusions about those process variables that have been supported by positive outcomes across a range of studies, as defined in those studies. A great many process variables have been shown to be influential that are not specific to feminist therapy, such as therapist warmth, skill, engagement, and credibility, as well as client talk production, problem focus, engagement, expressiveness, and the overall quality of the therapeutic bond.

Compatibility with feminist goals

Certain variables reviewed by Brehm & Smith (1986), Beutler, Crago, & Arizmendi (1986), and Orlinsky & Howard (1986) can be viewed as concordant with feminist therapy and were found to be effective in producing positive outcomes in psychotherapy. For each variable, we indicate in parentheses the match with one or more of the goals of the three Feminist Therapy Principles.

(1) *Similarity of therapeutic dyad on gender.* "The best controlled research investigations available consistently suggest that therapists' gender exerts a modest effect on the selection of patients, the nature of the therapeutic process, and therapeutic change . . ." Same-sex dyads "were rated as more helpful . . . patients felt more satisfied . . . reported greater improvement . . . and produced more favorable estimates of change" (Beutler, Crago, & Arizmendi, 1986, pp. 263–264). (Principles II and III.)

(2) *Implementation of the therapeutic contract.* "Understanding the rules and role expectations that govern each party's role performance vis-à-vis the other" (Orlinsky & Howard, 1986, p. 315). (Principle II.)

(3) *Collaborative roles.* "The more patients and therapists collaborate in sharing initiative and responsibility, avoiding dependency on the one hand and authoritarian direction on the other, the better is the outcome of their effort likely to be" (Orlinsky & Howard, 1986, p. 364). (Principle II.)

(4) *Egalitarian female role.* "The current findings suggest that female therapists, first, and therapists of the patients' gender, second, facilitate treatment benefit, especially if these therapists present a non-stereotypic sexual viewpoint . . . these findings may suggest the importance of

egalitarianism and role flexibility rather than gender attitudes per se"
(Beutler, Crago, & Arizmendi, 1986, pp. 264–265). (Principle II.)

(5) *Expression of anger.* "The experience of negative affect, such as distress
     and hostility, was fairly often associated with good outcomes . . .
     evidence also suggests that the occurrence of affective discharge in
     therapy is associated with good outcomes" (Orlinsky & Howard, 1986,
     p. 365). (Principle I.)

(6) *Empathy.* "There is very strong evidence indicating that therapist
     empathy makes an important contribution to patient benefit, when
     empathy is measured as perceived by patients" (Orlinsky & Howard,
     1986, p. 344). (Principles II and III.)

(7) *Affirmation.* "Reciprocal affirmation was significantly and positive asso-
     ciated with outcome in a startling 80% of the findings surveyed"
     (Orlinsky & Howard, 1986, p. 366)). (Principles II and III.)

(8) *Empowerment.* "Maximizing perceptions of personal control should be
     therapeutically desirable when the goal is motivated striving toward
     what will likely be positive experiences" (Brehm & Smith, 1986, p. 91).
     (Principles I, II and III.)

Summary and Conclusions

In this chapter, we reviewed the early beginnings of feminist writings and
research in psychology. We presented a model of feminist identity development and some validation for its application to personal change. Feminist
identity development contains stages similar to those proposed for Black
identity, and can be used to evaluate some of the outcomes of a gender-
sensitive curriculum. A model program of graduate training in feminist
counseling was outlined which included four factors: attitudes and values;
structures, resources; and outreach. Suggestions for preliminary evaluation
of a feminist training program, in the form of a Cascade Model, were offered,
and the possibilities for evaluation of feminist counseling and psychotherapy
were summarized.

The lack of research specifically addressing Feminist Therapy Principles
and outcomes is problematic. Both Lucia Gilbert (1980) and Brodsky &
Hare-Mustin (1980) have called for a research agenda that focuses on the
process or outcomes of psychotherapy and counseling with women. At the
present time, we have some evidence from traditional outcome research that
therapists who establish clear rules and expectations at the start (i.e. who
state their values), are egalitarian and non-stereotypic in sex-role orientation,
are empathic, affirming, and collaborative, who encourage client expressions
of anger, and who reinforce client empowerment through perceptions of

personal control, are likely to realize positive outcomes with their women clients. An agenda for further research on feminist therapy is needed.

Activities

A
With a partner, review the model training program and compare its contents and process with your current or past programs. How do they differ and how are they similar?

B
Prepare and present three suggestions for revising your current or former graduate program to match the goals of a feminist agenda.

C
Retake the "Self and World Views" Self-assessment (Feminist Identity Development Scale, FIDS) at the beginning of this book and compare your scores on each factor with your previous scores before you read this book. Please note that the scale presented here is a shortened version of the Bargad & Hyde (1991) scale, in that Stage IV was dropped. Otherwise, the stages are similar to those assessed by these authors. Share your observations with a partner and compare how each of you has changed.

Further Readings

Downing, N. E., & Rousch, K. L. (1985). From passive acceptance to active commitment: A model of feminist identity development for women. *Counseling Psychologist*, **13**, 665–670.

Kimmel, E. (1989). The experience of feminism. *Psychology of Women Quarterly*, **13** 133–146.

Paludi, M. A. (1989). *Exploring/Teaching the Psychology of Women: A Manual of Resources*. New York: State University of New York Press.

References

Abramson, L. Y., Seligman, M. E. P., & Teasdale, J. D. (1978). Learned helplessness in humans: Critique and reformulation. *Journal of Abnormal Psychology*, **87**, 49–74.

Alloy, L. B., & Abramson, L. Y. (1988). Depressive realism: Four theoretical perspectives. In L. B. Alloy (Ed.), *Cognitive Processes in Depression* (pp. 223–265). New York: Guilford.

Alsdurf, J. M. (1985). Wife abuse and the church: The response of pastors. *Response*, Winter, pp. 9–11.

Ambert, A. (1982). Differences in children's behavior toward custodial mothers and custodial fathers. *Journal of Marriage and the Family*, **44**, 730–736.

Amenson, C. S., & Lewinsohn, P. M. (1981). An investigation into the observed sex differences in prevalence of unipolar depression. *Journal of Abnormal Psychology*, **90**, 1–13.

American Association of University Professors (1990). *AAUP Report: 1990–1991*. Lexington: University of Kentucky.

American Psychiatric Association (1980). *Diagnostic and Statistical Manual of Mental Disorders* (2nd edn) Washington, D.C.

American Psychiatric Association (1987). *Diagnostic and Statistical Manual of Mental Disorders* (3rd edn—revised) Washington, D.C.

American Psychological Association (1975). Report of the Task Force on Sex Bias and Sex-Role Stereotyping in Psychotherapeutic Practice. *American Psychologist*, **30**, 1169–1175.

American Psychological Association (1978). Task Force on Sex Bias and Sex Role Stereotyping in Psychotherapeutic Practice. *American Psychologist*, **33**, 1122–1123.

American Psychological Association (1981). Ethical principles of psychologists. *American Psychologist*, **36**, 633–638.

American Psychological Association (1983). *Publication Manual* (3rd edn) (pp. 43–49). Washington, D.C.

American Psychological Association, Committee on Women in Psychology (1985). *Statement on Proposed Diagnostic Categories for DSM-III-R*. Washington, D.C.

Aneshensel, C. S., Frerichs, R. R., & Clark, V. A. (1981). Family roles and sex differences in depression. *Journal of Health and Social Behavior*, **22**, 379–393.

Arkes, H. (1981). Impediments to accurate clinical judgments and possible ways to minimize their impact. *Journal of Consulting and Clinical Psychology*, **49**, 323–333.

Ashmore, R., & Del Boca, F. (1984, May). *A rationally-derived working taxonomy of gender-related attitude objects*. Paper presented at the first Nag's Head Conference on Sex and Gender, Nag's Head, NC.

Astin, H. S. (1984). The meaning of work in women's lives: A sociopsychological model of career choice and work behaviors. *The Counseling Psychologist*, **12**, 117–126.

Atkinson, D. R., & Hackett, G. (Eds.) (1988). *Counseling Non-ethnic American Minorities*. Springfield: Charles C. Thomas.

Atkinson, R. R., Morten, G., & Sue, D. W. (Eds.) (1979). *Counseling American Minorities: A Cross-cultural Perspective*. Dubuque: William C. Brown.

Atkinson, A. K., & Rickel, A. U. (1984). Post-partum depression in primaparous patients. *Journal of Abnormal Psychology*, **93**, 115–119.

Axelson, J. A. (1985). *Counseling and Development in a Multicultural Society*. Monterey: Brooks-Cole.

Baltes, P. B., Reese, H. W., & Lipsett, L. P. (1980). Life-span developmental psychology. In M. R. Rosensweig & L. W. Porter (Eds.) *Annual Review of Psychology*, **31**, 65–110.

Bandura, A. (1977a). Self-efficacy: Toward a unifying theory of behavior change. *Psychological Review*, **84**, 191–215.

Bandura, A. (1977b). *Social Learning Theory*. Englewood Cliffs, NJ: Prentice-Hall.

Bandura, A. (1978). The self system in reciprocal determinism. *American Psychologist*, **33**, 344–358.

Bandura, A. (1986). *Social Foundations of Thought and Action*. Englewood Cliffs, NJ: Prentice-Hall.

Bargad, A., & Hyde, J. S. (1991). Women's studies: A study of feminist identity development. *Psychology of Women Quarterly*, **15**, 181–201.

Barnett, P. A., & Gotlib, I. H. (1988). Psychosocial functioning and depression: Distinguishing among antecedents, concomitants, and consequences. *Psychological Bulletin*, **104**, 97–106.

Barnett, R. C., & Baruch, G. K. (1986). Role quality, multiple involvement, and psychological well-being in midlife women. *Journal of Personality and Social Psychology*, **51**, 578–585.

Barnett, R. C., & Baruch, G. K. (1987). Social roles, gender, and psychological stress. In R. C. Barnett, L. Biener, & G. K. Baruch (Eds.), *Gender and Stress* (pp. 122–143). New York: Free Press.

Barry, R. J. (1980). Stereotyping of sex role in preschoolers in relation to age, family structure, and parental sexism. *Sex Roles*, **6**, 975–976.

Bar Tal, D., & Frieze, I. (1978). Achievement motivation for males and females as a determinant of attributions for success and failure. *Sex Roles*, **3**, 301–313.

Basoff, E. S., & Glass, G. V. (1982). The relationship between sex roles and mental health: A meta-analysis of twenty-six studies. *The Counseling Psychologist*, **10**, 105–112.

Basow, S. A. (1986). *Gender Stereotypes: Traditions and Alternatives* (2nd edn). Monterey: Brooks-Cole.

Beck, A. T., Ward, C. H., Mendelson, M., Mock, J., & Erbaugh, J. (1961). An inventory for measuring depression. *Archives of General Psychiatry*, **4**, 561–571.

Beck, A. T. (1976). *Cognitive Therapy and the Emotional Disorders*. New York: International Universities Press.

Beckman, L. J. (1978). The relative rewards and costs of parenthood and employment for employed women. *Psychology of Women Quarterly*, **2**, 215–234.

Belenky, M. F., Clinchey, B. M., Goldberger, N. R., & Tarule, J. M. (1986). *Women's Ways of Knowing: Development of Self, Voice, and Mind*. New York: Basic Books.

Belk, S. S., & Snell, W. E. Jr (1986). Beliefs about women: Components and correlates. *Personality and Social Psychology Bulletin*, **12**, 403–413.

Bellak, A. S., & Hersen, M. (Eds.) (1985). *Dictionary of Behavior Therapy Techniques*. New York: Pergamon.

Bem, S. L. (1974). The measurement of psychological androgyny. *Journal of Consulting and Clinical Psychology*, **47**, 155–162.

Bem, S. L. (1975). Sex-role adaptability: One consequence of psychological androgyny. *Journal of Personality and Social Psychology*, **31**, 634–643.

Bem, S. L. (1981). *The Bem Sex-role Inventory (BSRI), Short Form*. Western Psychological Press.

Bem, S. L. (1983). Gender schema theory and its implications for child development: Raising gender-aschematic children in a gender schematic society. *Signs*, **8**, 598–616.

Bem, S. L. (1985). Androgyny and gender schema theory: A conceptual and empirical integration. In T. B. Sonderegger (Ed.), *Nebraska Symposium on Motivation: Psychology of gender*. Lincoln: University of Nebraska Press.

Bem, S. L., & Lenney, E. (1976). Sex typing and the avoidance of cross-sex behavior. *Journal of Personality and Social Psychology*, **33**, 48–54.

Bem, S. L., Martyna, W., & Watson, C. (1976). Sex typing and androgyny: Further exploration of the expressive domain. *Journal of Personality and Social Psychology*, **44**, 1016–1023.

Benokraitis, N. V., & Feagin, J. R. (1986). *Modern Sexism: Blatant, Subtle, and Covert Discrimination*. Englewood Cliffs, NJ: Prentice-Hall.

Berman, J. R. S. (1985). Ethical feminist perspectives on dual relationships with clients. In L. B. Rosewater & L. E. A. Walker (Eds.), *Handbook of Feminist Therapy* (pp. 287–296). New York: Springer.

Berzon, B. (1988). *Permanent Partners: Building Gay and Lesbian Relationships that last*. New York: Dutton.

Betz, N. E., & Hackett, G. (1981). The relationship of career-related self-efficacy expectations to perceived career options in college women and men. *Journal of Counseling Psychology*, **28**, 399–410.

Betz, N. E., & Hackett, G. (1987). Concept of agency in educational and career development. *Journal of Counseling Psychology*, **34**, 299–308.

Beutler, L. E., Crago, M., & Arizmendi, T. G. (1986). Research on therapist variables in psychotherapy. In S. L. Garfield & A. E. Bergin (Eds.), *Handbook of Psychotherapy and Behavior Change* (pp. 257–310). New York: Wiley.

Birk, J. M. (1975). Reducing sex bias: Factors affecting the client's view of the use of career interest inventories. In E. Diamond (Ed.), *Issues of Sex Bias and Sex Fairness in Career Interest Measurement* (pp. 101–122). Washington, D.C.: National Institute of Education.

Blankenship, M. L. (1984, May). *Adolescent and Adult Women's Perceptions of Social Rules Based on Gender*. Paper presented to the Midwestern Society for Research in Life-span Development, Akron, Ohio.

Blatner, H. A. (1973). *Acting-in: Practical Applications for Psychodramatic Methods*. New York: Springer.

Blatner, A., & Blatner, A. (1988). *Foundations of Psychodrama: History, Theory, & Practice*. New York: Springer.

Bleier, R. (1984). *Science and Gender: A Critique of Biology and its Theories on Women*. Elmsford, New York: Pergamon.

Bleier, R. (1988). Sex differences research: Science or belief? In R. Bleier (Ed.), *Feminist Approaches to Science*. (pp. 147–164). New York: Pergamon.

Block, C. B. (1984). Diagnostic and treatment issues for Black patients. *The Clinical Psychologist*, **37**, 51–54.

Block, J. H. (1979). Another look at sex differentiation in the socialization behavior of mothers and fathers. In J. Sherman & F. F. Denmark (Eds.), *Psychology of Women: Future Directions for Research*. New York: Psychological Dimensions.

Block, J. H. (1983). Differential premises arising from differential socialization of the sexes: Some conjectures. *Child Development*, **54**, 1335–1354.

Block, J. H., Block, J., & Harrington, D. (1975). Sex-role typing and instrumental behavior: A developmental study. Cited in J. H. Block (Ed.), *Child Development*, **54**, 1335–1354.

Bloom, B. I., Asher, S. J., & White, S. W. (1978). Marital disruption as a stressor: A review and analysis. *Psychological Bulletin*, **85**, 867–874.

Blumstein, P., & Schwartz, P. (1983). *American couples: Money, Work, and Sex*, New York: William Morrow.

Bograd, M. (1986). A feminist examination of family therapy: What is women's place? In D. Howard (Ed.), *The Dynamics of Feminist Therapy* (pp. 95–106). New York: Haworth.

Bograd, M. (1988). Feminist perspectives on wife abuse: An introduction. In K. Yllo & M. Bograd (Eds.) *Feminist Perspectives on Wife Abuse* (pp. 11–26). Newbury Park: Sage.

Bowker, L. H. (1982). *Beating Wife-beating*. Lexington: D. C. Heath.

Bowker, L. H., Arbitell, M., & McFerron, J. R. (1988). On the relationship between wife beating and child abuse. In K. Yllo & M. Bograd (Eds.), *Feminist Perspectives on Wife Abuse* (pp. 158–174). Newbury Park: Sage.

Boyd-Franklin, N. (1989). *Black Families in Therapy*. New York: Guilford.

Bram, S. (1984). Voluntary childless women: Traditional or non-traditional? *Sex Roles*, **10**, 195–206.

Brehm, S. S., & Smith. T. W. (1986). Social psychological approaches to psychotherapy and behavior change. In S. L. Garfield & A. E. Bergin (Eds.), *Handbook of Psychotherapy and Behavior Change*. (pp. 69–116). New York: Wiley.

Brickman, J. (1984). Feminist, non-sexist, and traditional model of therapy: Implications for working with incest. *Women and Therapy*, **3**, 49–67.

Brickman, P., Rabinowitz, V. C., Karuza, J., Coates, D., Cohn, E., & Kidder, L. (1982). Models of helping and coping. *American Psychologist*, **37**, 368–384.

Bridges, J. C., & Bower, M. S. (1985). The effects of perceived job availability for women on college women's attitudes towards prestigious male-dominated occupations. *Psychology of Women Quarterly*, **9**, 265–276.

Briere, J. (1984). The effects of childhood sexual abuse on later psychological functioning: Defining a post-sexual-abuse syndrome. Paper presented at Third National Conference on Sexual Victimization of Children, Washington, D.C.

Briere, J., & Malamuth, N. (1983). Self-reported likelihood of sexually aggressive behavior: Attitudinal vs. sexual explanations. *Journal of Research in Personality*, **17**, 315–323.

Bristow, A., Frieman, J., & Dickson, D. (1984, August). *Evaluation of Abnormal Psychology Textbooks*. Paper presented at the annual meeting of the American Psychological Association, Toronto, CA, August.

Brockner, J., & Rubin, J. Z. (1985). *Entrapment in Escalating Conflicts: A Social Psychological Analysis*. New York: Springer.

Brodsky, A. M. (1973). The consciousness-raising group as a model for therapy with women. *Psychotherapy: Therapy, Research, and Practice*, **10**, 24–29.

Brodsky, A. M., & Hare-Mustin, R. T. (1980). *Psychotherapy with Women: An Assessment of Research and Practice*. New York: Guilford.

Brooks-Gunn, J. (1986). The relationship of maternal beliefs about sex-typing to maternal and young children's behavior. *Sex Roles*, **14**, 21–35.

Brooks-Gunn, J., & Fisch, M. (1980). Psychological androgyny and college students' judgments of mental health. *Sex Roles*, **6**, 575–580.

Brophy, J. E., & Good, T. L. (1974). *Teacher–student Relationships: Causes and Consequences*. New York: Holt.

Broverman, I. K., Broverman, D., Clarkson, F. E., Rosenkrantz, P. S., & Vogel, S. R. (1970). Sex-role stereotypes and clinical judgments of mental health. *Journal of Consulting and Clinical Psychology*, **34**, 1–7.

Brown, G. W., & Harris, T. (1978). *The Social Origins of Depression: A Study of Psychiatric Disorder in Women*. London: Tavistock.

Brown, L. S. (1987). *Towards a New Conceptual Paradigm for the Axis II Diagnoses*. New York: Annual Meeting of the American Psychological Association.

Brown, L. S. (1991). Ethical issues in feminist therapy: Selected topics. *Psychology of Women Quarterly*, **15**, 323–336.

Brownell, A., & Shumaker, S. A. (1984). Social support: An introduction to a complex phenomenon. *Journal of Social Issues*, **40**, 1–19.

Brush, L. R., Gold, A. R., & White, M. G. (1978). The paradox of intention and effect: A woman's studies course. *Signs*, **3**, 870–883.

Burchardt, C. J., & Serbin, L. A. (1982). Psychological androgyny and personal adjustment in college and psychiatric populations. *Sex Roles*, **8**, 835–851.

Burgess, A. W., & Holmstrom, L. L. (1979). *Rape: Crisis and Recovery*. Bowie, Robert J. Brady.

Burnam, M. A., Stein, J. A., Golding, J. M., Siegel, J. M., Sorenson, S. B., Forsythe, A. B., & Telles, C. A. (1988). Sexual assault and mental disorders in a community population. *Journal of Consulting and Clinical Psychology*, **56**, 843–850.

Caldwell, M. A., & Peplau, L. A. (1984). The balance of power in lesbian relationships. *Sex Roles*, **10**, 587–599.

Cancian, F. M. (1987). *Love in America: Gender and Self-development*. Cambridge: Cambridge University Press.

Caplan, P. J. (1985). *The Myth of Women's Masochism*. New York: Signet.

Caplan, P. J., & Hall-McCorquodale, I. (1985). Mother-blaming in major clinical journals. *American Journal of Orthopsychiatry*, **55**, 345–353.

Cass, V. (1979). Homosexual identity formation: A theoretical model. *Journal of Homosexuality*, **4**, 219–235.

Cate, R. M., Henton, J. M., Koval, J., Christopher, F. S., & Lloyd, S. (1982). Premarital abuse: A social psychological perspective. *Journal of Family Issues*, **3**, 79–90.

Chesler, P. (1972). *Women and Madness*. New York: Avon Books.

Chodorow, N. (1978). *The Reproduction of Mothering: Psychoanalysis and the Sociology of Gender*. Berkeley: University of California Press.

Chronicle of Higher Education (1988, January 13). Fact file: Earned degrees conferred in 1985–1986. *The Chronicle of Higher Education*, **34**, A36.

Clance, P. R., & Imes, S. A. (1978). The imposter phenomenon in high-achieving women: Dynamics and therapeutic intervention. *Psychotherapy: Theory, Research, and Practice*, **15**, 241–247.

Clance, P., R., & O'Toole, M. A. (1987). The imposter phenomenon: An internal barrier to empowerment and achievement. *Women & Therapy*, **6**, 51–64.

Clarey, J. H., & Sanford, A. (1982). Female career preference and androgyny. *Vocational Guidance Quarterly*, **30**, 258–264,

Coie, J. D., Pennington, B. F., & Buckley, H. H. (1974). Effects of situational stress and sex roles on the attribution of psychological disorder. *Journal of Consulting and Clinical Psychology*, **42**, 559–568.

Colao, F., & Hunt, M. (1983). Therapists coping with sexual assault. *Women & Therapy*, **2**, 205–214.

Cole, N. S., & Hansen, G. R. (1978). Impact of interest inventories on career choice. In L. S. Hansen & R. S. Rapoza (Eds.), *Career Development and Counseling of Women* (pp. 487–509). Springfield: Charles C. Thomas.

Coles, F. S. (1986). Forced to quit: Sexual harassment complaints and agency response. *Sex Roles*, **14**, 81–95.

Collin, J., Reardon, M., & Waters, L. K. (1980). Occupational interest and perceived success: Effects of gender, sex-role orientation, and the sexual composition of the occupation. *Psychological Reports*, **47**, 1155–1159.

Comas-Diaz, L. (1987). Feminist therapy with mainland Puerto Rican women. *Psychology of Women Quarterly*. **11**, 461–474.

Comas-Diaz, L. (1988). Cross-cultural mental health treatment. In L. Comas-Diaz & L. Griffith (Eds.), *Clinical Guidelines in Cross-cultural Mental Health* (pp. 335–362). New York: Wiley.

Condry, J., & Dyer, S. (1976). Fear of success: Attribution of causes to the victim. *Journal of Social Issues*, **32**, 63–83.

Constantinople, A. (1973). Masculinity–femininity: An exception to a famous dictum? *Psychological Bulletin*, **80**, 309–407.

Constantinople, A. (1979). Sex-role acquisition: In search of the elephant. *Sex Roles*, **5**, 121–134.

Cook, A. S., West, J. S., & Hammer, T. J. (1982). Changes in attitudes toward parenting in college women: 1972 and 1979 samples. *Family Relations*, **31**, 109–113.

Cook, E. P. (1985). *Psychological Androgyny*. New York: Pergamon.

Cowan, G., Lee, C., Levy, D., & Snyder, D. (1988). Dominance and inequality in X-rated videocassettes. *Psychology of Women Quarterly*, **12**, 299–311.

Crawford, J. D. (1978). Career development and career choice in pioneer and traditional women. *Journal of Vocational Behavior*, **12**, 129–139.

Crawford, M., & Marecek, J. (1989). Psychology reconstructs the female: 1968–1988. *Psychology of Women Quarterly*, **13**, 147–167.

Crosby, F. J. (1991). *Juggling: The Unexpected Advantages of Balancing Career and Home for Women and their Families*. New York: Free Press.

Cross, W. E. (1980). Models of psychological nigrescence. In R. L. Jones (Ed.), *Black Psychology* (pp. 81–98). New York: Harper & Row.

Deaux, K. (1984). From individual differences to social categories: Analysis of a decade's research on gender. *American Psychologist*, **39**, 105–116.

Deaux, K. (1985). Sex and gender. In M. R. Rosensweig & L. W. Porter (Eds.), *Annual Review of Psychology*, Volume 36 (pp. 49–82). Palo Alto, CA: Annual Reviews.

Denmark, F. (1983). Integrating the psychology of women into introductory psychology. In C. J. Sheirer & A. Rogers (Eds.), *The G. Stanley Hall Lecture Series*, Volume 3 (33–75). Washington, DC: American Psychological Association.

Dewey, C. R. (1974). Exploring interests: A non-sexist method. *Personnel and Guidance Journal*, **52**, 311–315.

Dobash, E. R., & Dobash, R. (1981). *Violence Against Wives: A Case Against Patriarchy*. New York: Free Press.

Dobash, E. R., & Dobash, R. (1988). In K. Yllo & M. Bograd (Eds.), *Feminist Perspectives on Wife Abuse*. Newbury Park: Sage.

Doherty, M. A. (1978). Sexual bias in personality theory. In L. W. Harmon, J. M. Birk, L. E. Fitzgerald, & M. F. Tanney (Eds.), *Counseling Women* (pp. 94–105). Monterey CA: Brooks-Cole.

Douglas, M. A. (1985). The role of power in feminist therapy: A reformulation. In L. B. Rosewater & L. E. A. Walker (Eds.), *Handbook of Feminist Therapy* (pp. 241–249). New York: Springer.

Douglas, M. A. (1987). The battered woman syndrome. In D. J. Sonkin (Ed.), *Domestic Violence on Trial: Psychological and Legal Dimensions of Family Violence* (pp. 39–54). New York: Springer.

Douglas, M. A., & Strom, J. (1988). Cognitive therapy with battered women. *Journal of Rational–Emotive and Cognitive–Behavioral Therapy*, **6**, 33–49.

Downing, N. E., & Rousch, K. L. (1984). From passive acceptance to active commitment: A model of feminist identity development. *The Counseling Psychologist*, **13**, 695–709.

Dutton, D., & Painter, S. L. (1981). Traumatic bonding: The development of emotional attachments in battered women and other relationships of intermittent abuse. *Victimology*, **6**, 139–155.

Dweck, C. S. (1986). Motivational processes affecting learning. *American Psychologist*, **10**, 1040–1048.

Dweck, C., Davidson, W., Nelson, S., & Enna, B. I. (1978). Sex differences in learned helplessness: II. The contingencies of evaluative feedback in the classroom; and III. An experimental analysis. *Developmental Psychology*, **14**, 268–276.

Dziech, B. W., & Weiner, L. (1984). *The Lecherous Professor: Sexual Harassment on Campus*. Bonton: Beacon.

Eagly, A. H. (1987). *Sex Differences in Social Behavior: A Social Role Interpretation*. Hillsdale: Erlbaum.

Eccles, J. S., & Hoffman, L. W. (1984). Sex roles, socialization, and occupational behavior. In H. W. Stevenson & A. E. Siegel (Eds.), *Child Development Research and Social Policy*, Volume I. Chicago: University of Chicago Press.

Eichler, A., & Parron, D. L. (1987). *Women's Mental Health: Agenda for Research*. Rockville: National Institute of Mental Health.

Ellis, A. (1962). *Reason and Emotion in Psychotherapy*. New York: Lyle Stuart.

Emery, R. E., Hetherington, E. M., & DiLalla, L. (1985). Divorce, children, and social policy. In H. W. Stevenson & A. E. Siegel (Eds.), *Child Development Research and Social Policy*, Chicago: University of Chicago Press.

Enns, C. Z., & Hackett, G. (1990). Comparison of feminist and non-feminist women's reactions to variants of non-sexist and feminist counseling. *Journal of Counseling Psychology*, **37**, 33–40.

Epstein, C. (1970). Encountering the male establishment: Sex status limits on women's careers in professions. *American Journal of Sociology*, **75**, 965–982.

Epstein, N., Schlesinger, S. E., & Dryden, W. (1988). *Cognitive–behavioral Therapy with Families*. New York: Brunner-Mazel.

Erez, E. (1986). Police reports of domestic violence. In D. J. Sonkin (Ed.), *Domestic Violence on Trial*. New York: Springer.

Erikson, E. (1963). *Childhood and Society* (2nd edn) New York: Norton.

Erikson, E. (1968). *Identity; Youth and Crisis*. New York: Norton.

Etaugh, C. ((1980). Effects of non-maternal care on children: Research evidence and popular views. *American Psychologist*, **35**, 309–319.

Fagot, B. (1978). The influence of sex of child on parental reactions to toddler behaviors. *Child Development*, **49**, 459–465.

Faunce, P. S. (1985). Teaching feminist therapies: Integrating feminist therapy, pedagogy, and scholarship. In L. B. Rosewater & L. E. A. Walker (Eds.), *Handbook of Feminist Therapy: Women's Issues in Psychotherapy* (pp. 309–320). New York: Springer.

Faux, M. (1984). *Childless By Choice*. Garden City: Anchor.

Feather, N. T. (1985). Masculinity, femininity, self-esteem, and subclinical depression. *Sex Roles*, **12**, 491–501.

Feminist Therapy Institute (1987). *Feminist Therapy Code of Ethics*. Denver: Feminist Therapy Institute, Inc.

Feminist Therapy Network (1988). *Feminist Therapy Network Code of Ethics*. Milwaukee: Feminist Therapy Network.

Fenema, E., & Sherman, J. (1977). Sex-related differences in mathematics achievement, spatial visualization and affective factors. *American Educational Research Journal*, **14**, 51–71.

Figler, H. E. (1979). *Path: A Career Workbook for Liberal Arts Students*. Cranston: Carroll.

Figley, C. R. (1985). From victim to survivor: Social responsibility in the wake of catastrophe. In C. R. Figley (Ed.), *Trauma and Its Wake: The Study and Treatment of Post-traumatic Stress Disorder* (pp. 398–415). New York: Brunner-Mazel.

Figueira-McDonough, J., & Sarri, R. (Eds.) (1987). *The Trapped Woman: Catch 22 in Deviance and Control*. Newbury Park: Sage.

Fine, L. J. (1979). Psychodrama. In R. Corsini (Ed.), *Current Psychotherapies* (pp. 428–459). Ithaca: F. E. Peacock.

Finkelhor, D. (1986). *A Sourcebook on Child Sexual Abuse*. Beverly Hills, CA: Sage.

Finn, J. (1986). The relationship between sex role attitudes and attitudes supporting marital violence. *Sex Roles*, **24**, 235–244.

Fitzgerald, L. F., & Crites, J. O. (1980). Toward a career psychology of women: What do we know? What do we need to know? *Journal of Counseling Psychology*, **27**, 44–62.

Fitzgerald, L. F., & Nutt, R. (1986). The Division 17 principles concerning the counseling/psychotherapy of women: Rational and implementation: *The Counseling Psychologist*, **14**, 180–216.

Fitzgerald, L. F., Gold, Y., Ormerand, A. J., & Weitzman, L. M. (1988). Academic harassment: Sex and denial in scholarly garb. *Psychology of Women Quarterly*, **12**, 329–340.

Flerx, V. C., Fidler, D. S., & Rogers, R. W. (1976). Sex-role stereotypes: Developmental aspects and early intervention. *Child Development*, **47**, 998–1007.

Ford, M., & Widiger, T. (1989). Sex bias in the diagnosis of histrionic and antisocial personality disorders. *Journal of Counsulting and Clinical Psychology*, **57**, 301–305.

Fox, M. F. (1987). Women in the labor force: Position, plight, prospects. In J. Figueira-McDonough & R. Sarri (Eds.), *The Trapped Woman: Catch 22 in Deviance and Control* (pp. 197–215). Newbury Park: Sage.

Fox, L. H., Brody, L., & Tobin, D. (1980). *Women and the Mathematical Mystique*. Baltimore: Johns Hopkins University Press.

Foxley, C. H. (1979). *Non-sexist Counseling: Helping Women and Men Redefine Their Roles*. Dubuque: Kendall/Hunt.

Franks, V. (1986). Sex-stereotyping and diagnosis of psychopathology. *Women & Therapy*, **5**, 219–232.

Franks, V., & Burtle, V. (1974). *Women in Therapy: New Psychotherapies for a Changing Society*. New York: Brunner-Mazel.

Freud, S. (1948). Some psychological consequences of the anatomical distinction between the sexes. In *Collected Papers*, Volume 5. London: Hogarth.

Freud, S. (1965). *New Introductory Lectures on Psychoanalysis*. New York: Norton.

Frieze, I. H., Bailey, S., Mamula, P., & Noss, M. (1989). Perceptions of daily life scripts and their effects on college women's desires for children. In R. K. Unger (Ed.), *Representations: Social Constructions of Gender* (pp. 222–235). Amityville: Baywood.

Ganley, A. L. (1987). Perpetrators of domestic violence: An overview of counseling the court-mandated client. In D. J. Sonkin (Ed.), *Domestic Violence on Trial: Psychological and Legal Dimensions of Family Violence* (pp. 156–173). New York: Springer.

Gardner, M. A. (1989). *Prevalence and Correlates of Depressive Symptoms in Aged Black Females: Some Preliminary Findings. Dissertation Abstracts International*, **50**, 12B–5879. (University Microfilms No. AAC 8918927.)

Garfield, S. L. (1986). Research on client variables in psychotherapy. In S. L. Garfield, & A. E. Bergin (Eds.). Handbook of psychotherapy and behavior change, 3rd edn (pp. 213–256). New York: Wiley.

Garfield, S. L., & Kurtz, R. (1974). A survey of clinical psychologists: Characteristics, activities, and orientations. *The Clinical Psychologist*, **28**, 7–10.

Garfield, S. L., & Kurtz, R. (1977). A study of eclectic views. *Journal of Consulting and Clinical Psychology*, **45**, 78–83.

Gartrell, N. (1984). Combating homophobia in the psychotherapy of lesbians. *Women and Therapy*, **3**, 13–29.

Gelles, R. J., & Strauss, M. A. (1988). *Intimate Violence: The Definitive Study of the Causes and Consequences of Abuse in the American Family*. New York: Simon & Shuster.

Gergen, K. J. (1985). The social constructionist movement in modern psychology. *American Psychologist*, **40**, 266–275.

Gigy, L. L. (1980). Self-concept of single women. *Psychology of Women Quarterly*, **5**, 321–340.

Gilbert, L. A. (1980). Feminist therapy. In A. M. Brodsky & R. T. Hare-Mustin (Eds.), *Women and Psychotherapy* (pp. 245–265). New York: Guilford.

Gilbert, L. A. (1985). *Men in Dual-career Families: Current Realities and Future Prospects*. Hillsdale: Erlbaum.

Gilligan, C. (1982). *In a Different Voice: Psychological Theory and Women's Development*. Cambridge: Harvard University Press.

Glick, P. C. (1979). Children of divorced parents in demographic perspective. *Journal of Social Issues*, **35**, 177–182.

Goldfried, M. R. (Ed.) (1982). *Converging Themes in Psychotherapy: Trends in Psychoanalytic, Humanistic, and Behavioral Practice*. New York: Springer.

Goldman, E. E., & Morrison, D. S. (1984). *Psychodrama: Experience and process*. Dubuque: Kendal-Hunt.

Goldner, V. (1985). Warning: Family therapy may be dangerous to your health. *The Family Therapy Networker*, **9**, 19–23.

Golub, S., & Freedman, J. R. (1987). *Psychology of Women: Resources for a Core Curriculum*. New York: Garland.

Gondolph, E. W. (1988). *Battered Women as Survivors: An Alternative to Treating Learned Helplessness*. Lexington: Lexington Books.

Good, T., Sikes, J. N., & Brophy, J. E. (1973). The effects of teacher sex and student sex on classroom interaction. *Journal of Educational Psychology*, **65**, 74–87.

Goodrich, T. J., Rampage, C., Elman, B., & Halstead, K. (1988). *Feminist Family Therapy*. New York: W. W. Norton.

Gotlib, I. H., & Hooley, J. M. (1988). Depression and marital distress: Current status and future directions. In S. W. Duck (Ed.), *Handbook of Personal Relationships*. New York: Wiley.

Grady, K. E. (1981). Sex bias in research design. *Psychology of Women Quarterly*, **5**, 628–636.

Graham, D. L. R., Rawlings, E. I., Halpern, H. S., & Hermes, J. (1984). Therapists' needs for training in counseling lesbians and gay men. *Professional Psychology: Research and Practice*, **15**, 482–496.

Graham, D. L. R., Rawlings, E., & Rimini, N. (1988). Survivors of terror: Battered women, hostages, and the Stockholm syndrome. In K. Yllo & M. Bograd (Eds.), *Feminist Perspectives on Wife Abuse*, (pp. 217–233). Newbury Park: Sage.

Gray-Little, B., & Burks, N. (1983). Power and satisfaction in marriage: A review and critique. *Psychological Bulletin*, **93**, 513–538.

Greene, B. A. (1986). When the therapist is White and the patient is Black: Considerations for psychotherapy in the feminist heterosexual and lesbian communities. In D. Howard (Ed.), *The Dynamics of Feminist Therapy*, (pp. 41–66). New York: Haworth.

Greenspan, M. (1983). *A New Approach to Women and Therapy*. New York: McGraw-Hill.

Greenspan, M. (1986). Should therapists be personal? Self disclosure and therapeutic distance in feminist therapy. *Women & Therapy*, **5**, 5–18.

Groth, A. N., Burgess, A. W., & Holmsrom, L. L. (1977). Rape: Power, anger, and sexuality. *American Journal of Psychiatry*, **134**, (11), 1239–1243.

Grunebaum, H., & Chasin, R. (1978). Relabeling and reframing reconsidered: The beneficial effects of a pathological label. *Family Process*. **17**, 449–456.

Gump, J. (1980). Reality and myth: Employment and sex-role ideology in Black women. In F. Denmark and J. Sherman (Eds.), *Psychology of Women: Future Directions for Research*. New York: Psychological Dimensions.

Guttentag, M., & Bray, M. (1976). *Undoing Sex-role Stereotypes*. New York: McGraw-Hill.

Guttentag, M., Salasin, S., & Belle, D. (1980). *The Mental Health of Women*, New York: Academic Press.

Hackett, G. & Betz, N. E. (1981). A self-efficacy approach to the career development of women. *Journal of Vocational Behavior*, **18**, 326–339.

Hamilton, J. A., Alagna, S. W., King, L. S., & Lloyd, C. (1987). The emotional consequences of gender-based abuse in the workplace: New counseling programs for sex discrimination. *Women & Therapy*, **6**, 155–182.

Hamilton, S., Rothbart, M., & Dawes, R. M. (1986). Sex bias, diagnosis, and DSM-III. *Sex Roles*, **15**, 269–274.

Hammen, C. (1982). Gender and depression. In I. Issa (Ed.), *Gender and Psychopathology*.

Hammen, C. (1988). Depression and personal cognitions about personal stressful life events. In L. B. Alloy (Ed.), *Cognitive Processes in Depression* (pp. 77–108). New York: Guilford.

Hansen, J. C., Stevic, R. R., & Warner, R. W. (1986). *Counseling Theory and Process*. Boston: Allyn and Bacon.

Hansen, L. S., & Keierleber, D. L. (1978). Born free: A collaborative consultation model for career development and sex-role stereotyping. *Personnel and Guidance Journal*, **56**, 395–399.

Hare-Mustin, R. (1978). A feminist approach to family therapy. *Family Process*, **17**, 181–194.

Hare-Mustin, R. (1980). Family therapy may be dangerous for your health. *Professional Psychology*, **11**, 935–938.

Hare-Mustin, R. T. (1983). An appraisal of the relationship between women and psychotherapy; 80 years after the case of Dora. *American Psychologist*, **38**, 594–601.

Hare-Mustin, R. T., Bennett, S. K., & Broderick, P. C. (1983). Attitudes toward motherhood: Gender, generational, and religious comparisons. *Sex Roles*, **9**, 643–661.

Hare-Mustin, R. T., & Marecek, J. (1988). The meaning of difference: Gender theory, post-modernism, and psychology. *American Psychologist*, **43**, 455–464.

Hare-Mustin, R. T., Marececk, J., Kaplan, A. G., & Liso-Levinson, N. (1979). Rights of clients, responsibilities of therapists. *American Psychologist*, **34**, 3–16.

Harmon, L. (1978). Career counseling for women. In L. S. Hansen & R. S. Rapoza (Eds.), *Career Development and Counseling of Women* (pp. 338–353). Springfield: Charles C. Thomas.

Harrigan, B. L. (1977). *Games Your Mother Never Taught You: Corporate Gamesmanship for Women*. New York: Warren Books.

Harris, B., & Lightner, J. (1980). The image of women in abnormal psychology: Professionalism vs. psychopathology. *Psychology of Women Quarterly*, **4**, 396–422.

Harway, M. (1979). Training counselors. *The Counseling Psychologist*. **8**, 8–10.

Harway, M. (1980). Sex bias in educational–vocational counseling. *Psychology of Women Quarterly*, **4**, 396–411.

Hayes, S. C. (1987). A contextual approach to therapeutic change. In N. S. Jacobson (Ed.), *Pschotherapists in Therapeutic Practice: Cognitive and Behavioral Perspectives* (pp. 327–387). New York: Guilford.

Henley, N. M. (1977). *Body Politics: Power, Sex, and Non-verbal Communication*. Englewood Cliffs: Prentice-Hall.

Herman, J. (1981). Father–daughter incest. *Professional Psychology*, **12**, 76–80.

Herr, E. L., & Cramer, S. H. (1988). *Career Guidance and Counseling Through the Life Span: Systematic Approaches*. Boston: Little, Brown.

Herzog, A. R., & Bachman, J. G. (1982). *Sex-role Attitudes Among High School Seniors: Views about Work and Family Roles*. Ann Arbor: Institute for Social Research, University of Michigan.

Herzog, J. G., Bachman, A. R., & Johnson, L. D. (1983). Paid work, childcare, and housework: A national survey of high school seniors' preferences for sharing responsibilities between husband and wife. *Sex Roles*, **9**, 109–113.

Hess, A. K. (1980). *Psychotherapy Supervision: Theory, Research, and Practice*. New York: Wiley.

Hetherington, E. M., Cox, M., & Cox, R. (1982). The effects of divorce on parents and children. In M. Lamb (Ed.), *Non-traditional Families*. Hillsdale: Erlbaum.

Hoffman, L. W. (1977). Changes in family roles, socialization, and sex differences. *American Psychologist*, **32**, 644–657.

Hoffman, L. W. (1979). Maternal employment: 1979. *American Psychologist*, **34**, 644–657.

Hoffman, L. W., & Nye, I. F. (1974). *Working Mothers*. San Francisco: Jossey-Bass.

Holland, D., & Davidson, D. (1984). Prestige and intimacy: The folk models behind

Americans' talk about gender types. In N. Quinn & D. Holland (Eds.), *Cultural Models in Language and Thought*. New York: Cambridge University Press.

Holland, J. L. (1966). *The Psychology of Vocational Choice*. Waltham: Blaisdell.

Holland, J. L. (1974). *Self-directed Search*. Palo Alto: Consulting Psychologist Press.

Hollender, J., & Shafer, L. (1981). Male acceptance of female career roles, *Sex Roles*, 7, 1199–1203.

Holroyd, J. (1978). Psychotherapy and women's liberation. In L. W. Harmon, J. M. Birk, L. E. Fitzgerald, & M. F. Tanney (Eds.), *Counseling Women* (pp. 193–207). Monterey: Brooks/Cole.

Horner, M. S. (1972). Toward an understanding of achievement-related conflicts in women. *Journal of Social Issues*, 28, 157–175.

Horowitz, M. J. (1979). Psychological responses to serious life events. In V. Hamilton and D. Warburton (Eds.), *Human Stress and Cognition: An Information Processing Approach* (pp. 235–263). New York: Wiley.

Horowitz, M. J. (1986). *Stress Response Syndromes* (2nd edn). Northvale: Jason Aronson.

Horowitz, M., Wilner, N., & Alvarez, W. (1979). Impact of Event Scale: A measure of subjective distress. *Psychosomatic Medicine*, 41(3), 209–218.

House, J. S. (1974). Occupational stress and coronary heart disease: A review and theoretical integration. *Journal of Health and Social Behavior*, 15, 12–27.

Houseknecht, S. K. (1979). Timing of the decision to remain voluntarily childless: Evidence for continuing socialization. *Psychology of Women Quarterly*, 4, 81–96.

Houser, B. B., Berkman, S. L., & Beckman, L. J. (1984). The relative rewards and costs of childlessness for older women. *Psychology of Women Quarterly*, 8, 395–398.

Hunt, P. (1987). Black clients: Implications for supervision of trainees. *Psychotherapy*, 24, 114–119.

Huston, A. C. (1983). Sex-typing. In P. H. Mussen & E. M. Hetherington (Eds.), *Handbook of Child Psychology, Volume 4: Socialization, personality, and social development*, 4th edn, (pp. 387–468). New York: Wiley.

Huston, A. C. (1988). Gender, socialization, and the transmission of culture. In S. S. Brehm (Ed.), *Seeing Female: Social Roles and Personal Lives* (pp. 7–19). New York: Greenwood Press.

Hyde, J. S., & Linn, M. (1986). *The Psychology of Gender: Advances Through Meta-analysis*. Baltimore: Johns Hopkins University Press.

Ickes, W., & Barnes, R. D. (1978). Boys and girls together—and alienated: On enacting stereotyped sex roles in mixed-sex dyads. *Journal of Personality and Social Psychology*, 36, 669–683.

Institute for Social Research (1976). Twenty-year comparison of family roles. *ISR Newsletter (Winter)*. Ann Arbor: University of Michigan.

Jackson, L. A., Ialongo, N., & Stollak, G. E. (1986). Parental correlates of gender roles: The relation between parents' masculinity, femininity, and childrearing behaviors and their children's gender roles. *Journal of Social and Clinical Psychology*, 4, 204–224.

Jacobson, N. (Ed.) (1987). *Psychotherapists in Clinical Practice: Cognitive and Behavioral Perspectives*. New York: Guilford.

Jacobson, N. S., & Margolin, G. (1979). *Marital Therapy: Strategies Based on Social Learning and Behavior Exchange Principles*. New York: Brunner/Mazel.

Jacobson, N. S., Holzworth-Munroe, A., & Schmaling, K. B. (1989). Marital therapy and spouse involvement in the treatment of depression, agoraphobia, and alcoholism. *Journal of Consulting and Clinical Psychology*, 57, 5–10.

Jakubowski, P. A. (1977). Self-assertion training procedures for women. In E. I. Rawlings & D. K. Carter (Eds.), *Psychotherapy for Women* (pp. 168–190). Springfield: Charles C. Thomas.

Janoff-Bulman, R. (1979). Characterological versus behavioral self-blame: Inquiries into depression and rape. *Journal of Personality and Social Psychology*, **37**, 1798–1809.

Janoff-Bulman, R. (1985). The aftermath of victimization: Rebuilding shattered assumptions. In C. R. Figley (Ed.), *Trauma and Its Wake: The Study and Treatment of Post-traumatic Stress Disorder* (pp. 15–35). New York: Brunner-Mazel.

Johnson, P. B. (1976). Women and power: Toward a theory of effectiveness. *Journal of Social Issues*, **32**, 99–100.

Jones, A. (1980). *Women Who Kill*. New York: Fawcett Columbine Books.

Kahn, A. (1984). The power war: Male response to power loss under equality. *Psychology of Women Quarterly*, **8**, 234–247.

Kahn, S. E., & Theurer, G. M. (1985). Evaluation research in a course on counseling women: A case study. In L. B. Rosewater & L. E. A. Walker (Eds.), *Handbook of Feminist Therapy: Women's Issues in Psychotherapy* (pp. 321–331). New York: Springer.

Kanfer, F. H., & Goldstein, A. P. (Eds.) (1986). *Helping People Change: A Textbook of Methods* (3rd edn). New York: Pergamon.

Kanfer, F. H., & Schefft, B. K. (1988). *Guiding the Process of Therapeutic Change*. Champaign: Research Press.

Kanter, R. M. (1977). *Men and Women of the Corporation*. New York: Basic Books.

Kaplan, M. (1983). A woman's view of DSM-III. *American Psychologist*, **38**, 786–792.

Kaslow, N. (1989, August). *Treatment of depressed women*. Symposium paper presented at the annual convention of the American Psychological Association, New Orleans, LA.

Katz, J. (1984). *No Fairy Godmothers, No Magic Wands: The Healing Process After Rape*. Saratoga: R & E Publishers.

Katz, P. A. (1979). The development of female identity. *Sex Roles*, **5**, 155–178.

Katz, P. A., & Boswell, S. L. (1986). Flexibility and fractionality in children's gender roles. *Genetic, Social, and General Psychology Monographs*, **112**, 105–147.

Kazak, A. E., & Linney, J. A. (1983). Stress, coping, and life changes in the single parent family. *American Journal of Community Psychology*, **11**, 207–220.

Keith, P. M., & Shafer, R. B. (1982). Comparison of depression among single-parent and married women. *The Journal of Psychology*, **110**, 239–247.

Kellerman, E. R., & Katz, E. R. (1978). Attitudes toward the division of child-rearing responsibility. *Sex Roles*, **4**, 505–512.

Kelly, J. A., O'Brien, G. G., & Hosford, R. (1981). Sex roles and social skills: Considerations for interpersonal adjustment. *Psychology of Women Quarterly*, **5**, 759–766.

Kelly, J. A., & Worell, L. (1976). Parent behaviors related to masculine, feminine, and androgynous sex-role orientations. *Journal of Consulting and Clinical Psychology*, **44**, 843–851.

Kelly, J. A., & Worell, J. (1977). New formulations of sex roles and androgyny: A critical review. *Journal of Consulting and Clinical Psychology*, **45**, 1101–1115.

Kelly, G. A. (1955). *The Psychology of Personal Constructs*. New York: W. W. Norton.

Kendall, P. C., & Hollon, S. D. (1979). *Cognitive–behavioral Interventions: Theory, Research, and Procedures*. New York: Academic Press.

Kendrick, D. T., & Trost, M. R. (1989). A reproductive model of heterosexual relationships: Putting proximate economics in ultimate perspective. In C. Hendrick (Ed.), *Close Relationships. 10: Review of Personality and Social Psychology* (pp. 92–117). Newbury Park: Sage.

Kentucky Psychological Association (1982). *Sex-fair Guidelines.* Lexington.

Kerr, B. (1985). Barriers to achievement. In B. Kerr (Ed.), *Smart Girls, Gifted Women* (pp. 125–144). Columbus, Ohio: Psychology Publishing.

Kessler, R. C., & McRae, J. A. Jr (1981). Trends in the relationship between stress and psychological stress. *American Sociological Review*, **47**, 216–227.

Kessler, R. C., & Neighbors, H. W. (1986). A new perspective on the relationships among race, social class, and psychological distress. *Journal of Health and Social Behavior*, **27**, 107–115.

Kilpatrick, D. G., Resick, P. A., & Veronen, L. J. (1981). Effects of a rape experience: A longitudinal study. *Journal of Social Issues*, **37**, 105–122.

Kimmel, E. (1989). The experience of feminism. *Psychology of Women Quarterly*, **13**, 133–146.

Kinloch, G. C. (1979). *The Sociology of Minority Group Relations.* Englewood Cliffs: Prentice Hall.

Kingdon, M. A. (1979). Lesbians. *The Counseling Psychologist*, **8**, 44–45.

Kinsey, A. C., Pomeroy, W. B., Martin, C. R., & Gabhard, P. H. (1953). *Sexual Behavior in the Human Female.* Philadelphia: W. B. Saunders.

Komoravsky, M. (1976). *Dilemmas of Masculinity: A Study of College Youth.* New York: Norton.

Koss, M. P. (1985). The hidden rape victim: Personality, attitudinal, and situational characteristics. *Psychology of Women Quarterly*, **9**, 193–212.

Koss, M. P., & Burkhart, B. R. (1989). A conceptual analysis of rape victimization: Long-term effects and implications for treatment. *Psychology of Women Quarterly*, **13**, 27–40.

Krantz, S. E. (1985). When depressive cognitions reflect negative realities. *Cognitive Theory and Research.* **9**, 595–610.

Krause, N. (1983). Conflicting sex-role expectations, housework dissatisfaction, and depressive symptoms among full-time housewives. *Sex Roles*, **9**, 1115–1125.

Kravetz, D. (1980). Consciousness-raising and self-help. In A. M. Brodsky & R. T. Hare-Mustin (Eds.), *Women and Psychotherapy: An Assessment of Research and Practice* (pp. 268–284). New York: Guilford.

Kurdek, L. A., & Schmitt, J. P. (1986). Relationship quality of partners in heterosexual married, heterosexual cohabiting, gay, and lesbian relationships. *Journal of Personality and Social Psychology*, **51**, 711–720.

LaCroix, A. Z., & Haynes, S. G. (1987). Gender differences in the health effects of workplace roles. In R. C. Barnett, L. Biener, & G. K. Baruch (Eds.), *Gender and Stress*, (pp. 96–121). New York: The Free Press.

Lafontaine, E., & Tredeau, L. (1986). The frequency, sources, and correlates of sexual harassment among women in traditional male occupations. *Sex Roles*, **15**, 433–442.

Lambert, M. J., Shapiro, D. A., & Bergin, A. E. (1985). The effectiveness of psychotherapy. In S. L. Garfield & A. E. Bergin (Eds.), *Handbook of Psychotherapy and Behavior Change.* (pp. 157–212). New York: Wiley.

Landrine, H. (1989). The politics of personality disorder. *Psychology of Women Quarterly*, **13**, 325–329.

Laner, M. R., & Thompson, J. (1982). Abuse and aggression in courting couples. *Deviant Behavior: An Interdisciplinary Journal*, **3**, 229–244.

Lange, S. J., & Worell, J. (1990, August). *Satisfaction and Commitment in Lesbian and Heterosexual Relationships.* Paper presented at the annual meeting of the American Psychological Association, Boston, MA.

Langlois, J. H., & Downs, A. C. (1980). Mothers, fathers, and peers as socialization agents of sex-typed play behavior in young children. *Child Development,* **51,** 1237–1247.

Lazar, J. (1987, March). *Sex Differences in Depression: A Review of Recent Findings and Future Directions.* Paper presented at the annual meeting of the Southeastern Psychological Association, Atlanta, GA.

Lazarus, A. A. (1981). *The Practice of Multimodal Therapy.* New York: McGraw-Hill.

Lazarus, R. S., & Folkman, S. (1984). *Stress, Appraisal, and Coping.* New York: Springer.

Leigh, W. A. (1989). Barriers to fair housing for Black women. *Sex Roles,* **21,** 69–84.

Lemkau, J. P. (1986). Themes in psychotherapy with women in male-dominated professions. In D. Howard (Ed.), *The Dynamics of Feminist Therapy* (pp. 29–40). New York: Haworth.

Lenwin, E. (1981). Lesbianism and motherhood: Implications for child custody. *Human Organization,* **40,** 6–14.

Leslie, L. A., & Grady, K. (1985). Changes in mothers' social support networks and social support following divorce. *Journal of Marriage and the Family,* **47,** 663–673.

Levant, R. F. (1984). *Family Therapy: A Comprehensive Overview.* Englewood Cliffs: Prentice-Hall.

Levine, F. M., & Sandeen, E. (1985). *Conceptualization in Psychotherapy: The Models Approach.* Hillsdale: Erlbaum.

Levy, L. (1970). *Conceptions of Personality: Theories and Research.* New York: Random House.

Lewinsohn, P. M. (1974). A behavioral approach to depression. In R. Friedman & M. Katz (Eds.), *The Psychology of Depression; Contemporary Theory and Research.* New York: Wiley.

Lewinsohn, P. M., Antonuccio, D. O., Steinmetz, J. L., & Teri, L. (1984). *Coping with Depression: A Psychoeducational Intervention for Unipolar Depression.* Eugene, OR: Castalia.

Lewinsohn, P. M., Munoz, R. F., Youngren, M. A., & Zeiss, A. M. (1978). *Control Your Depression,* Englewood Cliff, NJ: Prentice-Hall.

Lewinsohn, P. M., Youngren, M. A., & Grosscup, S. J. (1979). Reinforcement and depression. In R. A. Depue (Ed.), *The Psychobiology of Depressive Disorders: Implications for the Effects of Stress.* New York: Academic Press.

Liberman, R. P., & Roberts, J. (1976). Contingency management of neurotic depression and marital disharmony. In H. J. Eysenck (Ed.), *Case Studies in Behavior Therapy.* London: Routledge & Kegan Paul.

Liljestrand, P., Gerling, E., & Saliba, P. A. (1978). The effects of social sex-role stereotypes and sexual orientation in psychotherapeutic outcomes. *Journal of Homosexuality,* **3,** 361–372.

Linz, D., Donnerstein, E., Bross, M., & Chapin, M. (1986). Mitigating the influence of violence on television and sexual violence in the media. In R. J. Blanchard & D. C. Blanchard (Eds.), *Advances in the Study of Aggression,* Volume 2 (pp. 165–194). New York: Academic Press.

Lipman-Blumen, J., & Leavitt, H. J. (1978). Vicarious and direct achievement patterns in adulthood. In L. S. Hansen & R. S. Rapoza (Eds.). *Career Development and Counseling of Women* (pp. 132–148). Springfield: Charles C. Thomas.

Lips, H. M. (1981). *Women, Men, and the Psychology of Power.* Englewood Cliffs: Prentice-Hall.

Locksley, A. (1980). On the effects of wives' employment on marital adjustment and companionship. *Journal of Marriage and the Family,* **42,** 337–346.

Lott, B. (1981). A feminist critique of androgyny: Toward the elimination of gender attributions for learned behavior. In C. Mayo & N. M. Henley (Eds.), *Gender and Non-verbal Behavior* (pp. 171–180). New York: Springer.

Lott, B. (1985a). The potential enrichment of social/personality psychology through feminist research and vice versa. *American Psychologist,* **40,** 155–164.

Lott, B. (1985b). The devaluation of women's competence. *Journal of Social Issues,* **41,** 43–60.

Lott, B. (1987). *Women's Lives: Themes and Variations in Gender Learning.* Monterey: Brooks-Cole.

Loewenstein, S. F. (1980). Understanding lesbian women. *Social Casework,* **61,** 29–38.

Loewenstein, S. F., Bloch, N. E., Campion, J., Epstein, J. S., Gale, P., & Salvatore, M. (1981). A study of satisfaction and stresses of single women in midlife. *Sex Roles,* **7,** 1127–1141.

Luchins, E. & Luchins, A. (1980). Female mathematicians: A contemporary appraisal. In L. Fox, L. Brody, & D. Tobin (Eds.), *Women and the Mathematical Mystique.* Baltimore: The Johns Hopkins University Press.

Lunneborg, P. W. (1982). Role model influencers of non-traditional professional women. *Journal of Vocational Behavior,* **20,** 276–281.

Lykes, M. B. (1983). Discrimination and coping in the lives of Black women: Analysis of oral history data. *Journal of Social Issues,* **39,** 79–100.

Lynn, D. B. (1979). *Daughters and Parents: Past, Present, and Future.* Monterey: Brooks-Cole.

Maccoby, E. E., & Jacklin, C. N. (1974). *The Psychology of Sex Differences.* Stanford: Stanford University Press.

MacDonald, M. L. (1984). Behavioral assessment with women clients. In E. A. Bleckman (Ed.), *Behavior Modification with Women* (pp. 60–93). New York: Guilford.

MacKay, D. G. (1980). Language, thought, and social attitudes. In H. Giles, P. Robinson, & P. M. Smith (Eds.), *Language: Social Psychological Perspectives.* Oxford: Pergamon.

Major, B. (1987). Gender, justice, and the psychology of entitlement. In P. Shaver & C. Hendrick (Eds.), *Sex and Gender. Review of Personality and Social Psychology,* Volume 7, (pp. 124–148). Newbury Park: Sage.

Makepeace, J. (1981). Courtship violence among college students. *Family Relations,* **18,** 150–158.

Makowsky, V. P., & Paludi, M. A. (1990). Feminism and women's studies in the academy. In M. Paludi & G. A. Stuernagel (Eds.), *Foundations for a Feminist Restructuring of the Academic Disciplines* (pp. 1–38) New York: Harrington Park Press.

Malamuth, N. M. (1981). Rape proclivity among males. *Journal of Social Issues,* **37,** 138–157.

Malovich, N. J., & Stake, J. E. (1990). Sexual harassment on campus: Individual differences in attitudes and beliefs. *Psychology of Women Quarterly,* **14,** 63–81.

Malson, M. R. (1983). Black women's sex roles: The social context for a new ideology. *Journal of Social Issues,* **39,** 101–113.

Marcus, B. F. (1987). Object relations theory. In R. Formanek & A. Gurian (Eds.), *Women and Depression: A Lifespan Perspective* (pp. 27–40). New York: Springer.

Marecek, J., & Hare-Mustin, R. T. (1987). Feminism and therapy: Can this relationship be saved? (Unpublished manuscript.)

Margolin, G. (1982). Ethical and legal considerations in marital and family therapy. *American Psychologist*, **37**, 788–801.

Martin, D., & Lyon, P. (1984). Lesbian women and mental health policy. In: L. E. Walker (Ed.), *Women and Mental Health Policy* (pp. 151–179). Beverly Hills: Sage.

Massad, C. M. (1981). Sex role, identity, and adjustment during adolescence. *Child Development*, **52**, 1290–1298.

Matlin, M. W. (1987). *The Psychology of Women*. New York: Holt, Rinehart & Winston.

McBride, A. B. (1987). Position paper. In A. Eichler & D. L. Perron (Eds.), *Women's Mental Health: Agenda for Research* (pp. 28–41). Rochville: National Institute of Mental Health.

McBride, A. B. (1990). Mental health effects of women's multiple roles. *American Psychologist*, **45**, 381–384.

McCann, I. L., Sakheim, D. K., & Abrahamson, D. S. (1988). Trauma and victimization: A model of psychological adaptation. *The Counseling Psychologist*, **16**, 531–594.

McCombs, H. G. (1989). The dynamics and impact of affirmative action processes on higher education, the curriculum, and Black women. *Sex Roles*, **21**, 127–144.

McDaniel, C. (1978). *The Practice of Career Guidance and Counseling INFORM*, **7**, 1–2, 7–8.

McGhee, P. E., & Freuh, T. (1980). Television viewing and the learning of sex role stereotypes. *Sex Roles*, **6**, 179–188.

McGrath, E., Keita, G. P., Strickland, B. R., & Russo, N. F. (1990). *Women and Depression: Risk Factors and Treatment Issues*. Washington, DC: American Psychological Association.

McHugh, M. C., Koeske, R. D., & Frieze, I. H. (1986). Issues to consider in conducting non-sexist psychological research. *American Psychologist*, **41**, 879–890.

McNett, I., Taylor, L., & Scott, L. (1975). Minority women: Doubly disadvantaged. In A. G. Sargent (Ed.), *Beyond Sex Roles* (2nd edn). New York: West Publishing Co.

Meichenbaum, D. (1977) *Cognitive–behavioral Modification: An Integrative Approach*. New York: Plenum.

Meichenbaum, D. (1986). Cognitive–behavioral Modifiation. In F. H. Kanfer & A. P. Goldstein (Eds.), *Helping People Change: A Textbook of Methods* (pp. 346–380). New York: Pergamon.

Meriam, S. B., & Hyer, P. (1984). Changing attitudes of young women toward family-related tasks in young adulthood. *Sex Roles*, **10**, 825–835.

Mednick, M. T. S., & Weissman, H. J. (1975). The psychology of women—selected topics. In M. R. Rosensweig & L. W. Porter (Eds.), *Annual Review of Psychology*, Volume 26 (pp. 1–18). Palo Alto: Annual Reviews.

Meyer, C. B., & Taylor, S. E. (1986). Adjustment to rape. *Journal of Personality and Social Psychology*, **50**, 1226–1234.

Miles, A. (1988). *The Neurotic Woman: The Role of Gender in Psychiatric Illness*. Worcester, England: New York University Press.

Miller, J. B. (1976). *Toward a New Psychology of Women*. Boston: Beacon.

Moreno, J. L. (1975). *Psychodrama: Second Volume: Foundations of Psychodrama*. Beacon: Beacon House. (First published 1959.).

Moreno, J. L. (1985). *Psychodrama: First Volume*. Amber: Beacon House. (First published 1946.)

Morgan, M. (1982). Television and adolescents' sex-role stereotypes: A longitudinal study. *Journal of Personality and Social Psychology*, **43**, 947–955.

Morgan, R. (1970). *Sisterhood Is Powerful*. New York: Random House.

Morowski, J. G. (1987). The troubled quest for masculinity, femininity, and andro-gyny. In P. Shaver & C. Hendricks (Eds.), *Sex and Gender: Review of Personality and Social Psychology*, Volume 7 (pp. 44–69). Beverly Hills: Sage.

Moses, H. E., & Hawkins, R. O. Jr (1982). *Counseling Lesbian Women and Gay Men: A Life-issues Approach*. St Louis: C. V. Mosby.

Myers, J. K., Weissman, M. M., Tischler, G., Holzer, C. E., Leaf, P. J. Orvashel, H., Anthony, J. C., Boyd, J. H., Burke, J. D., Kramer, M., & Stoltzman, R. (1984). Six month prevalence of psychiatric disorders in three communities. *Archives of General Psychiatry*, **41**, 959–970.

Nagely, D. L. (1971). Traditional and pioneer working mothers. *Journal of Vocational Behavior*, **1**, 331–341.

Nash, S. C., & Feldman, S. S. (1981). Sex-related differences in the relationship between sibling status and responsivity to babies. *Sex Roles*, **7**, 1035–1042.

Neal, A. M. (1989). The role of skin color and features in the Black community: Implications for Black women and therapy. *Clinical Psychology Review*, **9**, 323–333.

Nevill, D. D., & Schlecker, D. L. (1988). The relation of self-efficacy and assertive-ness to willingness to engage in traditional/non-traditional career activities. *Women & Therapy*, **12**, 91–98.

New York Chapter of National Organization of Women (1978). *A Consumer's Guide to Non-sexist Therapy*. New York: Service Fund of the National Organization of Women.

Nieva, V. F., & Gutek, B. A. (1981). *Women and Work: A Psychological Perspective*. New York: Praeger.

Nolen-Hoeksema, S. (1987). Sex differences in unipolar depression: Evidence and theory. *Psychological Bulletin*, **101**, 259–282.

Nolen-Hoeksema, S. (1990). *Sex Differences in Depression*. Stanford: Stanford University Press.

Nyquist, L., Sliven, K., Spence, J. T., & Helmreich, R. T. (1985). Household responsibilities in middle-class couples: The contribution of demographic and personality variables. *Sex Roles*, **12**, 15–34.

O'Hara, M. W. (1989, August). *Postpartum Depression*. Paper presented at the annual meeting of the American Psychological Association, New Orleans.

O'Hare, J., & Taylor, K. (1983). The reality of incest. *Women & Therapy*, **2**, 215–228.

Olmedo, E. L., & Parron, D. L. (1981). Mental health of minority women: Some special issues. *Professional Psychology*, **12**, 103–111.

Orlinsky, D. E., & Howard, K. I. (1986). Process and outcome in psychotherapy. In S. L. Garfield & A. E. Bergin (Eds.), *Handbook of Psychotherapy and Behavior Change* (pp. 311–384).

Orlofsky, J., & O'Heron, C. A. (1987). Stereotypic and non-stereotypic sex-role trait and behavior orientation: Implications for personal adjustment. *Journal of Person-ality and Social Psychology*, **52**, 1034–1042.

Orzek, A. M. (1989). The lesbian victim of sexual assault: Special considerations for the mental health profession. *Women & Therapy*, **8**, 107–117.

Ostertag, P. A., & McNemara, J. R. (1991). "Feminization" of psychology: The changing sex ratio and its implications for the profession. *Psychology of Women Quarterly*, **15**, 349–369.

Paludi, M. A. (1984). Psychometric properties and underlying assumptions of four objective measures of fear of success. *Sex Roles*, **10**, 765–781.

Paludi, M. (1990). *Exploring/teaching the Psychology of Women: A Manual of Resources*. New York: State University of New York Press.

Parham, T. A., & Helms, J. E. (1985). The relationship of racial identity attitudes to self-actualization and affective states of Black students. *Journal of Counseling Psychology*, **32**, 431–440.

Parsons, J. E., Adler, T. F., & Kaczala, C. (1983). Socialization of achievement attitudes and beliefs: Parental influences. *Child Development*, **53**, 310–321.

Parsons, J. E., Kaczala, C., & Meece, J. (1982). Socialization of achievement attitudes and beliefs: Classroom influences. *Child Development*, **53**, 322–339.

Pearson, J. C. (1985). *Gender and Communication*. Dubuque: William C. Brown.

Peplau, L. A., & Conrad, E. (1989). Beyond non-sexist research: The perils of feminist methods in psychology. *Psychology of Women Quarterly*, **13**, 379–400.

Peterson, R. A. (1983). Attitudes toward the childless spouse. *Sex Roles*, **9**, 321–331.

Petry, R. A., & Thomas, J. R. (1986). The effect of androgyny on the quality of psychotherapeutic relationships. *Psychotherapy: Theory, Research, and Practice*, **23**, 249–251.

Piasecki, J., & Hollon, S. D. (1987). Cognitive therapy for depression: Unexplicated schemata and scripts. In N. S. Jacobson (Ed.), *Psychotherapists in Clinical Practice: Cognitive and Behavioral Perspectives* (pp. 121–152). New York: Guilford.

Pleck, J. G. (1975). Masculinity–femininity: Current and alternative paradigms. *Sex Roles*, **1**, 161–178.

Pleck, J. H. (1985). *The Myth of Masculinity*. Cambridge: MIT Press.

Pope, K., & Vetter, V. A. (in press). Prior therapist–patient sexual involvement among patients seen by psychologists. *Psychotherapy*.

Porter, N. (1985). New perspectives on therapy supervision. In L. B. Rosewater & L. E. A. Walker (Eds.), *Handbook of Feminist Therapy: Women's Issues in Psychotherapy* (pp. 332–343.) New York: Springer.

Price-Bonham, S., & Skeen, P. (1982). Black and white fathers' attitudes toward children's sex roles. *Psychological Reports*, **50**, 1187–1190.

Ptacek, J. (1988). Why do men batter their wives? In K. Yllo & M. Bograd (Eds.), *Feminist Perspectives on Wife Abuse*, (pp. 133–157). Newbury Park: Sage.

Quinn, V. (undated). *Professional Therapy Never Includes Sex*. California: Office of State Printing.

Radloff, L. S. (1975). Sex differences in depression: The effects of occupation and marital status. *Sex Roles*, **1**, 249–265.

Rawlings, E. I., & Carter, D. K. (1977). *Psychotherapy for Women: Treatment Toward Equality*. Springfield: Charles C. Thomas.

Rawlings, E. I., & Carter, D. K. (1977). Feminist and non-sexist psychotherapy. In E. I. Rawlings & D. K. Carter (Eds.), *Psychotherapy for Women* (pp. 19–76). Springfield: Charles C. Thomas.

Rebecca, M., Heffner, R., & Olenshansky, B. (1976). A model of sex-role transcendence. *Journal of Social Issues*, **32**, 197–206.

Rehm, L. P. (1988). Self-management and cognitive processes in depression. In L. B. Alloy (Ed.), *Cognitive Processes in Depression* (pp. 143–176). New York: Guilford.

Reid, P. T. (1988). Racism and sexism: Comparisons and conflicts. In P. A. Katz & D. A. Taylor (Eds.), *Eliminating Racism*. New York: Plenum.

Reis, S. M. (1987). We can't change what we don't recognize: Understanding the special needs of gifted females. *Gifted Child Quarterly*, **31**, 2.

Rekdal, C. K. (1984). Guiding the gifted female through being aware: The math connection. *Gifted Child Today*, **35**, 10–12.

Rekers, G. A. (1985). The genogram: Herstory of a woman. *Women and Therapy*, **4**, 9–15.

Remer, P. (1986). Stages in coping with rape. Unpublished manuscript.

Remer, P., & O'Neill, C. D. (1978). *A Counseling Companion for Self-guided Career Decision-making*. Lexington, KY: Authors.

Remer, P., & O'Neill, C. D. (1980). Clients as change agents: What color could your parachute be? *Personnel and Guidance Journal*, **58**, 425–429.

Remer, P., O'Neill, C. D., & Gohs, D. E. (1984). Multiple outcome evaluation of a life-career development course. *Journal of Counseling Psychology*. **31**, 532–540.

Remer, P., & Ross, E. (1982). The counselor's role in creating a school environment that fosters androgyny. *The School Counselor*, **30**, 4–14.

Remer, R., & Witten, B. J. (1988). Conceptions of rape. *Violence and Victims*, **3**, 217–232.

Resick, P. A. (1983). Sex-role stereotypes and violence against women. In V. Franks & E. D. Rothblum (Eds.), *The Stereotyping of Women: Its Effects on Mental Health* (pp. 230–256). New York: Springer.

Ridley, C. R. (1984). Clinical treatment of the non-disclosing Black client. *American Psychologist*, **4**, 1234–1244.

Robinson, D., & Worell, J. (1991). *The Feminist Practice Scale (FPS): A Survey of Feminist Therapy Beliefs and Goals*. Unpublished manuscript, University of Kentucky, Lexington, KY.

Rosen, B. C., & Aneshensel, C. S. (1978). Sex differences in the educational–occupational expectation process. *Social Forces*, **57**, 164–186.

Rosenkrantz, P. S., Vogel, S. R., Bee, H., Boverman, I. K., & Broverman, D. M. (1968). Sex-role stereotypes and self-concepts in college students. *Journal of Consulting and Clinical Psychology*, **32**, 287–295.

Rosewater, L. B., & Walker, L. E. A. (1985). *Handbook of Feminist Therapy: Women's Issues in Psychotherapy*. New York: Springer.

Rosewater, L. B. (1985a). Schizophrenic, borderline, or battered? In L. B. Rosewater & L. E. A. Walker (Eds.), *Handbook of Feminist Therapy: Women's Issues in Psychotherapy* (pp. 215–225). New York: Springer.

Rosewater, L. B. (1985b). Feminist interpretation of traditional testing. In L. B. Rosewater & L. E. A. Walker (Eds.), *Handbook of Feminist Therapy: Women's Issues in Psychotherapy* (pp. 266–273). New York: Springer.

Rosewater, L. B. (1988). Battered or schizophrenic? Psychological tests can't tell you. In K. Yllo & M. Bograd (Eds.), *Feminist Perspectives on Wife Abuse* (pp. 200–216). Newbury Park: Sage.

Ross, J., & Kagan, J. P. (1983). Children by choice or by chance: The perceived effects of parity. *Sex Roles*, **9**, 69–77.

Ross, C. E., Mirowsky, J., & Huber, J. (1983). Dividing work, sharing work, and in-between: Marriage patterns and depression. *American Sociological Review*, **48**, 809–823.

Rosser, S. V. (1990). *Female-friendly Science: Applying Women's Studies Methods and Theories to Attract Students*. New York: Pergamon.

Rothblum, E. D. (1983). Sex-role stereotypes and depression in women. In V. Franks & E. D. Rothblum (Eds.), *The Stereotyping of Women: Its Effects on Mental Health* (pp. 83–111). New York: Springer.

Rothblum, E. D., & Cole, E. (Eds.) (1988). Lesbianism: Affirming non-traditional roles. *Women and Therapy*, **9**, 112.

Rothblum, E. D., & Franks, V. (1983). Warning: Sex-role stereotypes may be hazardous to your health. In V. Franks & E. D. Rothblum (Eds.), *The Stereotyping of Women: Its Effects on Mental Health* (pp. 3–10). New York: Springer.

Rothblum, E. D., & Franks, V. (1987). Custom-fitted straight-jackets: Perspectives on women's mental health. In J. Figueira-McDonough & R. Sharri (Eds.), *The Trapped Woman: Catch 22 in Deviance and Control*. Newbury Park: Sage.

Rotter, J. B. (1954). *Social Learning and Clinical Psychology*. Englewood Cliffs: Prentice-Hall.

Ruble, T. L., Cohen, R., & Ruble, D. N. (1984). Sex stereotypes: Occupational barriers for women. *American Behavioral Scientist*, **27**, 339–356.

Ruble, D. N., Croke, J. A., Frieze, I., & Parsons, J. E. (1975). A field study of sex-role-related attitudes change in college women. *Journal of Applied Social Psychology*, **5**, 116–117.

Ruble, D. N., & Ruble, T. L. (1982). Sex stereotypes. In A. G. Miller (Ed.), *In the Eye of the Beholder: Contemporary Issues in Stereotyping*. New York: Praeger.

Ruble, T. (1983). Sex stereotypes: Issues of change in the 1970's. *Sex Roles*, **9**, 397–402.

Rusbult, C. E. (1983). A longitudinal test of the investment model: The development and deterioration of satisfaction and commitment in heterosexual involvements. *Journal of Personality and Social Psychology*, **45**, 101–117.

Russell, D. (1982). *Rape in Marriage*. New York: McMillan.

Russell, D. (1984). *Sexual Exploitation: Rape, Child Sexual Abuse and Workplace Harassment*. Beverly Hills: Sage.

Russell, D. (1986a). Psychiatric diagnosis and the oppression of women. *Women & Therapy*, **5**, 83–98.

Russell, D. (1986b). *The Secret Trauma: Incest in the Lives of Girls and Women*. New York: Basic Books.

Russell, D. E. H., & Howell, N. (1983). The prevalence of rape in the United States revisited. *Signs: Journal of Women in Culture and Society*, **8**, 688–695.

Russell, M. (1977). Sisterhood is complicated. In A. G. Sargen (Ed.), *Beyond Sex Roles* (pp. 259–265). St Paul: West.

Ryne, D. (1981). Bases of marital satisfaction among men and women. *Journal of Marriage and the Family*, **43**, 941–955.

Sadker, M. P., & Sadker, D. M. (1982). *Sex Equity Handbook for Schools*. New York: Longman.

Sadker, M., & Sadker, D. (1985). Sexism in the schoolroom of the 80s. *Psychology Today*, 54–57.

Sales, E. (1978). Women's adult development. In I. H. Frieze, J. E. Parsons, P. B. Johnson, D. N. Ruble, & G. L. Zellman (Eds.), *Women and Sex Roles: A Social Psychological Perspective* (pp. 157–190). New York: W. W. Norton.

Sanday, P. R. (1981). *Female Power and Male Dominance: On the Origins of Sexual Inequality*. New York: Cambridge University Press.

Sandburg, D. E., Erhhardt, A. A., Mellins, C. A., Ince, S. E., & Meyer-Bahburg, H. F. L. (1987). The influence of individual and family characteristics upon career aspirations of girls during childhood and adolescence. *Sex Roles*, **16**, 649–667.

Sanders, C. J., & Steward, D. C. (1977). Feminist bibliotherapy—prescription for change: A selected and annotated bibliography. In R. I. Rawlings & D. K. Carter (Eds.), *Psychotherapy for Women* (pp. 328–342). Springfield: Charles C. Thomas.

Sandler, B. (1982). *Project on the Education and Status of Women.* Washington, D.C.: US Government Printing Office.

Scott, R., Richards, A., & Wade, M. (1977). Women's studies as change agent. *Psychology of Women Quarterly,* **1**, 377–379.

Schlossberg, N. K., & Pietrofesa, J. J. (1978). Perspectives on counseling bias: Implications for counselor education. In L. W. Harmon, J. M. Birk, L. E. Fitzgerald, & M. F. Tanney (Eds.), *Counseling Women* (pp. 59–74). Monterey: Brooks–Cole.

Scurfield, R. (1985). Post-trauma stress assessment and treatment: Overview and formulations. In C. R. Figley (Ed.), *Trauma and Its Wake: The Study and Treatment of Post-traumatic Stress Disorder* (pp. 219–256). New York: Brunner-Mazel.

Seager, J., & Olson, A. (1986). *Atlas: Women in the World.* New York: Simon & Schuster.

Seligman, M. E. P. (1975). *Helplessness: On Depression, Development, and Death.* San Francisco: W. H. Freeman.

Seligman, M. E. P. (1981). A learned helplessness point of view. In L. P. Rehm (Ed.), *Behavior Therapy for Depression.* New York: Academic Press.

Serbin, L. A., O'Leary, K. D., Kent, R. N., & Tonick, I. J. (1973). A comparison of teacher response to the preacademic and problem behavior of boys and girls. *Child Development.* **44**, 796–804.

Sherif, C. (1982). Needed concepts in the study of gender identity. *Psychology of Women Quarterly,* **6**, 375–398.

Sherman, J. A. (1971). *On the Psychology of Women: A Survey of Empirical Studies.* Springfield: Charles C. Thomas.

Sherman, J. A. (1980). Therapist attitudes and sex-role stereotyping. In A. M. Brodsky & R. T. Hare-Mustin (Eds.), *Women and Psychotherapy: An Assessment of Research and Practice* (pp. 35–66). New York: Guilford.

Sherman, J. (1982). Mathematics, the critical filter: A look at some residues. *Psychology of Women Quarterly,* **6**, 428–444.

Sherman, J. A. (1987). Achievement-related fears: Gender roles and individual dynamics. *Women & Therapy,* **6**, 97–105.

Sherman, L., & Berk, R. (1984). The deterrent effects of arrest for domestic assault. *American Sociological Review,* **49**, 261–272.

Shinar, E. H. (1975). Sexual stereotypes of occupations. *Journal of Vocational Behavior,* **7**, 99–111.

Siegel, R. J. (1985). Beyond homophobia: Learning to work with lesbian clients. In L. Walker & L. B. Rosewater (Eds.), *Handbook of Feminist Therapy: Women's Issues in Psychotherapy* (pp. 183–190). New York: Springer.

Smith, A. J., & Siegel, R. F. (1985). Feminist therapy: Redefining power for the powerless. In L. B. Rosewater & L. E. A. Walker (Eds.), *Handbook of Feminist Therapy: Women's Issues in Psychotherapy* (pp. 13–21) New York: Springer.

Snyder, D. K., & Fruchtman, L. A. (1981). Differential patterns of wife abuse: A data-based typology. *Journal of Consulting and Clinical Psychology,* **49**, 878–885.

Sobel, S. B., & Russo, N. F. (1981). Sex roles, equality, and mental health.: An introduction. *Professional Psychology,* **12**, 1–5.

Sonkin, D. J. (Ed.) (1987). *Domestic Violence on Trial.* New York: Springer.

Sonkin, D., Martin, D., & Walker, L. E. A. (1985). *The Male Batterer.* New York: Springer.

Sophie, J. (1982). Counseling lesbians. *Personnel and Guidance Journal,* **60**, 341–345.

Sophie, J. (1985/86). A critical examination of stage theories of lesbian identity development. *Journal of Homosexuality,* **12**, 39–51.

Spence, J. T., & Helmreich, R. L. (1978). *Masculinity and Femininity: Their Psychological Dimensions, Correlates, and Antecedents*. Austin: University of Texas Press.

Spence, J. T., & Helmreich, R. L. (1980). Masculine instrumentality and feminine expressivity: Their relationship with sex-role attitudes and behavior. *Psychology of Women Quarterly*, 5, 147–163.

Spence, J. T., Helmreich, R. L., & Stapp, J. (1975). Ratings of self and peers on sex-role attributes and their relation to conceptions of self-esteem and masculinity and femininity. *Journal of Personality and Social Psychology*, 32, 29–39.

Spence, J. T., & Sawin, L. L. (1985). Images of masculinity and femininity: A reconceptualization. In V. O'Leary, R. K. Unger, & B. S. Wallston (Eds.), *Women, Gender, and Social Psychology* (pp. 35–66). Hillsdale: Erlbaum.

Spielberger, C., Gorsuch, R., & Luchins, R. (1970). *Test Manual for the State–Trait Anxiety Inventory*. Palo Alto, CA: Consulting Psychologists Press.

Stacey, W. A., & Shupe, A. (1983). *The Family Secret: Domestic Violence in America*. Boston, MA: Beacon Press.

Stake, A. E., & Gerner, M. A. (1987). The women's studies experience: Personal and professional gains for women and men. *Psychology of Women Quarterly*, 11, 277–284.

Stake, J. (1979). The ability/performance dimension of self-esteem: Implications for women's achievement behavior. *Psychology of Women Quarterly*, 3, 365–377.

Stake, J. E., & Levitz, E. (1974). Career goals of college women and men and perceived achievement related encouragement. *Psychology of Women Quarterly*, 4, 151–159.

Steil, J. M., & Turetsky, B. A. (1987). Marital influence levels and symptomatology among wives. In F. J. Crosby (Ed.), *Spouse, Parent, Worker: On Gender and Multiple Roles* (pp. 74–90). New Haven: Yale University Press.

Stockard, J., Schmuck, P. A., Kempner, K., Williams, P., Edson, S. A., & Smith, M. A. (1980). *Sex Equity in Education*. New York: Academic Press.

Strange, C. C., & Rhea, J. S. (1983). Career choice considerations and sex-role self-concepts of male and female undergraduates in non-traditional majors. *Journal of Vocational Behavior*, 23, 219–226.

Straus, C., & Zoe, L. (1989). *Women and Poverty in Kentucky*. Lexington: University of Kentucky.

Strauss, M. A., Gelles, R. J., & Steinmetz, S. K. (1980). *Behind Closed Doors: Violence in the American Family*. New York: Doubleday.

Strube, M. J. (1989). The decision to leave an abusive relationship: Empirical evidence and theoretical issues. *Psychological Bulletin*, 104, 236–250.

Sturdivant, S. (1980). *Therapy with Women: A Feminist Philosophy of Treatment*. New York: Springer.

Sue, S. (1983). Ethnic minority issues in psychology: A re-examination. *American Psychologist*, 44, 583–592.

Sue, S. (1988). Psychotherapeutic services for ethnic minorities. *American Psychologist*, 43, 301–308.

Sundberg, N. S. (1977). *Assessment of Persons*. Englewood Cliffs: Prentice-Hall.

Super, D. E. (1957). *The Psychology of Careers*. New York: Harper & Row.

Super, D. E. (1976). *Career Education and the Meaning of Work*. Monographs on career education. Washington, DC: The Office of Career Education, US Office of Education.

Sutherland, S., & Scherl, D. J. (1970). Patterns of response among victims of rape. *American Journal of Orthopsychiatry*, 10, 503–511.

Sweeney, P. D., Anderson, K., & Bailey, S. (1986). Attributional style in depression: A meta-analytic review. *Journal of Personality and Social Psychology*, **50**, 974–991.

Taylor, D. A., & Smitherman-Donaldson, G. (1989). "And ain't I a woman?": African American women and affirmative action. *Sex Roles*, **21**, 1–12.

Terlau, Mary, T. (1991). Effects of career self-efficacy and sex-role beliefs on non-traditionality of women's occupational choices. *Dissertation Abstracts International*, **52**, 10A–1216. (University Microfilms No. DA 9126904.)

Terrell, F., & Terrell, S. (1984). Race of counselor, client sex, cultural mistrust level, and premature termination from counseling among Black clients. *Journal of Counseling Psychology*, **31**, 371–375.

Terrelonge, P. (1984). Feminist consciousness and black women. In J. Freeman (Ed.), *Women: A Feminist Perspective* (pp. 557–567). Palo Alto: Mayfield.

Thoits, P. (1987). Position paper. In A. Eichler & D. L. Parron, (Eds.), *Women's Mental Health: Agenda for Research* (pp. 80–102). Washington, DC: National Institute of Mental Health.

Thomas, D. A., & Weiner, R. L. (1987). Physical and psychological causality as determinants of culpability in sexual harassment cases. *Sex Roles*, **17**, 573–591.

Thoreson, C. E., & Mahoney, M. J. (1974). *Behavioral Self-control*. New York: Holt, Rinehart, & Winston.

Thyfault, R. K., Browne, A., & Walker, L. E. A. (1987). When battered women kill: Evaluation and expert witness testimony techniques. In D. J. Sonkin (Ed.), *Domestic Violence on Trial: Psychological and Legal Dimensions of Family Violence*. (pp. 71–85). New York: Springer.

Tittle, C. K. (1981). *Careers and Family: Sex Roles and Adolescent Life Plans*. Beverly Hills: Sage.

Touhey, J. C. (1974). Effects of additional women professionals on ratings of occupational prestige and desirability. *Journal of Personality and Social Psychology*, **29**, 86–89.

Towsen, S. M. J., Zanna, M. P., & MacDonald, G. (1989). Self-fulfilling prophecies: Sex-role stereotypes as expectations for behavior. In R. K. Unger (Ed.), *Representations: Social Constructions of Gender* (pp. 97–107). Amityville: Baywood.

Travis, C. B. (1988). *Women and Health: Mental Health Issues*. Hillsdale: Erlbaum.

Tresemer, D. (1976). The cumulative record of research on fear of success. *Sex Roles*, **2**, 217–236.

Trotman, F. K. (1984). Psychotherapy of Black women and the dual effects of racism and sexism. In C. M. Brody (Ed.), *Women Therapists Working with Women: New Theory and Process of Feminist Therapy* (pp. 96–108). New York: Springer.

Unger, R. K. (1979). *Female and Male: Psychological Perspectives*. New York: Harper & Row.

Unger, R. K. (1981). Sex as a social reality: Field and laboratory research. *Psychology of Women Quarterly*, **5**, 645–653.

Unger, R. K. (1982). Advocacy vs. scholarship revisited: Issues in the psychology of women. *Psychology of Women Quarterly*, **7**, 5–17.

Unger, R. K. (1983). Through the looking glass: No wonderland yet! *Psychology of Women Quarterly*, **8**, 9–32.

Unger, R. K. (1985/6). Explorations in feminist ideology: Surprising consistencies and unexamined conflicts. *Imagination, Cognition, and Personality*, **4**, 395–403.

Unger, R. K. (1989). Sex in psychological paradigms: From behavior to cognition. In R. K. Unger (Ed.), *Representations: Social Constructions of Gender* (pp. 15–20). Amityville, NY: Baywood.

United States Bureau of the Census (1980). *Statistical Abstracts of the United States.* Washington DC: US Government Printing Office.

United States Department of Labor, Bureau of Labor Statistics (1985). *Employment and Earnings.* Washington, DC: US Government Printing Office.

United States Department of Labor, Women's Bureau (1983). *Time of Change: 1983 Handbook on Women Workers.* Washington, DC: US Government Printing Office.

United States Merit Systems Protection Board (1981). *Sexual Harassment in the Federal Workplace: Is it a Problem?* Washington, DC.

VandenBos, G., Stapp, J., & Kilburg, R. H. (1981). Health service providers in Psychology: Results of the 1978 human services survey. *American Psychologist*, **36**, 1395–1418.

van Wormer, K. (1990). Co-dependency: Implications for women and therapy. *Women & Therapy*, **8**, 51–63.

Vedovato, S. L., & Vaughter, R. M. (1980). Psychology of women courses changing sexist and sex-typed attitudes. *Psychology of Women Quarterly*, **4**, 587–590.

Veronen, L. J., Kilpatrick, D. G., & Resick, P. A. (1979). Treating fear and anxiety in rape victims: Implications for the criminal justice system. In W. H. Parsonage (Ed.), *Perspectives on Victimology* (pp. 148–159). Beverly Hills: Sage.

Voyandoff, P. (1980). Perceived job characteristics and job satisfaction among men and women. *Psychology of Women Quarterly*, **5**, 177–185.

Wachtel, P. L. (1977). *Psychoanalysis and Behavior Therapy: Toward an Integration.* New York: Basic Books.

Walker, L. A. (1985). The American Psychiatric Association's work group to revise DSM-III: Statement on proposed diagnosis of masochistic personality disorder. Unpublished manuscript.

Walker, L. E. A. (1978). *Psychotherapy and Counseling with Battered Women.* Report to APA Division 17 (Counseling). Minimal competencies in counseling and psychotherapy project. Washington, D.C.: American Psychological Association.

Walker, L. E. A. (1979). *The Battered Woman.* New York: Harper Row.

Walker, L. E. A. (1984). *The Battered Woman Syndrome.* New York: Springer.

Walker, L. E. A. (1986, August). Diagnosis and politics: Abuse disorders. In R. Garfinkel (Chair), The politics of diagnosis: Feminist psychology and the DSM-III-R. Symposium conduct at the 94th Annual Convention of the American Psychological Assocation, Washington, DC.

Walker, L. E. A. (1989). Psychology and violence against women. *American Psychologist*, **44**, 695–702.

Wallston, B. S. (1981). What are the questions in the psychology of women? A feminist approach to research. *Psychology of Women Quarterly*, **5**, 597–617.

Wallston, B. S. (1986). *What's in a Name Revisited: The Psychology of Women vs. Feminist Psychology.* Invited address, Annual meeting of the Association for Women in Psychology, Oakland, CA.

Walsh, M. R. (1985). The Psychology of Women course: A continuing catalyst for change. *Teaching of Psychology*, **12**, 198–202.

Warburton, J., Newberry, A., & Alexander, J. (1989). Women as therapists, trainees, and supervisors. In M. McGoldrick, C. Anderson, & F. Walsh (Eds.), *Women in Families: A Framework for Family Therapy* (pp. 152–165). Scranton: Norton.

Washor-Liehaber, G. (1982). Women's career decision-making process: A feminist perspective. *Women & Therapy*, **1**, 51–58.

Webster's New World Dictionary of the English Language (1978). Collins, World Publishing Company.

Weinraub, M., & Brown, L. M. (1983). The development of sex-role stereotypes in children: Crushing realities. In V. Franks and E. D. Rothblum (Eds.), *The Stereotyping of Women: Its Effects on Mental Health* (pp. 30–58). New York: Springer.

Weinraub, M., & Wolf, B. M. (1983). Effects of stress and social supports on mother–child interactions in single and two-parent families. *Child Development*, **54**, 1297–1311.

Weinstein, E., & Rosen, E. (1988). *Sexuality Counseling: Issues and Implications.* Pacific Grove: Brooks-Cole.

Weis, K., & Borges, S. S. (1977). Victimology and rape: The case of the legitimate victims. In D. R. Nass (Ed.) *The Rape Victim* (pp. 35–75). Dubuque: Kendall-Hunt.

Weissman, M. M. (1980). Depression. In A. M. Brodsky & R. T. Hare-Mustin (Eds.), *Women and Psychotherapy: An Assessment of Research and Practice.* New York: Guilford.

Weissman, M. M., & Klerman, G. L. (1977). Sex differences and the epidemiology of depression. *Archives of General Psychiatry*, **34**, 98–111.

Weissman, M. M., & Klerman, G. L. (1987). Gender and depression. In R. Formanek & A. Gurian (Eds.), *Women and Depression: A Lifespan Perspective* (pp. 3–15). New York: Springer.

Weitzman, L. J. (1985). *The Divorce Revolution: The Unexpected Social and Economic Consequences for Women and Children.* New York: Free Press.

Weitzman, L. J., & Rizzo, D. (1974). *Images of Males and Females in Elementary School Text.* New York: Legal Defense and Education Fund.

Wells, K. (1980). Gender-role identity and psychological adjustment in adolescence. *Journal of Youth and Adolescence*, **9**, 59–72.

Westerveldt, E. M. (1978). A tide in the affairs of women: The psychological impact of feminism on educated women. In L. W. Harmon, J. M. Birk, L. E. Fitzgerald, & M. F. Tanney (Eds.), *Counseling Women* (pp. 1–33). Monterey: Brooks-Cole.

Whetsell, M. S. (1990). The relationship of abuse factors and revictimization to the long-term effects of childhood sexual abuse in women. *Dissertation Abstracts International*, **51**, 10B–5047. (University Microfilms No. AAC 9034199.)

White, L. K., Booth, A., & Edwards, J. N. (1986). Children and marital happiness: Why the negative correlations? *Journal of Social Issues*, **7**, 131–147.

Whitely, B. E. Jr (1983). Sex-role orientation and self-esteem: A critical meta-analytic review. *Journal of Personality and Social Psychology*, **44**, 765–778.

Whitely, B. E. Jr (1984). Sex-role orientation and psychological well-being: Two meta-analyses. *Sex Roles*, **12**, 207–225.

Widiger, T. A., & Spitzer, R. L. (1991). Sex bias in the diagnosis of personality disorders:, Conceptual and methodological issues. *Clinical Psychology Review*, **11**, 1–22.

Wilkinson, C. (1990). Cultural identity and the psychological well-being of professional Black women. *Dissertation Abstracts International*, **51**, 07A–2528. (University Microfilms No. AAC 9034200.)

Williams, J. B. W., & Spitzer, R. L. (1983). The issue of sex bias in DSM-III. A critique of "A Woman's View of DSM-III" by Marcie Kaplan. *American Psychologist*, **38**, 793–798.

Williams, J. M. G. (1984). *The Psychological Treatment of Depression: A Guide to the Theory and Practice of Cognitive–Behavioral Therapy.* New York: The Free Press.

Williams, S. W., & McCullers, J. C. (1983). Personal factors related to typicalness of career and success in active professional women. *Psychology of Women Quarterly*, **7**, 343–357.

Wilson, E. O. (1975). *Sociobiology: The New Synthesis.* Cambridge: The Belknap Press of Harvard University Press.

Wilson, E., & Ng, S. H. (1988). Sex bias in visual images evoked by generics: A New Zealand study. *Sex Roles*, **18**, 159–168.

Wise, G. W. (1978). The relationship of sex-role perception and levels of self-actualization in public school teachers. *Sex Roles*, **4**, 605–617.

Witt, V., & Worell, J. (1986, March). *Premarital and Marital Abuse: Factors in Common.* Paper presented at the annual meeting of the Southeastern Psychological Association, New Orleans, LA.

Witt, V., & Worell, J. (1988, March). *Antecedents and Correlates of Premarital Abuse.* Paper presented at the annual meeting of the Southeastern Psychological Association, New Orleans, LA.

Woody, B. (1989). Black women in the emerging services economy. *Sex Roles*, **21**, 45–68.

Worell, J. (1978). Sex roles and psychological well-being: Perspectives on methodology. *Journal of Consulting and Clinical Psychology*, **46**, 777–791.

Worell, J. (1980). New directions in counseling women. *The Personnel and Guidance Journal*, **58**, 477–484.

Worell, J. (1981). Lifespan sex roles: Development, continuity, and change. In R. M. Lerner and N. A. Busch-Rossnagel (Eds.), *Individuals as Producers of Their Development* (pp. 313–346). New York: Academic Press.

Worell, J. (1982). Psychological sex roles: Significance and change. In J. Worell (Ed.), *Psychological Development in the Elementary Years* (pp. 3–52). New York: Academic Press.

Worell, J. (1984). Will the Real Feminist Please Stand Up? Women's Attitudes Toward Feminism. Unpublished manuscript, University of Kentucky, Lexington.

Worell, J. (1986, November). *The DSM III-R: Controversies in Gender Bias.* Invited paper presented at the Annual meeting of the Association for the Advancement of Behavior Therapy, Chicago.

Worell, J. (1987, August). *Counseling Women: A Model of Training.* Paper presented at the annual meeting of the American Psychological Association.

Worell, J. (1988). Women's satisfaction in close relationships. *Clinical Psychology Review*, **8**, 477–498.

Worell, J. (1989a). Sex roles in transition. In J. Worell & F. Danner (Eds.), *The Adolescent as Decision-maker: Applications for Development and Education* (pp. 246–280). New York: Academic Press.

Worell, J. (1989b). Images of women in psychology. In M. A. Paludi & G. A. Stuernagel (Eds.), *Foundations for a Feminist Restructuring of the Academic Disciplines* (pp. 185–224). New York: Harrington Park.

Worell, J. (1990). Feminist frameworks. *Psychology of Women Quarterly*, **14**, 1–6.

Worell, J. (1991, April). *The psychology of women vs. feminist psychology.* Invited paper presented as part of a symposium titled: How can the psychology of women and gender be more politically relevant? (Arnold Kahn, Chair) at the annual convention of the Southeastern Psychological Association, New Orleans, LA.

Worell, J. (in press). Feminist journals: Academic empowerment or professional liability? In J. Williams (Ed.), *Gender in Academe.* Tampa: University of South Florida Press.

Worell, J. & Garret-Fulks, N. K. (1983). The resocialization of single-again women. In V. Franks & E. D. Rothblum (Eds.), *The Stereotyping of Women: Its Effects on Mental Health* (pp. 201–229). New York: Springer.

Worell, J., & Remer, P. (1979). A Cascade Model for Training Counselors of

Women. Research proposal submitted to the Department of Health, Education, and Human Welfare.

Worell, J., Romano, P., & Newsome, T. (1984, May). Patterns of nurturance in same and cross-sex friendships. Paper presented to the first Nag's Head Conference on Sex and Gender, Nag's Head, NC.

Worell, J., & Stilwell, W. S. (1981). *Psychology for Teachers and Students*. New York: McGraw-Hill.

Worell, J., Stilwell, D., & Robinson, D. (1991, May). *Constructions of Feminist Identity Development: Stages or Dimensions?* Paper presented at the Seventh Annual Nag's Head Conference on Gender Theory and Research, Highland Beach, FL.

Worell, J., & Worell, L. (1977). Support and opposition to the women's liberation movement: Some personality and parental characteristics. *Journal of Research in Personality*, 11, 10–20.

Wortman, C. B. (1983). Coping with victimization: Conclusions and implications for future research. *Journal of Social Issues*, 39, 195–221.

Wyatt, G. E., Notgrass, C. M., & Newcomb, M. (1990). Internal and external mediators of women's rape experiences. *Psychology of Women Quarterly*, 14, 153–176.

Yee, D., & Eccles, J. (1983, August). *A Comparison of Parents' and Children's Attributions for Successful and Unsuccessful Math Performances*. Paper presented at the annual meeting of the American Psychological Association, Anaheim, CA.

Yllo, K. (1988). Political and methodological debates in wife abuse research. In K. Yllo, & M. Bograd (Eds.), *Feminist Perspectives on Wife Abuse* (pp. 28–50). Newbury Park: Sage.

Yogev, S., & Vierra, A. (1983). The state of mothering among professional women. *Sex Roles*, 9, 391–396.

Yorburg, B., & Arafat, I. (1975). Current sex-role conceptions and conflict. *Sex Roles*, 1, 135–146.

Young, J. E. (1982). Loneliness, depression, and cognitive therapy. In L. A. Peplau and D. A. Perlman (Eds.), *Loneliness: A Sourcebook of Current Theory, Research, and Therapy* (pp. 379–404). New York: Wiley.

Yuen, L. M., & Depper, D. S. (1987). Fear of failure. *Women & Therapy*, 6, 21–39.

Zeldow, P. B. (1976). Effects of non-pathological sex-role stereotypes on student evaluations of psychiatric patients. *Journal of Consulting and Clinical Psychology*, 44, 304.

Zollicoffer, A. M. (1984). Issues for psychotherapists counseling lesbians. Unpublished manuscript.

Zollicoffer, A. M. (1989). Factors affecting long-term avoidant and intrusive responses and the process of resolution for women who have been raped. *Dissertation Abstracts International*, 50, 12A–4126. (University Microfilms No. AAC-9008-780).

Zollicoffer, A. M., & Remer, P. (1989). Untitled manuscript.

Zunker, V. C. (1982). *Using Assessment Results in Career Counseling*. Monterey: Brooks-Cole.

Zunker, V. C. (1986). *Career Counseling: Applied Concepts of Life Planning*. Monterey: Brooks-Cole.

Index

Index compiled by A. C. Purton